The WISE practical HOME FURNITURE BUILDER

by

Hubbard Cobb

Designs by

Sigman-Ward

1952

WM. H WISE & CO., INC.

NEW YORK

4523R

PRINTED IN THE UNITED STATES OF AMERICA

INTRODUCTION

There is no pleasure like making things for yourself — things that are useful *and* beautiful. The money you save can amount to a considerable sum, but that is a minor part of your pleasure. The satisfaction of a job well done with your own hands adds immeasurably to the years of enjoyment and use you will get from it.

And it's all the better if it's something you really need. A kitchen cabinet? — A work bench? — An outdoor chair?—they are all here, and for only the cost of materials and your pleasure in making them.

The first section tells you the tools you need and how to use them, the last section tells you how to paint or give a finish to all the articles you make. You should read these sections before you start to work on your first project: they give you important information, such as how to make allowance for the difference in dimensions between rough and dressed types of lumber.

After that—go to it! Even if you've never held a hammer in your hand before, there isn't one of these articles you can't build yourself from the complete plans and directions. Of course, if you are just beginning, it will be better to start off with a simple job like the *Hardware Shelves* or the *Plant Stand* before you tackle a project like the *Wardrobe Closet.* But even that you'll be able to handle amazingly soon, once you've got the feel of your tools and the habit of careful measuring.

You can add to the comfort of your living, the value of your home, and the enjoyment of your whole family with these articles. We wish you good luck and fun doing it.

ACKNOWLEDGMENTS: We take this opportunity to express our thanks to the following individuals, who developed and designed the projects in this book: Carl T. Sigman, William J. Ward, Jr., Lois Brand, William A. Patrick, Fergus Retrum, Carl R. Kinscherf, and Walter J. Karl.

CONTENTS

For the Workroom and Cellar

For the Bedroom

For the Bathroom

For the Garden and Outdoors

The WISE practical

HOME FURNITURE BUILDER

TOOLS AND HOW TO USE THEM

The tools listed below are all that are required to build the projects described in this book. Naturally, it is possible to build a wide variety of items with the same tools once you learn how to use them correctly. Many of these tools can be bought in home tool kits; only a few extras will have to be purchased separately.

THE BASIC TOOLS

Claw Hammer
Rip Saw
Crosscut Saw
Compass or Keyhole Saw
Jack Plane
Block Plane
Screwdriver
Wood Chisel
Wood Gouge
Brace and Bit
Compass
Level
Try Square
Framing Square
Combination Square

When you buy tools, get the better brands. Your hardware dealer will assist you in choosing what you need. The difference in cost between expensive and cheap equipment is slight, but the difference in quality is worth considering. Good tools not only last longer but, of course, produce better results. This is especially true with cutting tools such as planes, chisels, and gouges. Unless these can take and hold a sharp edge, they are useless to the amateur or professional furniture builder.

HAMMERS

While there is a wide variety of hammers, the type most popularly used in woodworking is the claw hammer. It is used for driving in nails, and the claws can be used for removing nails. A hammer should be selected on the basis of the weight of the head. A 16-oz. head is about right for most men. Women use a somewhat lighter head. Buy a hammer that feels right for you. Grip the handle by the end and take a few practice whacks at an old board. If the hammer is too heavy, get one with a lighter head. But get one with the heaviest head that is comfortable for you. This will work in your favor where much hammering is to be done. It is the weight of the hammer head and not force that drives in a nail.

Keep the face of the hammer free from rust and dirt. Soiled hammerheads may slip off the head of the nail. Be sure that the handle is firmly attached to the head. The portion of the handle flush with the top of the head is usually slotted to take a wood wedge. If the wedge becomes loose or falls out, replace it with a metal wedge obtainable at hardware stores.

Keep the handle of the hammer free from splintering rough spots. Many persons slip a rubber cap over the end of the hammer handle so that there is less chance that the handle will slip. Do not try to remove large spikes with the hammer claws—they are designed only for smaller nails. Trying to pull out a spike may break the claws. When removing a nail with a hammer, slip a piece of wood for a fulcrum between the hammerhead and the work. This prevents the head from damaging the work and also increases the leverage, making it easier to remove the nail.

Using a Hammer

It may seem elementary to tell you how to use a hammer, but a surprising number of persons don't know how to hammer correctly. To start a nail, hold it with one hand and tap the head gently with the hammer until the nail is far enough into the wood to support itself. Now the hammer can be held by the end of the handle and the nail driven in with a few firm strokes. Keep the hammer on the same plane as the nail. This prevents the nail from being bent over at an angle. Keep the face of the hammer centered on the head of the nail.

A little practice and you'll hit the button every time. If the nail starts to bend, remove it and use a fresh one—don't waste time straightening out bent nails. On finished work, stop hammering when the head of the nail is a fraction of an inch above the wood surface. The nail can be set in (see page 14) the rest of the way with a nail set, thus eliminating the chance that the hammerhead will dent the wood. Additional information on nailing is given under the section on wood fasteners (page 17).

HAND SAWS

Three kinds of handsaws are required for the basic tool kit. They are the rip, crosscut, and compass saws. A fourth, the coping saw, is optional. The ripsaw is used in cutting with the wood grain. The crosscut saw is used to cut against the wood grain, while the compass saw is used for cutting holes and circles, or small places where a rip or crosscut saw doesn't fit.

Crosscut Saw. The formation of the teeth is the basic difference between a rip and a cross saw. The teeth of a crosscut saw are triangular. The front of each tooth is cut to a 15 degree angle while the back of the tooth is cut to 45 degrees. The upper portion of the teeth are set alternately left and right. This is called "set" and is necessary to provide the proper degree of clearance between the saw teeth and the wood while the tool is in motion. A saw is measured by the number of teeth or points to the inch. The greater the number of teeth, the finer will the cut be. For average shopwork, an 8 point crosscut will serve most of your purposes.

Rip Saw. The rip saw has teeth which are chisel-shaped and the action is much like a series of small chisels working together. The front of each tooth is filed to an 8 degree angle. The rear of the tooth is set at a 52 degree angle. The teeth are set alternately. Like crosscut saws, rips are measured according to the number of points to

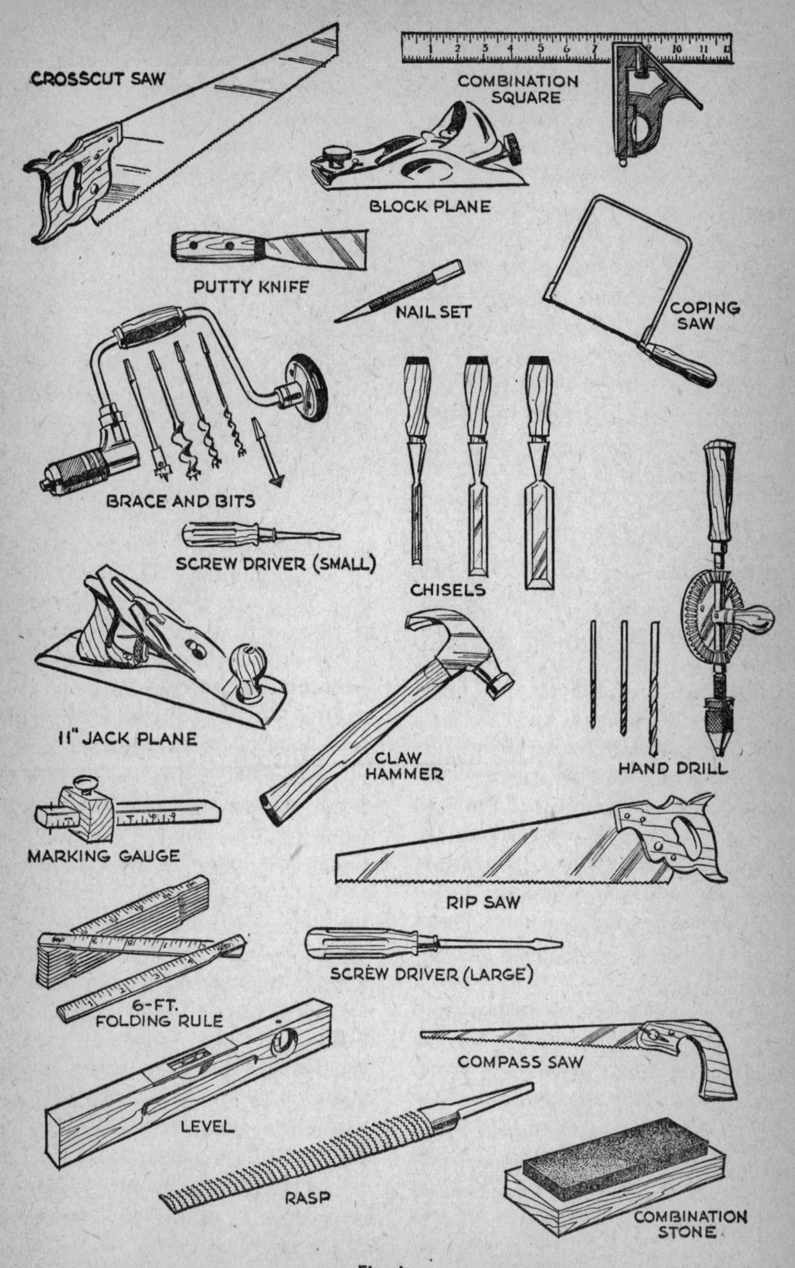
CROSSCUT SAW
COMBINATION SQUARE
BLOCK PLANE
PUTTY KNIFE
NAIL SET
COPING SAW
BRACE AND BITS
SCREW DRIVER (SMALL)
CHISELS
11" JACK PLANE
CLAW HAMMER
HAND DRILL
MARKING GAUGE
RIP SAW
SCREW DRIVER (LARGE)
6-FT. FOLDING RULE
COMPASS SAW
LEVEL
RASP
COMBINATION STONE

Fig. 1.

the inch. Seven points make a good all 'round saw.

Compass Saw. The compass saw is used for curves and for situations where other handsaws won't fit. Many manufacturers now make a compass saw with three interchangeable blades. One is suitable for fine crosscutting. Another does the work of a compass saw. The last blade is a keyhole saw, which is similar to a compass saw but smaller. A screw on the saw handle allows a blade to be removed and a new one installed according to the job you have in hand.

Coping Saw. This is the fourth saw shown in Figure 1. It is not necessary for most of the projects in this book but can often be used in place of the compass saw. In fact due to the very thin blade many small cuts can be made easier with a coping saw than with crosscut or rip saws if you are adept at using it.

Care of Saws

Saw blades should be wiped with a thin machine oil from time to time to prevent rusting. The saw should be hung by the handle in such a way that the teeth will not become dulled through contact with metal surfaces or metal tools. Next are a few "don'ts." Be careful when working with old wood not to let the saw teeth touch nails or wood screws. Also be careful not to let the saw blade become bent either through improper storage or by forcing it through dense wood. When sawing through wood that has been painted, place the wood with the painted side down, as this will not dull the saw blade as much as if the painted surface faces up.

Saws must be kept sharp if they are to do good work. Sharpening is divided into three operations: (1) Joining, which is filing the saw teeth to the same height; (2) shaping which is filing the teeth to the correct angle; and finally (3) setting, which is bending the teeth in the right direction. All these operations can be done by the amateur, provided he has the right assortment of files and a saw set. (Most saw manufacturers distribute literature telling how their products should be sharpened.) The fact remains, however, that sharpening a saw does require a good deal of skill as well as time. For about a dollar, the amateur would be wise to let a reliable hardware store or a firm specializing in sharpening tools do this work for him; their precision machines do an excellent job.

Sawing Technique

First select the proper saw for the job. Then place the work on a table or saw horse so that it can be held firmly in place. Grasp the saw in either hand by the handle, allowing the thumb and index finger to extend on each side of the handle to help guide the blade. The thumb of the free hand can be held on the work and used as a guide to help keep the blade in the correct place. Be sure that the saw blade is perfectly upright unless you are cutting the wood at an angle. The starting cut should be made with an upstroke — *never* a downstroke. The accuracy of the cut depends on how well it is started, so take things easy until you are sure that the cut is going correctly. The saw blade is flexible enough to allow for some bending to get back on the line should the blade drift slightly. Always make your cut on the outside, or waste side, of the line marked on the board. The blade of the saw has some thickness, and if you saw on the finish side, or inside, of the line or along the line itself, you may find that, in spite of your accuracy in measuring, the cut piece of wood is too short. It's easy enough to remove excess wood from the end of a board with a block plane or sandpaper—adding wood is another matter.

When cutting across the wood grain, hold the saw at a 45 degree angle to the wood. As you get close to the end of the cut, support the waste end of the board with your hand. You can then make a clean cut with the saw and the waste will not fall off and split the wood. When using a rip saw to cut a board to size, set the work up so that yau can get a full stroke with the saw blade. The saw should be held at 60 degrees to the wood. After sawing for some distance, put a small wood wedge or nail into the kerf—the opening left by the saw—to hold it open. This prevents the saw from binding.

Any saw will bind and often not work at all if the work is improperly

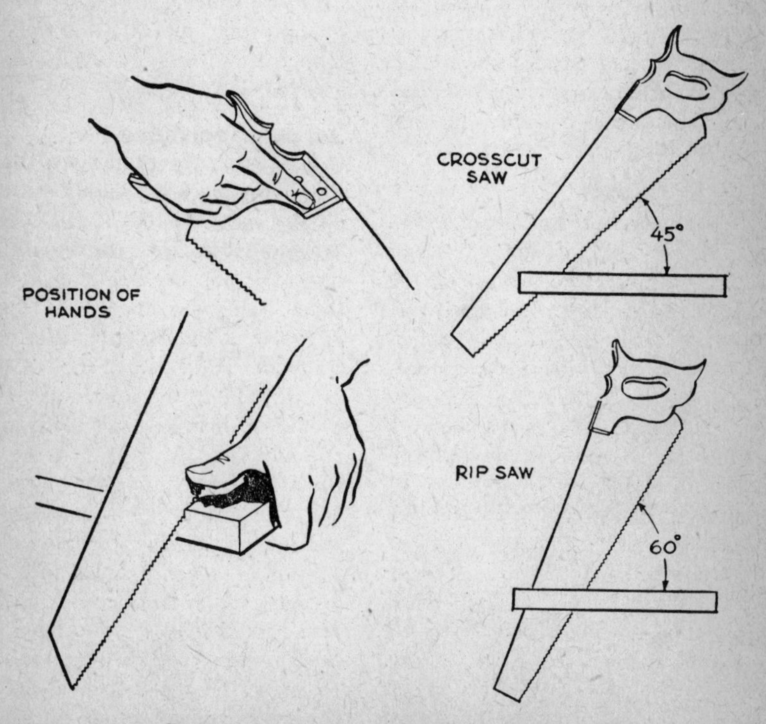

Fig. 2. Correct use of crosscut and rip saws.

supported and the kerf closes in on the blade. A saw will also bind if the angle to the wood is changed. In cutting small pieces of wood, avoid twisting off the waste piece with the saw blade.

SCREWDRIVERS

Screwdrivers for wood screws come in several sizes. It is important that the blade of the screwdriver fits snugly in the slot made for it in the screw head. If the tip of the blade is too thick, it will not fit into the slot; if to small, it will slip out of the slot as

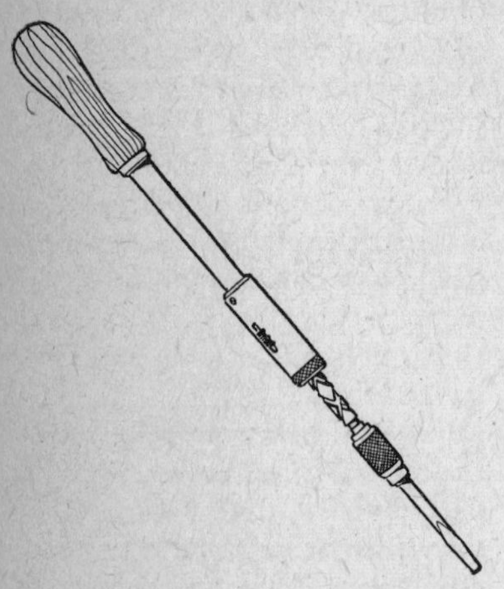

Fig. 3. A ratchet screwdriver.

the screwdriver is turned and possibly damage the screw head or the surface of the work. If the screwdriver blade is wider than the screw head, the edges will gouge the work when the screw is brought down flush with the surface. For these reasons, several sizes are required in the average home shop. The tip of the blade should be square. Rounded corners let the blade slip out of the screw-head notch. The blade can be kept in good condition with a metal file. Don't use a screwdriver for any purpose other than installing or removing screws, and don't use a light screwdriver on heavy work as you may twist the handle from the blade. For those who wish to spend a few extra dollars on a tool kit, ratchet screwdrivers with interchangeable blades are available. The ratchet is a great time saver when installing and removing screws.

When using either the standard or ratchet screwdriver, be sure the tool is held perpendicular to the work. If held at an angle, it will have a tendency to sink the screw in at an angle or to slip off the head. Keep firm pressure on the screwdriver so it won't slip off the screw head. When the head of the screw gets close to the wood surface, slow down to prevent the blade from slipping and spoiling the finish of the work. For instructions on installing screws, see wood screws, page 18.

PLANES

Planes are used for smoothing off the rough surface of wood and for bringing wood down to size when a saw cannot be used effectively. There are two basic types of planes—the bench, and the block. Bench planes are used when planing in the direction of the wood grain. Block planes are used when planing against the wood grain, for instance, on the end of a piece of wood.

There are a great many different bench planes used for various jobs, but the jack plane is suitable for ordinary shop work. The base of this plane is from 11″ to 15″. It is advisable to select the shortest one available for use on these furniture projects as most of the pieces of lumber are relatively short. You can always use a short plane on a long piece of wood, but it is sometimes rather difficult to do good work when trying to plane a short board with a long plane. A plane of this sort will remove any unevenness from a wood surface and also bring the wood down to a moderate degree of smoothness.

Adjusting Plane

There are three adjustments to make on a jack plane, depending on the work for which it is to be used. The first is the plane-iron cap. This is fastened to the plane iron, or blade, by means of a clamping screw. The purpose of this cap is to stiffen the blade and curve the shavings. When planing hardwood, this cap should be set down near the end of the blade to prevent the wood from splintering. When planing ordinary soft wood, the cap should be set about 1/16″ up from the tip of the blade.

The thickness of the cut is regulated by a knob which is connected to the blade by an adjusting lever. Hold the plane upside down as you turn the knob so you will be able to see exactly how far out of the plane body the blade protrudes. Above this knob is a lateral adjustment lever. This is used to center the blade in the plane; for if the blade sets at an angle, the cut naturally will turn out to be at a corresponding angle.

Using a Plane

To use a plane, first set the blade to the correct depth for the job at hand. If planing is required to smooth out a rough piece of wood before sanding, the blade should be set to take a very thin cut. If a considerable amount of wood must be removed, the blade should be set for a deep cut. Do not, however, allow the blade to extend out too far or the plane won't work at all.

The plane should be held perfectly level on the work. Tilting the plane to either side will produce an uneven surface. At the start of the planing operation, apply pressure to the front of the plane so that the blade cuts into the wood. When it rests flat on the wood, apply pressure to the center of the plane and end up the stroke by relieving the pressure on the front.

For good work, plane blades must be kept sharp and free from nicks. Instructions for sharpening the blade are given later in this section (page 10) along with information on sharpening other cutting tools. Never place a plane down so that the blade comes in contact with wood or metal. This will dull the blade. Either store it on its side or retract the blade so that the tip does not protrude out of the plane body. Try always to plane in the direction of the wood grain. If the plane produces a rough cut, change the direction of planing.

A block plane is designed for going across wood grain and is operated with one hand. There is no plane-iron cap over the blade. Adjustment for depth is made by means of a knob or lever. Planing end grain must be done with care to prevent splitting the wood at each end. The best procedure is to start from one end and plane to the center of the wood. Then, reverse the piece of wood and plane in from the opposite direction.

CHISELS AND GOUGES

Chisels and gouges are used to remove excess wood where this cannot be readily done with a saw, plane, or wood bit. Chisels have a square front edge, while gouges have a U-shaped or round edge for cutting hollows and curves. Chisels and gouges come in a wide variety of sizes. For the home workshop, a set of firmer socket chisels are suitable. The set should consist of 1/4″, 1/2″, 3/4″, and 1″ chisels. Similarly, a set of firmer gouges will prove useful.

The better quality chisels have a leather cap on the end of the handle. This protects the wood handle from direct contact with the mallet and prevents splitting of the wood. Always use a wood or plastic mallet when working with a chisel or gouge—never a steel hammer.

Using a Chisel

A chisel should be used only after as much of the wood as possible has been removed with a saw, plane, or wood bit. The rough cut is made with one or several of these tools, and the chisel is used for finishing off the work. For example, if you wish to cut a 1″ x 2″ hole in the center of a piece of wood, drill two 3/4″ holes side by side with a brace and bit. The excess wood around the holes can then be removed and the sides of the opening made square with the chisel.

In using a chisel, place the work on a wood bench or table where it can be held securely and the chisel blade will not be dulled should it slip off the work. Hold the chisel at a slight angle and don't try to remove too much of the wood at one time. If you trim the wood down in thin shavings, you will be able to make very accurate cuts. Always chisel slightly on the inside of the marking lines. It is much easier to cut with a chisel against the wood grain than with the grain. You also get a cleaner cut when working against the wood grain—so do as much of the cutting as possible in this manner. When you have to cut across the surface of a board, go only half way, and then change sides so that the chisel will not split the end wood.

The cutting edge of a chisel blade is easily dulled by coming into contact with metal. For this reason, chisels and gouges should be stored in separate slots. Such an arrangement is described on page 107.

Never work with a dull chisel. Not only will it do poor work but it may cause you an injury.

SHARPENING PLANE IRONS AND CHISELS

Plane irons and chisels can be easily sharpened in the home workshop. Sharpening involves two operations: grinding and whetting. Grinding is only necessary when the cutting edge has become nicked or when, after repeated whettings, the bevel on the end of the blade is short. Grinding the blade to the correct bevel and to the proper degree of smoothness is done on a hand or powered emery wheel—

sometimes, on a grindstone. The need to grind tools is infrequent. Hardware stores can grind your blades for you at a slight cost. If you do your own grinding, don't allow the blade to become too hot or it will lose its ability to hold a good edge.

The plane iron or chisel blade should be held on the stone at a 25 degree angle. Most power-operated grinders have an adjustable tool rest or holder that can be set to hold the blade at the correct angle. The bevel must be ground to an even depth across the width of the plane iron or chisel blade. You have finished when the bevel is free of nicks and is the correct depth.

Whetting the plane iron or chisel blade is done on a whetstone or oilstone. These stones have two surfaces, a coarse and a smooth. Light oil is applied to the stone before sharpening the tool. Place it on the stone with the bevel at the correct angle and move it along the stone in a figure "8" pattern. Be sure that the blade rests level on the stone. Most of the time you will only need to use the smooth side of the stone. If the blade is in very bad shape, work it down a bit on the coarse side and then finish up on the smooth side.

As the bevel edge of the blade is worked over the stone, a fine wire edge will appear on the edge of the blade. Remove this by turning the blade on its back and moving it across the stone a few times. The final sharpening is done by stropping the edge of the blade on a piece of leather. An old belt will serve.

Sharpening a wood gouge is done in much the same fashion as for plane irons and chisel blades. As the gouge is curved, the blade must be turned during grinding and whetting. An oil slip stone, which has a curved edge, is used to remove the burr from the inside of the gouge.

BRACE AND BIT

The brace and auger bit is used for making holes in wood and removing excess wood prior to chiseling or sawing. The brace is the tool used to hold the bit, and the bit is the portion that does the actual drilling. The brace has an adjustable chuck, which allows it to take many sizes of bits as well as other tools such as screwdriver bits and countersink bits.

The best type of brace for general woodworking purposes is the ratchet brace. The ratchet mechanism allows the brace to be operated in either direction and permits the tool to be used even when there is insufficient room for a 360 degree turn.

Auger bits are available in different sizes. They come in 1/16″ gradations. For the home workshop, a set of six single-twist bits should be adequate. These should be 1/4″, 3/8″, 1/2″, 5/8″, 3/4″, and 1″. Additional bits may be purchased as the need for them arises. Like other cutting tools, bits should be stored in such a fashion that the cutting edges will not be dulled. The portion of the bit that fits into the chuck of the brace is called the tang. Below this is the shank and then the twist. At the end of the twist are the spur, the lips, and the screw. The screw at the end draws the bit into the wood so that the lips and spur can make the cut.

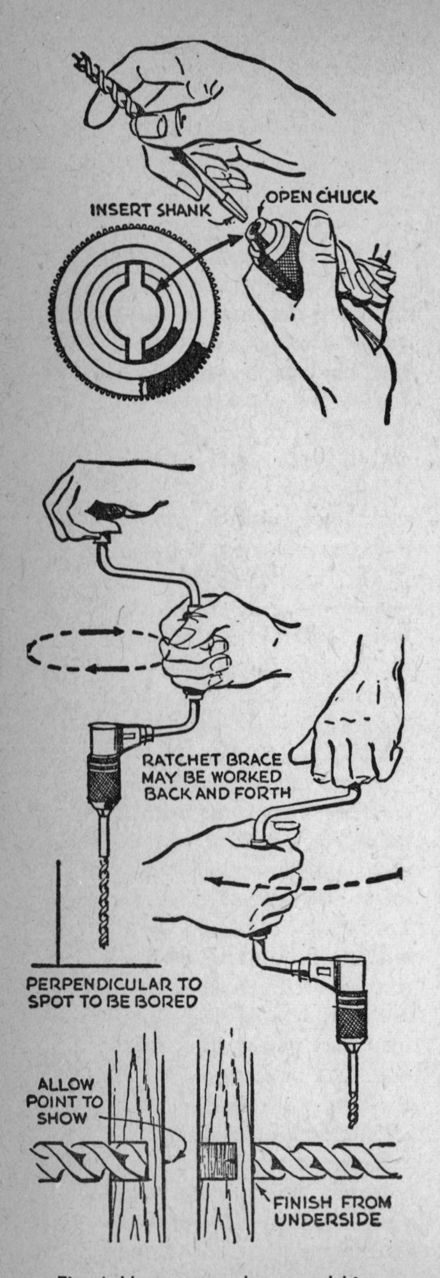

Fig. 4. How to use a brace and bit.

Using a Brace and Bit

The brace and bit is a simple tool to use. First select the correct size of bit and fasten it securely into the jaws of the brace chuck. If the bit is not held firmly, you may bend the bit while drilling. Set the point of the screw where the center of the hole is to be, and start rotating the brace in a clockwise direction, keeping one hand on the head of the brace so that you can apply sufficient pressure. Most of the holes you drill will be vertical. And unless you take special care, you may find yourself boring through at a slight angle. Sighting along the bit is one way to be sure you're working properly.

And the second method — and one that is much safer—is to set a small square on the work and against the bit. Once the bit is in the wood, it can be bent if the brace is moved out of line — avoid this by holding the brace as steadily as possible. Single-twist bits are supposed to clear themselves of waste wood. But when drilling through very thick stock, it is a good idea to remove the bit from time to time and clear away any waste in the hole or on the bit.

Do not bore a hole completely through a piece of wood. The wood is damaged by splintering when the bit breaks through on the other side. Bore through until you see the screw of the bit breaking through. Then remove the bit and start drilling from the other side. Centering the screw in the hole it has already made. In this way you will be sure of getting a clean opening. When it is necessary to bore a hole at an angle, set a bevel square to the correct angle and use this to guide the bit.

In many cases it is necessary to drill a number of holes of the same size and depth. Equal depth can be achieved by fastening a bit gauge to the side of the bit; the gauge prevents the bit from going further than the required distance. A block of wood with a hole drilled in its middle will also serve as a depth gauge. When fully inserted, the bit should extend beyond the block of wood to the depth of the hole.

Additional Bits

It is sometimes necessary to make a hole larger than 1″. This can be done with an expansion bit, which has an adjustable rack that can be set to the required size. Another type of bit—not necessary but useful—is the Forstner bit. This bit is used for drilling through thin wood that an ordinary bit might split and also for drilling close to the edge of a piece of wood.

It is also good for drilling very hard wood (which also might be split by an auger bit) and for drilling in end wood. As a Forstner bit has no screw or spur or lip, it makes accurate and clean cuts. It can also be used to enlarge a hole previously cut with an auger bit. This cannot be readily done with a larger size of auger bit because there is no wood for its screw to take hold of.

In addition to the wood-boring bits, a brace can be fitted with screwdriver bits, which are useful when a good many screws must be installed. There are also bits for countersinking screw heads, which have tangs that fit into the brace chuck.

HAND DRILLS

When you need to drill holes smaller than 1/4″, a twist drill is used. Twist drills have straight shanks and they range in size from 1/16″ up to 1/4″. Larger sizes are available but cannot be used in the ordinary hand drill or the 1/4″ power drill now found in many home workshops.

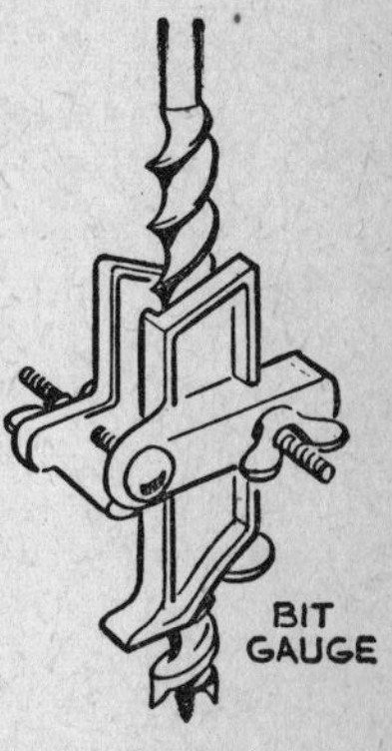

Fig. 5.

Twist drills are made for use either in wood or in metal. The least expensive type of drill with which to use them is the hand drill, which is suitable for the average workshop.

A breast drill—a type of hand drill—will take bits up to 1/2″ diameter and has a more rugged construction than ordinary hand drills.

Another type of small drill useful for making holes in wood is the automatic push drill. The rotary action of this drill is produced by pushing down on the handle. A spring pushes the handle back up, ready for the next stroke. Bits are usually enclosed in the push drill handle; they range in size from 1/16" to 11/64".

Using a Drill

Twist drills must be handled with care as they are not very thick and the bits can be easily bent or broken by moving the drill once it is in the wood. If the drill is rotated too quickly, it will heat up. This can spoil

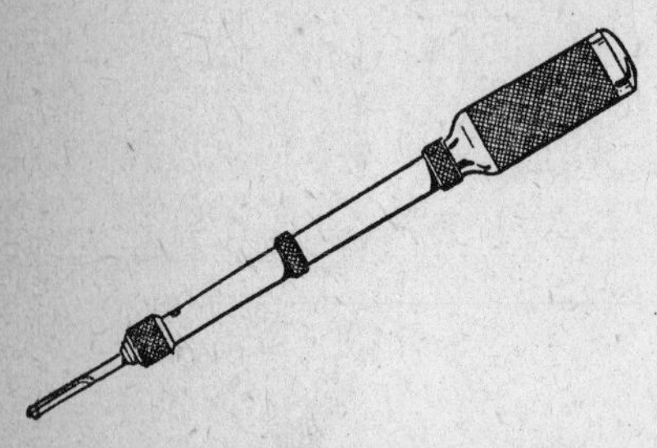

Fig. 6. An automatic push-pull drill.

the temper of the bit. This overheating is very easy when you are using an electric power drill. Also, twist drills do not clear themselves as easily as auger bits. Consequently, it is necessary to take out the bit from time to time and remove the waste from the bit and the hole.

OTHER TOOLS

Brad Awl

This tool consists of a metal shaft that is pointed at one end and has a wooden handle fastened to the other end. It is used in place of a hand drill or push drill to make holes in soft wood for screws and nails.

Files

Files are used in the wood workshop for sharpening and maintaining tools such as saws and screwdrivers. The exception is the rasp-cut file used on wood to produce a rounded surface —which cannot be done with a saw or plane. For example, if you wish to round off the edges of a board for a table top, you would use a rasp rather than a plane or saw. If you intend to do your own sharpening, you will need several files to fit the varying sizes of saw teeth.

Putty Knife

You'll need a putty knife in the home tool chest for applying putty, plaster, and plastic wood fillers. Keep the blade of the knife clean because if filler is allowed to accumulate and harden on it, you will be unable to smooth out a finish.

Nail Set

A nail set is a small metal punch used for forcing the heads of nails below the surface of the wood. The point of the nail set is centered on the nail head. Then the punch is struck with a hammer. By using a nail set you avoid damaging the wood surface with the face of the hammer. The depression over the countersunk nail head should be filled with plastic filler or wood putty.

Levels

Levels, as the name suggests, show you if a surface is perfectly flat or exactly upright. The location of a small air bubble in a liquid-filled glass tube tells the story. When the bubble is centered in the glass cylinder, the work on which the level is resting is either perfectly level or perfectly upright. Other readings show that the work is not true. Lines on the glass tube indicate its exact center.

Levels are made of wood or aluminum. The aluminum ones have several advantages over those made of wood—they are not as easily damaged and they won't warp; also, they are very light. Some types of levels have replaceable tubes. Other types give a reading of 45 degrees as well as the usual 0 degrees and 90 degrees. Place levels where there is no danger that another tool might break the glass tube.

Pliers

A pair of diagonal cutting pliers is handy for removing bent finishing nails and doing other odd jobs.

Clamps

There is a wide variety of jobs for clamps to do in the workshop. They hold articles firmly for cutting or chiseling as well as holding pieces together for gluing and accurate nailing. Clamps are made of wood or metal. Every shop should have at least four of each size—two inches and four inches. The correct use of clamps is covered in the instructions on using glue (page 20).

MEASURING TOOLS

You'll need measuring tools to produce well-made articles. All work should be carefully marked out before fitting begins, for even the most skilled craftsman cannot judge with the eye alone and not make mistakes now and then.

Rules

Rules are used to measure length or width. They are made of wood or metal. A folding rule is made up of 6″ sections that fold together when the rule is not in use; it is marked in sixteenths of an inch. Folding rules generally are six feet in length. Boxwood rules also fold in 6″ sections, but their total length is ony two or three feet.

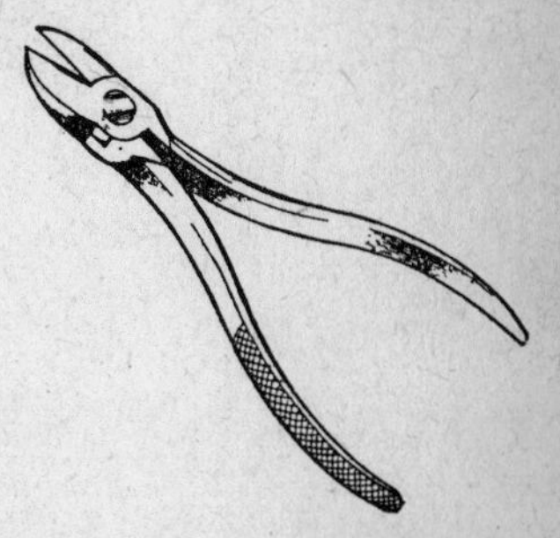

Fig. 7. Pliers for wire cutting.

These rules are marked off in eighths of an inch. The steel tape is still another kind of rule. It is made of flexible steel ribbon and winds into a small metal case. Steel tapes are very accurate and they are not as easily broken as wood rules. On the other hand, the steel rule can be bent and once it is creased it is no longer satisfactory for accurate measurements. Steel rules can be had in 6′, 8′, 10′, and 12′ lengths marked off in sixteenths of an inch. A workshop should have at least two rules, a boxwood type and either a folding wood rule or a steel tape.

Fig. 8. A framing square.

Squares

Three kinds of squares are required for woodworking: the framing or carpenter's square, the try square, and the combination square. The framing square and try square are fixed while the combination square is an adjustable instrument.

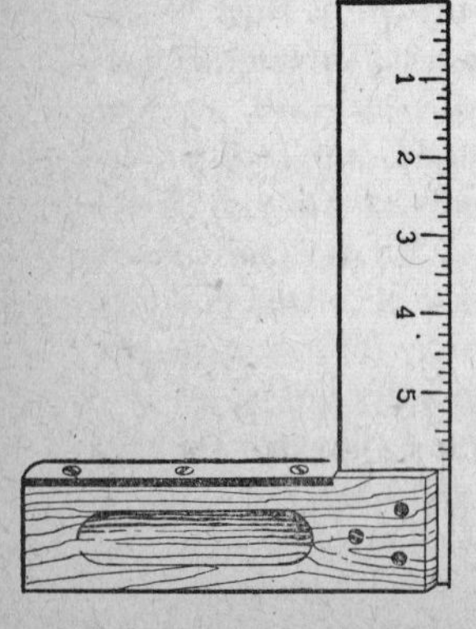

Fig. 9. A right-angle square.

Framing Square. The framing square is made of steel and comes in two sizes: 24″ x 16″ and 24″ x 18″. The difference is important only in house framing—elsewhere, either one will do. The long leg of the square is the "body," and the short leg is the "tongue." Framing squares can be used for measuring lengths and for making right-angle cuts.

Try Square. The try square is somewhat smaller than the framing square and is used to true a board for squareness. The blade of the square, which measures from 2″ to 12″, is fixed in a metal or wood handle. A 6″ try square is suitable for most woodworking requirements.

Combination Square. The combination square combines a try square with a miter square. The latter is used for cutting 45 degree angles. A lock nut fits in the stock of the square, when it is loosened the blade can be moved to the desired setting. Better grades of combination squares have spirit levels mounted in the stock.

Bevel Square. The bevel square has an adjustable blade which can be set for any desired angle. The handle of the square is marked off in graduations of common angle cuts. This tool is useful when making angle cuts for other than 45 degrees.

Squares and metal rules must be treated with care so that they won't get bent out of shape. Wipe them with oil from time to time so that they will not rust. A thin coating of rust can conceal the graduation marks and make the tool useless. Rust can be removed from the metal with a typewriter eraser.

Marking Gauge

A marking gauge is used to mark a line a set distance from the edge of a board. The bar of the gauge consists of a square piece of wood marked in fractions of an inch. The head of the gauge slips over the bar and can be locked by means of thumb screws. At the end of the bar is a metal pin point, which marks the wood. This gauge is used by first setting the head on the bar at the proper point. The head of the gauge is then pressed firmly against the edge of the wood and the bar tipped so that the pin point comes into contact with the wood. As the gauge is pushed away from along the board the pin point leaves a mark in the wood.

WOOD FASTENERS

Nails

Nails are the most common type of wood fasteners. They are used on both rough and finished work. While there are many different types of nails suitable for various special jobs, those most commonly used in woodworking are the common, finishing, and casing nails.

Common nails are used for all rough work where an exposed nail head doesn't matter. They have flat heads and pyramid-shaped points. Finishing and casing nails have smaller heads, which are driven below the wood surface where they will not show. This is called countersinking.

Nail sizes are measured by the symbol "d" or "penny." This derives from the old English system in which so many nails of a certain size could be purchased for one penny. The following list shows the penny measurements and their lengths in inches.

2d – 1″
3d – 1 1/4″
4d – 1 1/2″
5d – 1 3/4″
6d – 2″
7d – 2 1/4″
8d – 2 1/2″
9d – 2 3/4″
10d – 3″
12d – 3 1/4″
16d – 3 1/2″

Among the special nails you may find use for is the clinch nail, which is used where great holding power is required. The end of this nail, which extends beyond the wood surface, is bent over with the hammer against the wood grain. Brads are small nails —under 1″ in length—which are used to install thin trim, molding, and similar stock that would be split by a heavier type of fastener.

Fig. 10. An adjustable square, a very useful tool.

Using the Right Nail. Selecting the right size of nail for a job and deciding how many nails to use is a problem for the amateur. After you have made up a few projects, you will get the feel of things and know more or less which type and what quantity to use. A good rule of thumb for beginners is to use a nail three times as long as

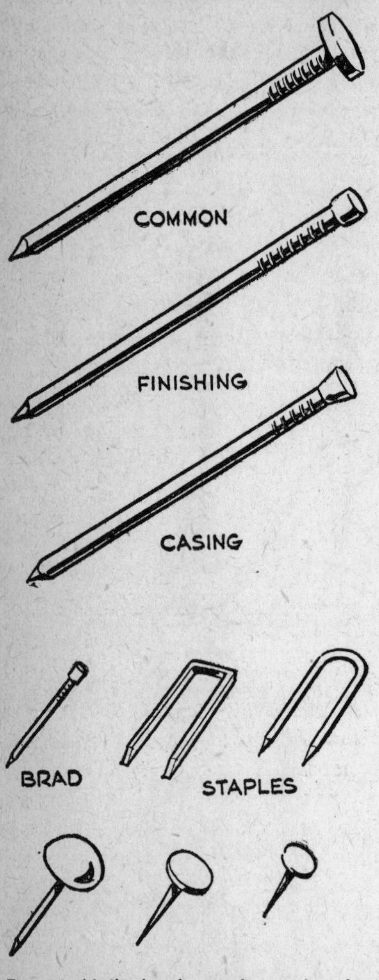

Fig. 11. Nails, brads, staples, and tacks.

the wood through which the nail is to be driven. For example, if you wish to nail a piece of wood 1″ thick, an 8d or 10d nail would be about right.

Nails should be staggered along a piece of wood because too many in line will start a split. This is especially true when nailing close to an edge. Nails with blunt ends are less likely to split the wood than those with sharp ends. This is because a sharp point will force the wood fibers apart, thus starting the split, while a blunt nail will merely break the fibers. If you find that a nail has a tendency to split the wood, blunt its end with your hammer. When nailing through very hardwood, it is wise first to drill a hole smaller than the diameter of the nail. This will reduce the chance of splitting. If a nail should bend while it is being driven in, remove it and use a new one.

Nails are much faster to install than screws but they do not have the same holding power and cannot be easily removed, once in place, without damage to the wood. For this reason, when great strength is required or when a piece may have to be removed at some later date for repairs or refinishing, use wood screws. Also always use wood screws on hardware such as hinges. *Never* use nails no matter how small the hinge.

Nails driven in at an angle, called toe-nailing, have greater strength than when they are upright. Clean nails also have a stronger holding power than those covered with dirt and rust. Up until a few years ago, all nails were made out of steel. Now aluminum nails are available and they are not only lighter but also will not rust—an important consideration for outdoor projects involving chairs and benches.

Wood Screws

As already mentioned, wood screws have several advantages over nails and should be used on all fine work. The most common screws are the flat-head and round-head types. Flat-head screws are used when the head must come flush with or below the wood surface. Round-head screws can be used where appearance doesn't count too much. Screws are measured in length by inches. The length of a flat-head screw is the over-all length from tip to top of head. For round-head screws the length runs from the tip to the underside of the head. The diameter is given either in a gauge number or in inches. Screws should be purchased by specifying the type of head, length, and diameter.

Screws are made of steel or brass. Steel screws are stronger than those of brass but will corrode if exposed to the weather. Brass screws should always be used where appearance is important.

Inserting a Screw. Before a screw can be installed, it is necessary to drill a hole in the wood. Usually two holes of different sizes are drilled in the two pieces of wood to be fastened together with the screw. The hole in the top piece of wood should be somewhat smaller in diameter than the shank of the screw above the threads. The hole in the lower piece should be slightly smaller than the diameter of the threads at the bottom of the screw and should be the same depth as the penetration of the screw. These are called pilot holes. The second pilot hole is not always necessary when working with very soft wood but it is necessary in hardwood. If you fail to drill these holes, the chances are that the head of the screw will be broken off or twisted by the screwdriver or that the wood will split. Also, with the holes the screws will go in with much less effort. When a screw is driven into end-grain wood, only a relatively small hole is required unless the wood is very dense and hard.

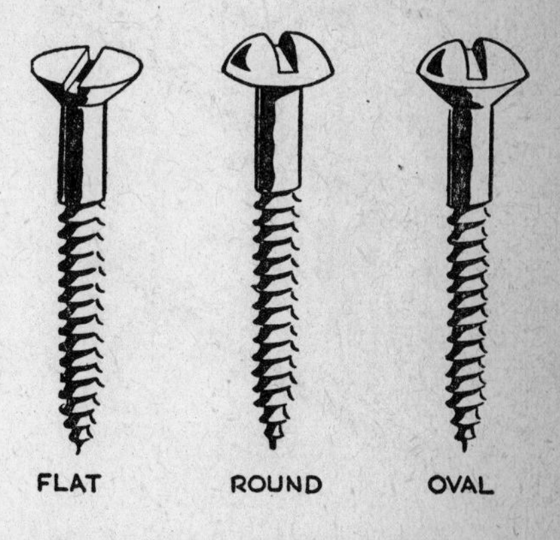

Fig. 12. Different types of screw heads.

If the screw head is to be sunk below the wood surface, a third hole is needed. This hole is drilled with a countersink on the surface of the wood and should be deep enough to allow the screw head to go below the wood surface. Wood filler is then applied over the screw head. In very fine work, a wood plug is glued in over the screw head, and in this case the countersink must be deep enough to take both screw head and plug. Always be sure that the countersink is deep enough to take the screw head, for if it is too shallow, the head will split the wood as it is driven down. When you have to run a screw through very hard wood, put a little soap on the tip of the screw. This acts as a lubricant and makes the screw go in more easily and with less chance of splitting the wood.

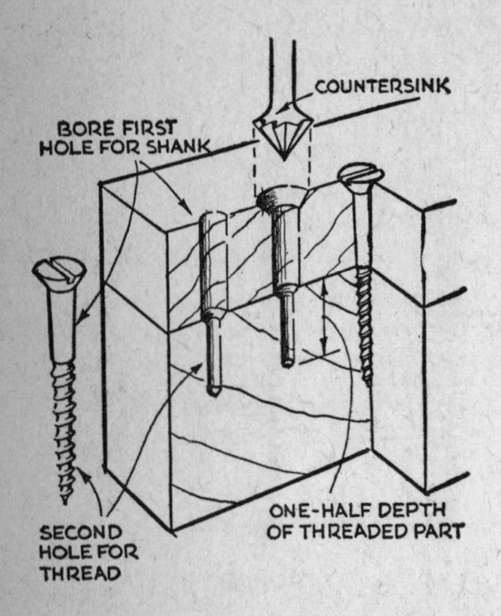

Fig. 13. Proper method of inserting a wood screw. The shank and thread holes prevent splitting the wood; the countersinking permits the screw head to go below the surface.

When it is necessary to run a line of screws near the edge of a piece of wood, stagger the screws to lessen the chance of splitting the wood.

Carriage Bolts

These bolts have an oval head and a square shank for a short distance from the head. They are fitted with nuts and washers and are used for heavy construction jobs. They are used in this book for the construction of the outdoor swing and see-saw.

Toggle Bolts

These are useful for attaching a heavy object to a wall where it is impossible or impractical to get at the far side of the wall to attach washers and nut. You drill a hole large enough to permit bolt and collapsed toggle to pass (see Fig. 14) and after toggle is opened you screw up the bolt until it is tight.

Glue

Glue is used for fastening wood together. It can be used alone or with wood screws if a very strong joint is desired. Two of the best glues for the home workshop are casein glue and resorcinol-formaldehyde. Casein glue comes in a dry powder form and is mixed with water before use. It is applied cold, requiring no heating as animal glues do. It makes a very strong joint. Resorcinol-formaldehyde glue—a resin glue—is waterproof and can be used for outdoor work. Follow the manufacturer's directions for using a particular brand.

Gluing. The strength of a glued joint depends to a great extent on a snug fit between the two pieces of wood. The wood surfaces must be planed or sanded until such a fit is obtained. Wood surfaces must not only be smooth but they must also be clean and dry. Apply a thin coat of glue to both surfaces and when almost dry apply a second light coat to each surface. When the second coat becomes tacky, place the two pieces together.

Clamps. The work must now be held together with clamps until the glue is dry. Clamps prevent the two pieces from slipping apart. Even more important, unless held tight until dry, the glued joint will not be very strong. Care must be taken, however, not to put too much pressure on the joint with the clamps as this would force out a lot of the glue. Clamps should be arranged on the work to provide an even pressure over the entire area. Do not try to glue together too many pieces of the same work at once—this would make it too difficult to clamp them properly. Allow the joint to sit for at least twenty-four hours with the clamps on. Avoid giving a glued joint a sharp blow—it may weaken the joint.

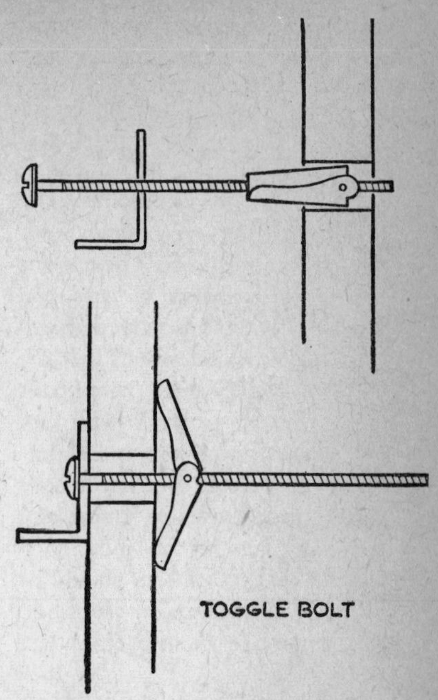

Fig. 14. How a toggle bolt works.

SANDPAPER

Sandpaper is an abrasive paper used for smothing down wood surfaces. A workshop should have a good supply of various grades for smoothing down surfaces prior to gluing or finishing and for removing excess wood that is too thin for saw or plane.

Sandpaper is graded by numbers. No. 3 1/2 is very coarse, it is suitable only for sanding down rough unfinished wood. No. 9/0 is very fine and is used only for polishing. For general shop work you should use such grades as No. 1, No. 0, No. 2/0, and No. 3/0. Steel wool is often used in place of sandpaper for smoothing out wood, particularly curved areas that are difficult to do with sandpaper.

Wood is always sanded *with* the wood grain. If you try to sand against the grain, it will produce a rough, scratchy surface. The best way to hold the sandpaper is to clip it around a block of wood that fits comfortably into your hand. Any piece of waste wood will do for this purpose, but you can buy a ready-made sandpaper holder, which is somewhat better. When bringing a piece of wood down to the desired smoothness, start out with a rather coarse grade of sandpaper. Then work down through the finer grades. Sandpaper should be stored where it will be kept dry. While sold in packages of assorted grades, you may find it wiser to buy only some grades.

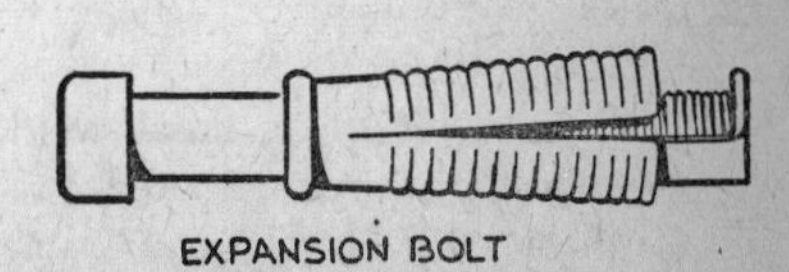

Fig. 15. Expansion bolts are useful for anchoring cabinets to plaster walls.

LUMBER

The two main classifications of lumber are: hardwood and softwood. Hardwoods are cut from deciduous trees like oak, maple, and hickory, which lose their leaves in the fall. The softwoods are the evergreens, or conifers, like pine and spruce. These terms are slightly misleading because you will run across hardwoods that are relatively soft and softwoods that are hard. For the most part, hardwoods are more difficult to work with and more expensive—but also more durable—than softwoods. The hardwoods also have more attractive grains and take finishes better than most softwoods. For this reason they should be used, when possible, on furniture where appearance and sturdiness are important factors.

In the composition of wood we find hundreds of small cells called pores. In most hardwoods these pores are very pronounced and must be taken into account when the wood is finished or else the finish will dry rough. Oak and ash, for example, have very noticeable pores. Such woods are called "open-grain" woods. Birch and maple, on the other hand, have small pores and are referred to as "close-grain" woods.

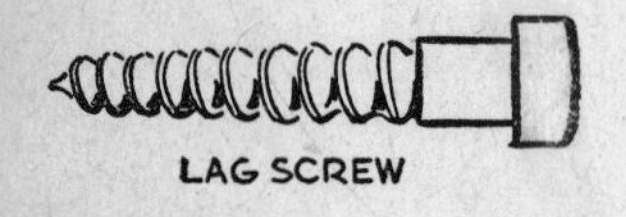

LAG SCREW

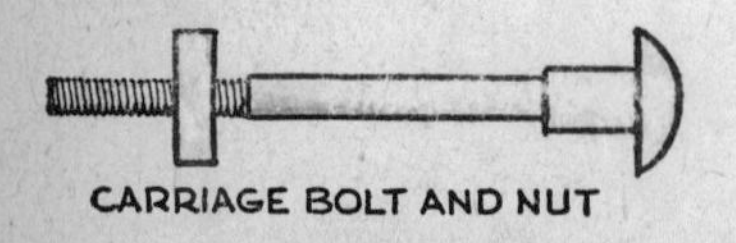

CARRIAGE BOLT AND NUT

Fig. 16.

Grading. Most cut lumber is classified by a grading system set up by the lumber industry. The best grades are called "select." They are almost completely free from such defects as knots and stains. Select lumber is graded A, B, C, or D, A being the best grade. "A Select" should be almost perfect, while "D Select" should have only a few minor flaws that can be covered with paint. The next major grade of lumber is called "Common," and this in turn is graded 1 to 5. Common 1 to 3 can be used for most structural purposes, such as rough carpentry.

Seasoning. Freshly-cut lumber contains a good deal of moisture. As this moisture disappears, the board shrinks somewhat. When the moisture content of a board gets to around 12 per cent, it remains at this point unless subject to artificial heat. When the moisture content is 12 per cent or so, the lumber is considered "seasoned," that is, suitable for use. Seasoning is sometimes speeded up by placing the wood in an oven and the lumber is then called "kiln-dried" (pronounced "kill") and is usually more expensive than lumber allowed to season naturally. Either type of seasoned lumber is suitable for use. Lumber in a yard is usually stored in a warm dry spot where it will not have a chance to absorb moisture. When you take a piece of seasoned lumber home, take precautions to store it in a warm dry

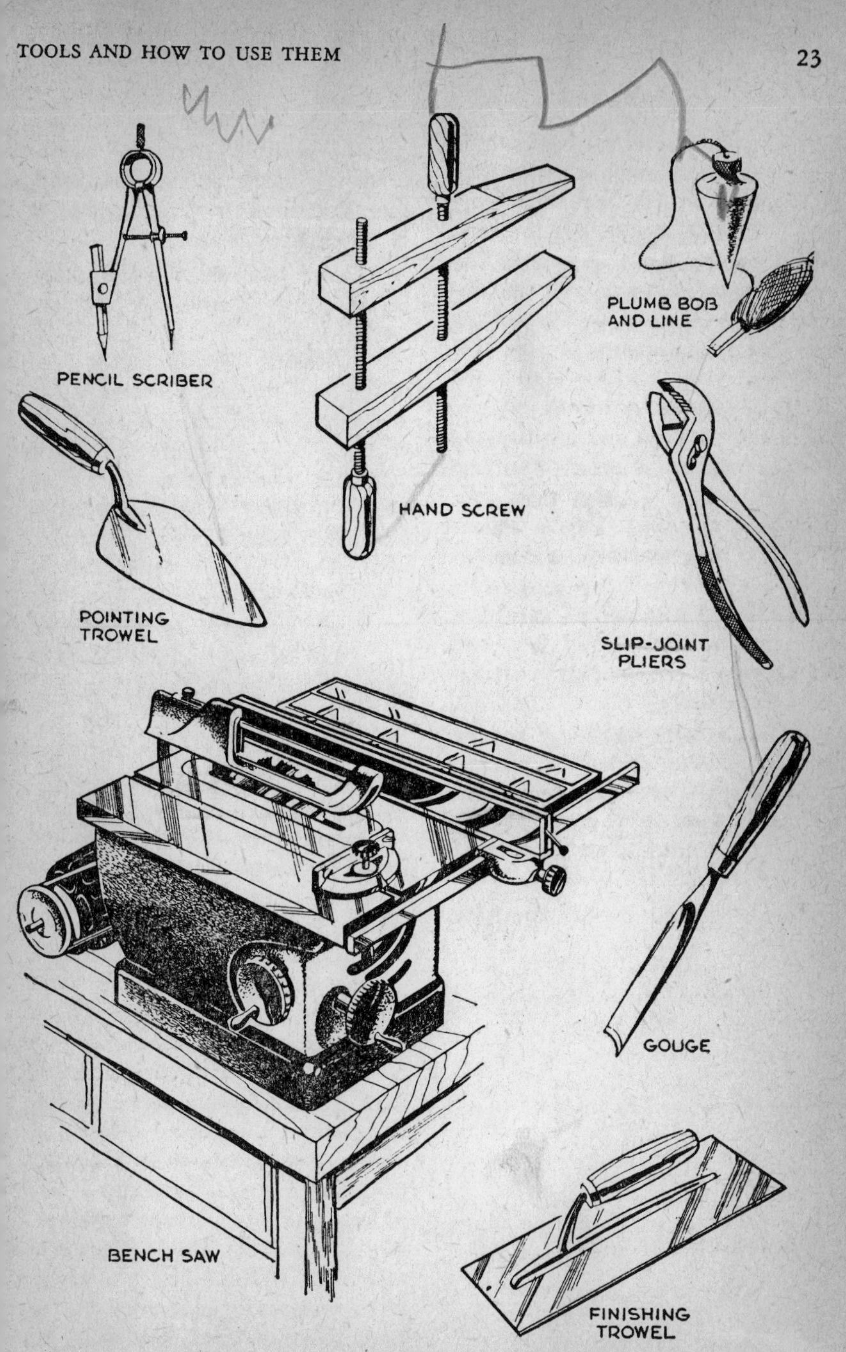
PENCIL SCRIBER
HAND SCREW
PLUMB BOB AND LINE
POINTING TROWEL
SLIP-JOINT PLIERS
GOUGE
BENCH SAW
FINISHING TROWEL

Fig. 17.

place. Lumber with a high moisture content is not only difficult to work with but, when the project is finished and the lumber begins to dry out, it will shrink and may open up glued joints and seams and may even crack.

Don't let boards sag or they will warp and twist out of shape. Keep them in a storage rack.

Lumber Sizes

Lumber is graded when in the rough state. After this the boards are run through a machine that planes down one or more surfaces. Lumber stamped S1S has been surfaced on one side. S2S means surfaced on two sides; S1E, surfaced on one edge; S1S1E, surfaced on one side and one edge; and S4S, surfaced on all four surfaces. Because board dimensions are graded in the rough state and then finished, surfaced lumber measures somewhat less than indicated. For example, a board 1″ x 6″ surfaced on all four sides actually measures only 25/32″ (3/4″ for most purposes) x 5 1/2″. This factor must be constantly taken into account when constructing projects where dimensions must be accurate. If the plans call for a board 6″ wide, it is necessary to take a 7″ board that actually measures 6 1/2″ and remove the excess 1/2″. If a board must be exactly 1″ thick you will have to order five-quarter (5/4) which measures 1 1/16″, and remove the extra 1/16″.

The accompanying table gives the thicknesses of rough and surfaced lumber that you are likely to use in woodworking.

Most of the projects in this book call for lumber dressed or surfaced on all four sides, that is S4S.

The unit of measurement for most lumber is the board foot. A board foot is equal to a piece of wood 1″ thick, 12″ wide, and 12″ long. Boards under 1″ thick are considered 1″

STANDARD WIDTHS AND THICKNESSES OF ROUGH AND SURFACED YARD LUMBER

Lumber described as nominal—		Actual dimensions when surfaced shall not be less than—	Actual dimensions when rough dry shall not be less than—
	Inches	Inches	Inches
Thickness	1	25/32	29/32
	1 1/4	1 1/16	1 5/32
	1 1/2	1 5/16	1 13/32
	1 3/4	1 7/16	1 9/16
	2	1 5/8	1 3/4
Width of finish	3	2 5/8	2 3/4
	4	3 1/2	3 5/8
	5	4 1/2	4 5/8
	6	5 1/2	5 5/8
	7	6 1/2	6 5/8
	8	7 1/4	7 3/8
	9	8 1/4	8 3/8
	10	9 1/4	9 3/8
	11	10 1/4	10 3/8
	12	11 1/4	11 3/8

boards; those between 1″ and 2″ are considered 2″ boards. To determine exactly how many board feet of lumber you require for a particular project, multiply the length in feet by the width in feet by the thickness in inches. For instance, the number of board feet in a piece of 1″ x 6″ that is 12′ long would be 1″ x 6/12′ x 12′, or 6 board feet.

The required amount of each size of lumber is given with each of the projects in this book and, if you wish, this list can be given to your lumber dealer. This eliminates the possibility of waste and also the storage problem for those who do not have facilities to store long pieces of lumber. It is wise to add 10 per cent to the list of materials to take care of waste to allow for trimming, and so on.

While most softwoods come in lengths of 8′, 10′, 12′, and on up, many lumber yards stock "shorts" — pieces of uneven length, which may be just what you require. Most of the hardwoods come in random lengths. The price of lumber is quoted by the 1000 (M) board feet. Lumber that sells for $160 a thousand costs 16 cents a board foot.

Wood molding such as quarter round (also written 1/4″ round) half round, and trim is sold by the foot. When you order this material, just give the total length required. It is not necessary to figure this out into board measure.

Plywood

Many of the projects in this book call for plywood. Plywood is made by taking thin sheets of wood veneer and gluing them together so that the grain of each sheet runs at right angles to the next one. It comes in 3-ply and 5-ply. The thicknesses available range from 1/4″ and 3/8″ up to 1″. For most purposes 3/8″, 1/2″, and 3/4″ plywood can be used. The standard sheet of plywood is 4′ x 8′ but it is possible to get the longer 10′ or 12′ sheets when required.

Special sheets are available for table-tennis table tops, which must measure 5′ x 9′. If your lumber dealer does not have these sheets in stock, he can order them for you. Plywood is much stronger than wood of comparable thickness, and the large-size sheets eliminate the need for many joints and seams that would be necessary if regular boards were used. Plywood can be worked with the same tools as are used for ordinary wood. A little extra care is advisable in cutting it, whether using saws or chisels.

Plywood comes in interior grade and exterior grade. The interior grade can be used for all inside projects. Outdoor projects must be made from the exterior plywood as the veneers of these sheets are fastened together with a waterproof glue that will not loosen up from dampness. If interior plywood is allowed to become very wet, the sheets of veneer will wrinkle and separate.

Some lumber yards stock plywood in random sizes or will saw a full sheet in half for you if a full-size sheet is not required. There is often a slight charge for this service. Plywood is priced by the square foot. A standard 4′ x 8′ sheet contains 32 square feet.

Hardboard

Hardboard is another wood product that can be used on many jobs. This material is made out of wood fibers mixed with an adhesive and rolled into hard sheets measuring 4′ x 8′. The sheets come in several thicknesses and are extremely tough and durable.

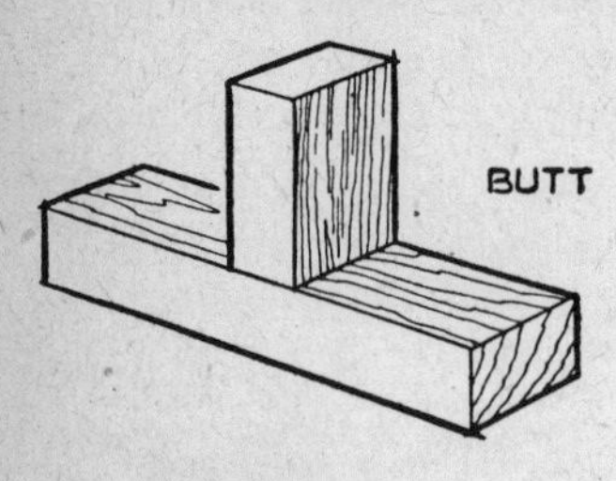

Fig. 18. Butt joint.

They are moisture-resistant and take a finish well. Hardboard, or pressed-wood as it is sometimes called, is much less expensive than plywood but does not have the same type of structural strength. It is used for such purposes as backing for shelves and cabinets and sliding doors. It is worked with woodworking tools and can be sawed, planed, and nailed with ease. Care must be taken in handling the large sheets, for while they will bend to some extent, too much bending will crack them. Hardboard comes in two grades, regular and tempered. Plywood, on the other hand, comes in several grades. The least expensive type of plywood has only one surface free from knots and cracks. The reverse side has flaws and cannot be exposed in finished work. The more expensive kinds of interior plywood come with a surface veneer cut from the more expensive kinds of woods, such as walnut, maple, or birch.

Kinds of Wood Used for Woodworking

Birch: This is a good wood to use for furniture. It is not difficult to work with and is hard and rather strong. It takes glue moderately well and is ideal for blonde finishes.

Butternut: Often used for furniture in place of the more expensive walnut or mahogany. It is easy to work with and takes glue very readily.

Cherry: Very good for all furniture.

Cypress: This wood is difficult to work with as it splinters easily. On the other hand, it is the must durable native American wood and is ideal for all outdoor work where it will be exposed to the weather.

Gum (Red): Another fine wood for furniture. It's moderately easy to work with, takes glue and nails well.

Hickory: This is an extremely hard wood but is very satisfactory for furniture.

Maple (Hard): Sometimes called sugar maple, this wood is extremely hard and one of the best for furniture.

Maple (Soft): Not as satisfactory as hard maple, the soft variety is used for less expensive furniture.

Oak (White): The best of the many oaks, this wood is excellent for furniture.

Oak (Red): Not as satisfactory as white oak but used in a good deal of cheaper work.

Walnut: An excellent wood for furniture and cabinet making.

Redwood: Like cypress, this wood is highly resistant to decay. It is more easily worked than cypress and makes an excellent material for outdoor furniture.

Pine (White): The best wood for painting. Very easy to work with and rather soft, therefore easily dented.

Pine (Ponderosa, Western, or Yellow): Not too satisfactory for furniture, but can be used for other projects such as shelves, molding, and trim.

JOINTS USED IN WOODWORKING

Properly constructed wood joints are essential for many of the wood projects described in this book. A well constructed joint not only adds to the over-all appearance of a piece of furniture or cabinet but it also provides additional support. Sharp cutting tools and accurate measurements and cutting are important to produce a really tight joint.

A description of the joints commonly used in woodworking follows.

Butt Joint

This is the most common [illegible] simplest of all wood joints. [illegible] ting or special shaping is required, therefore the joint is not particularly strong and must be assembled with nails or screws and not with glue alone. The end of the intersecting member must be cut off square to obtain a solid bearing along its entire width. Care must be taken when driving in nails or screws to see that they are placed in such a fashion as to strike the approximate center of the intersecting member. Butt joints are often used on such projects as shelves, where a horizontal member runs between two upright pieces. To insure that the horizontal member is perfectly level, mark lines an equal distance up on each of the uprights and use them to position the horizontal member.

Lap Joint

The two principal kinds of lap joints are the corner lap and the middle half-lap. These two joints are used in a variety of projects. The first step in laying out these joints is to place one piece on top of the other in the correct position. Use a clamp or vice to hold them in place and then mark off the width of each cut. Use a try or combination square to draw out the lines. The depth of each cut is then marked out with a marking gauge. Use a fine-toothed crosscut or back saw to make the cuts and then carefully remove the waste wood with a chisel. Be sure to saw on the waste side of the lines. Rather than try to remove a large solid piece of waste with the chisel, it is wise to make several saw cuts and then remove the remaining waste in small pieces. The extra minute is time well spent.

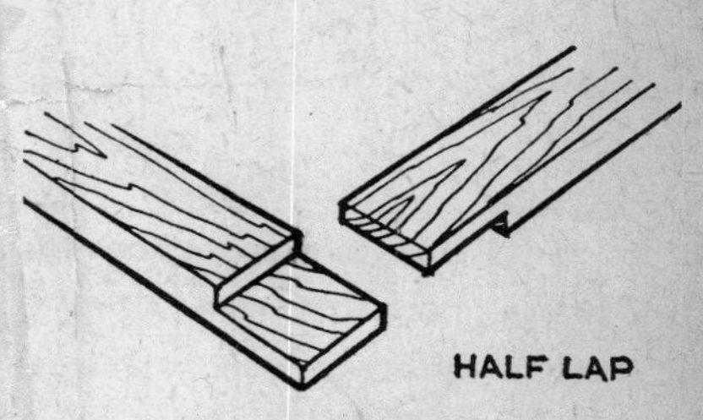

Fig. 19. Half lap joint.

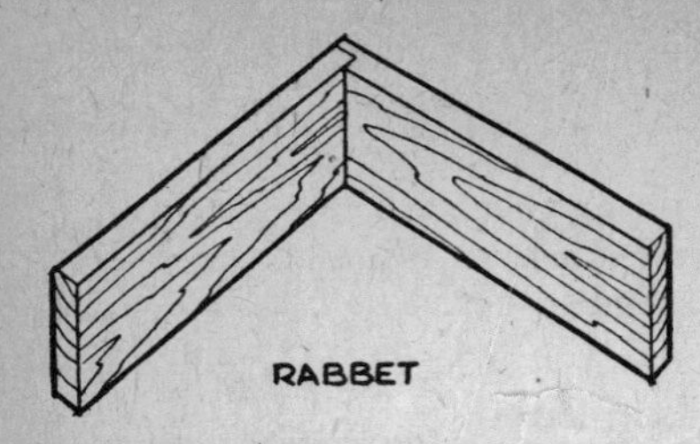

Fig. 20. Rabbet joint.

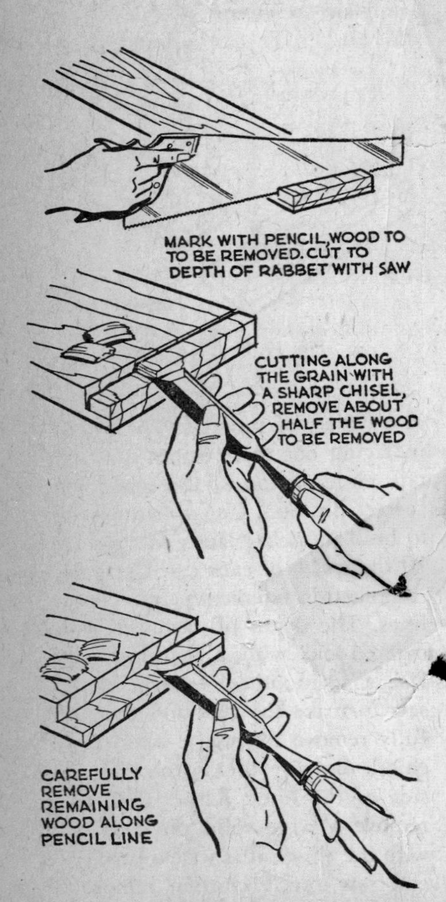

Fig. 21. Making a rabbet with a saw and chisel.

Rabbet Joint

Rabbet joints are made by cutting a recess or shoulder on the end of one or both pieces of wood that are to be joined together. The width and depth of each rabbet required is given on the drawings in this book. To lay out a rabbet, run a line with a try square the required distance from the end of the wood. This is for the width of the rabbet. Bring this line down along the sides of the stock the required depth. Cut along this line with a saw and then remove the waste with the chisel. A time saver in cutting this joint is a rabbet plane. This type of plane has a blade that extends flush with one edge of its frame and it has a gauge to regulate the width and depth of the cut.

Dado Joint

A dado is actually a groove cut in one member to take the width of another member. Dado joints are used for shelves and cabinets. A dado is laid out by drawing two parallel lines across the face of the stock the same distance apart as the width of the stock to be fitted. These lines are brought down along the side for the depth of the dado and a cut is made on each line with a saw. The waste is then removed with a chisel.

Miter Joint

Miter joints are a type of butt joint with the end of each piece cut to a 45 degree angle. The correct angle for the cut can be laid out with the 45 degree angle of a combination square. For greater accuracy it is best to use a miter box. Inexpensive miter boxes can be made up in the shop or purchased for around one dollar. The more expensive ones run up to $20 or $30.

Dowel Joint

Butt joints and miter joints are often reinforced by drilling holes in each of the members and inserting a wood dowel, which is held in place with glue. This makes a very strong joint. To make sure that the dowel is correctly centered, remove the head from a small brad and drive the brad into one member at the correct location for the dowel. Allow the brad to extend a fraction of an inch above the wood surface and then place the two pieces of wood firmly together. When they are taken apart the brad will leave an impression in the wood where the hole for the dowel should be centered.

MISCELLANEOUS MATERIALS

Hinges

Several types of hinges are required for some of the projects in this book. The most common type of hinge is the butt hinge. It consists of two leaves held together by a removable pin. To install this type of hinge, the edge of the door and of the door frame must be recessed so that the leaves of the hinge will set flush with the wood surface. Take the hinge apart by removing the pin and set one leaf on the edge of the door or frame where it is to be fastened. Holding the leaf securely, mark with a knife round the edges. Along the back edge mark a line to indicate the thickness of the hinge leaf. The recess is then cut with a wood chisel. Take very light cuts with the chisel against the wood grain because if the recess is deeper than the thickness of the hinge plate, the door will not fit correctly. When the

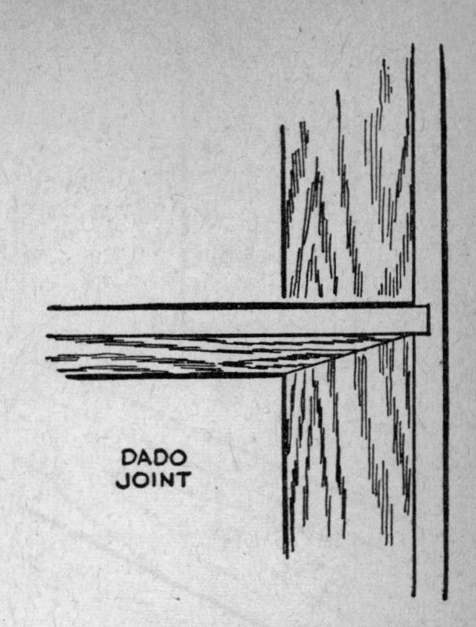

Fig. 22. Dado joint.

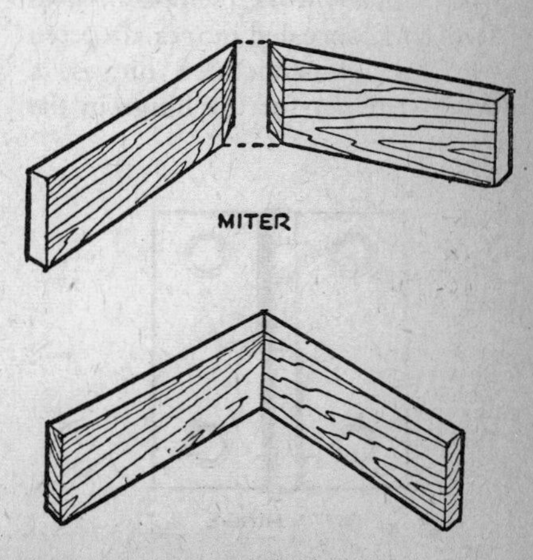

Fig. 23. Miter joint.

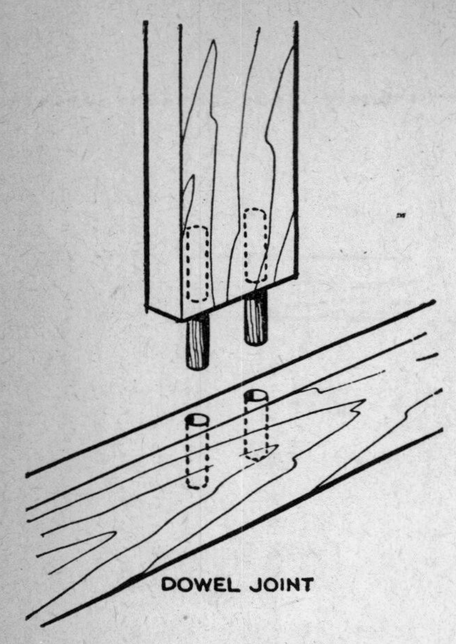

Fig. 24. Dowel joint.

recess has been cut on both door and door frame, the hinge can be assembled and installed.

For cabinet work, semi-concealed hinges and concealed hinges are often used. For semi-concealed hinges, a recess is cut out for the hinge in the same manner as for a butt hinge. Openings for concealed hinges are made with a brace and bit as well as a wood chisel because the opening must be deep enough to take the entire hinge.

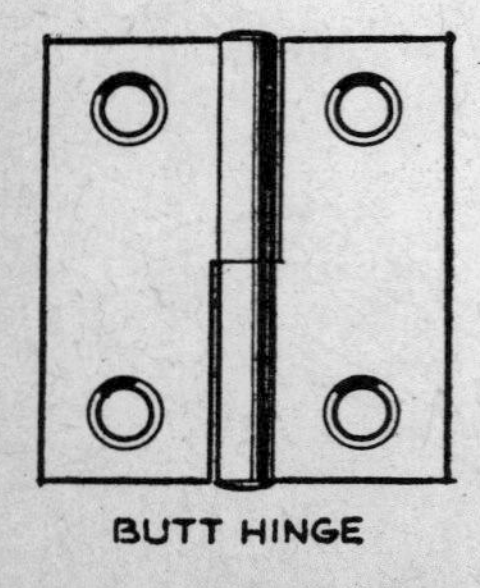

Fig. 25.

For heavy outdoor work, "T" or strap hinges are often used. These require no recess but are fixed over the wood surface.

Always used screws for fastening hinges in place, regardless of the size.

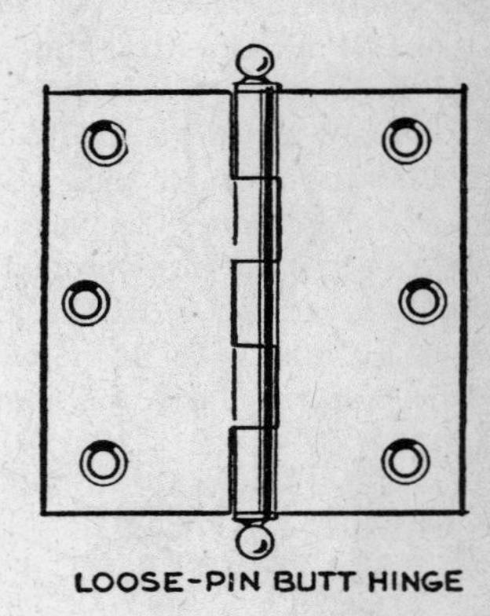

Fig. 26.

Latches

Hardware dealers stock a wide variety of latches suitable for cabinets. Cupboard catches and spring latches are screwed directly to the face of the wood. Bullet latches or catches are recessed into the wood, and friction catches are fastened to the inside of the cabinet door itself.

Mending Plates and Angle Irons

These metal plates come in several sizes and shapes and are very useful

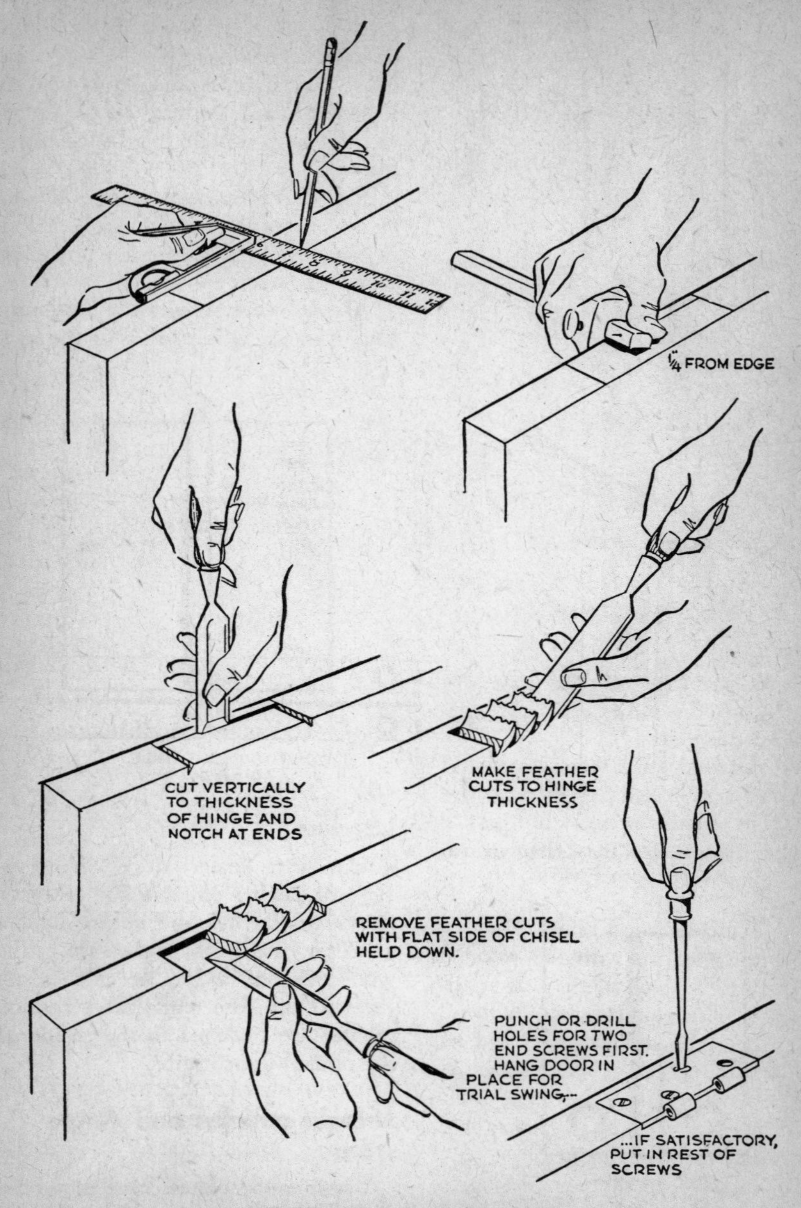

Fig. 27. How to attach a hinge.

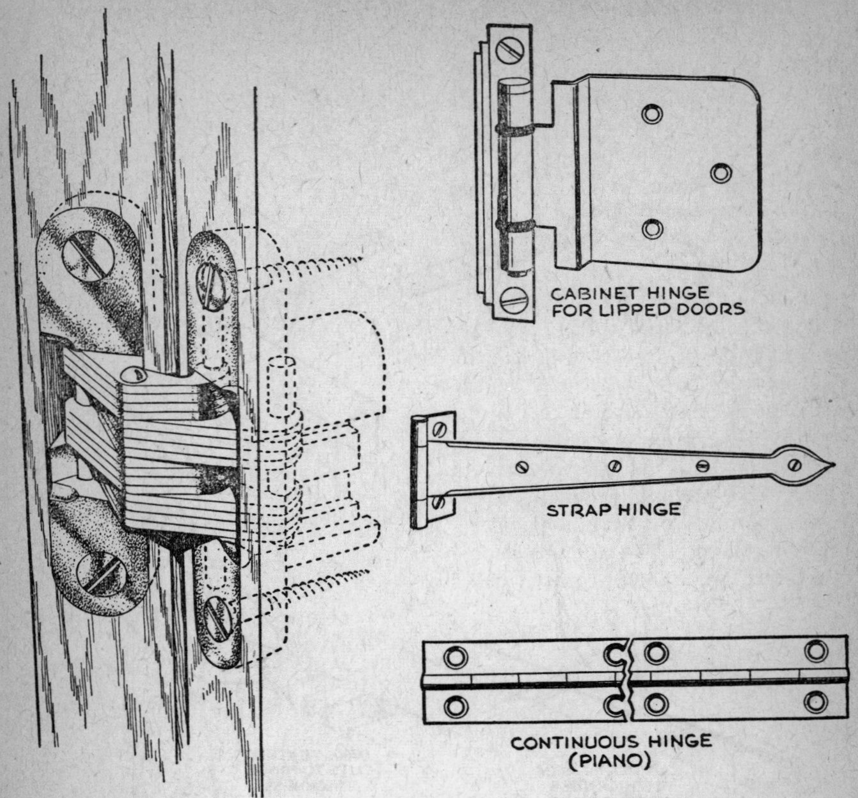

Fig. 28. How an invisible hinge is constructed and installed.

Fig. 29.

for reinforcing wood joints. They can either be set flush with the wood or on its face. They should always be installed with wood screws. A mending plate recessed into the wood has more holding power than when set on the wood surface.

Corrugated Fasteners

These fasteners are very useful for assembling miter joints. They are installed by driving them in against the wood grain with a hammer. The work should be placed on a solid surface and held together with clamps or in a vice while the fasteners are being driven in.

Screw Hooks, Screw Eyes, and Hooks and Eyes

These items come in several sizes. A mixed assortment of them should be kept on hand.

STARTING A PROJECT

The first step in making a project is to purchase the necessary material. The list at the end of each project gives you all the materials necessary. Add 10 per cent to these figures to account for waste. It is best, when possible, to pick out the materials yourself as this will eliminate the chance of getting a board which contains so much waste as to be useless.

Before doing any cutting, lay out the rough dimensions of the work on the boards. This will help reduce waste. It is often possible to use the scrap left over from one piece of lumber rather than to cut an unused board. This preliminary laying out is very important in cutting plywood because if you cut up a large sheet without careful thought on exactly what you need, you may find a good portion of the total is wasted.

Before laying out the final measurements on a board, check the end with

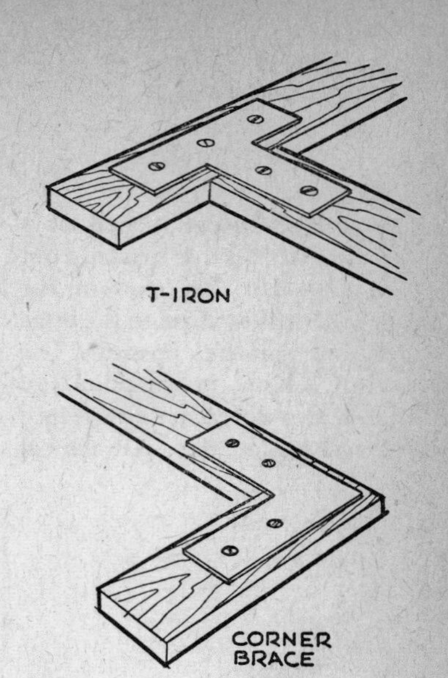

Fig. 31.

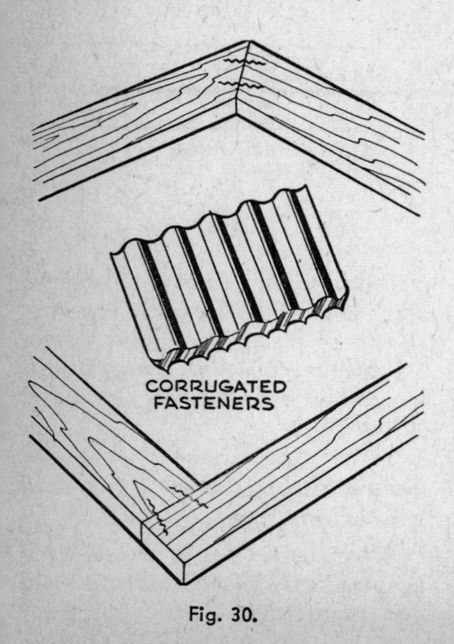

Fig. 30.

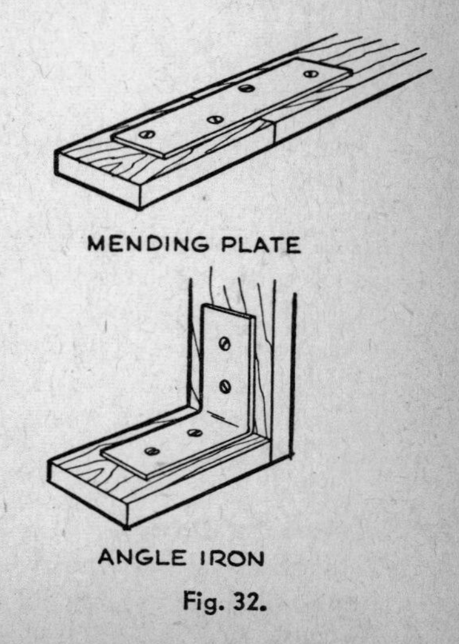

Fig. 32.

your square to be sure that it is perfectly true. In most cases it is best to remove this end. Even if it is smooth, it may be rough or damaged and might spoil your work.

Use a well-sharpened pencil or a knife or metal scriber for marking out lines. Be sure that the point of the pencil or scriber is as close to the edge of the rule or square as possible. The thickness of a blunt pencil point can often mean the difference between a good fit and a poor one. Always cut on the waste side of the line. When several pieces of the same size are to be cut, make one up and check it for size. Then use this as a pattern for the rest.

All measurements given for projects in this book are worked out for stock that has been surfaced on all four sides. If another size of stock is used, the necessary reductions or additions must be made to take care of the differences in thicknesses, lengths, and widths.

DETACHABLE BREAKFAST TABLE

When it is not in use, it is a simple matter to take this breakfast table down and store it out of the way.

The table top is made from a solid piece of 3/4″ plywood with the outside corners rounded off to a 6″ radius. At the bottom of the end which rests against the wall, fasten on edge a strip of 3/4″ stock 1 1/8″ wide. This should be cut the same length as the width of the table top — 24″.

Select a piece of 5″ stock 24″ long and round off the two upper corners. This is the portion of the table that will be fastened to the wall and will always remain in place, even when the table has been stored away. Along the bottom edge of this piece, fasten a strip of 3/4″ stock 7/8″ wide. This strip should be fastened in place on edge, and its bottom should be flush with the bottom edge of the 5″ x 24″ board. To this 3/4″ x 7/9″ strip, a 1/2″ x 1 7/8″ strip is fastened; the bottom edges of the two pieces should be flush.

At a distance 1″ in from the front end of the table top and at the midpoint of its width, install the leg, which is made of 3/4″ stock 4″ wide by 29 1/4″ long. The leg is attached in place with a hinge and supported by a folding metal bracket. Set the rear support for the table on the wall 32 1/4″ from the floor and fasten it in place with screws run through the plaster into the wall studding, or with expansion bolts. Now set the table top in place with the lip on its rear end extending down into the recess formed in the wall support. Center the table top and then drill a 1/4″ hole at each end through the wall support and table lip so that 1/4″ dowels can be inserted to hold the top tightly in place.

Materials List

1 piece 3/4″ plywood 24″ x 48″
1 " 3/4″ x 5″ x 24″
1 " 3/4″ x 4″ x 29 1/4″
1 " 3/4″ x 1 1/8″ x 24″
1 " 3/4″ x 7/8″ x 24″
1 " 1/2″ x 1 7/8″ x 24″
2 1/4″-dowels 2 1/2″
1 folding metal bracket

Materials Totals

1/4″ dowel — 5″
(Remainder as itemized above)

DETACHABLE BREAKFAST TABLE

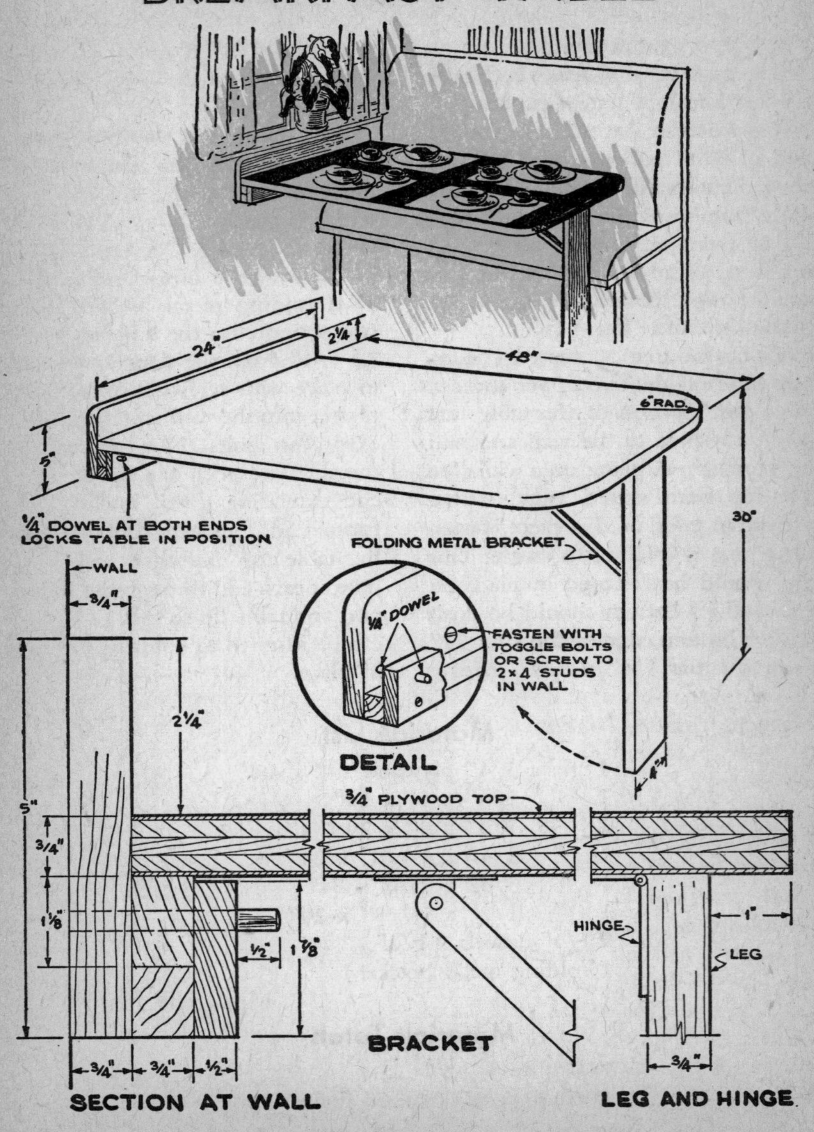

DROP-LEAF TABLE

This table is large enough when extended to serve as a dining room table for a sizeable family.

The first step is to make up the two side sections (see second illustration). These are made out of 3/4″ plywood and measure 32″ long and 28 1/4″ high. Draw a line across the bottom 4″ in from the edge of each side piece. 2″ in from the lower corner, set a bevel gauge at 60 degrees to get the correct angle for the legs, and then make the cuts. The next step is to make up the frameworks for the bottom of the table, the drawers, and the table top. The frames are made out of 3/4″ x 3/4″ stock. Each frame should be 10 1/2″ wide and 30 1/2″ long. The top framework is set flush with the top of the side pieces; set the middle frame 5 1/2″ down from the top and the bottom frame 17 1/2″ down from this. When the two side pieces have both been fastened to the three frames, cut and fit the 1/2″ plywood divider strip. This should be set at the exact midpoint of the frames, that is 15 1/4″ from the end. The plywood divider will have to be notched to fit around the middle and top frameworks. After the divider is in place, cut and fasten in place the 1/2″ plywood coverings for the frameworks. Each is 10 1/2″ x 15″.

The two gate legs can now be made up. 1″ x 3″ stock is used for this purpose and all joints are made with dowels. 7″ from the end of the table, the gate legs are attached to the sides with hinges. The two drawers for the table are made up with front pieces of 3/4″ or 1″ stock. Front pieces should be 6″ x 10 1/2″ and rear pieces are 1/2″ x 4 3/4″ x 15 1/2″. Drawer bottoms are 15 1/2″ x 9 3/16″ and are made out of 1/4″ plywood. Doors for the table are of 3/4″ stock 18 1/4″ x 10 1/2″.

The fixed portion of the table top, which is 3/4″ x 14″ x 34″, is now fastened in place and the two table leaves, 34″ x 24″, are hinged to the fixed portion of the top. A stop should be installed on the underside of each leaf to prevent the gate legs from extending more than 45 degrees from the table base.

Materials List

2 pcs. 1″ x3″ x28 1/4″
2 " 1″ x3″ x24 1/4″
4 " 1″ x3″ x15 1/2″
6 " 3/4″ x3/4″ x30″
6 " 3/4″ x3/4″ x10 1/2″
2 " 3/4″ plywood 32″ x28 1/4″
2 " 3/4″ plywood 24″ x24″
2 " 3/4″ plywood 19″ x10 1/2″
1 " 3/4″ plywood 14″ x34″
2 " 3/4″ plywood 4 1/4″ x10 1/2″
1 " 1/2″ plywood 10 1/2″ x23″
6 " 1/2″ plywood 10 1/2″ x15 1/2″
4 " 1/2″ plywood 4″ x15 1/2″
2 " 1/2″ plywood 4″ x9 1/2″
2 " 1/4″ plywood 10 1/2″ x15 1/2″
8 butt hinges 3″

Materials Totals

3/4″ x 3/4″ — 20′ 3″
1″ x3″ — 13′ 11″
(Remainder as itemized above)

DROP-LEAF TABLE

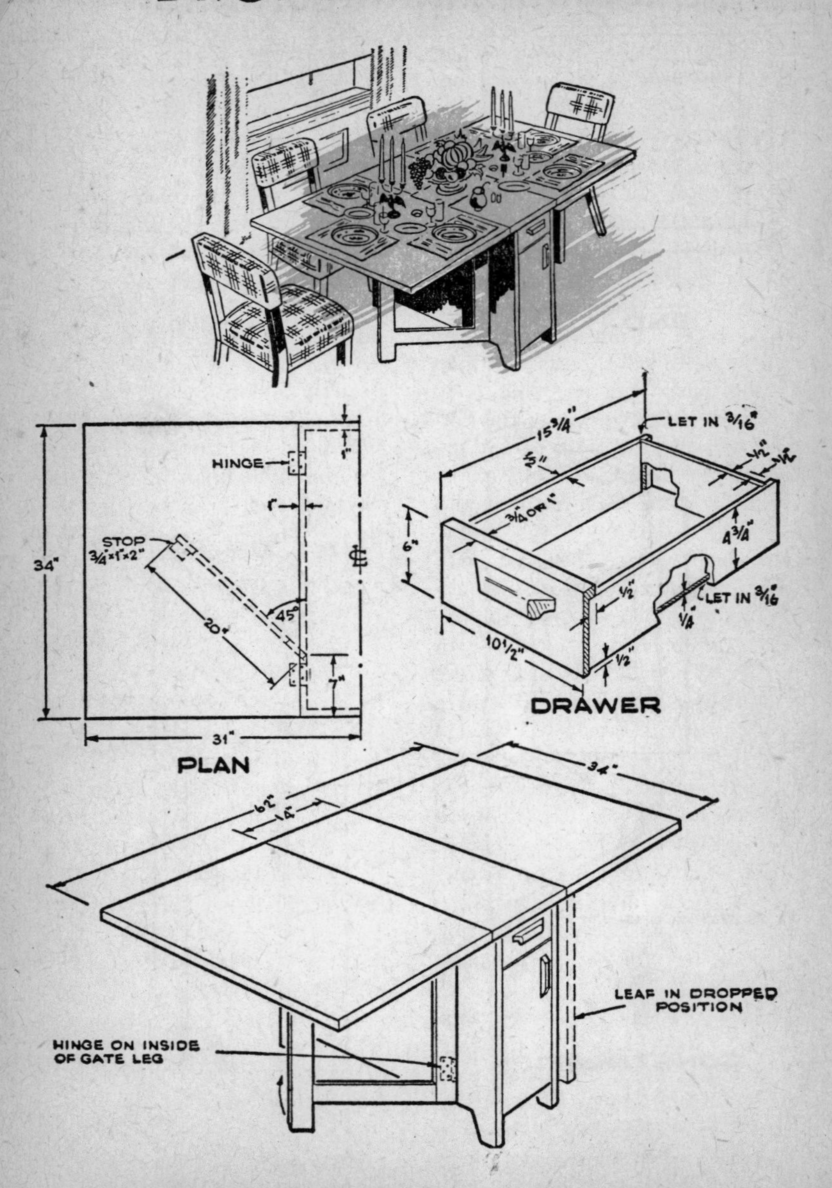

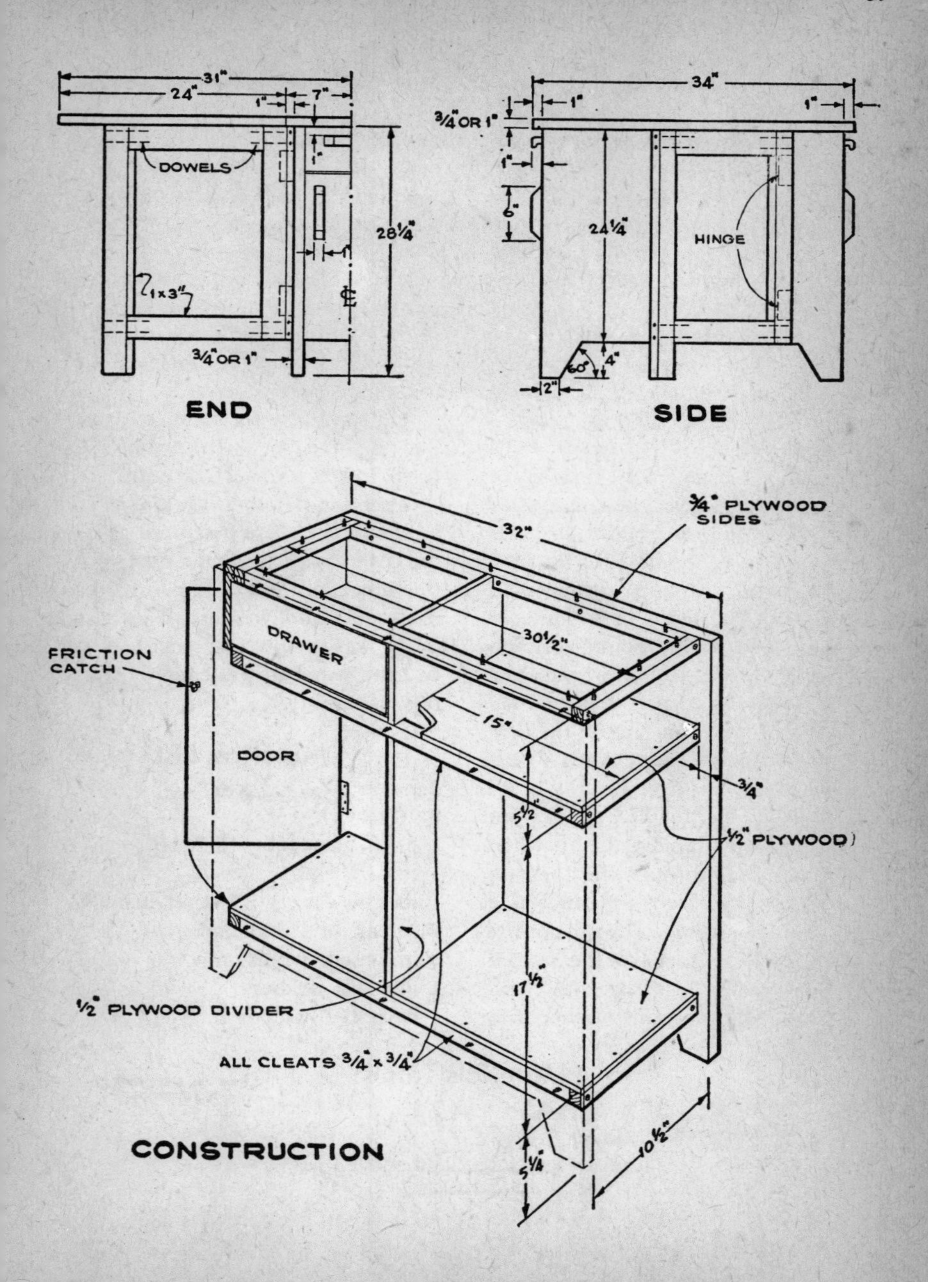
31"
24"
1"
7"
DOWELS
1x3"
3/4" OR 1"
28 1/4"
1"
END
34"
1"
1"
3/4" OR 1"
1"
6"
24 1/4"
HINGE
60°
4"
2"
SIDE
32"
3/4" PLYWOOD SIDES
DRAWER
30 1/2"
FRICTION CATCH
15"
DOOR
5 1/2"
3/4"
1/2" PLYWOOD
17 1/2"
1/2" PLYWOOD DIVIDER
ALL CLEATS 3/4" x 3/4"
CONSTRUCTION
5 1/4"
10 1/2"

MODERN TABLE LAMP

The top and base of this table lamp should be cut out of select hardwood. Cut out two pieces of stock that are square and roughly the right size. Then mark out the cutting line with a compass set for 4″. Cut slightly to the outside of this line with a compass saw and bring the wood down to the line with a wood rasp and sandpaper. Using the center of each block as a point, scribe a line with your compass set for 3 1/4″. This line indicates the middle of the holes to be drilled for the 1″ dowels. These holes should be 3/8″ deep and an equal distance apart. To line up the holes in the base with those in the top, drive small headless tacks through the middle of each base hole so the points stick up just above the surface. Now place the top over the base and press down. Remove the top and mark the impressions from the points with a pencil for future drilling. Drill a 3/8″ hole through the top and the bottom at the midpoint. Remove the bit when its tip just comes through the opposite side, and drill in from the other side to prevent splintering. The hole in the base should be enlarged on the bottom to a 5/8″ radius 3/8″ deep to form a recess for the nut and washer that holds the brass tube in place. Drill a 1/4″ hole through the side of the base at a slight downward angle so that it will meet the nut-and-washer hole.

Cut the hardwood dowels 12 3/4″ in length and glue them into the holes in the base and top. To be sure of the fit, check the top with a level before the glue is hard.

The hardware for the electric socket can be purchased at hardware or electrical stores. Thread the electric cord through the nut and tube and the hole in the base before assembling. Bring the cord out through the other end of the tube and install the ornamental brass nuts and washers. The base of the socket is now secured to the tube and the wires are fastened in place to the main body.

Materials List

2 pieces 1″ x 6″ x 6″
8 1″-dowels 13″
1 3/8″-brass tube 15 7/16″
1 brass socket
1 lock washer 3/8″ inner diameter
2 ornamental brass spacers
1 ornamental brass nut
1 nut and washer
1 harp 12″ wide

Materials Totals

1″ x 6″ – 1′
1″ dowel – 8′ 8″
(Remainder as itemized above)

MODERN TABLE LAMP

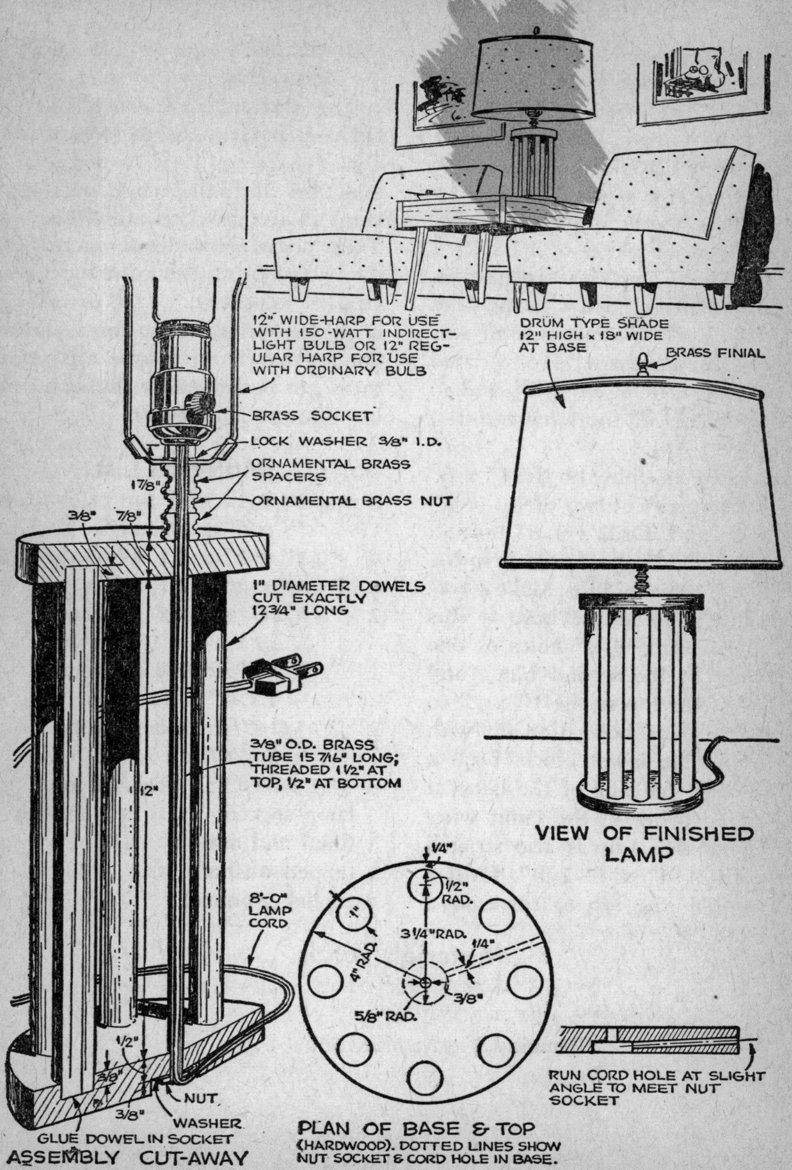

TABLE LAMP

This modern table lamp owes its attractive appearance to the interesting texture of the plywood.

The base is made from a piece of 1" x 6" x 14 1/8". The inside frame is made from two pieces 2" x 4" x 15 3/4". These pieces are fastened together with four pieces of 1" x 2" x 9 1/4". The 1" x 2" are placed on edge with the face flush with the sides of the 2" x 4". To one side of this assembly glue a piece of 5/16" striated plywood 13 1/8" x 15 3/4", and to the ends pieces of the same material 3 3/4" x 15 3/4".

Center the assembly on the 1" x 6" base and secure. Cut two pieces of 1" x 2" x 2 1/8". Drill a 3/8" hole in the center of one and fasten it to the base in the exact middle. Make a corresponding hole in the base at this point. Drill three 3/8" holes or one 7/8" hole in the second block and fasten it at the top to the 1" x 2" so that the hole or holes line up with the hole in the lower block. Drill a hole through the side of the lamp at the base to bring in the lamp wire. The top of the lamp is also striated plywood 4 1/4" x 13 1/8". Drill a hole through the top to correspond with the hole in the wood block. Glue the top in place.

The shaft is three pieces of 3/8" O.D. (outside diameter) brass tubing. The center piece is threaded at each end while the two that take the lamp sockets are threaded at one end. These pieces are soldered together and the two tubes to which the sockets are attached are cut off 2 1/2" or so shorter at the end than the third. This is done so that the wires running through them can be spliced to the wire coming into the lamp body.

Materials List

2 pcs. 2" x 4" x 15 3/4"
1 " 1" x 6" x 14 1/8"
4 " 1" x 2" x 9 1/4"
2 " 1" x 2" x 2 1/8"
2 " 5/16" striated plywood 13 1/8" x 15 3/4"
1 " 5/16" striated plywood 4 1/4" x 13 1/8"
2 " 5/16" striated plywood 3 3/4" x 15 3/4"
3 " 3/8" O.D. brass tubing
2 lamp sockets
1 finial and nut
1 tapped washer
1 rubber grommet

Materials Totals

2" x 4" — 2' 7 1/2"
1" x 2" — 3' 5 1/4"
(Remainder as itemized above)

TABLE LAMP

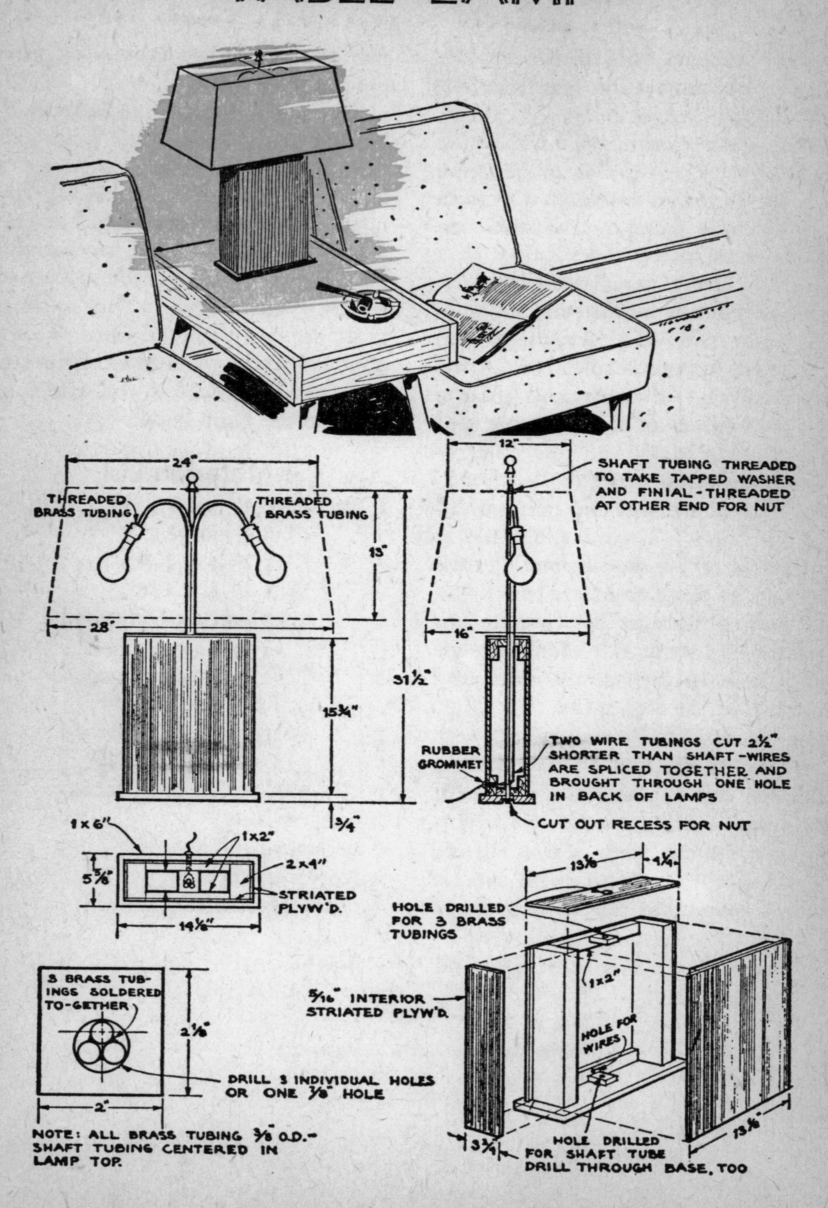
24"
THREADED BRASS TUBING
THREADED BRASS TUBING
13"
28"
31½"
15¾"
¾"
12"
SHAFT TUBING THREADED TO TAKE TAPPED WASHER AND FINIAL - THREADED AT OTHER END FOR NUT
16"
RUBBER GROMMET
TWO WIRE TUBINGS CUT 2½" SHORTER THAN SHAFT - WIRES ARE SPLICED TOGETHER AND BROUGHT THROUGH ONE HOLE IN BACK OF LAMPS
CUT OUT RECESS FOR NUT
1 x 6"
1x2"
2 x 4"
5⅝"
STRIATED PLYW'D.
14⅛"
13⅛"
4¼"
HOLE DRILLED FOR 3 BRASS TUBINGS
1x2"
5/16" INTERIOR STRIATED PLYW'D.
HOLE FOR WIRES
3 BRASS TUBINGS SOLDERED TO-GETHER
2⅛"
2"
DRILL 3 INDIVIDUAL HOLES OR ONE ⅞" HOLE
NOTE: ALL BRASS TUBING ⅜" O.D. - SHAFT TUBING CENTERED IN LAMP TOP.
3¾"
HOLE DRILLED FOR SHAFT TUBE DRILL THROUGH BASE, TOO
13⅛"

MODERN FLOOR LAMP

The base for this attractive floor lamp consists of three pieces of 1″ stock cut to circles of various diameters. The bottom circle of the base measures 12″, the middle 8″, and the top 3″. Cut these to rough size with a keyhole or coping saw and then bring them to the exact size with a rasp and sandpaper. The three parts of the base can be fastened together with glue and wood screws. At the exact center, bore a hole through the base 1/2″ in diameter and enlarge this at the bottom to take a nut and washer. The depth of this enlargement should be 3/8″.

The post for the lamp is made out of 4 pieces of 1″ quarter round molding. Plane 1/4″ off the apex of each piece of quarter round, and then glue the four pieces together. The post top assembly is cut out of 7/8″ hardwood. Cut one piece each of the following diameters: 2 1/4″, 2 1/2″, 2 3/4″, 3, 3 1/4″, and 2 1/4″.

Procure a piece of 1/8″ (nominal inside radius) pipe 48″ long with threads at each end 3/4″ deep. Slip the pipe through the base and the post and place the six parts of the top assembly over it. Slip a piece of 1″ (outside diameter) brass tubing 3 1/4″ long over the end of the pipe and then thread the lamp cord through the pipe. Install the husk and the three-way mogul socket at the top. Tighten the nut at the base of the post until the entire assembly is firm.

Materials List

4 pcs. 1″ quarter round 36″
1 " 1″ x 12″ x 12″
1 " 1″ x 8″ x 8″
1 " 1″ x 3″ x 3″
4 " 7/8″ hardwood 3 1/4″ diameter
1 " 7/8″ hardwood 3″ diameter
1 " 7/8″ hardwood 2 3/4″ diameter
1 " 7/8″ hardwood 2 1/2″ diameter
2 " 7/8″ hardwood 2 1/4″ diameter
1 " 1/8″ (inside radius) pipe 48″
1 " 1″ (outside diameter) brass tubing 3 1/4″
1 nut
1 lock washer
1 washer
1 3-way mogul socket
1 husk
4 chair glides

Materials Totals

1″ quarter round — 12′
(Remainder as itemized above)

MODERN FLOOR LAMP

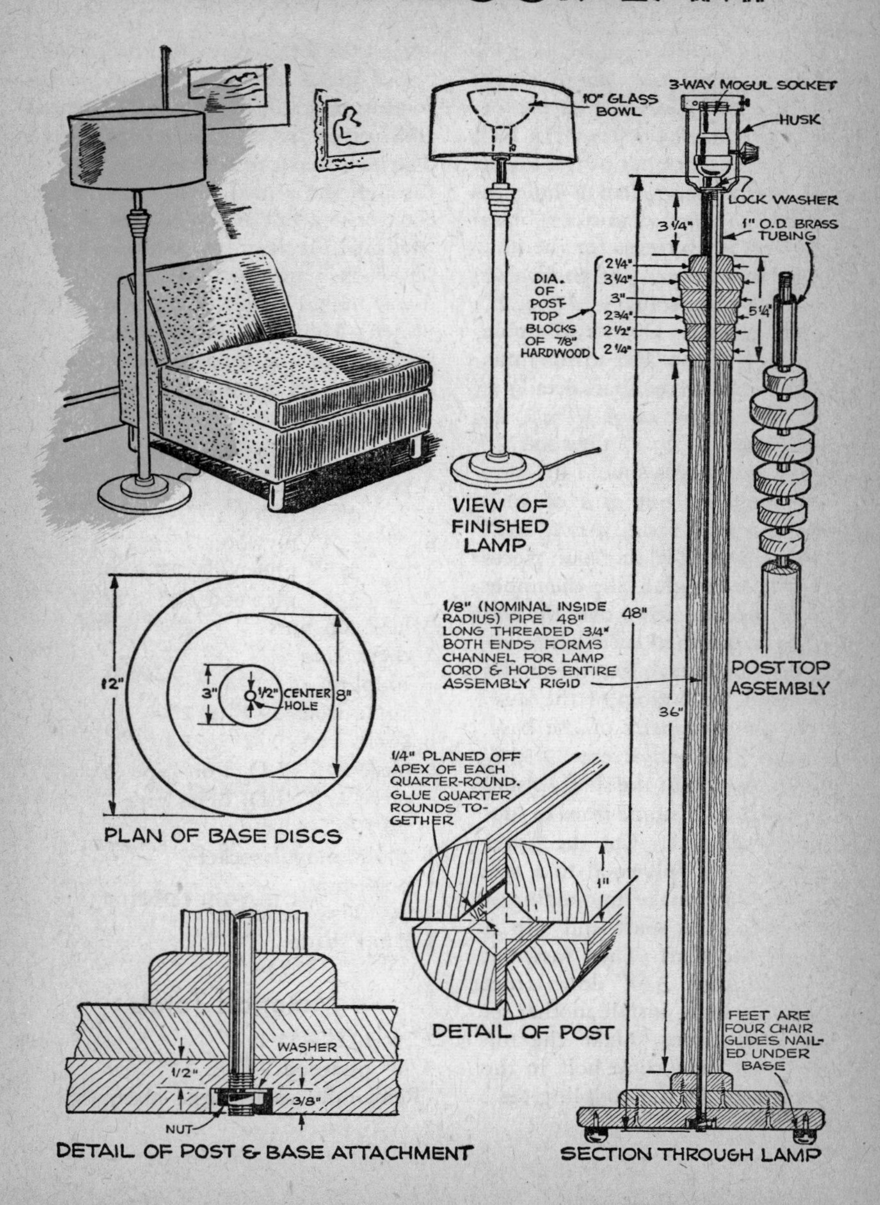

FLOOR LAMP

The base for the lamp (see plan of base) is made of one piece of 2" stock 19" x 14". Centered on top of this is a piece of plywood 3/4" x 10" x 8". At the exact center of the lower portion of the base, drill a hole to take a 3/8" (inner diameter) brass pipe and cut out a recess for the nut. At the center of the upper portion of the base, cut an opening 1 1/2" x 2" for the lamp shaft. Do not assemble the two parts of the base at this time.

The lamp shaft (see shaft detail) is made up of two pieces of 1" x 1/2" and two pieces of 1/4" plywood 2" wide. All four pieces should measure 27 5/8" long. At one end of each piece of 1" x 1/2" fasten a 1/2" x 2" angle iron. Assemble the four pieces of the shaft, using glue. Slip the upper portion of the base down over the end of the shaft and then cut shallow recesses in the bottom so that the angles fit flush with the bottom of the base. Assemble the two parts of the base, using wood glue and screws. 9 3/4" down from the top of the shaft, install four 1/2" x 1 1/2" angle irons to support the lower shelf. Cut the lower shelf out of 3/4" plywood to a size 19" x 14". Now, make an opening at the center for the shaft and slip it down over the shaft. Then fasten it to the angle irons. 3/4" down from the top of the shaft, install another set of four angle irons. Make the top shelf 10" x 8" and cut a hole in the exact center to fit the coupling size. Fasten the top shelf to the angle irons.

See detail A in the drawing for joining brass and iron pipe together. Both pipes are threaded at each end. The next step is to feed extension cord through the joined pipes. Attach the countersunk nut at the bottom of the iron pipe. At the top of the brass pipe, screw on a hexagon nut and then a 3-way mogul socket with a brass husk jacket. The 10" glass reflector is screwed into a shadeholder. Attach four silent glides on the bottom.

Materials List

2 pcs. 1" x 1/2" x 27 5/8"
1 " 2" x 14" x 19"
2 " 1/4" plywood 2" x 27 5/8"
1 " 3/4" plywood 19" x 14"
2 " 3/4" plywood 10" x 8"
3 hexagon nuts
1 check ring
1 coupling
2 angle irons 1/2" x 2"
6 angle irons 1/2" x 1 1/2"
1 piece 3/8" I.D. iron pipe 29 1/2"
1 piece 3/8" I.D. brass pipe 16 1/2"
1 3-way mogul socket
1 brass husk
1 10" glass reflector
1 lamp shade

Materials Totals

1" x 1/2"—55 1/4"
3/4" plywood 24" x 27"
(Remainder as itemized above)

FLOOR LAMP

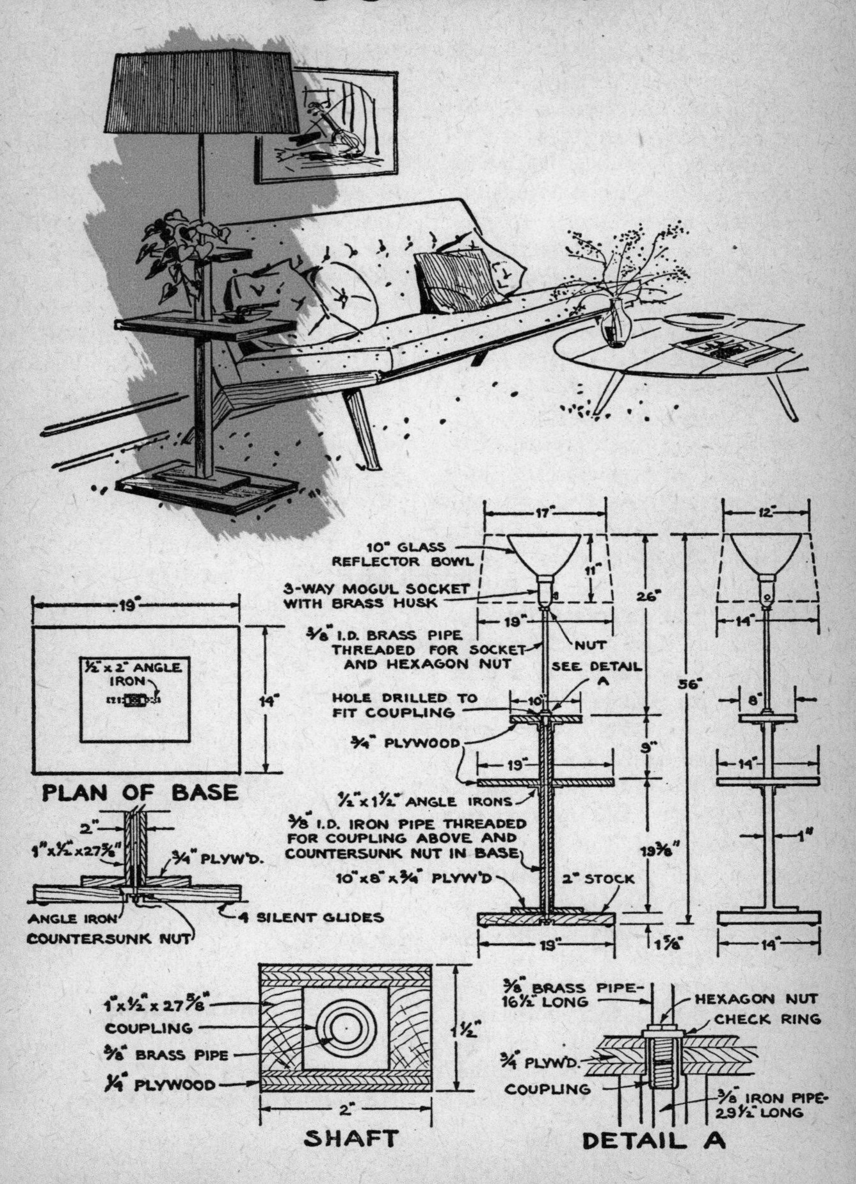

17"
12"
10" GLASS REFLECTOR BOWL
11"
3-WAY MOGUL SOCKET WITH BRASS HUSK
26"
19"
14"
3/8" I.D. BRASS PIPE THREADED FOR SOCKET AND HEXAGON NUT
NUT
SEE DETAIL A
56"
HOLE DRILLED TO FIT COUPLING
10"
8"
3/4" PLYWOOD
9"
19"
14"
1/2" x 1 1/2" ANGLE IRONS
3/8" I.D. IRON PIPE THREADED FOR COUPLING ABOVE AND COUNTERSUNK NUT IN BASE
19 3/8"
1"
10" x 8" x 3/4" PLYW'D
2" STOCK
19"
1 5/8"
14"
19"
1/2" x 2" ANGLE IRON
14"
PLAN OF BASE
2"
1" x 1/2" x 27 5/8"
3/4" PLYW'D.
ANGLE IRON
COUNTERSUNK NUT
4 SILENT GLIDES
1" x 1/2" x 27 5/8"
COUPLING
3/8" BRASS PIPE
1/4" PLYWOOD
1 1/2"
2"
SHAFT
3/8" BRASS PIPE-16 1/2" LONG
HEXAGON NUT
CHECK RING
3/4" PLYW'D.
COUPLING
3/8" IRON PIPE-29 1/2" LONG
DETAIL A

BOOKSHELVES AND CABINET

A combination such as this handy bookshelf and cabinet makes a very useful piece of furniture for small apartments, bedrooms, or a study. With the exception of the hardboard backing, 1" stock is used throughout the construction.

The bottom of the cabinet should be cut 8 1/4" x 34 1/2". 1 1/4" in from the outside edge along the bottom, fasten a strip of 1" x 2" on edge. This piece should be cut 34 1/2" long. The two side pieces should be 42" high and 9" wide. On the lower outside corner of each piece, cut a notch 2" x 2". The two shelves are supported at the ends by 1/2" quarter round cleats fastened to the side pieces. The cleats for the first shelf should be 8 1/4" long and those for the top 9" long. When the cleats have been installed, assemble the bottom and side pieces and the two shelves. The two shelves should be 9" wide and 34-1/2" long. The top of the cabinet, which is 9" x 36", is now fastened in place, and so is the 1/8" hardboard back, which measures 42 3/4" x 36".

The cabinet doors are 16 7/8" x 17 1/4". They should be hinged with flush door hinges. Each door is fitted with a friction catch to hold it shut and a stock doorpull.

Materials List

2 pcs. 1" x 9" x 42"
1 " 1" x 9" x 36"
2 " 1" x 9" x 34 1/2"
1 " 1" x 8 1/4" x 34 1/2"
1 " 1" x 2" x 34 1/2"
2 " 1" x 17" x 17 1/4"
1 " 1/8" hardboard 42 3/4" x 36"
1/2" quarter round 34 1/2"

Materials Totals

1" x 9"—15' 9"
(Remainder as itemized above)

BOOKSHELVES AND CABINET

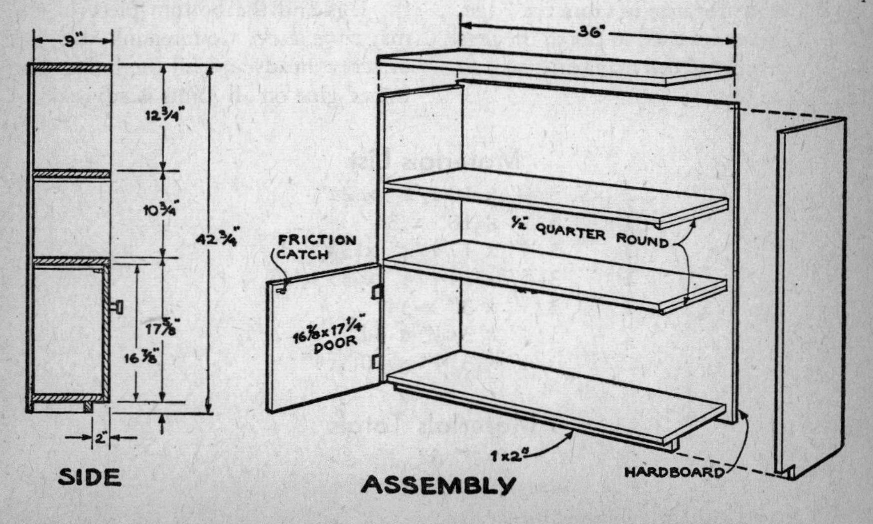

COFFEE TABLE AND MAGAZINE RACK

Here is a project that will give the amateur woodworker a good deal of satisfaction as well as many years of usefulness. And everyone visiting the house will see it.

Cut the legs for the table out of a solid piece of 3/4″ plywood. Note that the legs extend 1/2″ above the table top. This makes their over-all height 18 1/2″; their width is 22″. On the inside edge of each leg cut a miter as accurately as possible; or a simple butt joint as shown in the assembly drawing. Cut the table top to size and round off the outside corners. The top measures 18″ x 34″. At 3/4″ in from the inside edge of the table top, attach a strip of 3/4″ x 3/4″ along the bottom. Attach shorter strips of the same material along each end at the same distance in from the edge. These pieces are used to fasten the legs and the back of the magazine rack to the table top.

The back of the magazine rack is cut from a solid piece of stock. It should measure 17 1/2″ x 34″, and be beveled to fit. It serves to support one side of the table top. Four inches from the bottom of this piece, attach a piece 3″ x 34″ to act as the bottom of the magazine rack. The actual distance this piece is raised from the bottom edge of the magazine rack back is optional, and it can be varied to suit the size of the magazines to be placed in the rack. After this piece has been put in place, fasten the legs to the table top and the rack back to the table top and legs.

The front piece of the magazine rack should measure 14 1/4″ x 35 1/2″ and be beveled at top. Fasten it in place by nailing or screwing it to the legs and the bottom piece of the magazine rack. Countersink the nail or screw heads and fill the holes. The use of glue on all joints is advised.

Materials List

2 pcs. 3/4″ x 18 1/2″ x 22″
1 " 3/4″ x 18″ x 34″
1 " 3/4″ x 17 1/2″ x 34″
1 " 3/4″ x 14 1/4″ x 35 1/2″
1 " 3/4″ x 3″ x 34″
2 " 3/4″ x 3/4″ x 34″
2 " 3/4″ x 3/4″ x 10 3/4″

Materials Totals

3/4″ x 3/4″—7′ 6″
(Remainder as itemized above)

COFFEE TABLE AND MAGAZINE RACK

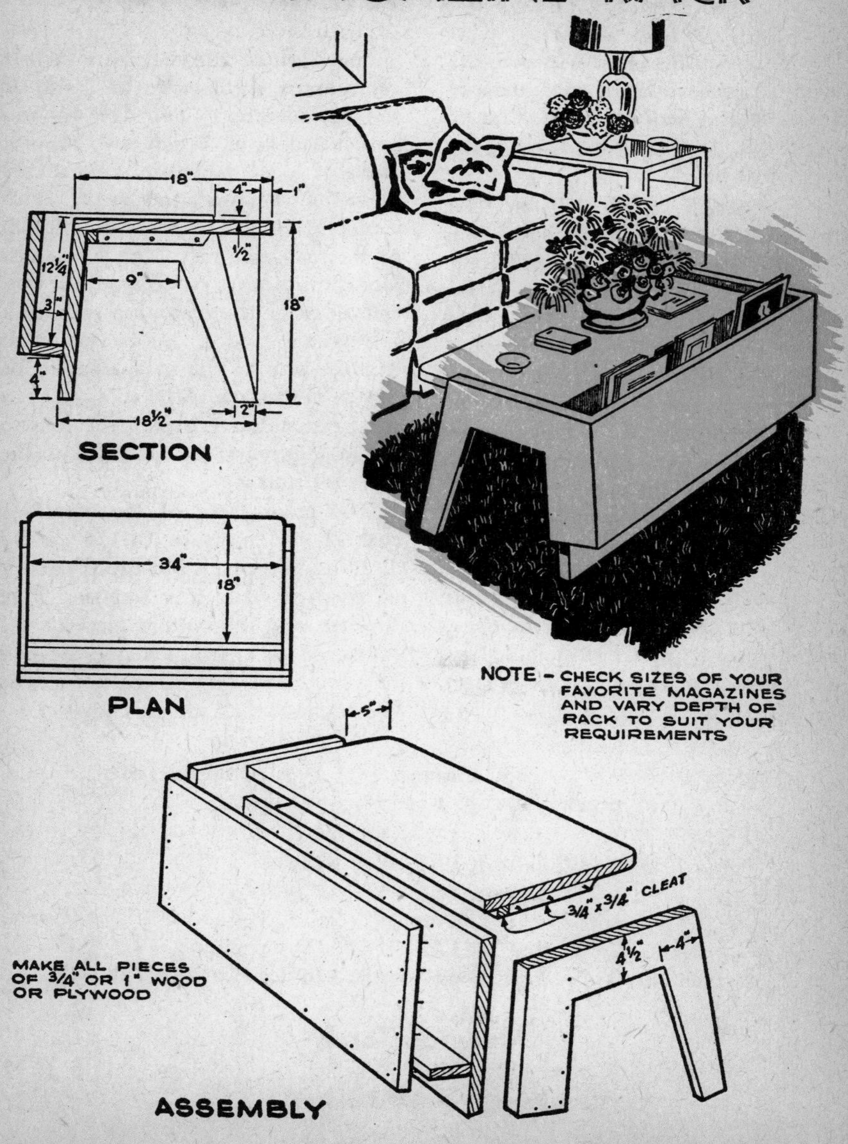

CARD AND GAME TABLE

Unlike the folding variety, this card and game table is a sturdy piece of furniture. The drawer provides a handy place to store various items of game equipment.

The sides of the table are made out of 1″ x 7″ (or nominal 1″ x 8″ stock). Two pieces are 34″ long; the other two, 36″ long. Cut the four legs out of 2″ x 2″ stock 28 1/2″ long. The legs should be fastened in the corners of the table 1 1/4″ from the top. Cut a piece of 1/2″ plywood 34 1/2″ x 34 1/2″ and fasten it over the tops of the legs. It should be fastened to the sides of the table as well as to the legs with flathead screws. A piece of 3/4″ plywood 28″ x 28″ should be fastened down on the 1/2″ plywood so that there is about a 3″ clearance on all sides. Cut out in the center of a side pieces a section 13″ x 5 1/2″ for the drawer. Fasten to the bottom of the 1/2″ plywood two 1 1/4″ x 1 1/4″ x 18″ rabbeted hardwood guides for the drawer. To be sure of getting these in the right spots, make up the drawer first, place it in position, and then fasten the guides in place.

The front of the drawer is made of 1″ stock 5 1/2″ x 13″. The two side pieces are 1/2″ plywood 5″ x 18 3/4″. The back piece is 1″ x 5″ that is 11″ long. The bottom is 1/4″ plywood measuring 12″ x 19″. Along the top of each side fasten a 1/2″ x 1/2″ runner. Joints between the sides and front piece are made with 5″ lengths of 1/2″ quarter round. The checkerboard can be stenciled on the table top.

Materials List

4 pcs. 2″ x 2″ x 28 1/2″
2 " 1″ x 7″ x 36″ (or 1″ x 8″ nominal stock)
2 " 1″ x 7″ x 34″ (or 1″ x 8″ nominal stock)
1 " 1″ x 5 1/2″ x 13″ (cut from 1 piece 1″ x 7″ x 36 above)
1 " 1″ x 5″ x 11″
2 " 1 1/4″ x 1 1/4″ x 18 3/4″ (hardwood guides)
2 " 1/2″ x 1/2″ x 18 3/4″ (runners)
1 " 3/4″ plywood 28″ x 28″
1 " 1/2″ plywood 34 1/2″ x 34 1/2″
2 " 1/2″ plywood 5 x 18 3/4″
1 " 1/4″ plywood 12″ x 19″
2 " 1/2″ quarter round 5″

Materials Totals

2″ x 2″ — 9′ 6″
1 1/4″ x 1 1/4″ — 3′ 1 1/2″ (hardwood)
1″ x 7″ — 11′ 8″
1/2″ x 1/2″ — 3′ 1 1/2″ (hardwood)
1/2″ quarter round — 10″
(Remainder as itemized above)

CARD AND GAME TABLE

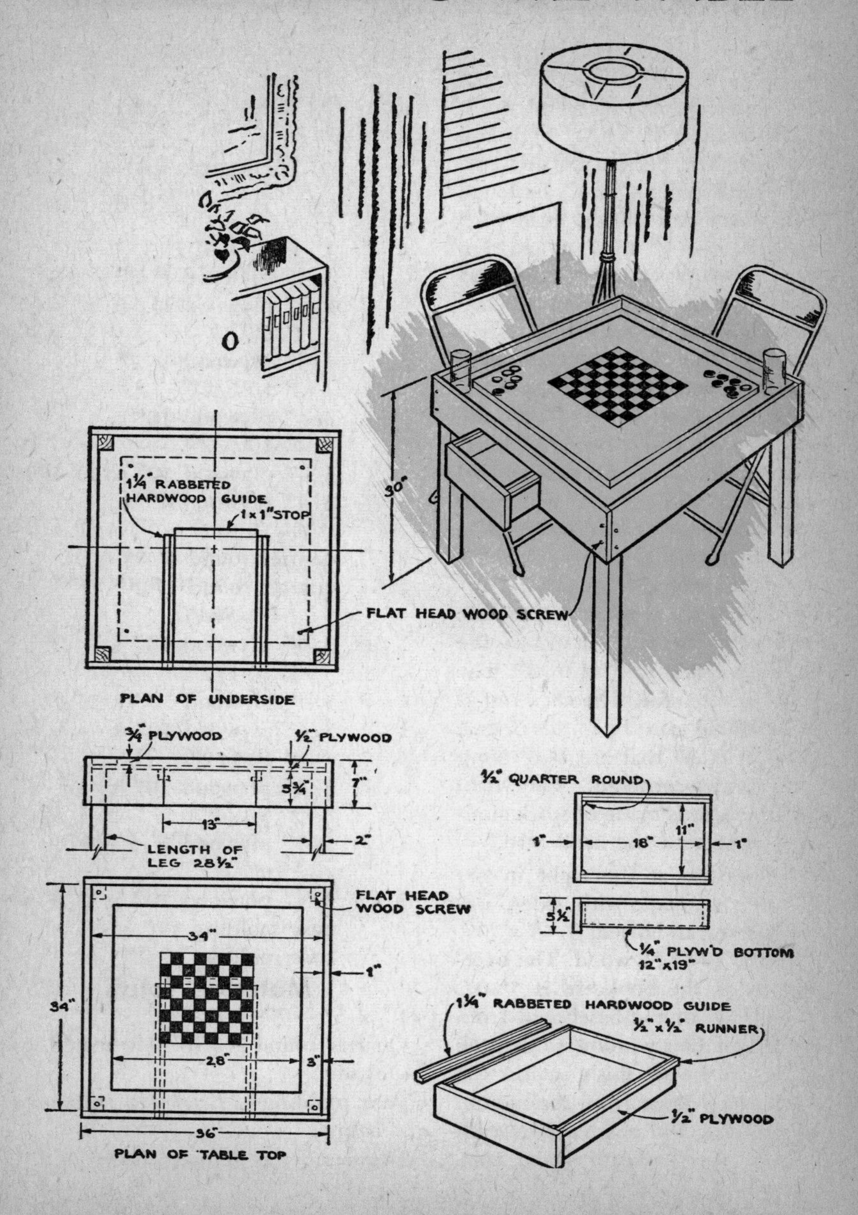

UNDER-WINDOW BOOKCASES

The combination window seat and bookcase is designed for use under windows no lower than 3′ 0″ from the floor line. The side pieces are made of 3/4″ plywood 1′ 5 1/4″ high and 1′ 6″ wide. The bottom outside corners are notched out 4″ x 4″. Fastened between these two pieces, flush with the back of the 4″ x 4″ notch, is a piece of 3/4″ plywood 4″ high and 4′ 10 1/2″ long. Side pieces are fastened together at the back with a strip of 1″ x 3″ that is 4′ 10 1/2″ long coming flush with the top of the sides. The shelf is made out of 3/4″ plywood 10″ wide and 4′ 10 1/2″ long. This is set in place and fastened to the side pieces and to the 4″ wide strip running between the side pieces. The back piece, 3/4″ x 1′ 2″ x 4′ 10 1/2″, is set in place; the divider piece, 3/4″ x 10″ x 12 1/2″, is set in the middle of the shelf. The seat, or top of the bookcase, is made 1′ 7″ x 5′ 2″. The back rest is the same. The back rest is given the slight slant by means of two strips of 1″ x 3″ that are 1′ 6″ long and cut cater-cornered. The trim around the base is made of stock similar to that around the baseboard.

The bookcase at the right in the illustration is made with sides, uprights, shelves, and top of 3/4″ x 10″. The back is 1/4″ plywood. The over-all length of the bookcase is 5′ 0″. Remove 5′ 0″ of the baseboard from the wall under the window so that the bookcase can be set flush against the wall. Measure down from the bottom of the window and make the over-all height of the bookcase equal this. After the bookcase has been assembled and moved into place, fasten the baseboard and quarter round molding along the sides and front to match the room trim.

Materials List

Bookcase with Seat

2 pcs. 1″ x 3″ x 1′ 6″
1 " 1″ x 3″ x 4′ 10 1/2″
2 " 3/4″ plywood 1′ 7″ x 5′ 2″
2 " 3/4″ plywood 1′ 5 1/4″ x 1′ 6″
1 " 3/4″ plywood 1′ 2″ x 4′ 10 1/2″
1 " 3/4″ plywood 10″ x 4′ 10 1/2″
1 " 3/4″ plywood 10″ x 12 1/2″
1 " 3/4″ plywood 4″ x 4′ 10 1/2″
1 " quarter round 5′ 2″
2 " quarter round 1′ 2″

Shelf

2 pcs. 3/4″ plywood 10″ x 4′ 10 1/2″
1 " 3/4″ plywood 10″ x 5′ 2″
2 " 3/4″ plywood 10″ x 4′ 10 1/2″
2 " 3/4″ plywood 10″ x 2′ 5 1/4″
1 " 1/4″ plywood 2′ 5 1/4″ x 5′ 0″
2 " 3/4″ plywood 10″ x 11 3/4″
2 " base molding 11″
1 " base molding 5′ 2″

Materials Totals

1″ x 3″ — 7′ 10 1/2″
Quarter round — 7′ 8″ (to match existing)
Base molding — 7′ 0″ (to match existing)
(Remainder as itemized above)

UNDER-WINDOW BOOKCASES

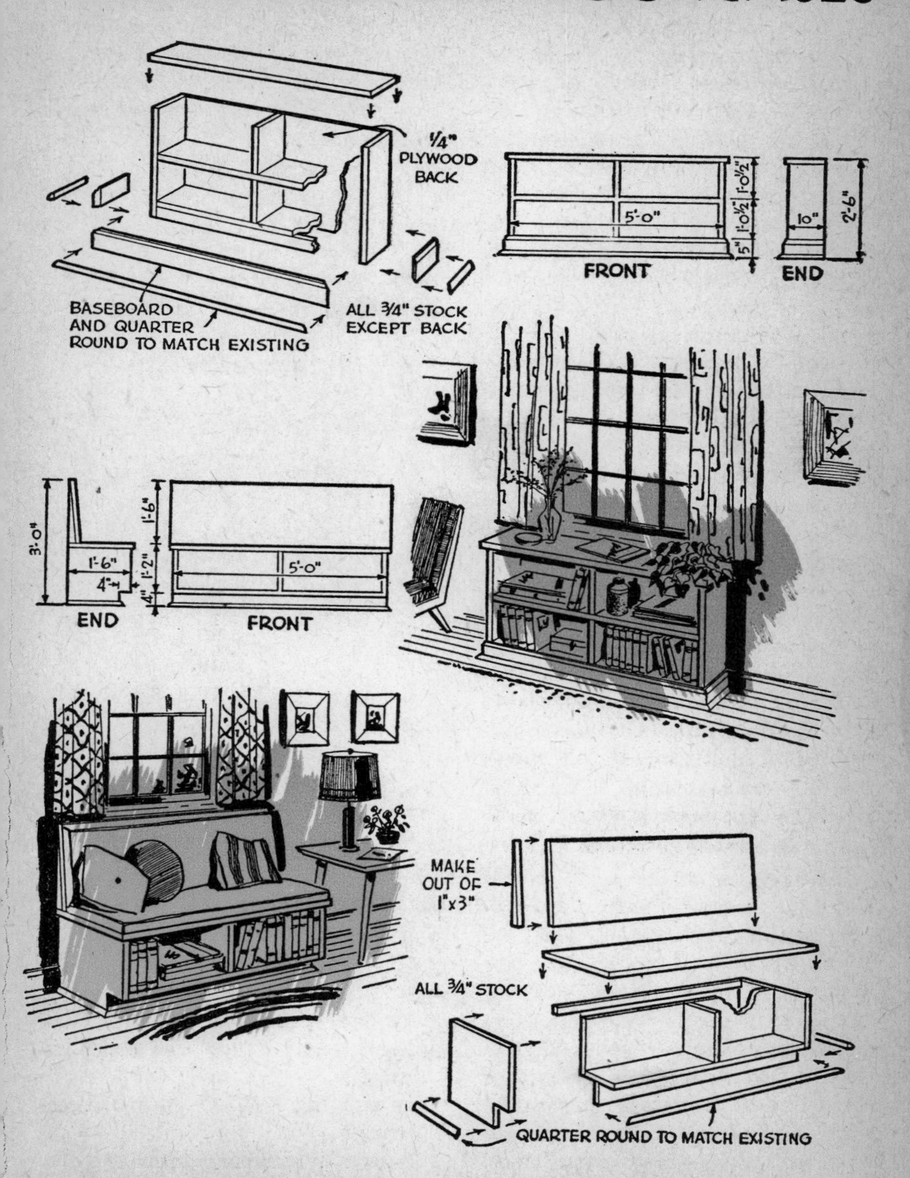

MAGAZINE STORAGE RACK

The base section of the rack consists of four shelves of 1″ x 12″. Each shelf is 50 1/4″ x 11 5/8″. Fasten a strip of 1″ x 2″ along the front end and sides of the bottom shelf to keep it off the floor. Make up the end piece 1″ x 12″ x 29 1/4″. The back is made out of 1/8″ hardboard 30″ x 50 1/4″. Assemble these three pieces. 9″ in from the end of the lower shelf install a support for the second shelf. This support should be 8 1/2″ high, cut from 1″ x 12″. Put the second shelf in place, use a level to see that it is true, and then nail it to the support. Nail it also to the side piece by driving nails through the side into the end grain of the shelf. Seams where the side piece and support join the shelf can be covered with strips of 1/2″ quarter round. The other shelves and supports are installed similarly. The second support is the same size as the first; the third is reduced in height to 8 3/8″. The top shelf must be 51″ long instead of 50 1/4″ as it rests on the side piece.

The magazine rack is made of 1″ x 6″. Top and bottom are 51″ long. Side pieces are 26 3/4″. The backing is made of 1/8″ hardboard 28 1/4″ x 50 1/4″. 13 3/4″ down from the top of the rack, install a shelf 1″ x 6″ x 49 1/2″. The back of the racks is made of 1/2″ plywood fastened to 1″ x 2″ and 1″ x 1″ beveled cleats. To prevent magazines from slipping off, 1/2″ quarter round should be tacked at the edge of each shelf.

Materials List

3 pcs. 1″ x 12″ x 50 3/4″
1 " 1″ x 12″ x 51″
1 " 1″ x 12″ x 29 1/4″
2 " 1″ x 12″ x 8 1/2″
1 " 1″ x 12″ x 8 3/8″
2 " 1″ x 6″ x 51″
1 " 1″ x 6″ x 49 1/2″
2 " 1″ x 6″ x 26 3/4″
1 " 1″ x 2″ x 50 3/4″
2 " 1″ x 2″ x 49 1/2″
1 " 1″ x 2″ x 10 7/8″
2 " 1″ x 1″ x 49 1/2″
2 " 1/2″ plywood 14 1/2″ x 49 1/2″
2 " 1/2″ quarter round 49 1/2″
9 " 1/2″ quarter round 11″

Materials Totals

1″ x 12″ — 21′ 5 7/8″
1″ x 6″ — 17′ 1″
1″ x 2″ — 13′ 4 5/8″
1/2″ quarter round 16′ 6″
(Remainder as itemized above)

MAGAZINE STORAGE RACK

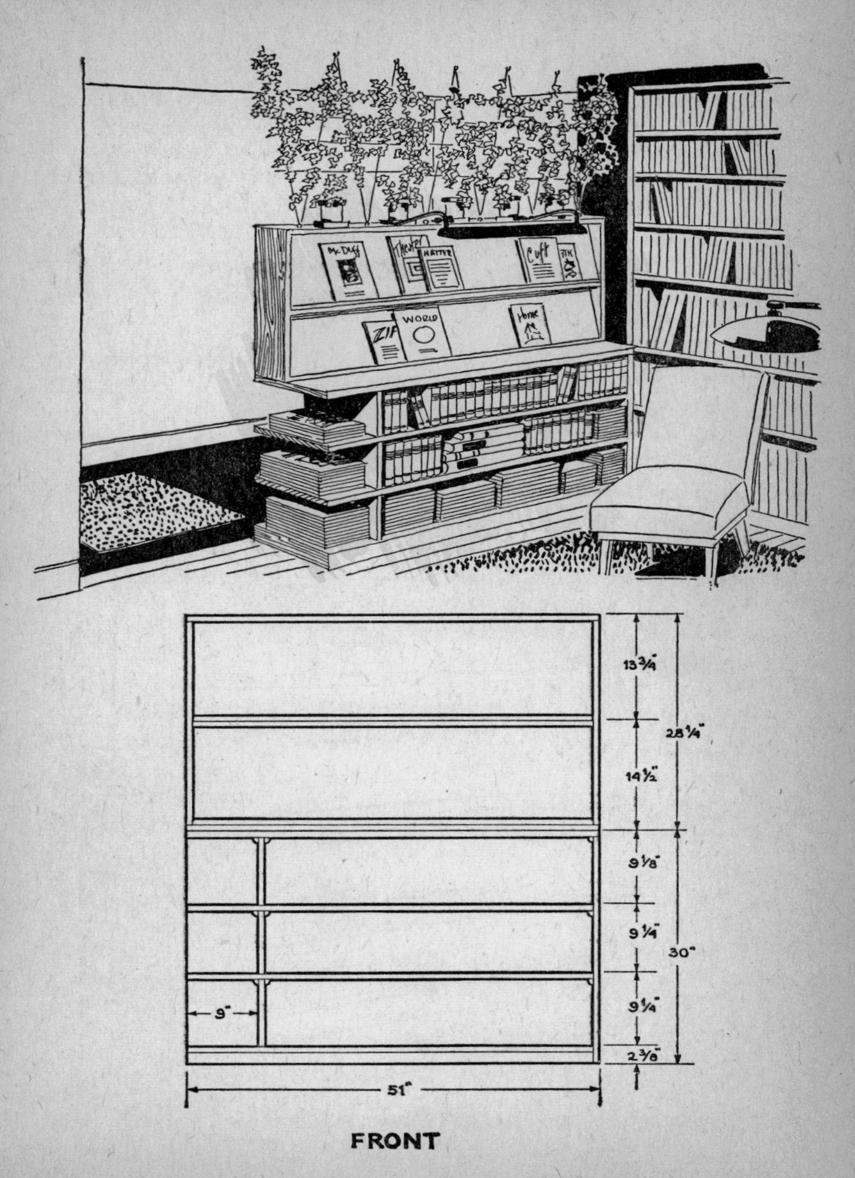

FRONT

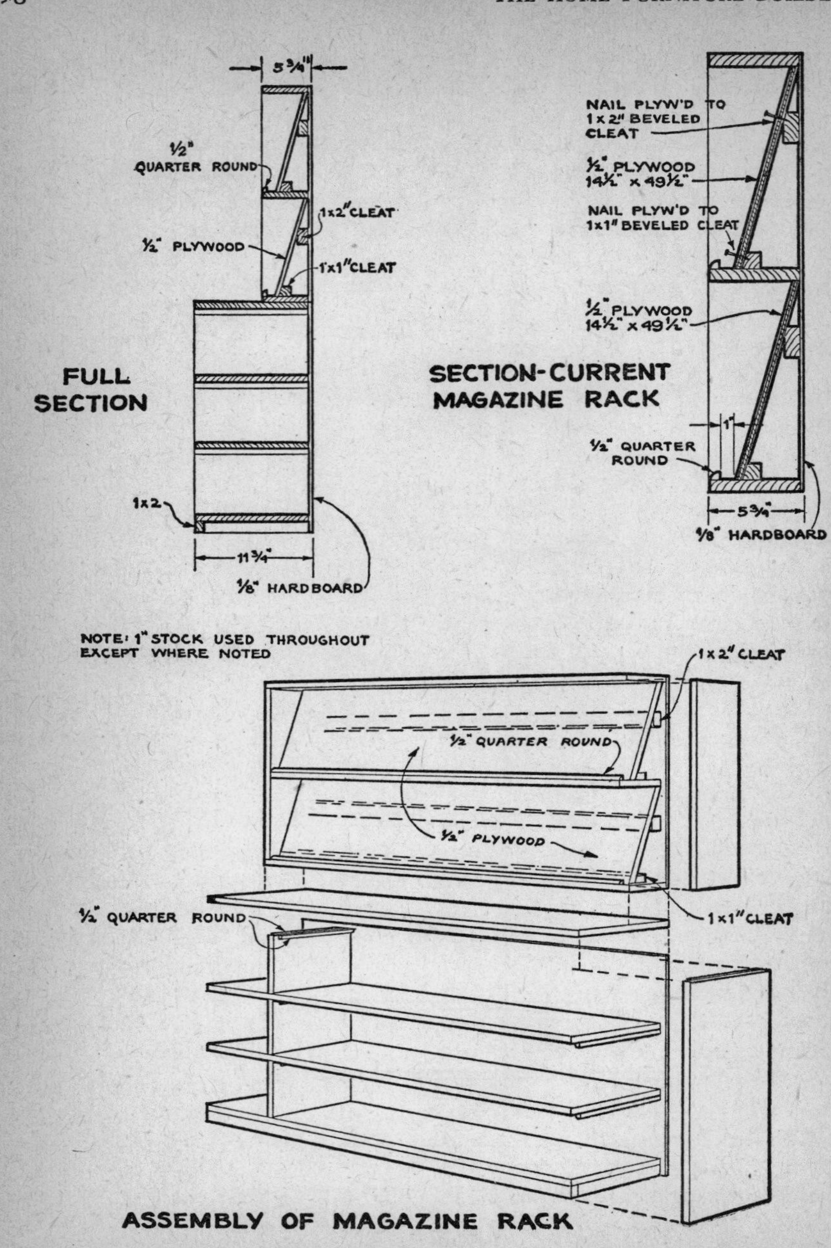
5 3/4"
1/2" QUARTER ROUND
1x2" CLEAT
1/2" PLYWOOD
1x1" CLEAT
FULL SECTION
1x2
11 3/4"
1/8" HARDBOARD
NAIL PLYW'D TO 1 x 2" BEVELED CLEAT
1/2" PLYWOOD 14 1/2" x 49 1/2"
NAIL PLYW'D TO 1x1" BEVELED CLEAT
1/2" PLYWOOD 14 1/2" x 49 1/2"
SECTION-CURRENT MAGAZINE RACK
1"
1/2" QUARTER ROUND
5 3/4"
1/8" HARDBOARD
NOTE: 1" STOCK USED THROUGHOUT EXCEPT WHERE NOTED
1 x 2" CLEAT
1/2" QUARTER ROUND
1/2" PLYWOOD
1/2" QUARTER ROUND
1 x 1" CLEAT
ASSEMBLY OF MAGAZINE RACK

TELEPHONE STAND & STOOL

Placed either in kitchen or living room, this combination makes a useful piece of furniture.

The sides of the stand are made out of 3/4″ plywood, 16″ x 32 1/2″. Cut the pieces to the correct size and then clamp them together for rounding off the outside top corner to form legs.

The back of the stand is a piece of 3/4″ plywood 23 1/4″ x 30 1/2″. The joint between the side pieces is made with a strip of 3/4″ x 3/4″.

4 1/2″ in from the righthand side, an additional upright cleat is installed to provide a base for the lefthand side of the cabinet. 3/4″ x 3/4″ cleats should now be fastened to the sides for the shelves. The lefthand side piece for the side compartment can now be cut and installed. This is 3/4″ plywood 15″ x 22 1/2″. Cleats of 3/4″ x 3/4″ stock should be installed on the inside face for the shelves. Shelves for the side compartment are 3/4″ plywood 4 1/2″ x 14 1/4″. The rear corners will have to be notched out 3/4″ x 3/4″ to fit around the two upright cleats. The two upper shelves are 3/4″ plywood 15″ x 23 1/4″. The pencil trough is made on the upper shelf by fastening a strip of 1/4″ half round 15 1/2″ long 2″ from the back.

The door for the side compartment is 3/4″ plywood 5 1/4″ x 22 1/2″. A 1″ x 1″ x 4″ makes its handle.

The legs for the stool are made of 2″ x 2″ that is 17 1/4″ long. The frame at the top is made of two pieces of 1″ x 4″ measuring 14″ long and two pieces of the same stock 12 1/2″ long. If a miter box is available, these can be joined with miter joints. In this event, make all four pieces 14″ long. The top of the stool is 1/4″ plywood 14″ x 14″. Cover with cloth, etc., if desired.

Materials List

Stand

3 pcs. 3/4″ x 3/4″ x 26″
1 " 1″ x 1″ x 4″
9 " 3/4″ x 3/4″ x 13 1/2″
1 " 3/4″ plywood 23 1/4″ x 30 1/2″
2 " 3/4″ plywood 16″ x 32 1/2″
2 " 3/4″ plywood 15″ x 23 1/4″
1 " 3/4″ plywood 15″ x 22 1/2″
1 " 3/3″ plywood 5 1/4″ x 22 1/2″
2 " 3/4″ plywood 4 1/2″ x 14 1/4″
1 " 1/4″ half round 15 1/2″
2 butt hinges 1 friction catch

Stool

4 pcs. 2″ x 2″ x 17 1/4″
4 " 1″ x 4″ x 14″
1 " 1/4″ plywood 14″ x 14″

Stand Without Side Compartment

2 pcs. 3/4″ plywood 18″ x 15″
1 " 3/4″ plywood 18″ x 30 1/2″
2 " 3/4″ plywood 16″ x 32 1/2″
2 " 3/4″ x 3/4″ x18″
4 " 3/4″ x 3/4″ x 13 1/4″
1 " 1/4″ half round 11″

Materials Totals

Stand

3/4″ x 3/4″ — 16′ 7 1/2″

Stool

2″ x 2″ — 5′ 9″
1″ x 4″ — 4′ 8″
(Remainder as itemized above)

TELEPHONE STAND & STOOL

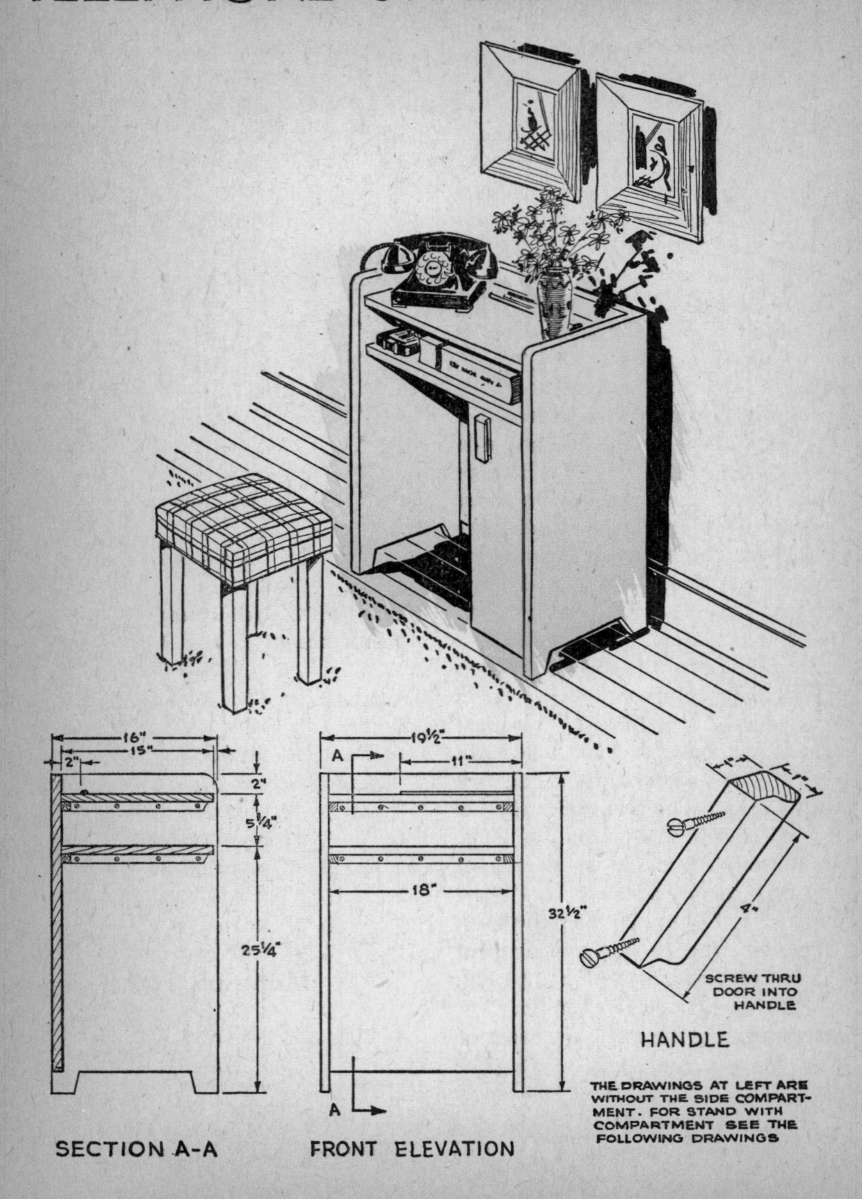

THE DRAWINGS AT LEFT ARE WITHOUT THE SIDE COMPARTMENT. FOR STAND WITH COMPARTMENT SEE THE FOLLOWING DRAWINGS

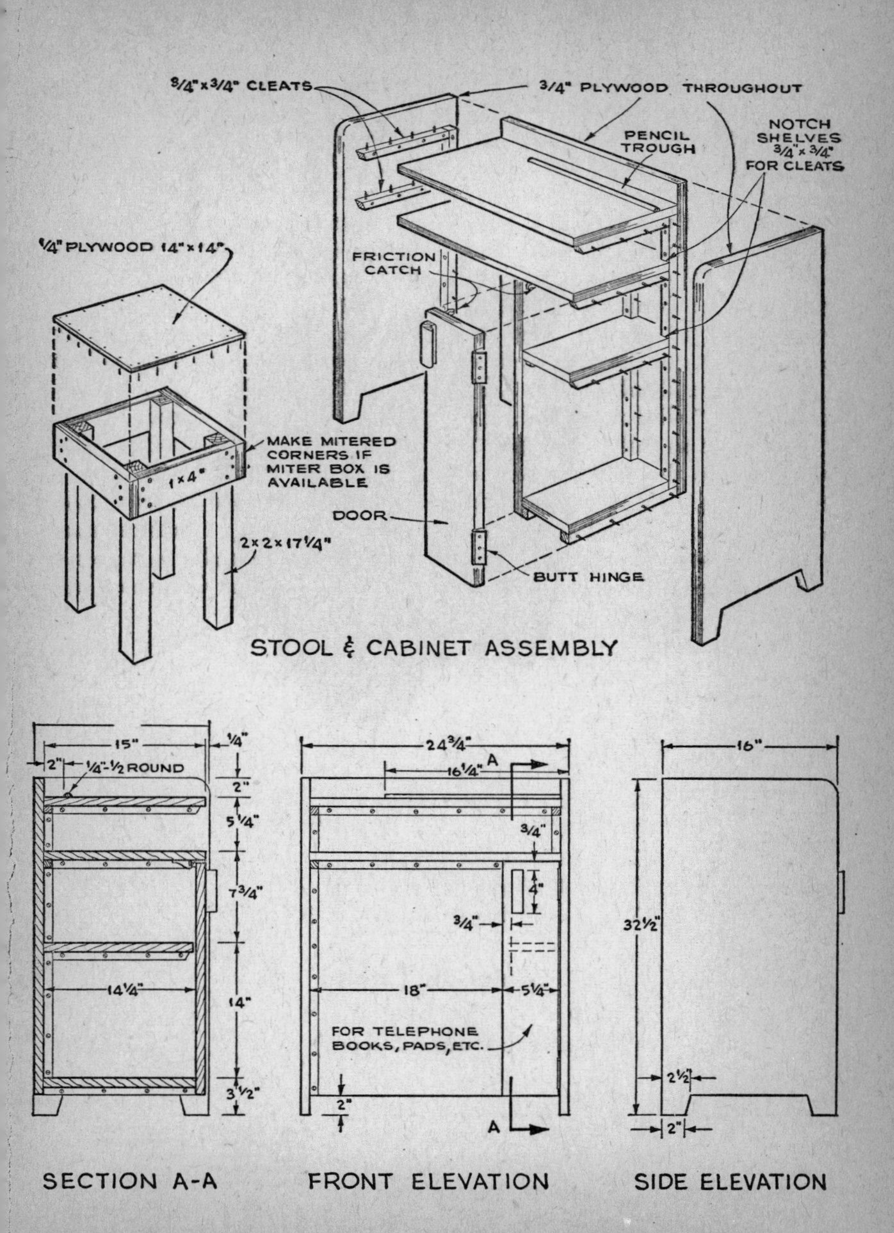

STOOL & CABINET ASSEMBLY

PLANT STAND

A modern plant stand makes an interesting piece of furniture for the home. It also offers a solution for the problem of storing potted plants during the winter months.

The bottom of the stand is 9 5/8″ wide and 36″ long. The short end piece is 9 5/8″ wide and 12 3/4″ high, while the long end piece is 9 5/8″ x 23 3/4″. Fasten these together and then cut the first shelf to size. This piece should be 35 1/4″ long and 9 5/8″ wide at one end. Rip the board down so that the far end is 6″ wide. Fasten this in place with a cleat of 1/2″ quarter round molding to hold it to the long end piece. The top shelf measures 25″, and this should be ripped down so that it tapers from 9 5/8″ to 6″. One end of this piece is nailed to the top of the high end piece. The other end is supported by an upright 6″ wide and 9 3/4″ long. 1/8″ hardboard is used for backing.

Holes should be cut in the shelves before assembly. They are made by first making an opening with a brace and bit and then cutting out with a keyhole saw. The size of the openings should be varied to take different sizes of pots. Plants to be put in the stand should be placed in glazed flower pots — ordinary clay pots are not suitable as they will leak. It is advisable to remove the pots from the stand for watering unless the stand is finished with a durable water-resistant finish, such as spar varnish or enamel paint.

Materials List

1 pc. 1″ x 9 5/8″ x 35 1/4″
1 " 1″ x 9 5/8″ x 34 1/2″
1 " 1″ x 9 5/8″ x 25″
1 " 1″ x 9 5/8″ x 23 3/4″
1 " 1″ x 9 5/8″ x 12 3/4″
1 " 1″ x 6″ x 9 3/4″
1 " 1/2″ quarter round 6″
1 " 1/8″ hardboard 24″ x 36″

Materials Totals

1″ x 9 5/8″ — 10′ 11 1/4″
(Remainder as itemized above)

PLANT STAND

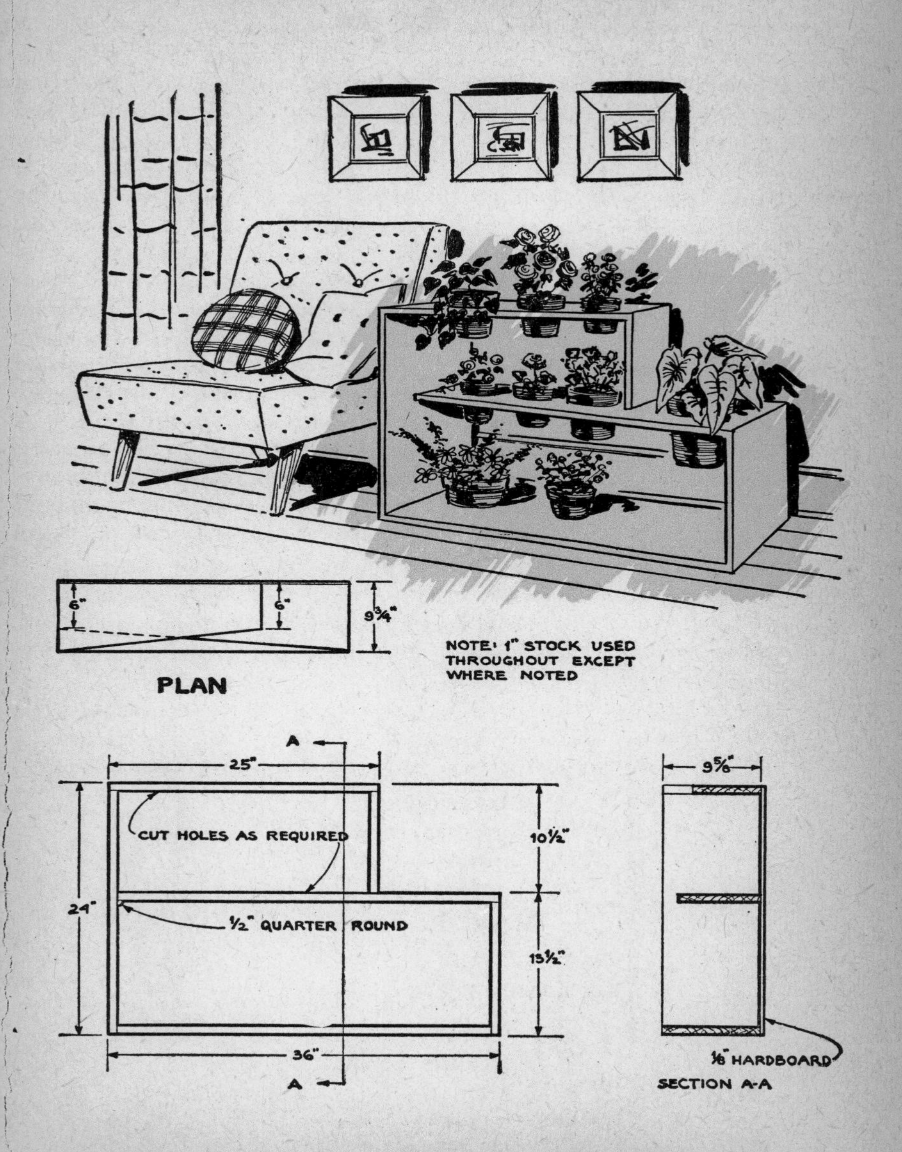
6"
6"
9¾"
PLAN
NOTE: 1" STOCK USED THROUGHOUT EXCEPT WHERE NOTED
A
25"
CUT HOLES AS REQUIRED
10½"
24"
½" QUARTER ROUND
13½"
36"
A
9⅝"
⅛" HARDBOARD
SECTION A-A

TELEPHONE AND DIRECTORY WALL SHELF

A telephone wall shelf is a handy solution to where to keep the 'phone and directories.

The width of the shelf is 14", which allows it to fit between wall studding spaced 16" on center. Locate the position of the studding by "sounding" the wall with your fist. Mark off the area of the plaster that is to be removed. Cut through the plaster with a cold chisel and hammer, and then cut through the lath with a compass saw, or with a hack saw if the lath is metal. Make the opening in the wall with clean straight edges so that they can be easily covered by the trim.

The sides, top, and bottom of the shelf are made out of 1/2" plywood joined with butt joints. The shelves are made 9" wide so that they extend out 1" beyond the sides of the cabinet. The vertical rack between the bottom and first shelf is made with 1" long spacers and 1/4" plywood panels. The back of the shelf is covered with a sheet of 1/4" plywood.

Once the shelf has been assembled, fit it into the wall opening. Let it extend into the wall cavity as far as possible. Use a level to get it perfectly plumb, and then fasten it in place by running nails or screws through the sides into the wall studding. Small wedges may be required in order to make the shelf sit level in the opening. The joint between plaster wall and shelf is covered over with a strip of 1/2" quarter round molding. These strips are joined at the ends with miter joints. The molding should be attached to the sides, top, and bottom of the shelf—not to the plaster wall—with finishing nails. If the plaster opening has rough edges that the quarter round molding will not cover, patch up the edges of the plaster with spackle or patching plaster. This should be done before the quarter round trim is fastened in place.

Materials List

2 pcs. 1/2" plywood 8" x 16 1/2"
2 " 1/2" plywood 8" x 14"
3 " 1/2" plywood 9" x 13"
1 " 1/4" plywood 14" x 17 1/2"
3 " 1/4" plywood 8" x 8"
6 " 1/2" x 1" x 8"
2 " 1/2" quarter round 17 1/2"
2 " 1/2" quarter round 15"

Materials Totals

1/2" x 1" — 4'
1/2" quarter round — 5'5"
(Remainder as itemized above)

TELEPHONE AND DIRECTORY WALL SHELF

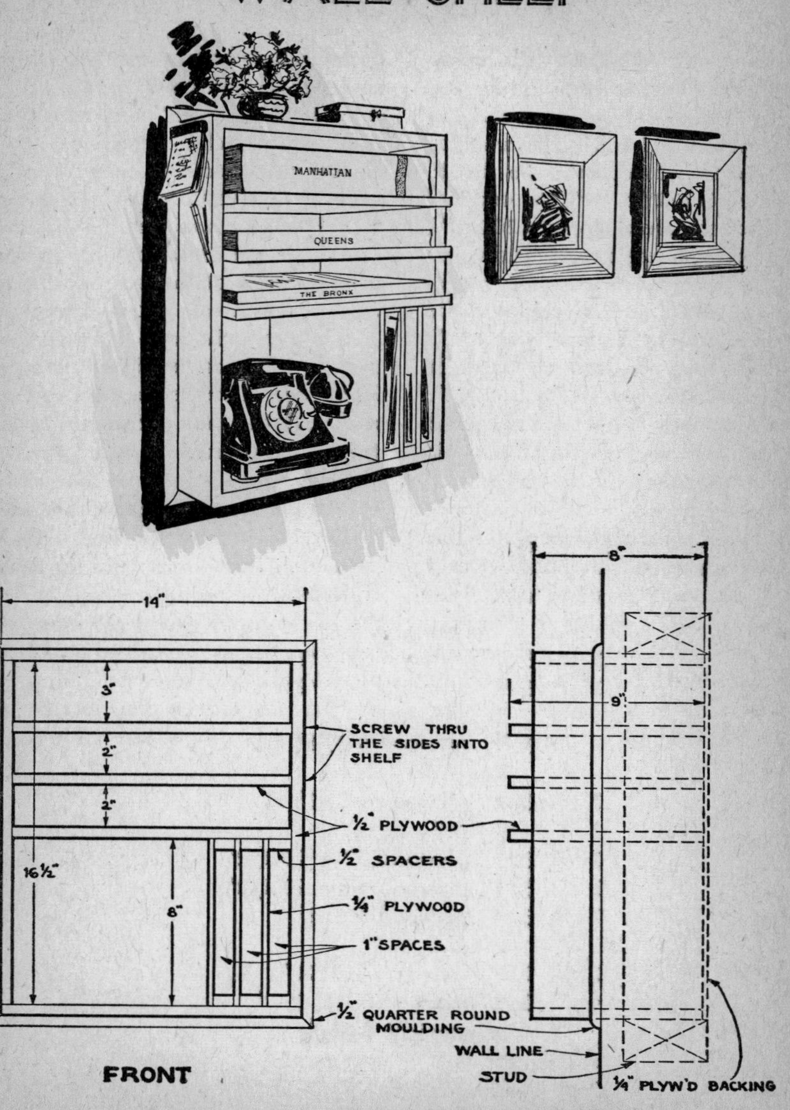

END TABLE AND LIGHT STAND

A valuable piece of furniture for the living room, this combination end table and light stand has space for magazines and a plant box.

Start assembly by cutting out the base. Assuming that 3/4" plywood or 3/4" stock is used, the base should measure 20 1/2" x 30". At one end fasten the end piece, 9 3/4" x 20 1/2". 10" from this piece, fasten the divider, which serves as the back of the magazine rack and as a support for the table top. The divider is 4" x 20 1/2". The table top is now installed; it should measure 20 1/2" x 26 1/4". The light stand is assembled next, and then the back piece is installed. This back measures exactly 5" x 20 1/2".

The side pieces for the table are now cut to size and put in place. The edges of these pieces should extend 1/4" above the top of the rack.

The legs for the table are made out of 3/4" x 2 1/4", and are tapered down so that the ends are 1 1/4" wide. The legs are attached to cleats made of 1 1/4" x 1 3/4" stock 20" long. The ends of each cleat are cut in 1/2" so that the legs can be let in. The legs should be given a slight outward slant. After the legs have been attached to the cleats, the cleats can be fastened to the bottom of the table with wood screws. The cleats should be spaced 5" in from each end of the table and 2 1/2" in from the sides. After the legs are in place, set the table upright and mark the ends of the legs for any trimming required to make them all perfectly level.

If plants are to be used in the plant box, it should be lined with sheets of either zinc or copper and the joints should be soldered.

Materials List

1 pc. 3/4" plywood 20 1/2" x 30"
1 " 3/4" plywood 20 1/2" x 26 1/4"
1 " 3/4" plywood 9 3/4" x 20 1/2"
1 " 3/4" plywood 8 1/2" x 7 1/4"
1 " 3/4" plywood 5" x 20 1/2"
1 " 3/4" plywood 4" x 20 1/2"
1 " 3/4" plywood 3 1/2" x 8 1/2"
2 " 1 1/4" x 1 3/4" x 20"
4 " 3/4" x 2 1/4" x 15 1/2"

Materials Totals

1 1/4" x 1 3/4" — 40"
3/4" x 2 1/4" — 5' 2"
(Remainder as itemized above)

END TABLE AND LIGHT STAND

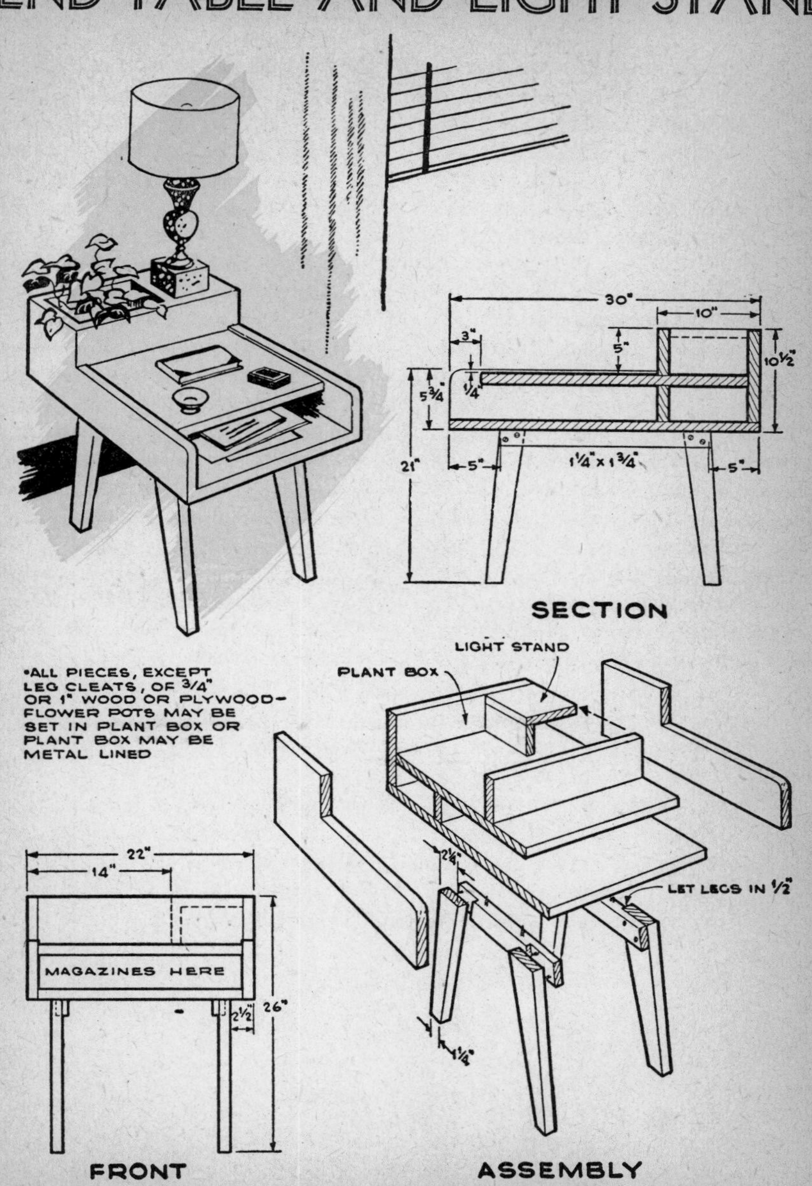

FIREPLACE MANTEL

Many an otherwise attractive living room has been ruined by an unsightly fireplace mantel. For those who enjoy working with wood this situation is easily fixed.

Remove the old mantel and trim. Install nailing bases as shown in Section A-A and in Plan B-B. 1″ x 2″ and 2″ x 2″ stock are used for this purpose. Fasten these bases to the fireplace masonry with expansion bolts and to the plaster wall with toggle bolts. Before you start on the mantel, check the dimensions of the fireplace, as these may vary somewhat from those given in the drawing.

The mantel is assembled as a unit and then moved into place and secured to the bases provided around the fireplace. The only exception to this is the pine board mantle shelf, which is attached directly to the base over the opening.

The outside corners of the mantel assembly are held together with a strip of 1″ x 1″ stock running up on the inside of the corner. Screws are run through this piece into the 4″ V-joint pine boards. A 3/4″ quarter round molding is used to cover up the outside ends of the boards as shown in Plan B-B. Be sure to leave a 4″ clearance between the woodwork and the fireplace opening on all three sides. Allowing the woodwork to come any closer to the opening is a fire hazard. When the mantel has been assembled, place it in position and secure it to the nailing bases with finishing nails. The nailheads should be countersunk and the holes filled with a wood filler.

Some trouble may be encountered in getting a good fit along the top edge between the mantel shelf and the V-joint pine boards due to the fact that the fireplace or floor is slightly out of plumb. This can be corrected by trimming down the top of the mantel assembly until it fits snugly.

Materials List

4 pcs. 2″ x 2″ x 3′ 6″
2 " 1″ x 2″ x 3′ 6″
1 " 1″ x 1″ x 5′ 4″
2 " 1″ x 1″ x 3′ 6″
1 mantel shelf 1 1/4″ x 8″ x 5′ 5 1/2″
2 pcs. 3/4″ quarter round 38″
2 " 3/4″ quarter round 30″
2 V-joint boards 4″ x 5′ 4″
14 V-joint boards 4″ x 10″
14 V-joint board 4″ x 3 1/4″

Materials Totals

2″ x 2″ — 14′
1″ x 2″ — 7′
1″ x 1″ — 12′ 4″
3/4″ quarter round — 11′ 4″
4″ V-joint boards — 25′ 10 3/4″
(Remainder as itemized above)

FIREPLACE MANTEL

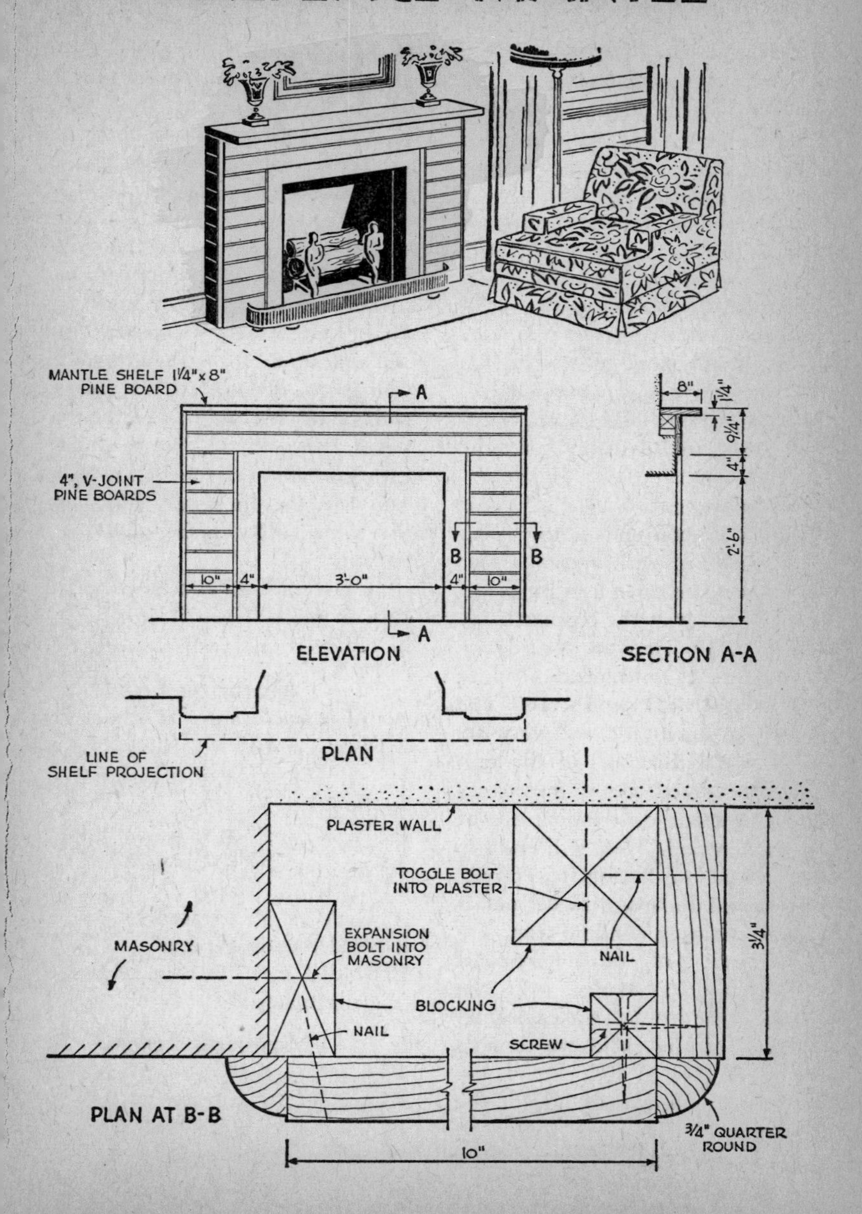

RADIATOR ENCLOSURE

The entire appearance of a room can be transformed and brought up to date by covering old-fashioned and unsightly radiators with this enclosure. Unlike some improperly designed enclosures, this one will not reduce the radiator's efficiency.

As radiators may differ greatly as to size, no dimensions are given. The note in the illustration, however, shows how to find the dimensions for any radiator.

Use only kiln-dried hardwood for the enclosure. Unseasoned wood will shrink when the radiator is on, opening up seams and possibly cracking.

The base of the front of the enclosure is made out of 1″ x 6″ stock. The curves at each end of the opening can be made with a compass or keyhole saw. The three upright pieces and the piece across the top are made out of 1″ x 3″. They are secured together at the back with metal mending plates fastened with wood screws. The sides of the enclosure will vary according to the thickness of the radiator to be covered, but in most cases they can be made of a solid piece of wood or plywood. They will have to be cut out at the bottom to fit over the baseboard and possibly cut out at the top to fit over window trim. Expanded metal lath or architectural grille material is stapled over the openings in the front of the enclosure.

The top of the enclosure consists of a strip of 1″ x 3″ that extends beyond the front and each side of the enclosure by 1″. This strip should be nailed with finishing nails to the front and side sections of the enclosure. The horizontal grille work in back of this piece is made with 1″ x 1″ strips and spacers cut out of 1″ x 3″ stock in 1″ sections. The exact width of these spacers will depend on the width of the radiator; they must be adjusted to make the grill even. The grille assembly is fastened together with 8d finishing nails driven in at the sides so that the heads are concealed. The final piece of the top assembly should come flush to the rear edges of the side pieces. Round off the front and ends of the top with a rasp and sandpaper then smooth. Set and fill all exposed nailheads and then apply a finish to the enclosure. Finish it in the same color as the walls of the room.

If possible, do not nail the enclosure in place. Keep it free so it can be removed easily for cleaning.

Materials List

(For Enclosure 3′ 0″ x 4′ 6″)

2 pcs. 1″ x 10″ x 2′ 11 1/2″
1 " 1″ x 6″ x 4′ 6″
1 " 1″ x 3″ x 4′ 8″
1 " 1″ x 3″ x 4′ 6″
3 " 1″ x 3″ x 2′ 2 1/2″
4 " 1″ x 1″ x 4′ 8″
9 " 1″ x 3″ (spacers)
8 metal mending plates
Expanded metal lath or architectural grille material.

Materials Totals

1″ x 10″ — 5′ 9″
1″ x 3″ — 16′ 6 1/2″
1″ x 1″ — 18′ 8″
(Remainder as itemized above)

RADIATOR ENCLOSURE

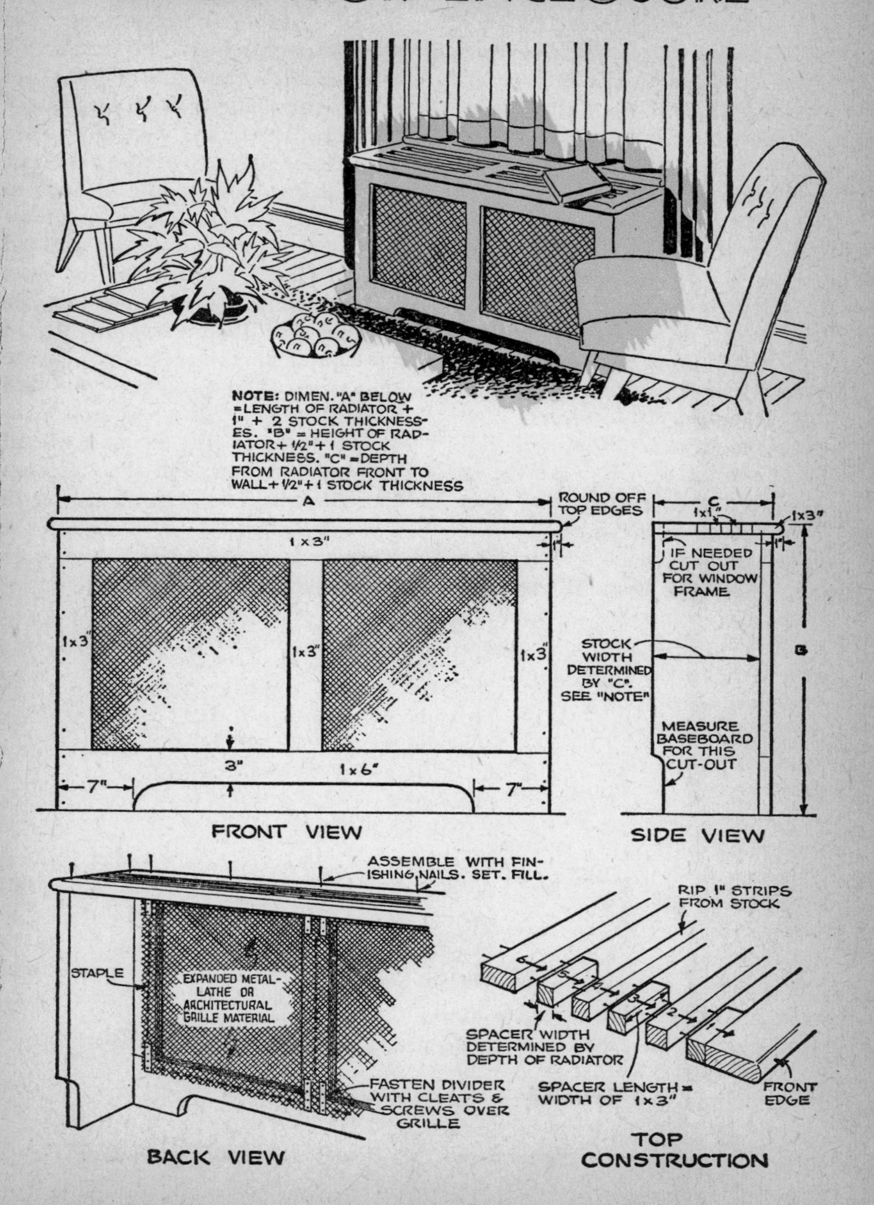

RECORD CABINET

The record cabinet pictured here has been designed to take 33 1/3, 45, and 78 R.P.M. 10″ and 12″ records. There is storage space for both record albums and record literature.

The bottom of the cabinet is made out of 3/4″ plywood 22 1/2″ x 13″. Fasten a piece of 1″ x 2″ along the bottom of this piece 3″ from the outside edge. The lefthand side of the cabinet is 29 1/8″ x 13″ wide. On the lower outside edge, a notch 1 5/8″ deep and 4″ wide should be cut. The righthand side is also made 29 1/8″ x 13″. The lower outside corner is notched out in the same fashion as the lefthand side piece. 16 1/8″ from the bottom, the width of this piece is reduced from 13″ to 8″. This forms the recess for the 45 L.P.R. and the record literature shelf. The top of the cabinet is 24″ x 13″. 10 3/4″ in from the lefthand side, the width is reduced from 13″ to 8″. The next operation involves assembling these four pieces.

The lower shelf in the cabinet is 22 1/2″ x 13″. It is supported by 1/2″ quarter round cleats fastened to the side pieces. A divider piece, 13″ x 13″, is placed between the bottom and first shelf 9 1/4″ in from the righthand side piece. A second divider, also 13″ x 13″, is run 9 1/4″ in from the lefthand side piece from the first shelf to the top. The 8″ wide shelf for 45 R.P.M. records is run between this piece and the righthand side and is 12 1/2″ long.

The back of the cabinet is made out of 1/8″ hardboard, 24″ x 29 7/8″.

Materials List

2 pcs. 3/4″ plywood 29 1/8″ x 13″
1 " 3/4″ plywood 24″ x 13″
2 " 3/4″ plywood 22 1/2″ x 13″
2 " 3/4″ plywood 13″ x 13″
1 " 3/4″ plywood 8 x 12 1/2″
1 " 1/8″ hardboard 24″ x 29 7/8″
1 " 1″ x 2″ x 24″
3 " 1/2″ quarter round 13″
3 " 1/2″ quarter round 8″

Materials Totals

1/2″ quarter round — 5′ 3″
(Remainder as itemized above)

RECORD CABINET

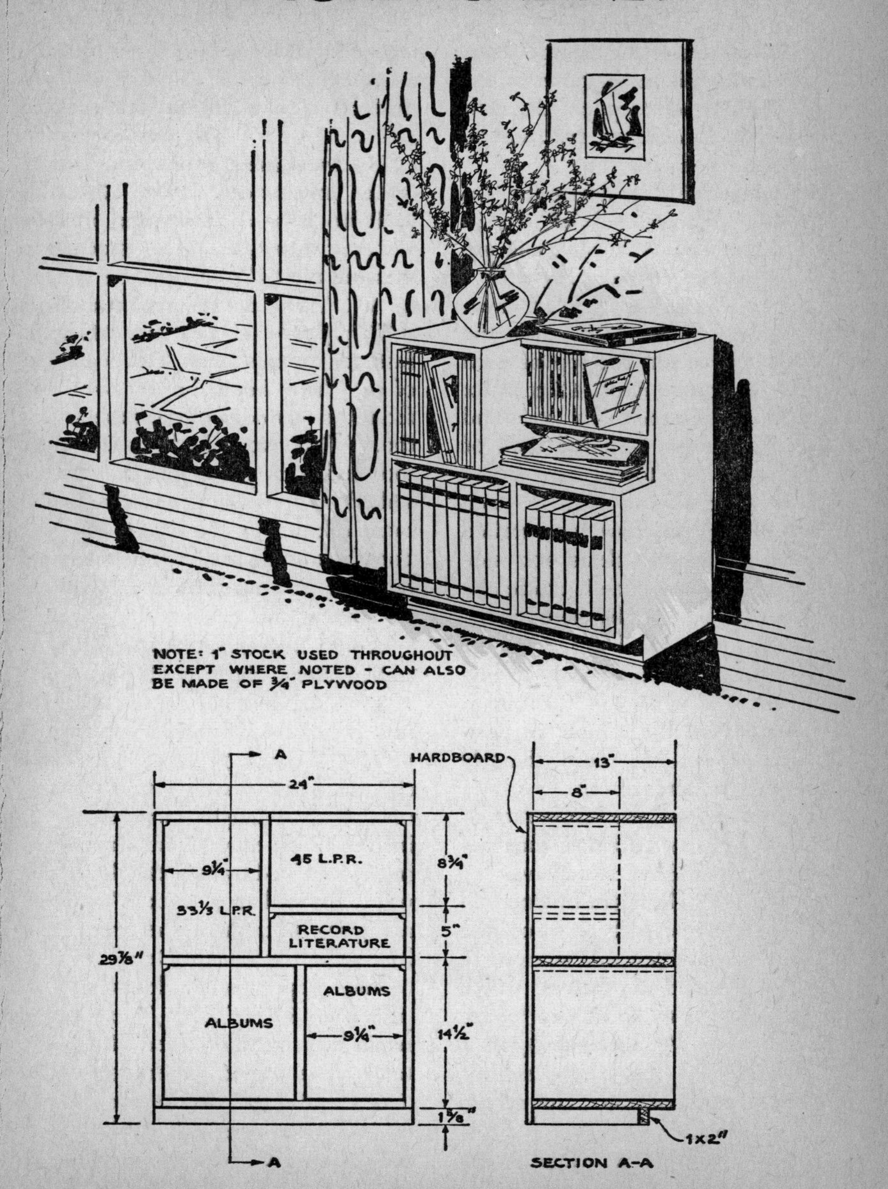

WALL CABINET

For either the living room or recreation room, this wall cabinet brings home entertainment equipment, such as TV set, record changer, and records, into one compact unit.

The first step is to make up the two side pieces. They are made of 1″ x 6″ and 1″ x 8″, each 87″ long, and are fastened together at the top by a 1″ x 2″ x 11 3/4″ cleat set 3 1/2″ down from the top and 1/4″ in from the back. 36 1/4″ from the top of each side piece another cleat, 1″ x 2″ x 12 1/8″, is fastened. Its rear end should come flush with the back of the side piece. The top of the cabinet, made of 1″ x 6″ and 1″ x 8″ each 57 3/4″ long, can now be installed and fastened to the cleats and side pieces. The bottom shelf, made the same size, can be installed between the two lower cleats. The backing for the upper part of the cabinet is 1/4″ plywood 33 1/2″ x 57 3/4″. Fasten it in place and set the cabinet in position. If there is a baseboard, the side pieces must be notched out.

18 3/4″ in from the inside face of each side piece, a partition runs between the top and bottom shelves. 1″ x 2″ x 11 3/4″ cleats are fastened on the outside face of each partition and the inside face of the side sections to take the intermediate shelves, which are made of 1″ x 6″ and 1″ x 8″, each 18 3/4″ long. An upright 3/4″ x 3/4″ x 18 3/8″ runs up the side of the center top opening. The record storage compartment between the first two shelves is made by installing upright pieces of 1/4″ plywood 12 1/2″ x 13″ with spacers at top and bottom made of 1/4″ plywood 4 1/2″ x 12 1/2″.

The two base cabinets can be made up as independent units. They are built up from a base made of three pieces of 1″ x 4″. The two side pieces measure 8 3/4″ long and the front is 13 1/2″. The bottom shelf, made of 3/4″ plywood 12 1/2″ x 12 1/2″, is fastened to this base. The rear edge of the shelf should be set 1/4″ back from the rear edge of the base to take the 1/4″ plywood backing. The side, top, and back pieces can now be installed and the unit secured to the main cabinet by the cleats that support the middle and top shelves. Runners for the top drawer can also be installed at this time.

A 48″ fluorescent light unit is installed along the top of the cabinet 1 3/4″ in from the back edge. The unit is concealed from view by a strip of 1″ x 3″ stock 57 3/4″ long with a strip of 3/4″ quarter round molding of the same length fastened to the inside lower edge. Additional lighting is provided by two 24″ fluorescent units fastened to a 1″ x 3″ attached along the bottom of the lower shelf by an angle iron (see Detail A).

Four upper corner doors of 3/4″ plywood 18 5/8″ x 8 5/8″ should be made and installed (see Hinge Detail). The upper center door is 18 5/8″ x 18 1/8″. Doors for the base cabinet are 11 5/8″ x 26″. The drawer required for each of these cabinets is

11 1/2″ deep (see Drawer Detail). Drawer and door pulls are made of 9/16″ stock cut to a 1 1/4″ diameter and beveled down to 7/8″ on the inside edge.

Materials List

2 pcs. 1″ x 8″ x 87″
2 " 1″ x 8″ x 57 3/4″
2 " 1″ x 8″ x 32″
2 " 1″ x 8″ x 30 1/2″
5 " 1″ x 8″ x 18 3/4″
2 " 1″ x 6″ x 87″
2 " 1″ x 6″ x 57 3/4″
2 " 1″ x 6″ x 32″
2 " 1″ x 6″ x 30 1/2″
5 " 1″ x 6″ x 18 3/4″
2 " 1″ x 4 3/8″ x 11 5/8″
2 " 1″ x 4″ x 13 1/2″
4 " 1″ x 4″ x 11 3/8″
2 " 1″ x 4″ x 10 1/8″
4 " 1″ x 4″ x 8 3/4″
2 " 1″ x 3″ x 57 3/4″
2 " 1″ x 2″ x 12 1/8″
8 " 1″ x 2″ x 11 3/4″
4 pcs. 1 3/4″ x 1 3/4″ x 11 3/4″ (hardwood runners)
1 " 3/4″ x 3/4″ x 18 3/8″
9 " 9/16″/x/1 1/4″ x 1 1/4″
4 " 3/4″ plywood/18 5/8″/ x 8 5/8″
1 " 3/4″ x plywood/18 1/8″ x 18 5/8″
4 " 3/4″ plywood/12 1/2″ x 12 1/2″
2 " 3/4″ plywood 12 1/2″ x 11 3/4″
2 " 3/4″ plywood 11 5/8″ x 26″
1 " 1/4″ plywood 33 1/2″ x 57 3/4″
2 " 1/4″ plywood 12 1/2″ x 31 1/4″
9 " 1/4″ plywood 12 1/2″ x 13″
2 " 1/4″ plywood 10 1/8″ x 11″
24 " 1/4″ plywood 4 1/2″ x 12 1/2″
1 " 3/4″ quarter round 57 3/4″
1 3/8″-angle iron 2″ x 2″
7 pairs cabinet hinges
1 fluorescent light unit 48″
2 fluorescent light units 24″

Materials Totals

1″ x 8″ — 42′ 4 1/4″
1″ x 6″ — 42′ x 4 1/4″
1″ x 4 3/8″ — 1′ 11 1/4″
1″ x 4″ — 10′ 7 3/4″
1″ x 3″ — 9′ 7 1/2″
1″ x 2″ — 9′ 10 1/4″
1 3/4″ x 1 3/4″ — 3′ 11″
9/16″ x 1 1/4″ — 11 1/4″
(Remainder as itemized above)

WALL CABINET

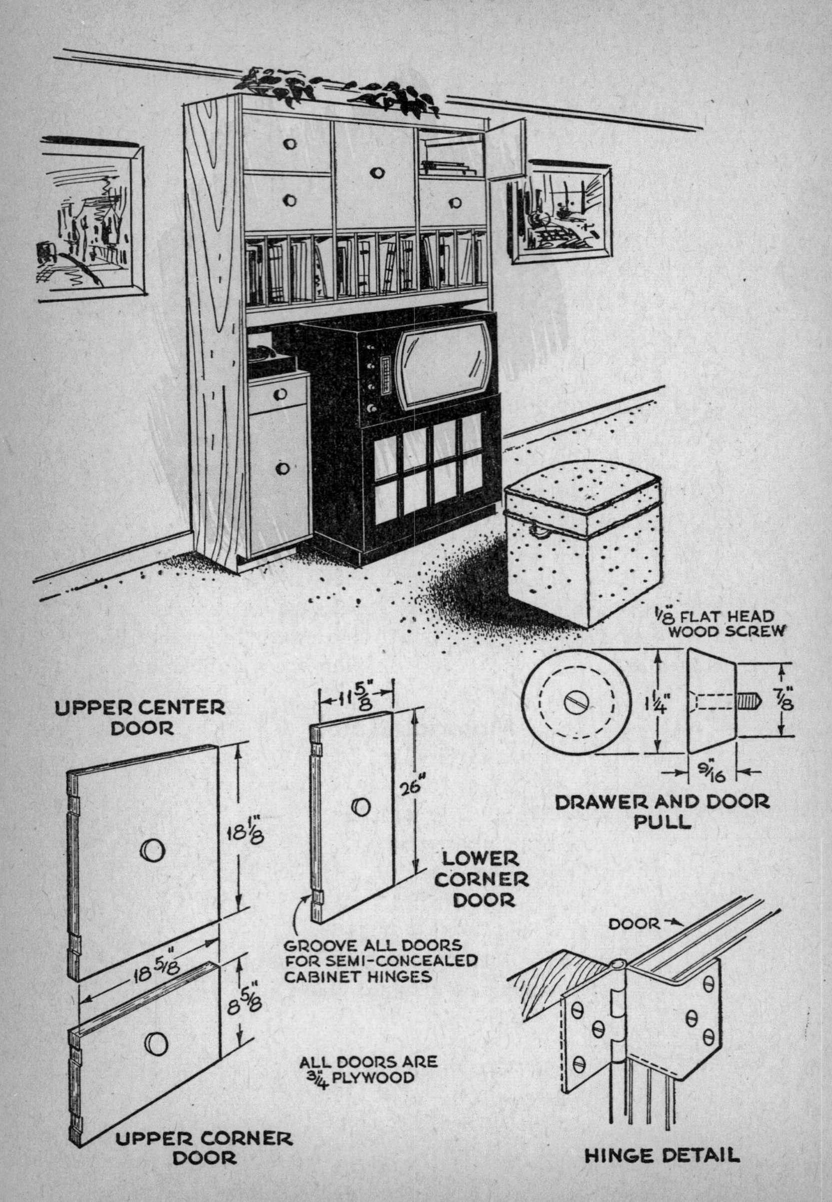

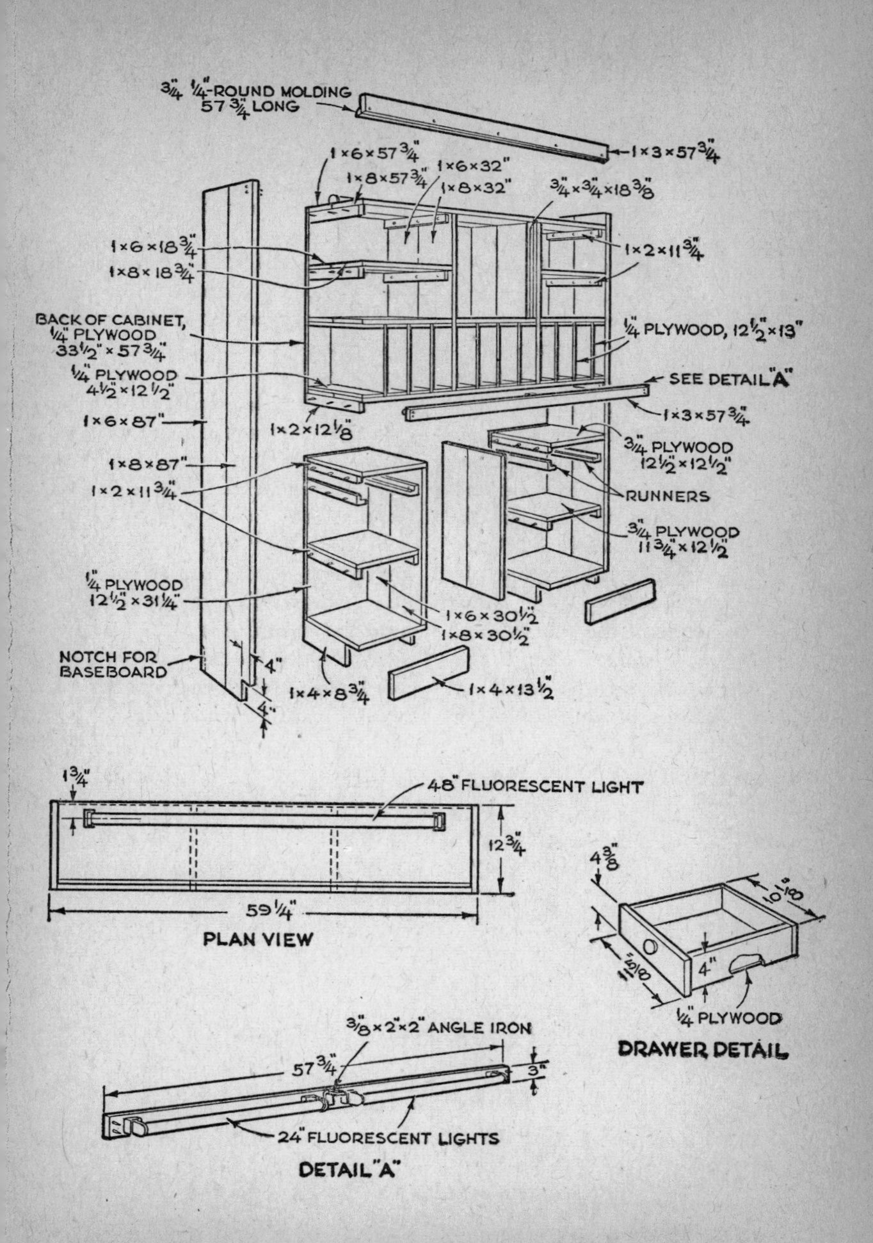

3/4" 1/4"-ROUND MOLDING 57 3/4" LONG
1×3×57 3/4"
1×6×57 3/4"
1×8×57 3/4"
1×6×32"
1×8×32"
3/4"×3/4"×18 3/8"
1×6×18 3/4"
1×8×18 3/4"
1×2×11 3/4"
BACK OF CABINET, 1/4" PLYWOOD 33 1/2"×57 3/4"
1/4" PLYWOOD, 12 1/2"×13"
1/4" PLYWOOD 4 1/2"×12 1/2"
SEE DETAIL "A"
1×6×87"
1×2×12 1/8
1×3×57 3/4
3/4 PLYWOOD 12 1/2"×12 1/2"
1×8×87"
1×2×11 3/4"
RUNNERS
3/4 PLYWOOD 11 3/4"×12 1/2"
1/4" PLYWOOD 12 1/2"×31 1/4"
1×6×30 1/2"
1×8×30 1/2"
NOTCH FOR BASEBOARD
4"
4"
1×4×8 3/4
1×4×13 1/2"
1 3/4"
48" FLUORESCENT LIGHT
12 3/4
59 1/4"
PLAN VIEW
4 3/8"
10 3/8
11 5/8
4"
1/4" PLYWOOD
DRAWER DETAIL
3/8"×2"×2" ANGLE IRON
57 3/4
3"
24" FLUORESCENT LIGHTS
DETAIL "A"

STEP-UP LADDER STOOL

You'll find many uses for this step-up ladder stool in the kitchen, pantry, and workshop.

The assembly of the legs for the ladder stool is begun by cutting the straight one to the correct size — 21 3/4″ long.

At inside of this leg, attach a 1″ x 4″ support at the top. Make sure that the top of this support is flush with the top of the leg and that they join at exactly 90 degrees. Now tack the other leg, which runs off at an angle, to the other end of this support and position it so that the top outside edge of this leg is exactly 9″ from the rear edge of the straight leg while the bottom outside edge is 15″ away from the rear edge of the straight leg. Now, laying a square along the straight leg, mark off the angle at which the bottom of the other leg must be cut to rest level. Use the same procedure for cutting off the top end of this leg. The top support should have its end cut off flush with the outside edge of the leg. Install the two additional 1″ x 2″ supports, and then make up the other leg assembly in the same manner. The two pairs of legs are joined in the back by two strips of 1″ x 4″. One of these fits flush under the top, the other flush with the bottom rung support.

Steps for the ladder can now be cut and installed. The top for the stool is cut from 1″ stock 10 3/4″ x 14 1/2″. A 1″ x 2″ is nailed on the underside of the top in such a way that it can be fastened to the top support between the legs.

After the ladder has been assembled, round off all edges or bevel them with a plane or wood rasp.

Materials List

2 pcs. 1″ x 4″ x 24″
2 " 1″ x 4″ x 21 3/4″
2 " 1″ x 4″ x 13 1/2″
2 " 1″ x 4″ x 12″ (steps)
2 " 1″ x 4″ x 10″
2 " 1″ x 2″ x 13″
2 " 1″ x 2″ x 11″
2 " 1″ x 2″ x 9″
1 " 1″ x 10 3/4″ x 14 1/2″ (top)

Materials Totals

1″ x 4″ — 13′ 6 1/2″
1″ x 2″ — 5′ 6″
(Remainder as itemized above)

STEP-UP LADDER STOOL

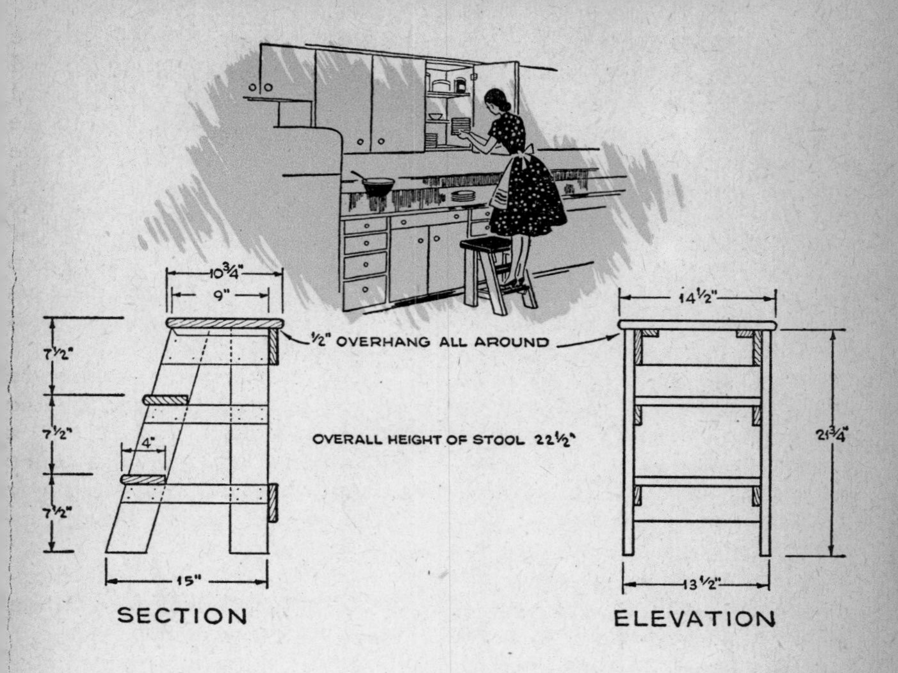

STOOL MAY BE ASSEMBLED WITH NAILS OR SCREWS – THE USE OF GLUE AT THE JOINTS WILL STRENGTHEN STOOL CONSIDERABLY

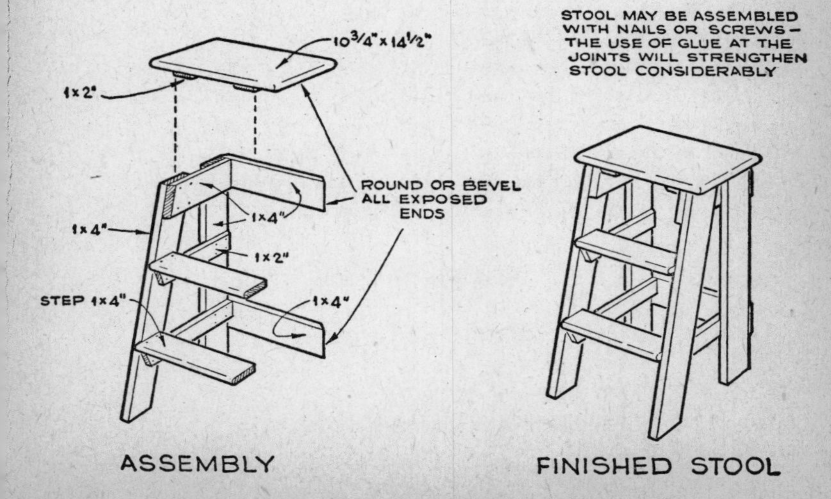

BREAKFAST BAR

This breakfast bar can be attached to existing kitchen cabinets, or to the wall and base cabinet illustrated elsewhere, or directly to a wall.

The top of the bar is made up of two pieces of 3/4" plywood. These should be fastened together with screws and wood glue. The top is then fastened to the wall or cabinet with a 3" x 3 1/2" angle iron at each end. The dimensions of the bar top can be varied to meet individual requirements. The outer edge of the bar top is supported at one end by means of a 2" x 2" leg. The other end is supported by the tray storage rack and a short leg. To install the long leg, first set a strip of 2" x 3" that is 8" long on the floor, and then place the 2" x 2" leg against this and the bar top to get the proper angles for the end cuts on the leg. Cut the leg to size — 25 1/2" — and then fit a 1/2" dowel into the 2" x 3" base. The dowel should extend 2" or so above the 2" x 3" base and should run at the same angle as the leg. Drill a hole in the leg the same depth as the portion of the dowel above the base, fit the dowel into the leg, and slip the leg in under the bar top. Fasten the leg to the top by running a long screw down through the top and then install a 3/4" angle iron.

The tray rack on the other side of the bar top is fastened to the top with two 1" x 1" wood cleats. Cut the two sides of the rack and the bottom piece and fasten in place. A 2" x 3" base should be fastened to the floor under the tray, and a strip of 2" x 2" that is 10 1/2" long run between this and the bottom of the tray storage rack. Angles of short and long legs must be equal.

The bar top can be covered with linoleum or stainless steel with steel or aluminum edging. The seam where the back of the bar joins the wall can be covered with a strip of 1/2" quarter round.

Materials List

2 pcs. 2" x 3" x 8 1/2"
1 " 2" x 2" x 25 1/2"
1 " 2" x 2" x 7 1/2"
2 " 1" x 1" x 12"
2 " 3/4" plywood 13" x 56"
1 " 1/2" plywood 13" x 28 1/2"
1 " 1/2" plywood 13" x 18"
1 " 1/2" plywood 10" x 3"
2 " angle irons 3" x 3 1/2"
1 angle iron 3/4"

Materials Totals

2" x 3" — 1' 5"
2" x 2" — 2' 9"
1" x 1" — 2'
3/4" plywood 56" x 26"
(Remainder as itemized above)

BREAKFAST BAR

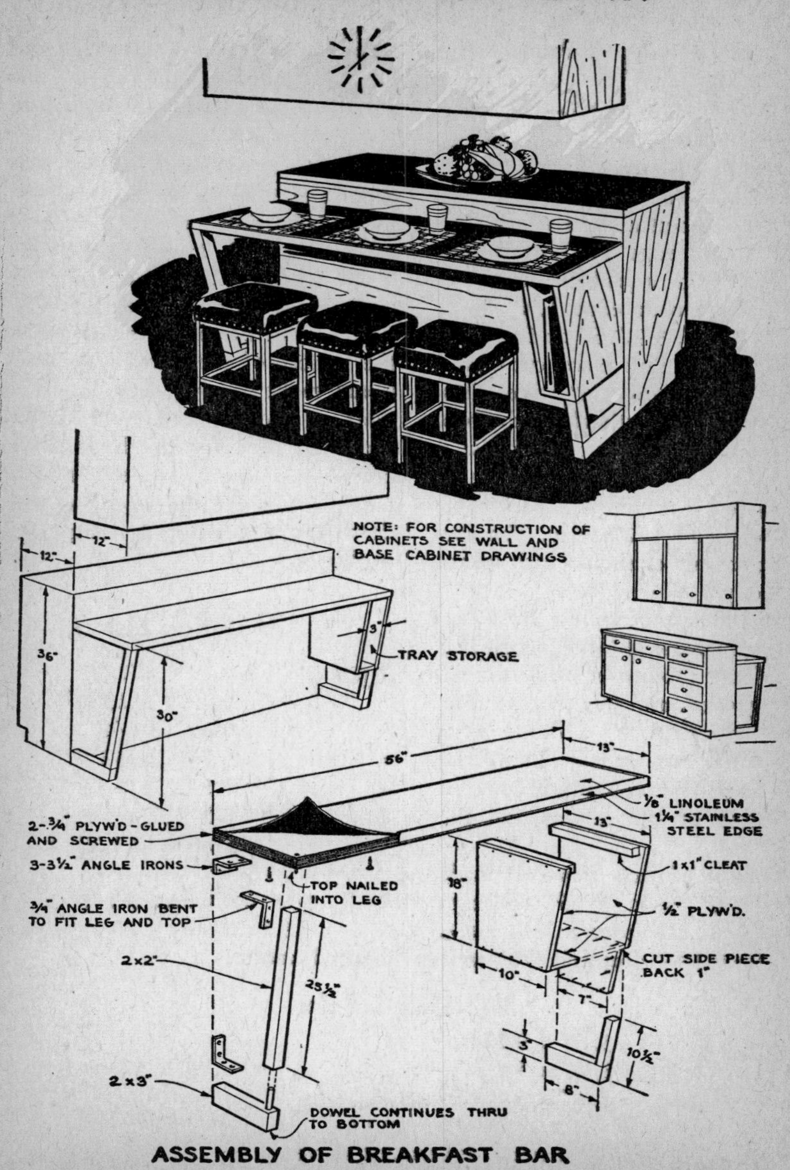

ASSEMBLY OF BREAKFAST BAR

COOK BOOK AND RECIPE FILING SHELF

This cook book and recipe filing shelf makes an excellent addition to your kitchen cabinets.

Cut the two side pieces to size, and then cut a rabbett along the top and bottom inside edge 1/4″ deep and 3/4″ wide. Cut a rabbett along the inside of the back edge 1/4″ deep and 1/2″ wide. 3 9/16″ up from the bottom edge of each piece, cut a rabbett 1/4″ deep and 3/4″ wide. This is for the shelf directly above the two small drawers. Now cut the top and bottom piece of the cabinet to size and cut a rabbett in each on the back edge 1/4″ deep and 1/2″ wide. The top and bottom pieces should each measure exactly 9 1/4″ wide by 13 1/4″ long. Cut the center shelf to this same size, and then assemble the pieces. The back of the cabinet is made out of 1/4″ plywood, and this too can now go into place. A 9″ dividing strip between the two drawers should be cut out of 3/4″ stock midway between the bottom of the cabinet and the shelf.

The front of each drawer is made out of 3/4″ stock. 3/16″ up from the bottom inside edge in this piece, cut a rabbett 1/4″ deep and 1/8″ wide for the bottom piece of the drawer. On the inside surface of each end of the front piece, cut a rabbett 1/2″ deep and 3/8″ wide for the side pieces. The sides of each drawer are made out of 3/8″ stock, and each needs a rabbett 1/4″ deep and 1/8″ wide on the bottom inside edge 3/16″ up from the bottom to accommodate the bottom of the drawer. An additional rabbett, 1/4″ deep and 3/8″ wide, is also required 1/4″ in from the back edge for the back of the drawer. Cut the back piece and bottom piece to size and assemble. Sand down any high points or rough spots in the drawers.

Materials List

2 pcs. 3/4″ x 9 1/4″ x 18″
2 " 3/4″ x 9 1/4″ x 13 1/4″
1 " 3/4″ x 9″ x 13 1/4″
2 " 3/4″ x 5 7/8″ x 3 1/2″
4 " 3/8″ x 3 1/2″ x 8 3/4″
2 " 3/8″ x 3 5/16″ x 5 1/8″
1 " 1/4″ plywood 17 1/2″ x 13 3/4″
2 " 1/8″ hardboard 5 1/8″ x 8 1/2″
2 wood knobs

Materials Totals

3/4″ x 9 1/4″ — 5′ 2 1/2″
3/4″ x 5 7/8″ — 7″
3/8″ x 3 1/2″ — 2′ 11″
3/8″ x 3 5/16″ — 10 1/4″
(Remainder as itemized above)

COOK BOOK AND RECIPE FILING SHELF

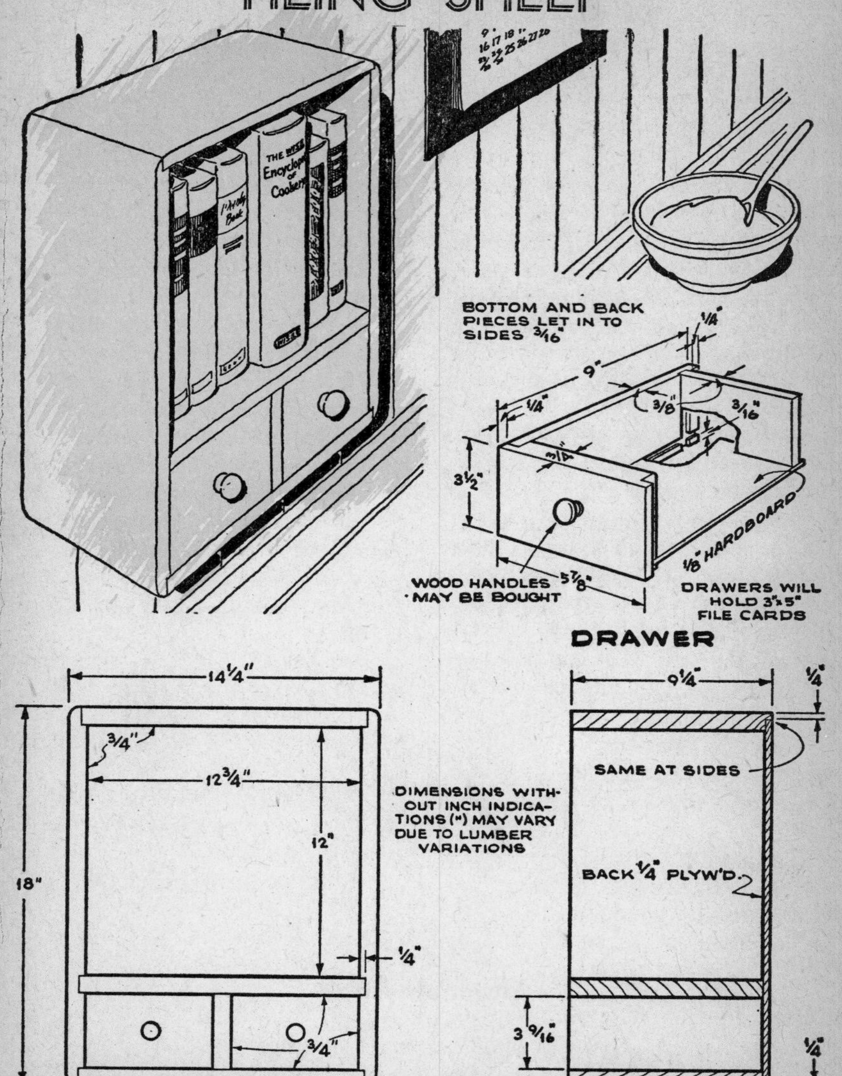

KNIFE RACK

Kitchen knives will keep their cutting edge much longer if they are placed in a knife rack rather than in a drawer with other metal objects that dull and knick the blades. This procedure is also a good safety measure, for the rack is out of a child's reach.

The top of the rack is made out of a piece of 3/4" stock. The ends can be rounded down with a plane and a wood rasp. Slots in the top for the knives are made by first drilling a series of holes with a twist drill and then squaring up the sides with a small wood chisel carefully.

The back and face of the rack are made out of 1/4" plywood. Cut them to size, leaving the top flat. After they are in place, the top can be rounded down to conform with the rounded top containing the knife slots. Tack the slotted top to the plywood back, and then install the side sections of the rack, securely fastening it also with tacks.

The upper section of each side piece is 5" long and extends down along the sides in a straight line. The lower sections of the sides are brought in at a slight angle so that the outside bottom dimension is 3". A tight fit where the two sections of the sides join can be made by cutting the ends of the side pieces at a slight angle. Sections of the sides are held in place by nailing them to the back of the rack. When the sides are in place, round off the top with a wood rasp to match the curvature at top of rack.

Holes should be drilled at the top and bottom of the back piece for nails or screws to attach the rack to the wall.

The divider strips can now be cut to size and fastened to the back plywood. After this, the front or face plywood can go on, and the top of the front and back plywood can be rounded off with a rasp. No bottom is required on the rack — it would only serve to catch dust and dirt.

Materials List

2 pcs. 1/4" plywood 6" x 12 7/8"
1 " 3/4" x 1 3/4" x 6"
2 " 1/2" x 1 3/4" x 9"
2 " 1/2" x 1 3/4" x 5 1/8"
2 " 1/2" x 1 3/4" x 4"
2 " 1/2" x 1 3/4" x 3"

Materials Totals

1/2" x 1 3/4" — 3' 6 1/4"
1/4" plywood — 12" x 12 7/8"
(Remainder as itemized above)

KNIFE RACK

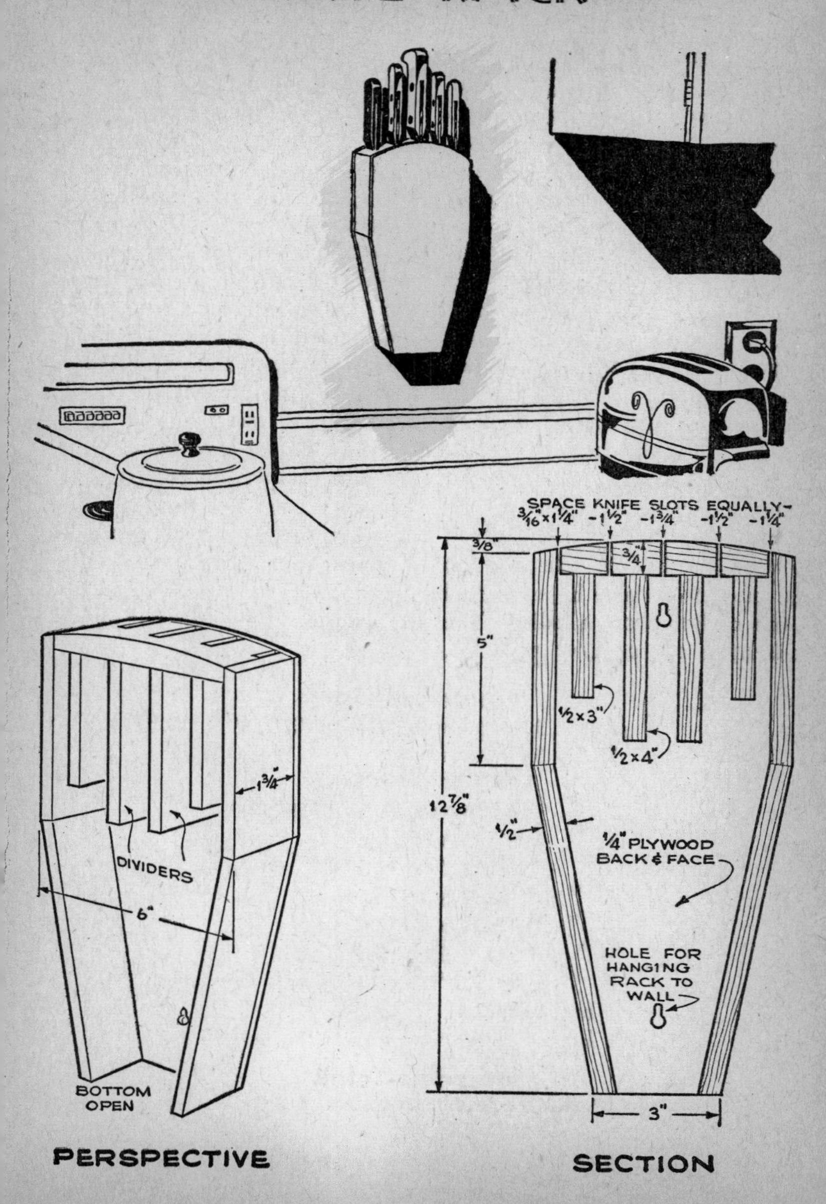

PERSPECTIVE

SECTION

BROOM CABINET

Keeping all of the house cleaning equipment in order is a good deal easier if you have a good roomy broom cabinet for storage. The cabinet shown has ample room for brooms, mops, dustpans, and other cleaning materials.

The cabinet is built up from a base made out of 1″ x 2″ stock. The side pieces of the base are 18″ long and its ends measure 11″. The bottom of the cabinet, made out of 3/4″ plywood and measuring 12″ x 18″, is fastened to this base.

The sides of the cabinet measure 12″ x 72 3/4″. 10″ from the top, a wood cleat 1″ x 1 1/2″ x 11″ is attached to the inside surface to support the shelf, This cleat should be attached with wood screws. The sides and top of the cabinet can now be assembled and the back section installed. The back is made out of 1/4″ plywood. Fasten the 11″ x 18″ shelf to the wood cleats.

A door stop is fastened along the inside edge of the lefthand side of the cabinet. It is made out of 1″ x 1 1/2″ stock and measures 59″. It should be set 3/4″ from the edge of the side, so that the door, when closed, will fit flush with the side pieces. The door itself is made from 3/4″ plywood and is fastened in place with three hinges. The middle hinge is necessary to prevent the door from buckling or warping. A door latch should also be installed.

The cabinet can be left resting on the floor, but it is wise to fasten the back to the plaster wall to prevent the cabinet from being moved out of position. This can be done either by using expansion bolts or by using raw plugs.

Materials List

2 pcs. 3/4″ plywood 12″ x 72 3/4″
1 " 3/4″ plywood 17 7/8″ x 69 1/8″
2 " 3/4″ plywood 12″ x 18″
1 " 1/4″ plywood 19 1/2″ x 72 3/4″
2 " 1″ x 2″ x 18″
2 " 1″ x 2″ x 11″
1 " 1″ x 1 1/2″ x 59″
2 " 1″ x 1 1/2″ x 11″
3 butt hinges
1 latch

Materials Totals

1″ x 2″ — 4′ 10″
1″ x 1 1/2″ — 6′ 9″
(Remainder as itemized above)

BROOM CABINET

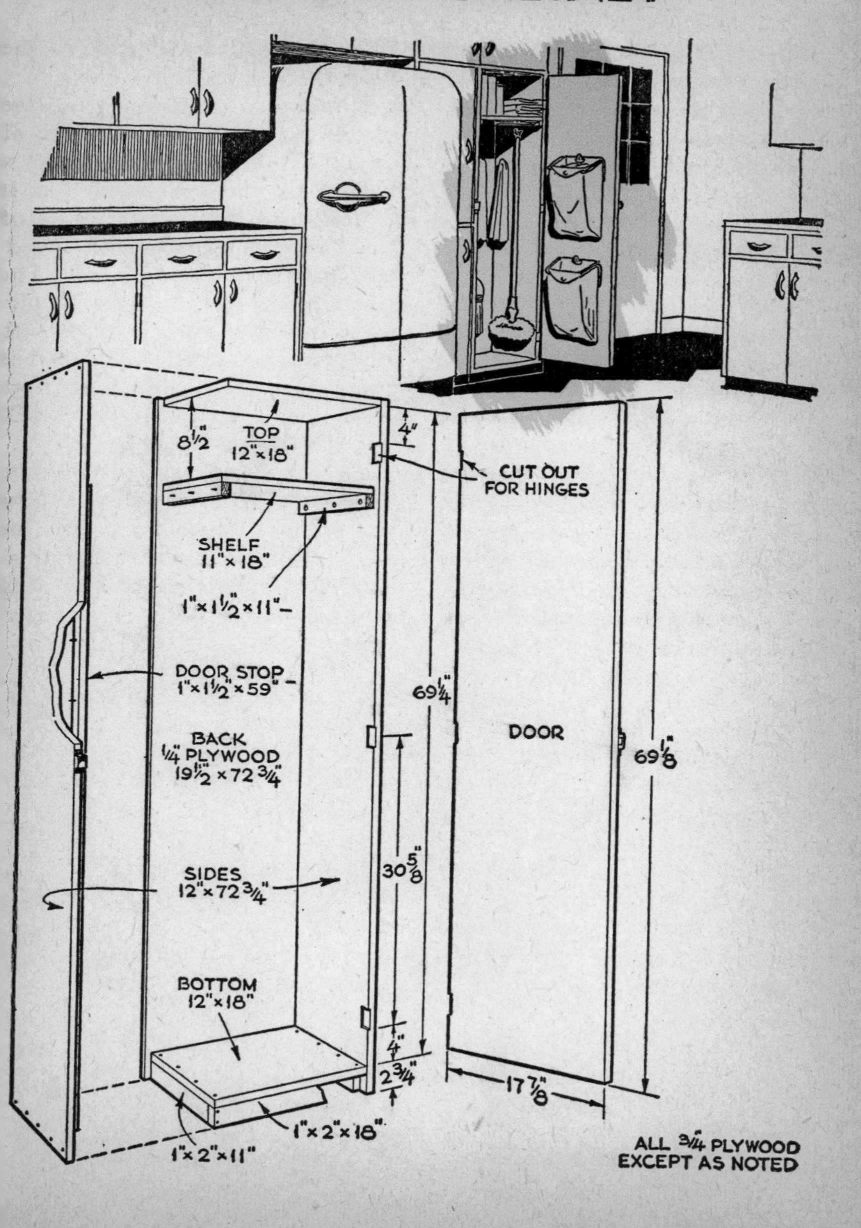

BUILT-IN IRONING BOARD

Before starting work on the cabinet, have a 20-amp duplex convenience outlet roughed into the wall in back of where the board is to be.

The sides, top, and bottom of the closet for the board are made out of 3/4″ plywood. Notch out the two side pieces at the bottom outside edge for a 3″ x 3″ toe space. Cut a rabbett 1/4″ deep and 3/4″ wide above the notch and at the top of each side piece for the top and bottom pieces. Assemble these pieces and install the 1/4″ plywood back. Cut and install a 3/4″ strip of plywood to cover up the base of the cabinet where the sides were notched out. The cabinet can then be placed in position, a hole cut in the back for the electrical outlet, and the cabinet anchored to the wall by running screws through the back into the wall studding.

The shelves in the cabinet are supported by 1″ x 1″ cleats attached to the inside surface of the sides. The shelf to which the ironing board is attached has a strip of 2″ x 2″ fastened across the front and flush with the top of the shelf. The 2″ x 2″ strip should be firmly anchored in place by means of screws run in through the sides of the cabinet. The ironing board is attached to this strip with a section of piano hinge (see page 90).

The front of the ironing board i supported by a leg made out of 1 1/8 x 4″ stock 31 7/8″ long. The top en of this leg should fit snugly betwee two 1″ x 1″ cleats attached to th bottom of the board and space 1 1/8″ apart. A folding extensio hinge between the board and leg pe mits the single leg to be pulled ou from between the cleats and folde up against the board. The board held folded upright by a strap an ring.

Materials List

2 pcs. 3/4″ plywood 17″ x 16″
3 " 3/4″ plywood 16 1/2″ x 8 3/4″
2 " 3/4″ plywood 16″ x 7′
1 " 3/4″ plywood 14 1/2″ x 6′ 9″
1 " 2″ x 2″ x 16 1/2″
1 " 1 1/4″ x 4″ x 30 3/4″
8 " 1″ x 1″ x 8 3/4″
2 " 1″ x 1″ x 4″
1 " 3/4″ x x3″ x 18″
1 ironing board 12″ x 48″
1 piano hinge 11″
1 folding extension hinge
1 strap with ring
1 hook
3 semi-concealed door hinges
1 door latch

Materials Totals

1″ x 1″ – 6′ 6″
(Remainder as itemized above)

BUILT-IN IRONING BOARD

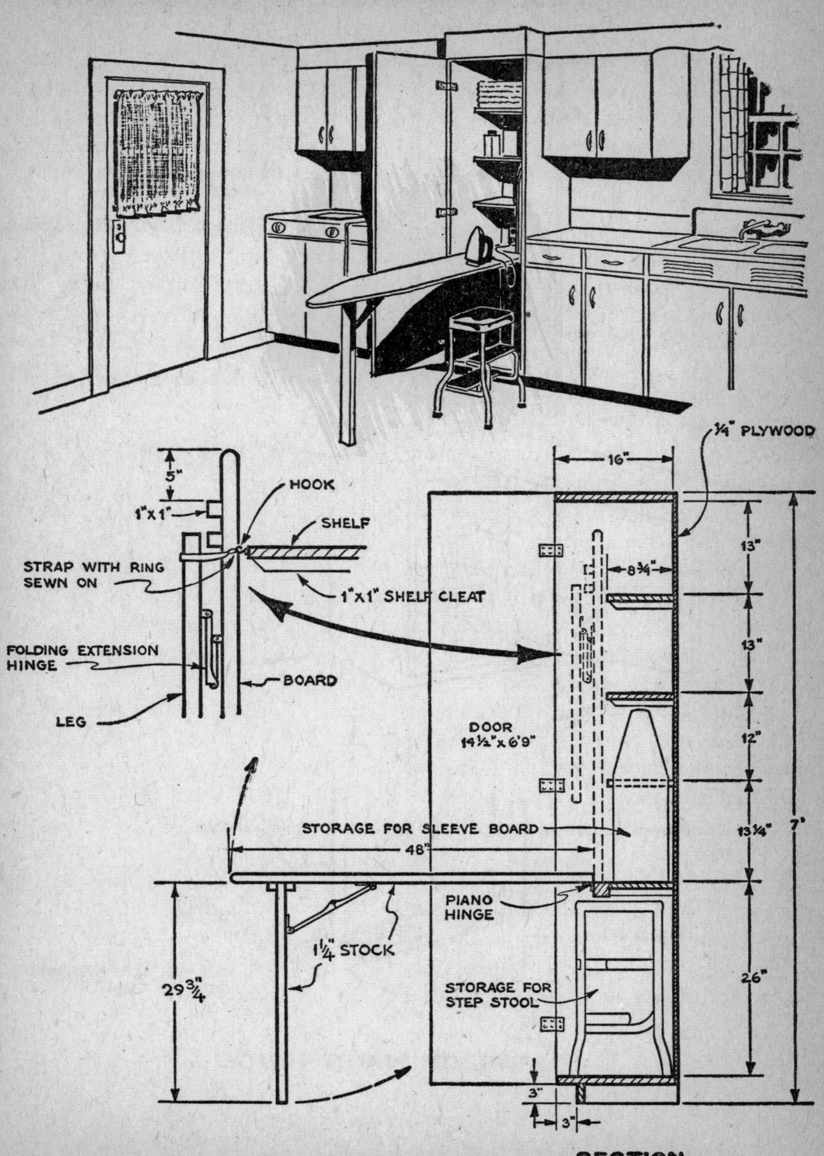

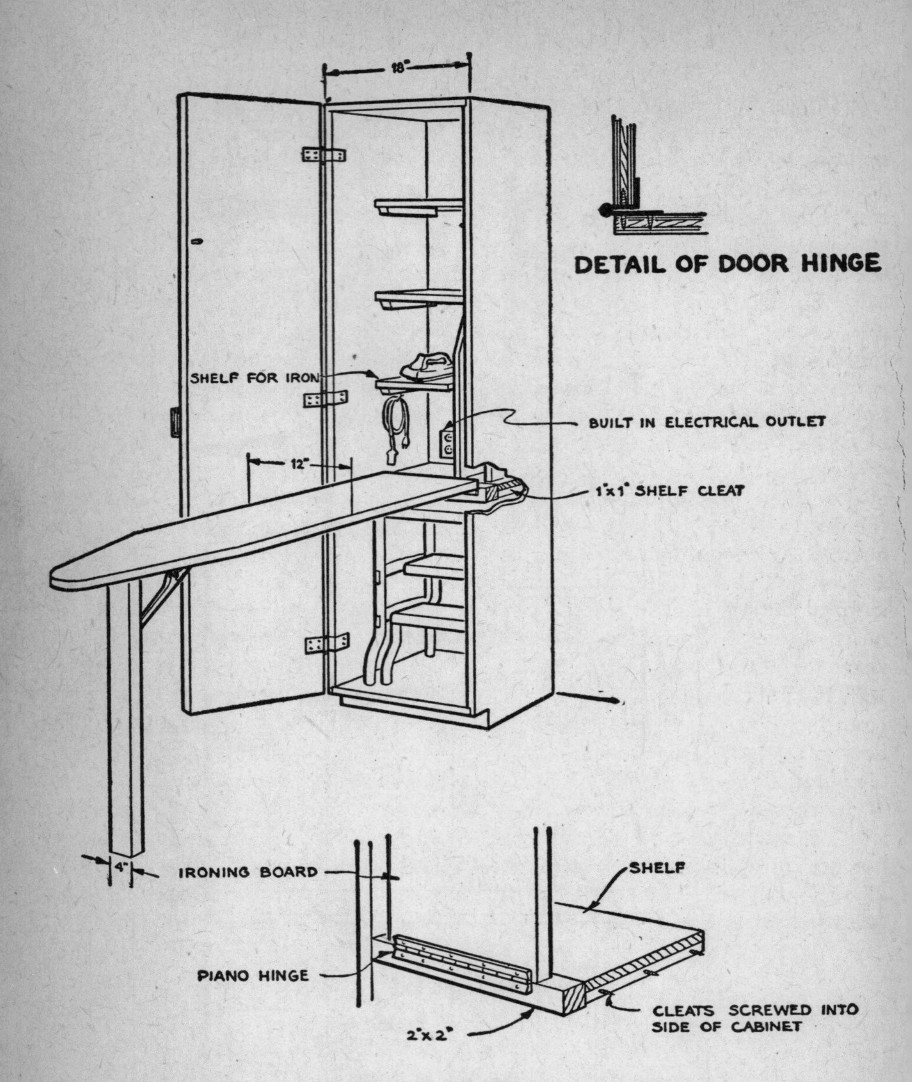

DETAIL OF PIANO HINGE

SINK ENCLOSURE

Hanging kitchen sinks can be converted into modern cabinet sinks by building an enclosure around the base.

Measure the straight surfaces on the rim of the sink. Make up the two side sections of the enclosure using the width of the straight portion of the side. To determine height, compute the distance from the edge of the sink to the floor. The rear uprights for the end sections are 2″ x 2″. The front uprights are 2″ x 4″. The bottom end of each is notched out to take a 1″ x 4″ board at the base. The 2″ x 4″ is also notched out along the bottom of the front endge to take a 1″ x 3″ baseboard that runs along the front of the enclosure. The top of the uprights are notched out 2″ to take the 1″ x 6″ board at the top. End sections are held apart at the back with a strip of 1″ x 10″. In the center a length of 2″ x 2″ from the top of the back brace to the floor is fastened. The end sections are separated along the front by the 1″ x 4″ baseboard. This is notched out 1″ x 4″ at each end and fits into the notches cut on the outside face of the 2″ x 4″ uprights. The frame for the front section, top, and sides is made of 1″ x 3″ stock with a 1″ x 2″ across the bottom as a center divider. It should be 3″ shorter than the side frames. After the frame has been made, fasten a 1″ x 6″ across the top in which four 1/2″ x 10″ vents have been cut. Fasten a second 1″ x 2″ across the bottom and fit two 1″ x 4″ at the sides and a 1″ x 3″ at the center. Assemble the front frame to the sides in proper relationship to the rim of the sink. Now nail the notched out 1″ x 4″ base piece at the bottom at both ends.

Fasten a piece of 1″ x 4″ along the floor between the front section and the 2″ x 2″ piece nailed to the 1″ x 10″ back piece. If you want a shelf, fasten 12″ x 12″ metal shelf hangers to the 2″ x 2″ rear uprights and the 2″ x 2″ middle piece. The shelf can be made out of a piece of 1″ x 12″ or 1″ x 10″. The end sections and the bottom of the enclosure are 1/2″ plywood. Doors are made of 1/2″ plywood cut 3/4″ larger than the opening. Along the edges a rabbet 3/8″ wide and 1/4″ deep is cut. The outside edge of the plywood is then rounded off.

Materials List

Because of the wide variation in sizes and shapes of kitchen sinks, a material list is not presented. The sink shown in the illustrations is 42″ over-all.

SINK ENCLOSURE

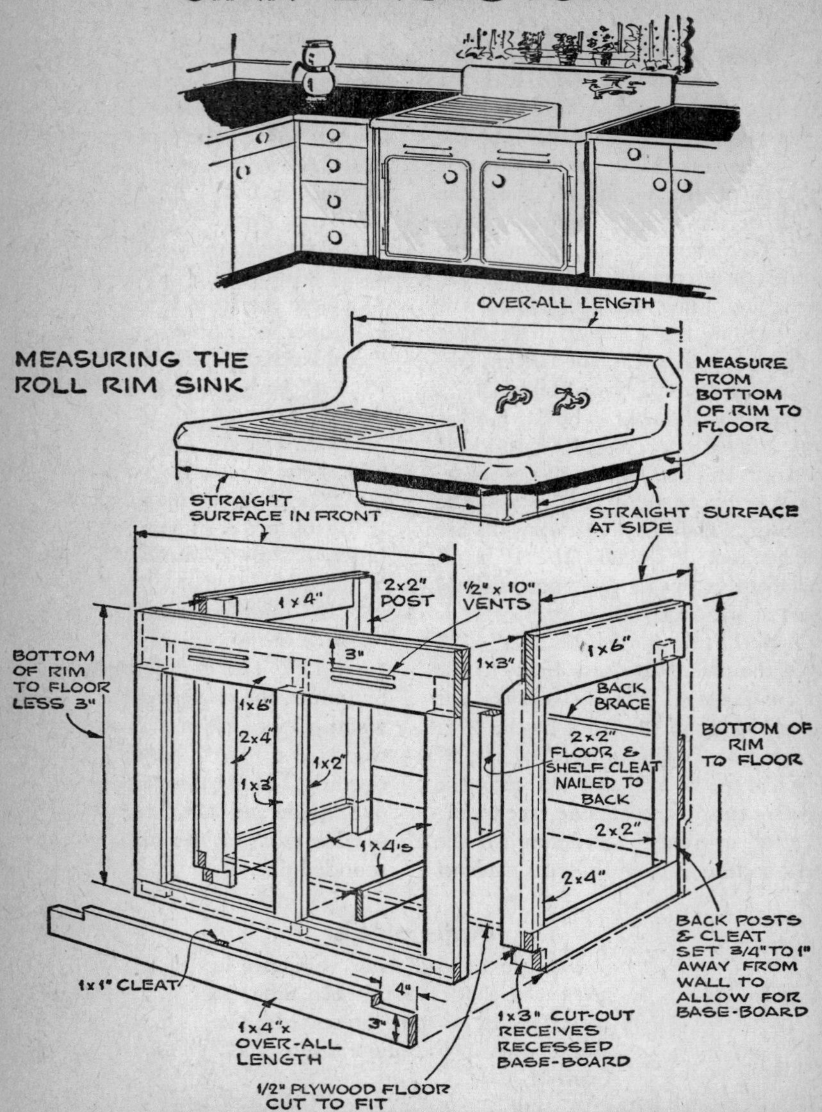

EXPLODED VIEW OF ENCLOSURE WITH RIGHT 1/2" PLYWOOD END PANEL & DOORS REMOVED.

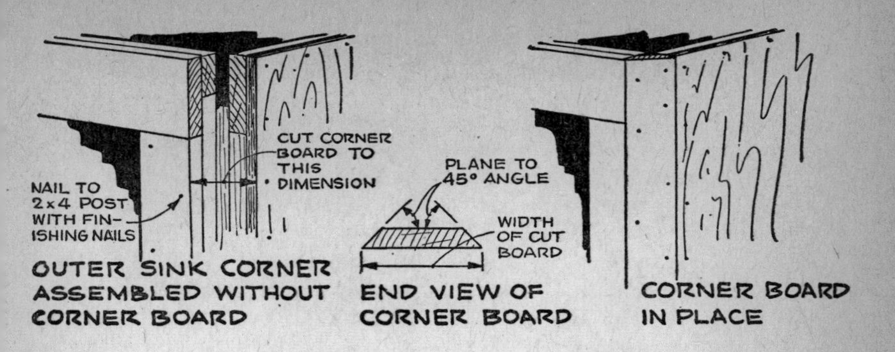
CUT CORNER BOARD TO THIS DIMENSION
NAIL TO 2x4 POST WITH FINISHING NAILS
OUTER SINK CORNER ASSEMBLED WITHOUT CORNER BOARD
PLANE TO 45° ANGLE
WIDTH OF CUT BOARD
END VIEW OF CORNER BOARD
CORNER BOARD IN PLACE

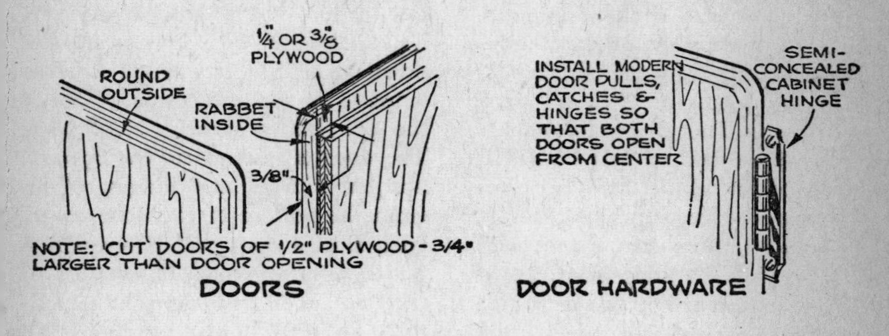
1/4" OR 3/8" PLYWOOD
ROUND OUTSIDE
RABBET INSIDE
3/8"
NOTE: CUT DOORS OF 1/2" PLYWOOD - 3/4" LARGER THAN DOOR OPENING
DOORS
INSTALL MODERN DOOR PULLS, CATCHES & HINGES SO THAT BOTH DOORS OPEN FROM CENTER
SEMI-CONCEALED CABINET HINGE
DOOR HARDWARE

INSTALL MIXING FAUCET LIKE THE ONE SHOWN HERE TO MAKE THIS A COMPLETELY UP-TO-DATE SINK
VIEW OF FINISHED ENCLOSURE

UPPER CORNER CABINET

Corners in the kitchen are often a neglected source of valuable space, which can be used with this cabinet.

The shelf and bottom of the cabinet are made of 3/4″ plywood 23″ x 23″ The plan in the drawing shows how these pieces should be cut out to take the uprights. The top of the cabinet is 3/4″ plywood 23 1/2″ x 23 1/2″. The plan in the illustration shows the dimensions of the various cuts. The uprights for the cabinet consist of five pieces of 2″ x 2″ stock 29 1/4″ long. They fit into the notches cut out of the bottom and the shelf. The top of the cabinet fits down over them. Joints between uprights and top, shelf, and bottom are made with 1 1/2″ x 1 1/2″ angle irons. 24 of these are required. The two large side pieces of the cabinet are made of 1/4″ plywood—one piece 23 1/4″ x 30″ and the other 23″ x 30″. The two smaller pieces are 1/4″ plywood 13″ x 30″. The cabinet door is made out of 3/4″ plywood 20 1/2″ x 30″. The two edges are beveled to a 45 degree angle to make a tight joint with the sides of the cabinet. There may be a difference of 1/4″ in the size of the door to allow for hinges and "ply" of the door. Two pieces of 1″ x 2″ are beveled down to a 45 degree angle and fastened to the top and bottom of one of the uprights to serve as door stops. The door is fastened to the opposite upright with cabinet hinges. 3″ up from the bottom of the door on the latch side, a door pull is screwed in place. A spring catch is installed on the door and on an upright to hold the door in the closed position.

Materials List

5 pcs. 2″ x 2″ x 29 1/4″
2 " 1″ x 2″ x 2″
1 " 3/4″ plywood 23 1/2″ x 23 1/2″
2 " 3/4″ plywood 23″ x 23″
1 " 3/4″ plywood 20 1/2″ x 30″
1 " 1/4″ plywood 23 1/4″ x 30″
1 " 1/4″ plywood 23″ x 30″
2 " 1/4″ plywood 13″ x 30″
24 angle irons 1 1/2″ x 1 1/2″
2 cabinet hinges
1 friction catch
1 door pull

Materials Totals

2″ x 2″ — 12' 2 1/4″
1″ x 2″ — 4″
(Remainder as itemized above)

UPPER CORNER CABINET

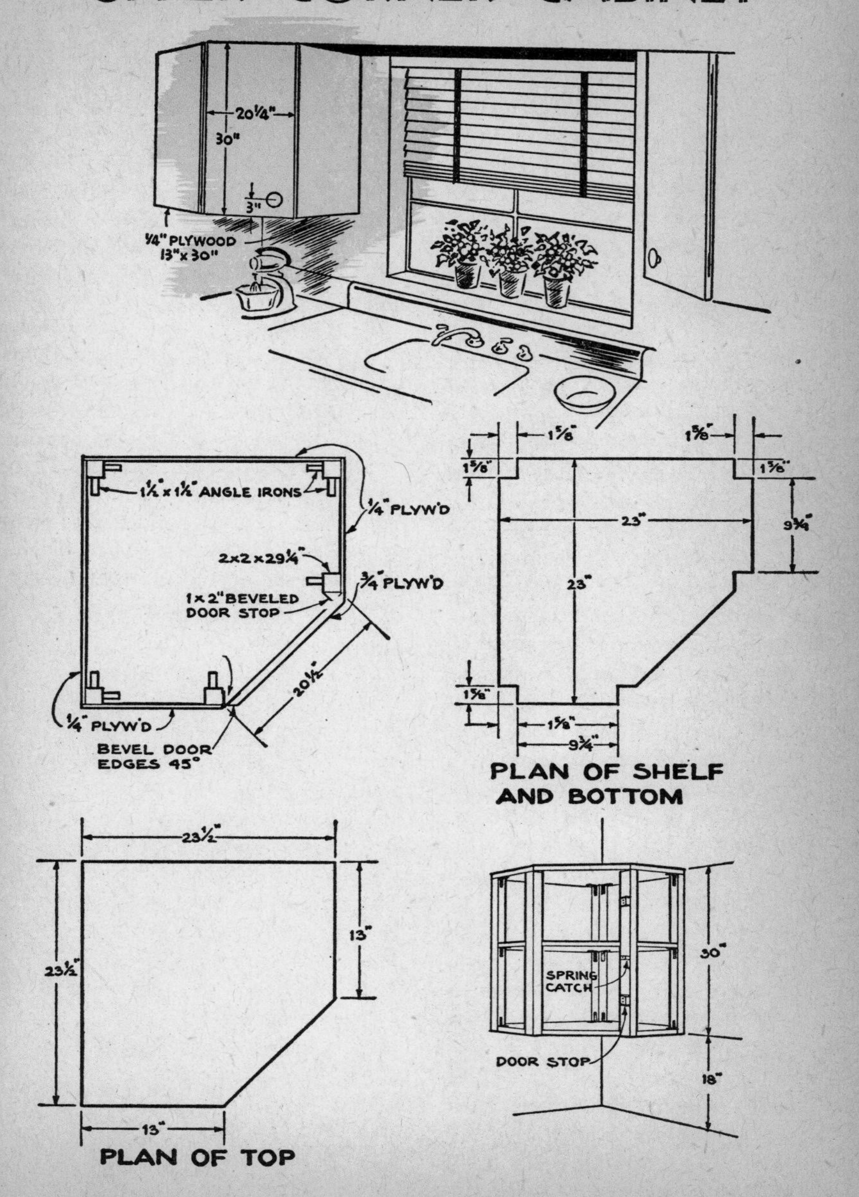

KITCHEN CORNER CABINET

Cut out the two shelves from 1/2″ plywood 35″ x 35″ as indicated in the plan. These will be useful as guides for making up the framework. The three rear uprights are made 2″ x 2″ x 35 1/4″. The two uprights in the front that serve as a frame for the door are 2″ x 2″ x 34 1/2″. These two pieces rest on a piece of 1″ x 6″ notched out. Uprights are fastened together with pieces of 1″ x 3″. The lower pieces of 1″ x 3″ are set 3/4″ up from the ends of the rear three uprights and flush with the ends of the two front uprights that rest on the 1″ x 6″ A piece of 1/2″ plywood 3 3/8″ x 14″ with the ends beveled to 45 degree angles should be installed between the front uprights at the base. Place the lower shelf in position and fasten it to the 1″ x 3″ strips and to the uprights. 18″ from the bottom shelf, install four more pieces of 1″ x 3″ for the second shelf. Along the back of the cabinet, fasten two pieces of 1″ x 8″, one 35 1/8″ and the other 35 7/8″ long. These pieces should extend above the top of the uprights 6 3/4″. Notch out the lower portions of the ends so that they come flush with the edges of the 2″ x 2″ uprights. The top of the cabinet, 3/4″ plywood 35 1/8″ x 35 1/8″, is then cut to size and fastened in place.

The latch side of the cabinet is made of 3/8″ plywood 24 3/8″ x 35 1/4″. The panel on this side should be beveled to a 45 degree angle. The hinged side of the cabinet is made of 3/8″ plywood 24 1/4″ x 35 1/4″.

The cabinet door is made out of 3/4″ plywood. The hinge side of the door is beveled to 45 degrees and the door is hinged to the upright with two 3″ x 3″ hinges. Two 1″ x 2″ beveled door stops are fastened to the upright on the latch side of the door, and a cabinet spring catch is also installed. The top of the counter is covered with linoleum in the same manner as for the base cabinet.

Materials List

3 pcs. 2″ x 2″ x 35 1/4″
2 " 2″ x 2″ x 34 1/2″
1 " 1″ x 8″ x 35 7/8″
1 " 1″ x 8″ x 35 1/8″
1 " 1″ x 6″ x 26 3/4″
2 " 1″ x 3″ x 35″
2 " 1″ x 3″ x 34 1/4″
6 " 1″ x 3″ x 23 1/4″
2 " 1″ x 2″ x 2″
1 " 3/4″ plywood 35 1/8″ x 35 1/8″
1 x 3/4″ plywood 15 1/4″ x 41 3/4″
2 " 1/2″ plywood 35″ x 35″
1 " 1/2″ plywood 3 3/8″ x 14″
1 " 3/8″ plywood 24 3/8″ x 35 1/4″
1 " 3/8″ plywood 24 1/4″ x 35 1/4″
1 " linoleum 35 1/8″ x 35 1/8″
Metal counter trim 25′ 1 7'8″
1 pair hinges 3″ x 3″
1 door pull
1 friction latch

Materials Totals

2″ x 2″ — 14′ 6 3/4″
1″ x 8″ — 5′ 11″
1″ x 3″ — 23′ 2″
1″ x 2″ — 4″

KITCHEN CORNER CABINET

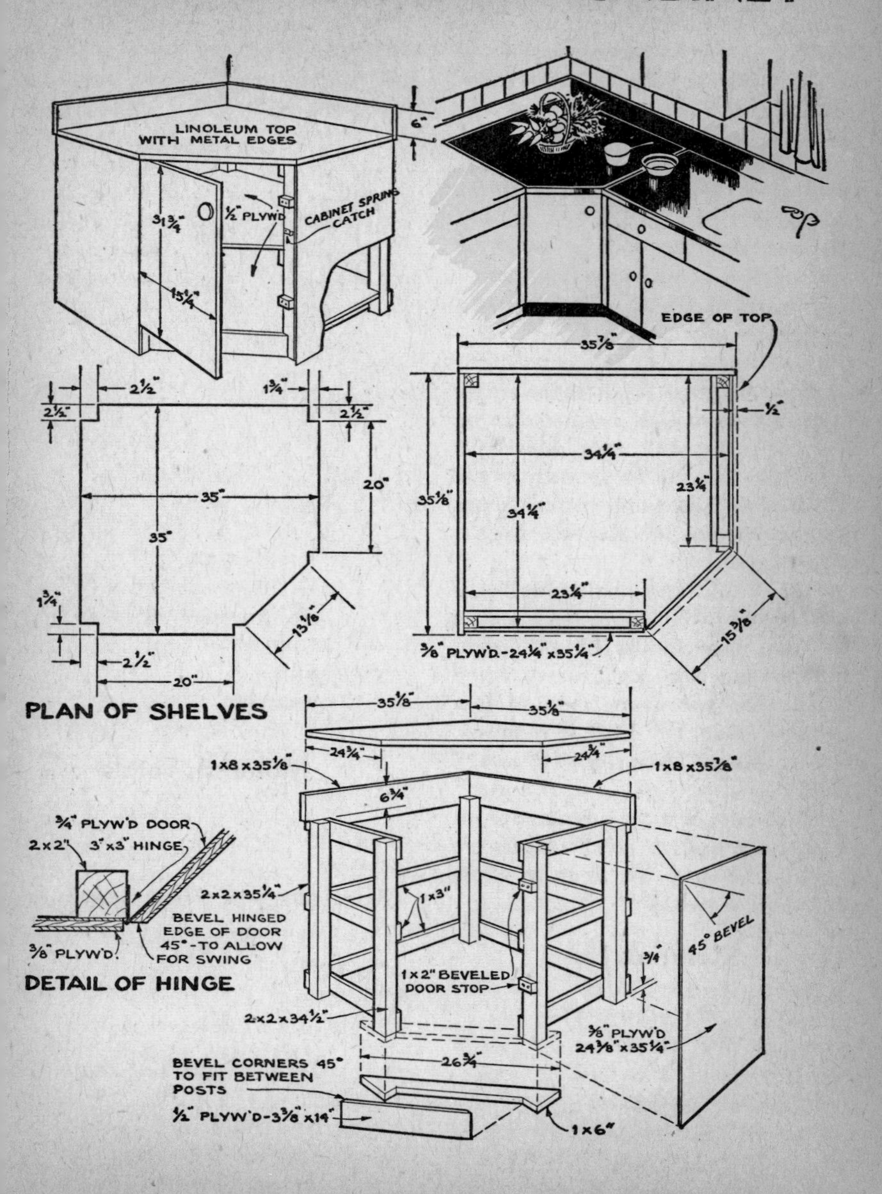

KITCHEN WALL CABINETS

Single Cabinets

Although the cabinet shown in the drawing is 15″ wide, single wall cabinets can be 12″, 18″, 21″, or 24″ wide. The sides, top, and bottom are made of 1″ x 12″ stock. The shelves are also of 1″ x 12″. The back is 1/4″ plywood and the door is made of 3/4″ plywood. Shelves are supported at each end by 1″ x 2″ cleats fastened to the sides of the cabinet.

Double Cabinets

Made the same depth as the single cabinet, these double cabinets can be 24″, 36″, and 42″ wide as well as 30″ wide, like the one shown in the illustration. The same materials are used for the double cabinet as for the single ones.

For use over base cabinets, wall cabinets should be 30″ high. For use over the sink, they should be 24″ high. For use over the range or over the refrigerator and deep freeze, a low double cabinet 18″ high is required. These cabinets can be from 24″ to 42″ wide.

When two or more cabinets are installed as a unit, 1″ x 2″ spacers are required between the units to allow the doors to swing.

Materials List

Single Cabinet

2 pcs. 1″ x 12″ x 29 1/4″
1 " 1″ x 12″ x 15″
3 " 1″ x 12″ x 13 1/2″
4 " 1″ x 2″ x 11 1/2″
1 " 3/4″ plywood 15″ x 30″
1 " 1/4″ plywood 15″ x 30″
2 cabinet hinges
1 door pull
1 friction latch

Double Cabinet

2 pcs. 1″ x 12″ x 29 1/4″
1 " 1″ x 12″ x 30″
2 " 1″ x 12″ x 28 1/2″
2 " 1″ x 2″ x 11 1/2″
2 " 3/4″ plywood 15″ x 30″
1 " 1/4″ plywood 30″ x 30″
4 cabinet hinges
2 door pulls
2 friction latches

Small Double Cabinet

2 pcs. 1″ x 12″ x 28 1/2″
1 " 1″ x 12″ x 30″
2 " 1″ x 12″ x 23 1/4″
2 " 1″ x 2″ x 11 1/2″
2 " 3/4″ plywood 15″ x 24″
1 " 1/4″ plywood 30″ x 24″
4 cabinet hinges
2 door pulls
2 friction catches

Materials Totals

Single Cabinet

1″ x 12″ — 9′ 6″
1″ x 2″ — 3′ 10″
(Remainder as itemized above)

Double Cabinet

1″ x 12″ — 1 1/2″
1″ x 2″ — 1′ 11″
(Remainder as itemized above)

Small Double Cabinet

1″ x 12″ — 11′ 1 1/2″
1″ x 2″ — 1′ 11″
(Remainder as itemized above)

KITCHEN WALL CABINETS

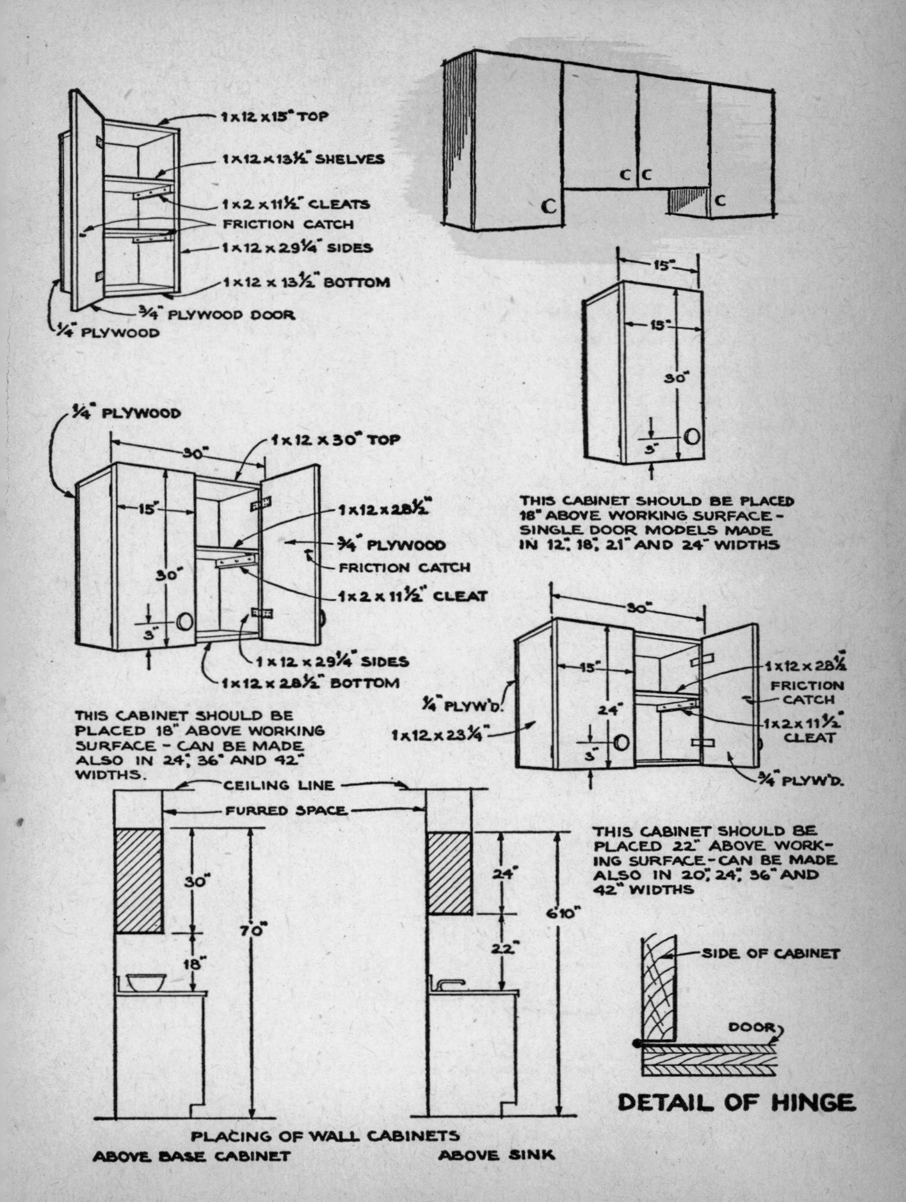

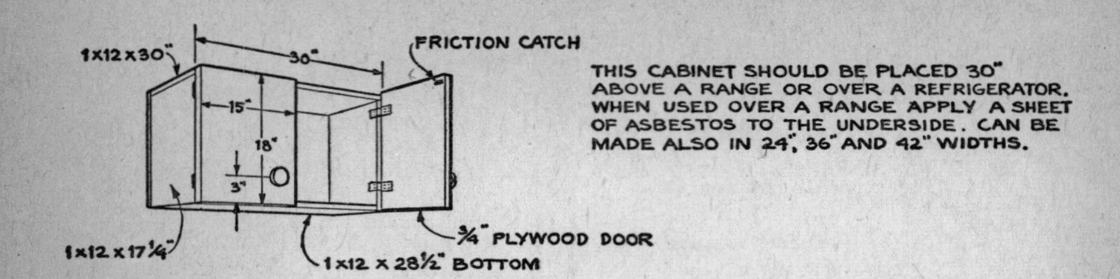

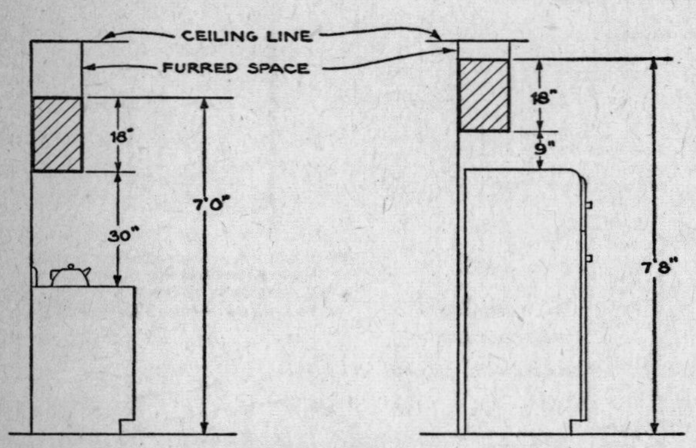

PLACING OF WALL CABINETS

ABOVE RANGE

ABOVE TWO-DOOR COMBINATION DEEP FREEZE AND REFRIGERATOR UNIT

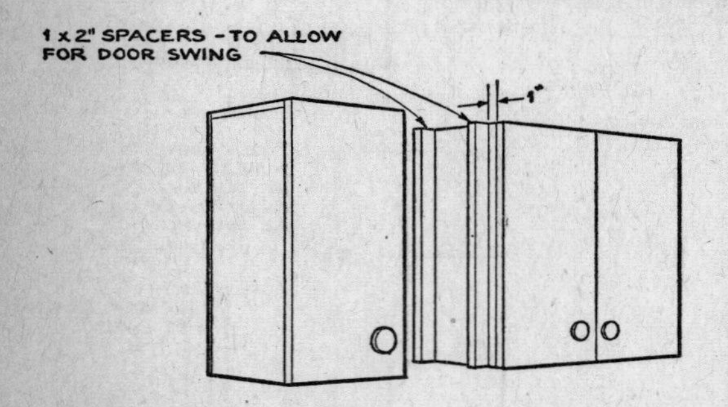

METHOD OF ASSEMBLING CABINET UNITS WITH SPACERS BETWEEN.

BASE KITCHEN CABINET

The first step in making up a complete set of kitchen cabinets is the building of the base cabinet — the most useful of the entire group. This cabinet provides ample storage space as well as a linoleum-covered counter top.

The two side pieces of the cabinet are made out of 3/4″ plywood 24″ x 35 1/4″. The lower outside corner of each is notched out 3″ wide and 2 3/4″ deep to take the base strip. The base strip is made from 1/2″ plywood or 1/2″ stock and is 3″ wide and 48″ long. Two glue blocks are fastened to the back of this piece flush with the top. The bottom of the cabinet is 3/4″ plywood 46 1/2″ x 24″. The back of the cabinet is made of 1/4″ plywood 48″ x 35 1/4″. Assemble these pieces.

29 7/8″ in from the inside surface of the lefthand side, install a 1″ x 3″ stile 31 1/2″ long. In back of this piece and 29 7/8″ in from the side, install a 3/4″ plywood partition. This piece should be 31 1/2″ high and 23 1/4″ wide. 5″ down from the top of the sides, install a piece of 1″ x 2″ between the sides and the stile. The righthand piece of 1″ x 2″ should be 14″ long, the lefthand piece 29 7/8″. 5″ down from the top, install 1″ x 2″ strips along the sides and on both sides of the center partition. On the lefthand side of the partition it will be necessary to fasten thin blocks of wood so that the strips of 1″ x 2″ are brought out beyond the 1″ x 3″ stile. These blocks should run the entire height of the partition as they will be needed to fasten the drawer guides into the correct position. 1″ x 1″ drawer guides are now fastened into place as indicated in the drawing.

Drawers for the righthand side should have an over-all length of 24″. The over-all width is 13 3/4″ and the width of the front pieces is 15 1/2″. The sides of the drawers are made of 1/2″ plywood or 1/2″ stock, the back of 1/4″ plywood, and the fronts of 3/4″ plywood. Corners are made with strips of 1/2″ quarter round, and strips of 1/4″ quarter round are fastened on the bottom. However, the drawers vary in lepth. The upper righthand drawer side is 2 3/4″ and its front is 3 7/8″. The second drawer side is 4 1/2″ and its front is 6 1/2″. The third drawer side is 7 1/2″ and its front is 8 5/8″. The bottom drawer is shown in section and plan. The side should be 9 3/4″ and the front 11 5/8″. The upper lefthand drawer has the same length as the others but the over-all width is 29 5/8″; the drawer side is 4 1/2″ in depth and its front 5 7/8″.

Materials List

2 pcs. 3/4″ plywood 27″ x 15 5/8″
1 " 3/4″ plywood 46 1/2″ x 24″
1 " 3/4″ plywood 31 1/2″ x 23 1/4″
1 " 3/4″ plywood 25 1/2″ x 49″
2 " 3/4″ plywood 24″ x 35 1/4″
1 " 3/4″ plywood 13 3/4″ x 23 1/4″ (cutting board)
1 " 3/4″ plywood 6″ x 48″

(continued on next page)

Materials List (Cont.)

1 pcs. 1/2″ plywood or 1/2″ stock 3″ x 48″
1 " 1/4″ plywood 48″ x 35 1/4″
1 " 1″ x 3″ x 31 1/2″
1 " 1″ x 2″ x 29 7/8″
4 " 1″ x 2″ x 23 1/4″
1 " 1″ x 2″ x 14″
6 " 1″ x 1″ x 23 1/4″
1 " 3/4″ x 3/4″ x 15 1/2″
2 " 1/4″ quarter round 28 5/8″
10 " 1/4″ quarter round 22 3/4″
8 " 1/4″ quarter round 12 3/4″
1 " linoleum 24 5/8″ x 49
1 " linoleum 6″ x 48″
Metal linoleum counter trim 21′ 5″
4 cabinet hinges
8 door pulls
2 friction catches

Upper Righthand Drawer

1 pcs. 3/4″ plywood 3 7/8″ x 15 1/2″
2 " 1/2″ plywood 2 3/4″ x 23 1/4″
1 " 1/4″ plywood 12 3/4″ x 23 1/4″
1 " 1/4″ plywood 2 1/2″ x 12 3/4″
4 " 1/2″ quarter round 2 1/2″

Second Drawer

1 pcs. 3/4″ plywood 6 1/2″ x 15 1/2″
2 " 1/2″ plywood 4 1/2″ x 23 1/4″
1 " 1/4″ plywood 12 3/4″ x 23 1/4″
1 " 1/4″ plywood 4 1/4″ x 12 3/4″
4 " 1/2″ quarter round 4 1/4″

Third Drawer

1 pcs. 3/4″ plywood 8 5/8″ x 15 1/2″
2 " 1/2″ plywood 7 1/2″ x 23 1/4″
1 " 1/4″ plywood 12 3/4″ x 23 1/4″
1 " 1/4″ plywood 12 3/4″ x 7 1/2″
4 " 1/2″ quarter round 7 1/4″

Bottom Drawer

2 pcs. 1/2″ plywood 9 3/4″ x 23 1/4″
1 " 3/4″ plywood 11 5/8″ x 15 1/2″
1 " 1/4″ plywood 12 3/4″ x 23 1/4″
1 " 1/4″ plywood 9 1/2″ x 12 3/4″
4 " 1/2″ quarter round 9 1/2″

Upper Lefthand Drawer

2 pcs. 1/2″ plywood 4 1/2″ x 23 1/4″
1 " 3/4″ plywood 31 3/8″ x 5 7/8″
1 " 1/4″ plywwood 28 5/8″ x 23 1/4″
1 " 1/4″ plywood 4 1/4″ x 28 5/8″
4 " 1/2″ quarter round 4 1/4″

Materials Totals

1″ x 2″ — 11′ 4 7/8″
1″ x 1″ — 11′ 7 1/2″
1/2″ quarter round — 9′ 3″
1/4″ quarter round — 32′ 2 3/4″
(Remainder as itemized above)

BASE KITCHEN CABINET

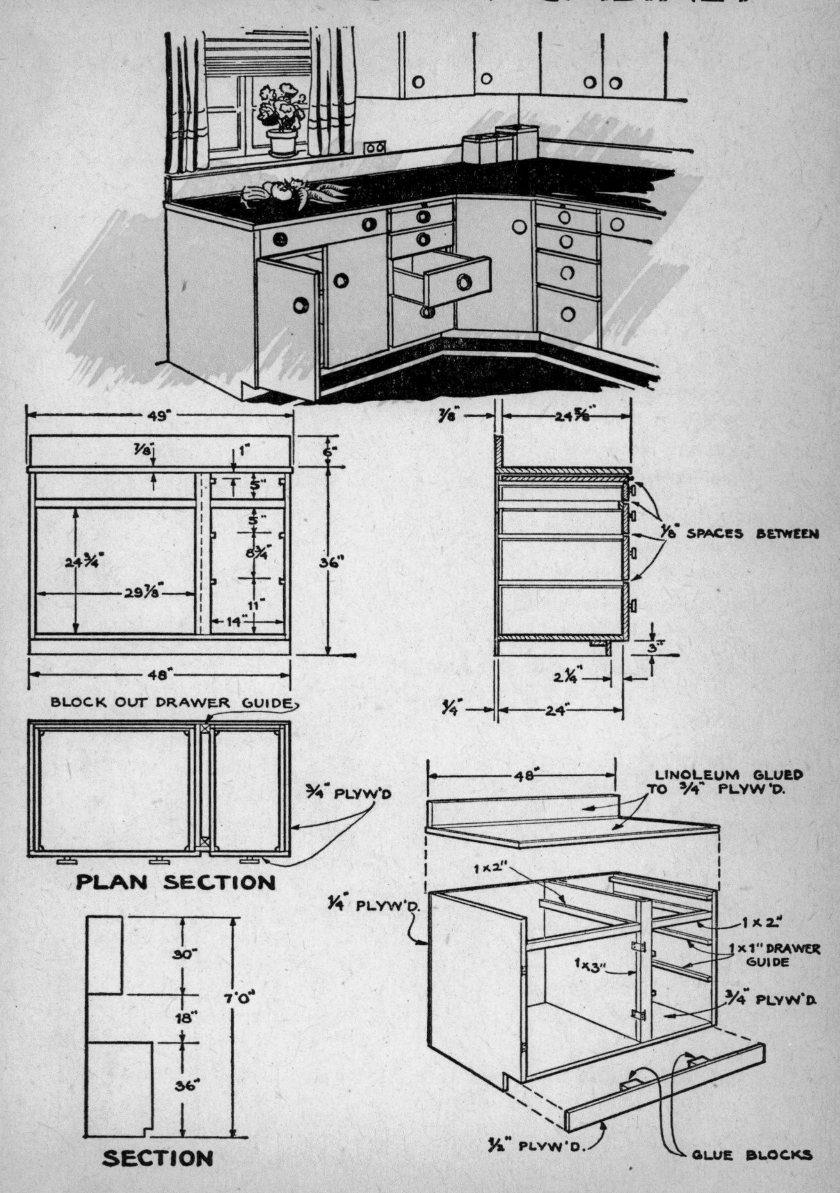

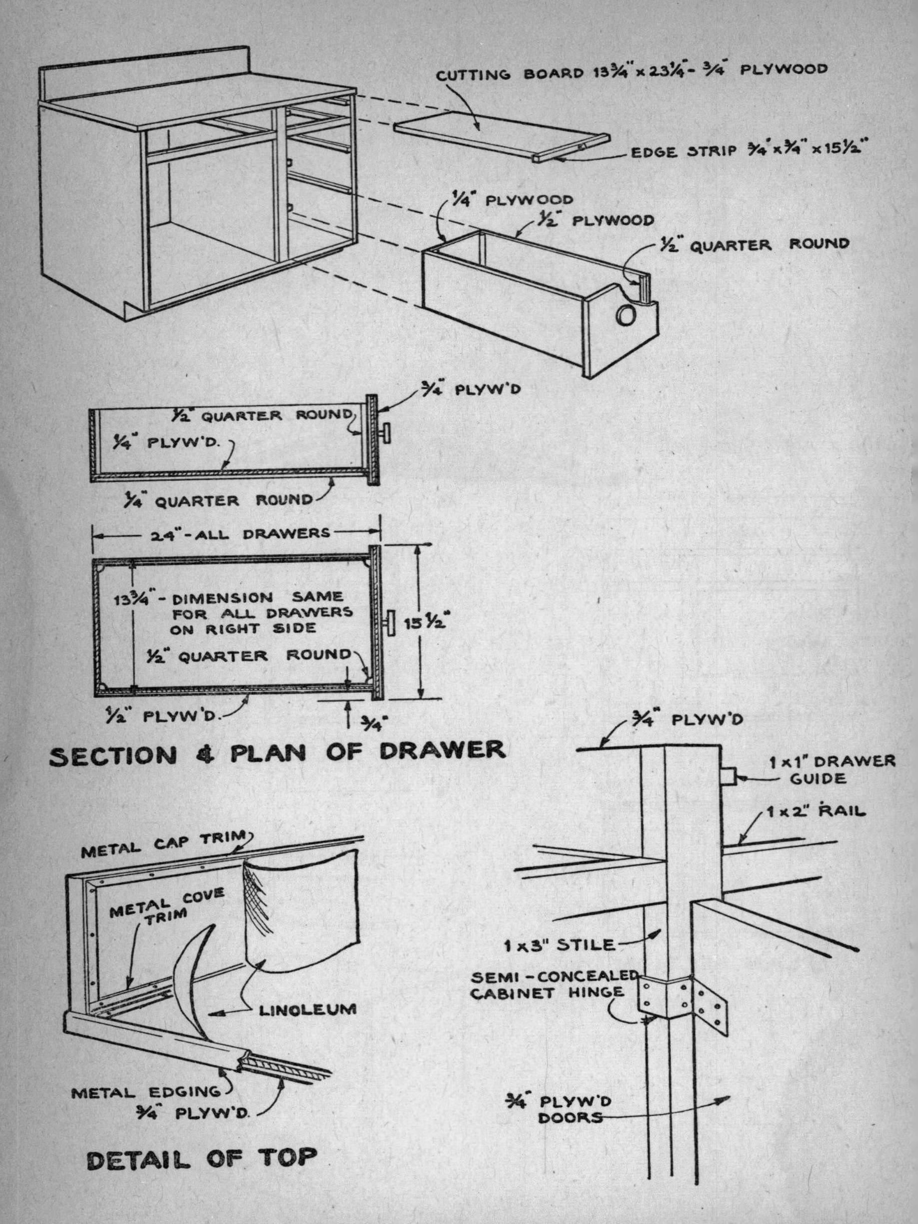

SECTION & PLAN OF DRAWER

DETAIL OF TOP

DETAIL OF HINGE

PORTABLE TOOL BOX

An excellent project for the beginner in woodworking is this portable tool box or tray, a handy container for the tools necessary for doing most small home-repair jobs.

The bottom and two side pieces as well as the ends are made out of 1″ x 8″ stock, which can be sawed or planed down to a uniform width of 7″. The top of the end sections can be pointed either by sawing or by planing. The rounded points are made with a rasp, followed by sandpapering. It is best to drill the holes in the end sections for the handle before cutting to size in order to prevent the possibility that the wood might split. These holes must correspond in size to the dowel used for the handle which is 1 1/8″. After the end pieces have been formed, clamp them together and make the saw kerfs on the sides.

Before assembling the pieces, procure, if possible, a small wood cheese box and tack this to the bottom of the tool box. It will make a useful place to store small items such as bits and chisels. If the box splits when nailed, use glue or small wood screws in place of nails.

The sections of the box are assembled with 8d nails or wood screws. Next, the dowel handle is inserted and cut off at the proper length. The dowel is secured in place with two small finishing nails at each end — 6d should be sufficient. The box is now ready for a finish, either paint or stain. When the finish is dry, cut a piece of canvas to size and tack it to the box along one edge for the cover.

Materials List

3 pcs. 1″ x 7″ x 28″
2 " 1″ x 7″ x 14 1/2″
1 1/8″ dowel 28″
1 empty cheese box
1 canvas cover

Materials Totals

1″ x 7″ — 9′ 5″
(Remainder as itemized above)

PORTABLE TOOL BOX

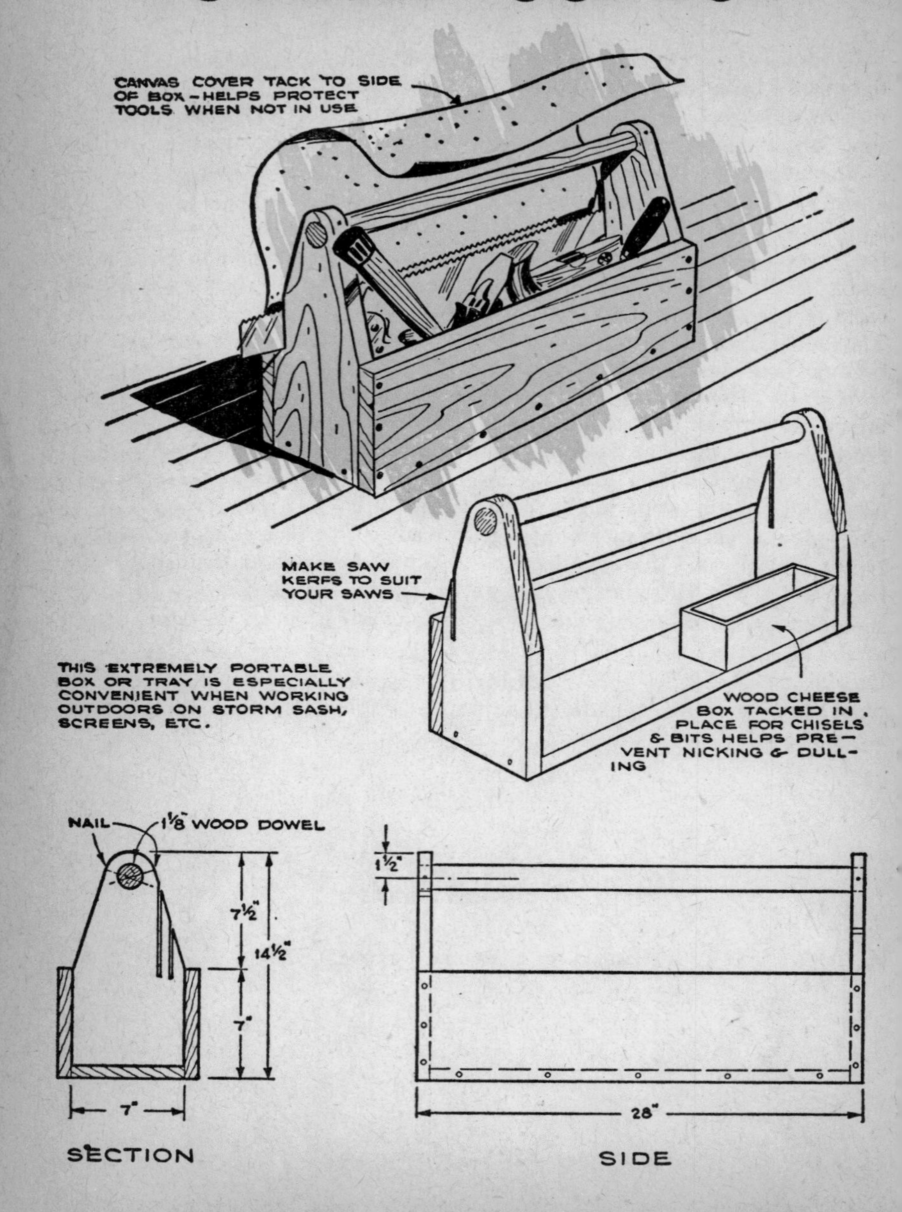

TOOL CABINET

This tool cabinet has been designed to hold the basic tools for woodworking. As more tools are added to your shop, a similar cabinet can be made.

The two side pieces of the cabinet are made of 1″ x 7″ stock 32″ in length. Along the top and bottom of these pieces cut a rabbet 25/32″ wide and 1/4″ deep. Along the back edge cut a rabbet 1″ wide and 1/4″ deep. The rabbets can be cut with a miter or back saw and chisel or a rabbet plane.

The top and bottom of the cabinet are made of 1″ x 7″ that is 23″ long. No rabbets are required in these two pieces. Assemble the four sections — two sides, top, and bottom — using glue and screws to make the joints. Now, out of 1″ plywood, cut the back piece 23″ x 30 1/2″. This piece should fit snugly against the shoulders of the rabbets cut along the edges of the side pieces. It should be glued in place and reinforced with screws along the sides and top and bottom.

The two doors, measuring 11 1/4″ x 30 1/2″ and 1″ in width, are cut from plywood. They are fastened to the frame with 2″ chest hinges. Make two door stops, as shown in the detail, and fasten one at the center of the top and one at the bottom 1″ in from the outer edge. On the left hand side of the bottom stop, attach a screw eye for a hook fastened to the left-hand door. To the right of the stop, attach a friction catch.

The second illustration shows a suggested method for hanging the tools in the cabinet and on the insides of the doors. All edged tools are placed in such a fashion that there is no danger of their being dulled through contact with metal. Note the wood block under the plane to prevent the blade from being dulled. Hammers, hatchet, measuring tools, and brace bit are hung from dowels fitted into holes drilled into the back of the cabinet and held with glue and screws.

Materials List

2 pcs. 1″ x 11 1/4″ x 30 1/2″
1 " 1″ x 23″ x 30 1/2″
2 " 1″ x 7″ x 32″
2 " 1″ x 7″ x 23″
1 " 1/2″ x 1 1/2″ x 2 1/2″
4 cabinet hinges
1 friction catch
1 hook and eye

Materials Totals

1″ x 11 1/4″ — 5′ 1″
1″ x 7″ — 9′ 2″
(Remainder as itemized above)

TOOL CABINET

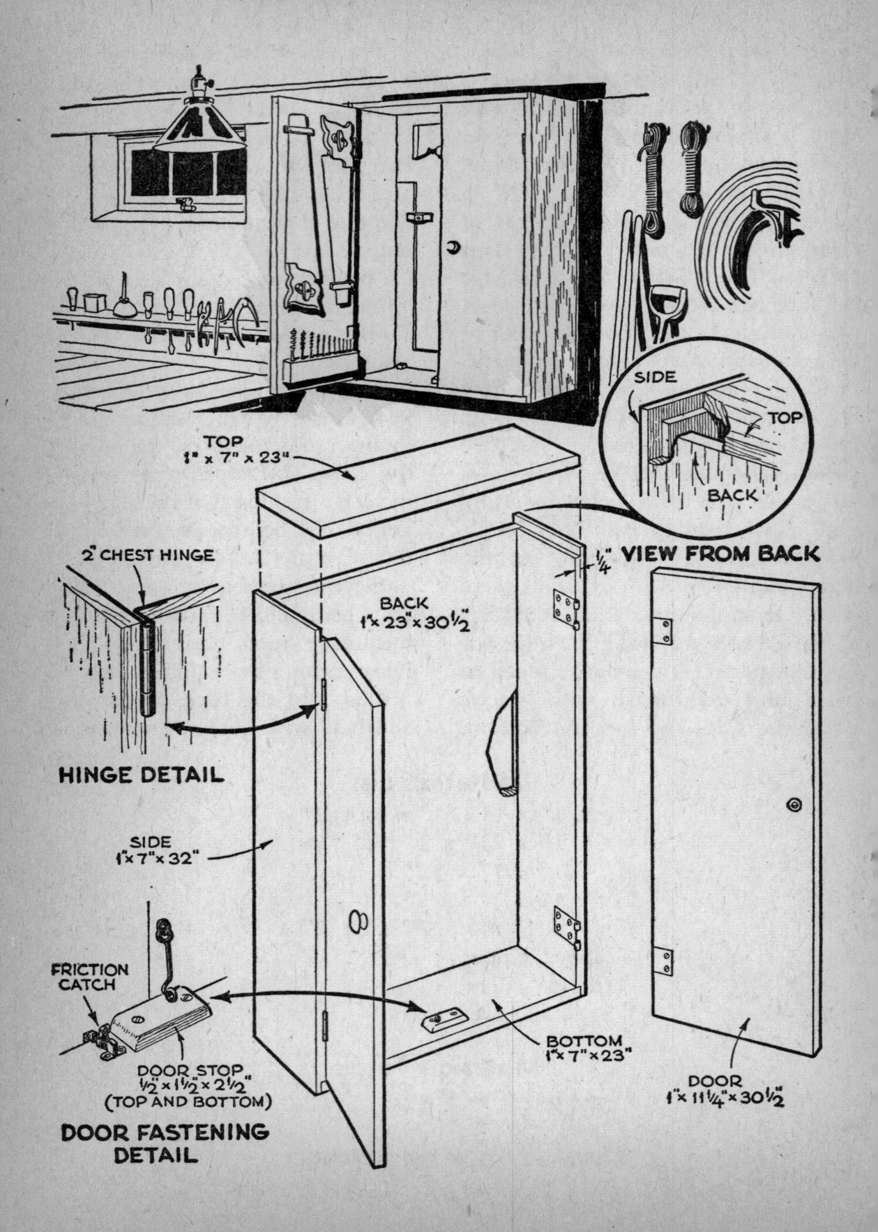

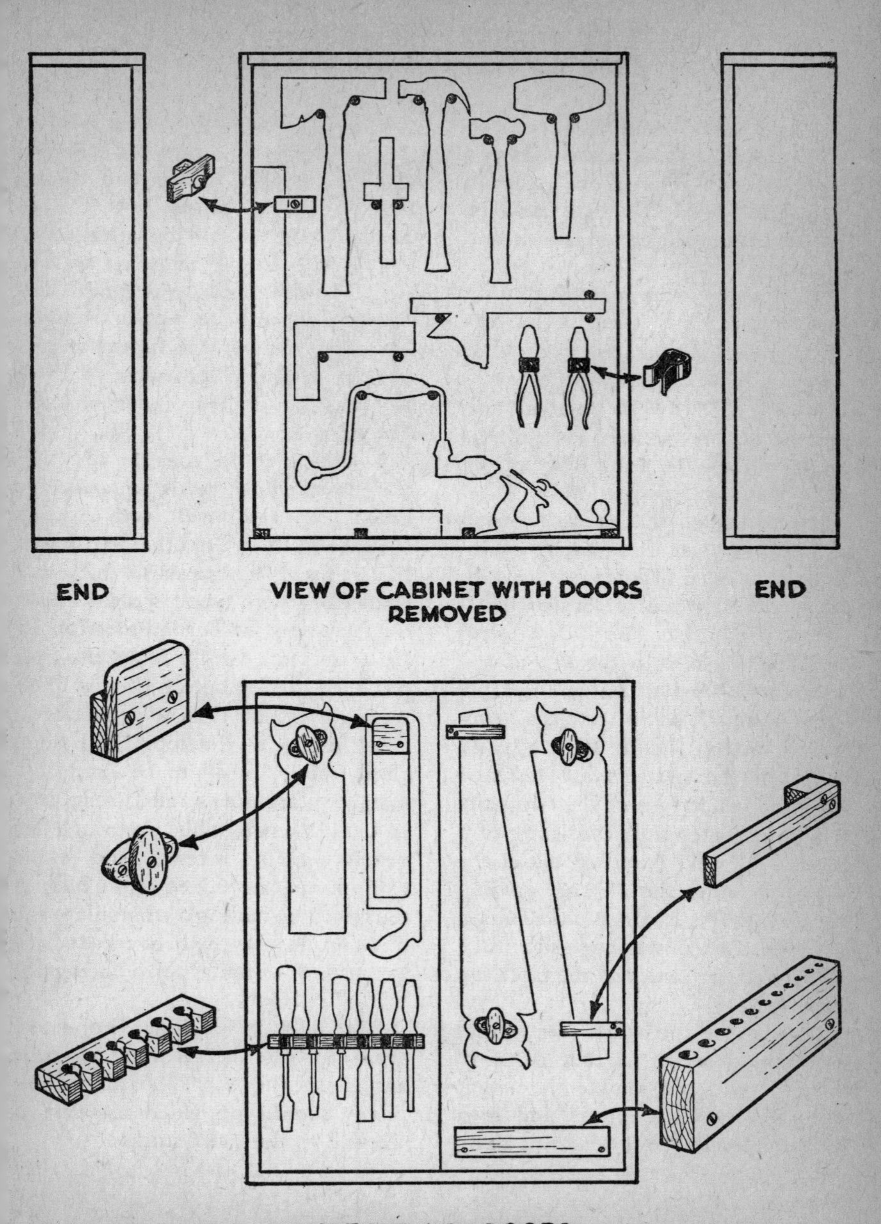
END
VIEW OF CABINET WITH DOORS REMOVED
END
INSIDE VIEW OF DOORS

WORK BENCH

A good work bench is as necessary for woodworking and repair jobs as a good set of tools. Here is one made out of standard materials that can't be beat for serviceability, ruggedness, and simplicity.

The legs are made out of 2″ x 4″ stock with a 2″ x 2″ spacer at the top. The legs are held together at the base by means of a strip of 1″ x 4″. Another strip of 1″ x 4″ is fastened flush with the top of the legs and projects 3 1/2″ beyond the front edge of the bench. Bevel this projection.

The two pairs of legs are fastened the required distance apart by an inside strip of 2″ x 2″ and an outer strip of 1″ x 4″ at the top, and a strip of 1″ x 4″ near the base. The 2″ x 2″ strip should be flush with the top of the legs as it is used to fasten the table top in place. 1″ down from the lower edge of the top 1″ x 4″ strip, 1″ x 2″ slides for the drawers are fastened along the inside face of the two pairs of legs. A center slide consisting of a piece of 1″ x 6″ (notched out at the top to fit under the 2″ x 2″ nailing strips) and 1″ x 2″ strips nailed along each side at the lower edge should be installed at the center of the table top framework.

Drawers for the bench (see second illustration) are made out of 3/4″ stock 5″ wide. Assemble the front, back, and two side pieces and then nail and glue 1/2″ x 1/2″ strips along the inside lower edge of each piece to support the 1/4″ plywood bottom. Cut the plywood to size and nail to the 1/2″ x 1/2″ strips. 3/4″ x 3/4″ corner blocks should be installed as well as 3/4″ x 3/4″ slides on the outside top edge of each side piece. The drawer should be approximately 15 5/8″ wide, but this dimension will have to be varied somewhat to allow for variations in the thickness of stock. The drawer front is 17 1/8″.

The bench top consists of 7/8″ tongue-and-groove or square-edge boards covered over with 1 1/8″ square-edge maple or other hardwood. Fasten the 7/8″ boards to the bench framework with wood screws. Allow the top to project beyond the front of the framework by 4″. Make the back piece for the top out of 1″ x 10 1/2″ with a piece of 1″ x 4″ attached at right angles to the top. Drill holes along the 1″ x 4″ to be used as a storage place for screwdrivers, bits, and other small tools. A trough for pencils, nails, screws, and other equipment is fashioned at the back of the bench by nailing a triangular strip of wood flush to the back piece of the bench and a similar strip facing the first 4″ in front.

The top 1/8″ thick hardwood covering for the bench runs at right angles to the 7/8″ boards. These pieces should be glued as well as screwed to the 7/8″ stock.

Materials List

1 1/8″ hardwood 12 1/2″ sq. ft.
4 pcs. 7/8″ x 8″ x 60″
4 " 3/4″ x 5″ x 23″
2 " 3/4″ x 5″ x 17 1/8″
2 " 3/4″ x 5″ x 15 5/8″
5 " 3/4″ x 3/4″ x 23 3/4″
8 " 3/4″ x 3/4″ 4 1/4″
4 " 1/2″ x 1/2″ x 23″
4 " 1/2″ x 1/2″ x 13 1/8″
2 " 1/4″ plywood 14 1/8″ x 23″
4 " 2″ x 4″ x 32″
2 " 2″ x 2″ x 35 1/4″
2 " 2″ x 2″ x 16 1/2″
1 " 1″ x 10 1/2″ x 60″
1 " 1″ x 6″ x 23 3/4″
1 " 1″ x 4″ x 60″
2 " 1″ x 4″ x 40″
1 " 1″ x 4″ x 38 1/2″
2 " 1″ x 4″ x 27 1/4″
2 " 1″ x 4″ x 23 3/4″
4 " 1″ x 2″ x 23 3/4″
2 " 1 1/8″ x 1 1/8″ x 60″

Materials Totals

2″ x 4″ — 10′ 8″
2″ x 2″ — 8′ 7 1/2″
1″ x 4″ — 23′ 4 1/2″
1″ x 2″ — 7′ 11″
1 1/8″ x 1 1/8″ — 10′
7/8″ x 8″ — 20′
3/4″ x 5″ — 13′ 1 1/2″
3/4″ x 3/4″ — 9′ 10 3/4″
1/2″ x 1/2″ — 12′ 1/2″
1/4″ plywood — 28 1/4″ x 46″
(Remainder as itemized above)

WORK BENCH

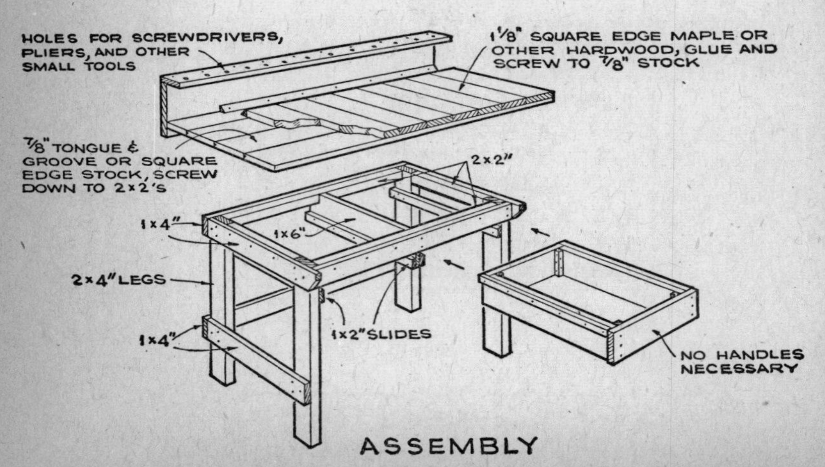

ASSEMBLY

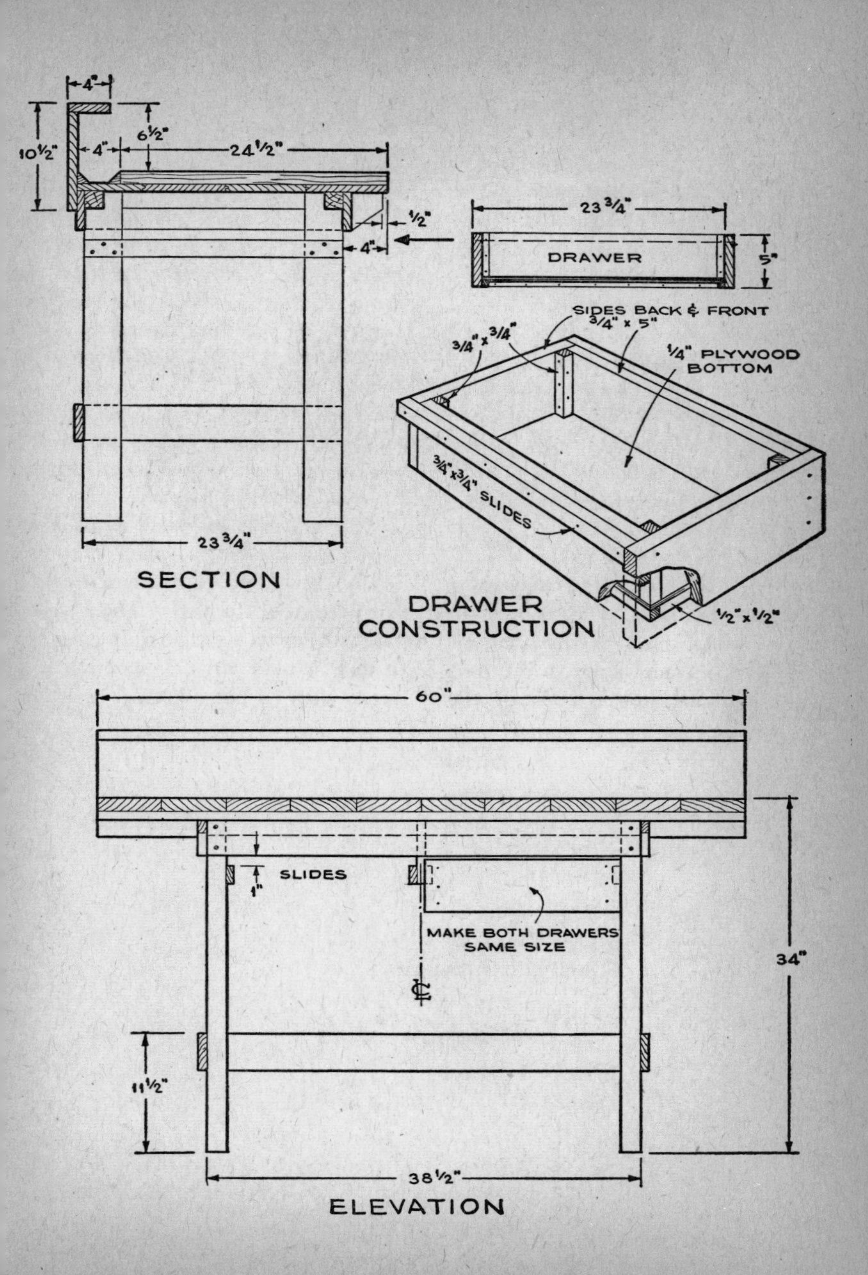
4"
10½"
6½"
4"
24½"
½"
4"
23¾"
SECTION
23¾"
DRAWER
5"
SIDES BACK & FRONT
¾" x 5"
¾" x ¾"
¼" PLYWOOD
BOTTOM
¾" x ¾" SLIDES
½" x ½"
DRAWER
CONSTRUCTION
60"
SLIDES
1"
MAKE BOTH DRAWERS
SAME SIZE
34"
11½"
38½"
ELEVATION

HANGING SHELVES FOR HARDWARE

Here is a perfect solution to the problem of where to store small quantities of nails, screws, and other hardware required for various jobs.

The shelf is constructed of 1″ stock. The bottom and back pieces are 8″ wide and the front piece is 4″ wide. When these three pieces are assembled, the two end pieces and the partition pieces for the storage bins can be cut to size and installed. The size of the bins can be varied to suit individual requirements.

The shelf is fastened to the wall by means of a 2″ x 2″ strip along the bottom of the shelf. This is held in place by angle irons. If the walls of the workshop are masonry, strap irons can be fastened to the back of the shelf and attached to the ceiling joists. The front of the shelf is supported by 1″ pipe straps or strap irons fastened to the bottom of the shelf and to the ceiling joists. If the joists are covered by a ceiling material, a strip of 2″ x 2″ can be spiked through the ceiling into the joists and the straps attached to this. Be certain that the shelf is given adequate support as it will weigh a good deal when the bins are filled with hardware.

Storage space for small items is provided by means of glass jars with metal caps. The caps are screwed to the bottom of the shelf tightly enough so that they will not turn. It takes only a flick of the wrist to remove a jar from place or put it back.

Materials List

2 pcs. 1″ x 8″ x 33″
5 " 1″ x 8″ x 7 1/4″
1 " 2″ x 2″ x 33″
1 " 1″ x 4″ x 33″
4 angle irons 2″
3 pipe straps 1″
6 jars with screw tops

Materials Totals

1″ x 8″ – 8′ 6 1/4″
(remainder as itemized above)

HANGING SHELVES FOR HARDWARE

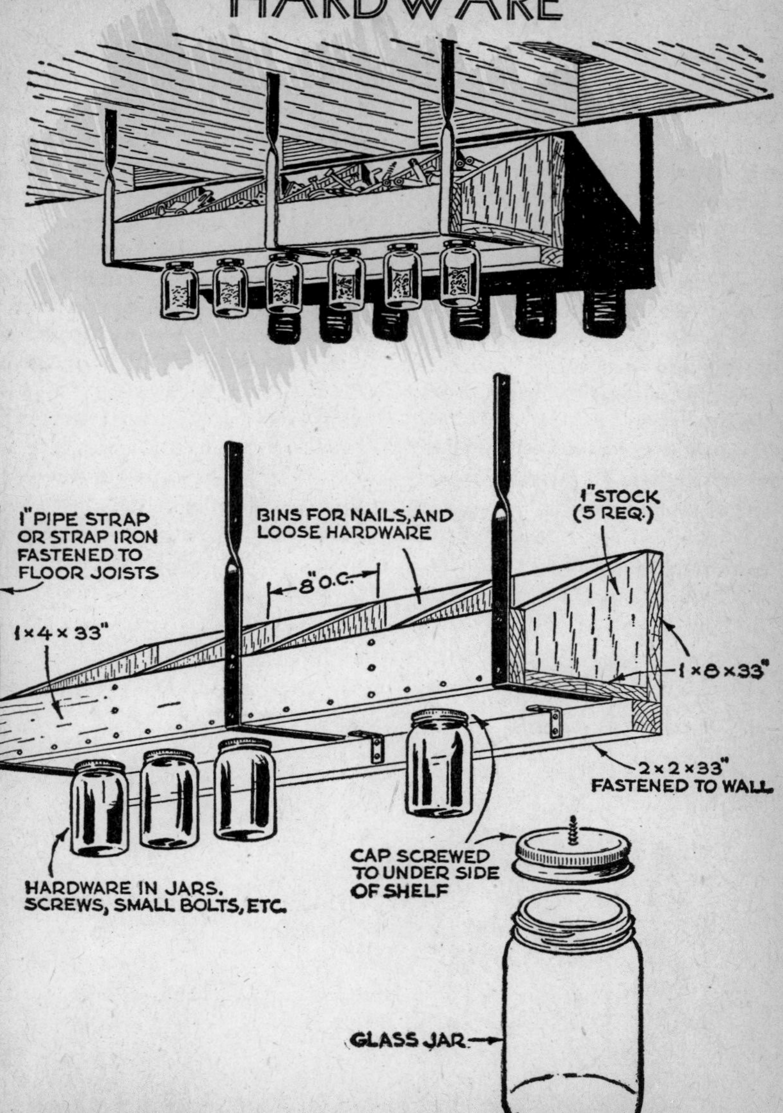

SAW HORSE AND TRESTLE

Saw Horse

A pair of saw horses makes very handy pieces of workshop equipment. They can be used to support scaffolding for painting and decorating jobs as well as to carry long pieces of wood or plywood for cutting and shaping.

The crossbar of the horse shown in the drawing is 2″ x 4″ x 30″. 4″ in from each end of the 2″ x 4″, fasten the legs. The legs are made out of 2″ x 4″ stock 27″ long. The inside surface of each leg is beveled down so that the ends of each pair of legs are 16″ apart. The legs are nailed or screwed into the crossbar and then reinforced with a 1/2″ plywood gusset 8″ high.

Materials List

4 pcs. 2″ x 4″ x 27″
1 " 2″ x 4″ x 30″
2 " 1/2″ plywood 8″ x 8 1/2″

Materials Totals

2″ x 4″ — 11′ 6″
(Remainder as itemized above)

Trestle

Trestles are used for cutting fireplace cordwood and stove wood. The one pictured here consists of two X's made of 2″ x 4″ that are 39 1/2″ long and beveled at the ends. Fasten them together with a 5/8″ x 5″ bolt and nut with washer at the midpoint. They are held the correct distance apart — 30″ — by a length of sash chain. The two X's are fastened together on each side with a strip of 1/4″ plywood 8″ x 30″. At the base of the legs, a strip of 1″ x 3″ x 30″ is installed.

Materials List

4 pcs. 2″ x 4″ x 39 1/2″
1 " 1″ x 3″ x 34″
1 " 1″ x 3″ x 30″
1 " 1/4″ plywood 8″ x 34″
1 " 1/4″ plywood 8″ x 30″
2 " sash chain 30″
2 machine bolts 5/8″ x 5″, with nuts and washers

Materials Totals

2″ x 4″ — 13′ 2″
1″ x 3″ — 5′ 4″
Sash chain — 5′
(Remainder as itemized above)

SAW HORSE AND TRESTLE

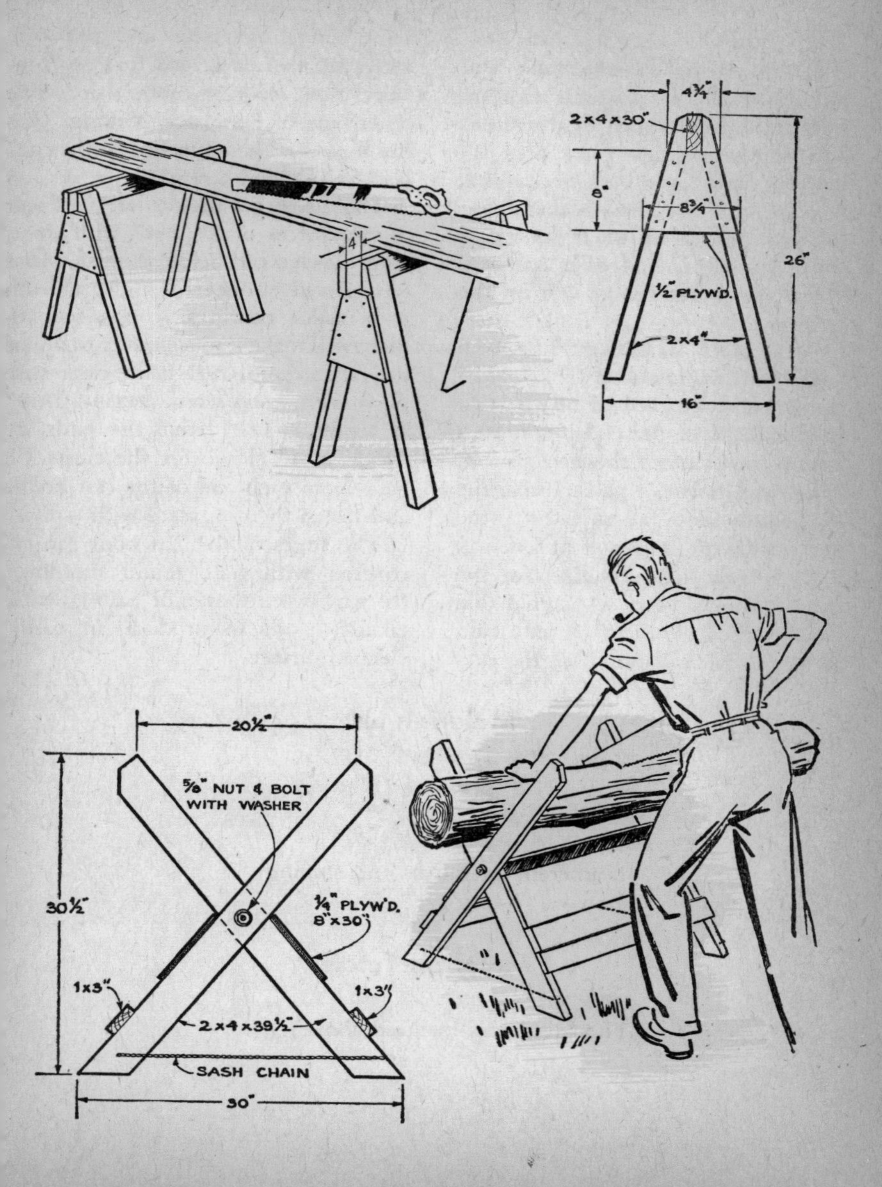

AUTOMOBILE REPAIR CART

Any man who does his own automobile repair and maintenance will find this repair cart a useful addition to the garage. The body of the cart is made out of a single piece of 1/2″ plywood. Select the best side of the plywood and use this as the upper surface. Sand out all rough spots and fill cracks with wood filler so there will be no splinters to catch on the clothing.

The headrest for the cart is built up from a base made out of 1″ x 5 1/2″ that is 18″ long. Round off the two upper corners of the end blocks to a 2″ radius and attach these to the end of the base with 8d nails. Drive the heads flush with the surface of the base so that the base will fit level on the cart body. The covering for the headrest should be of a material that is easily wiped clean. Leatherette, canvas, or plastic will do. Tack the covering along one edge and partially along the two ends, and then stuff in hair, moss, sponge rubber, or some other kind of upholstery stuffing. The headboard is then attached to the cart body with wood screws.

The casters for the cart are attached to two pieces of 2″ x 4″ with their ends beveled off. Select the flat, plate type of swivel casters — and get them with roller bearings if possible, as these will make it much easier to move the cart around. Attach the casters in place with wood screws setting them, at center, 3 1/2″ from the ends of the 2″ x 4″ cleats. Set the cleats 4″ back from each end of the cart body, and fasten them in place with screws.

The edges of the cart body can be covered with half round molding. the woodwork should be painted with enamel paint to produce an easily cleaned surface.

Materials List

2 pcs. 2″ x 4″ x 18″
1 " 1/2″ plywood 18″ x 43″
2 " 2″ x 4″ x 5 1/2″
1 " 1″ x 5 1/2″ x 18″
Leatherette or canvas and stuffing
4 swivel casters

Materials Totals

2″ x 4″ — 3′ 11″
(Remainder as itemized above)

AUTOMOBILE REPAIR CART

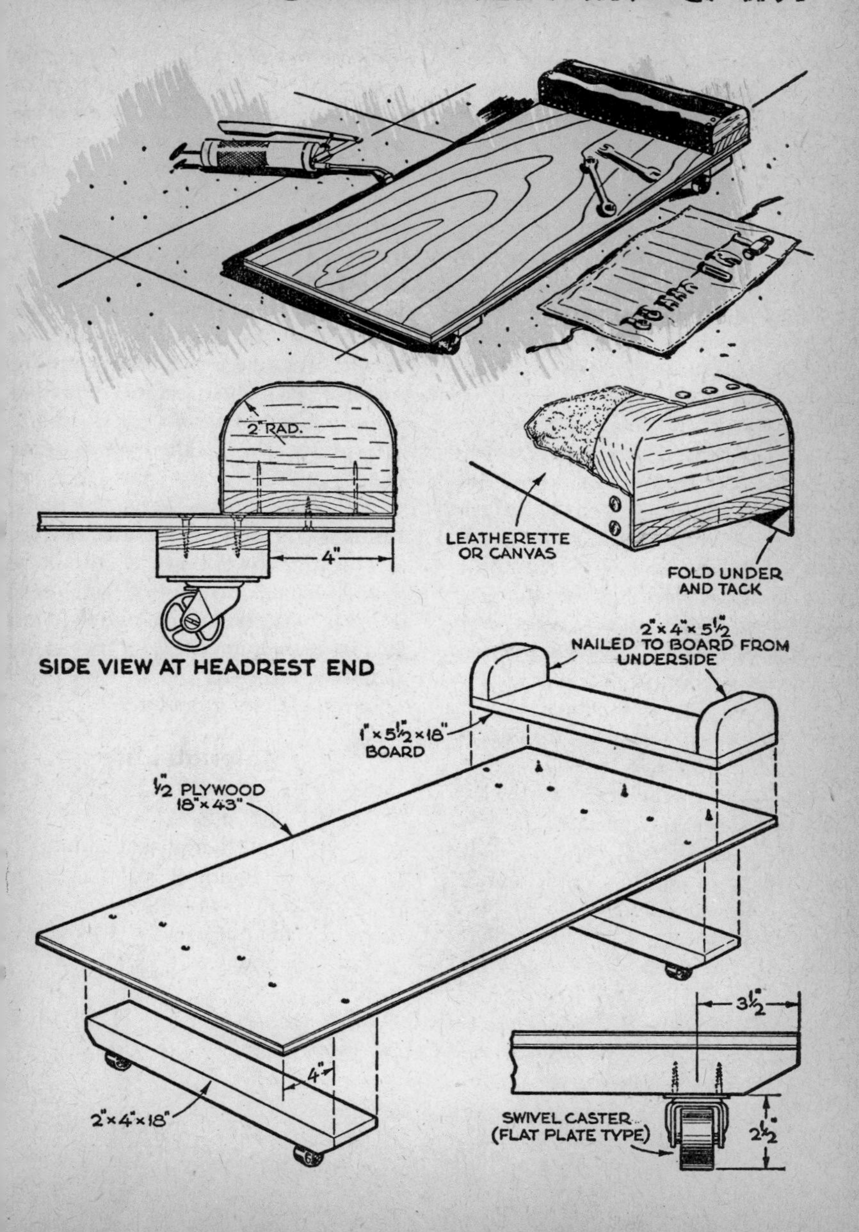

STORING SCREENS AND STORM SASH

Window screens and storm sash are more apt to be damaged while stored during the off-season than when in use. One excellent spot to store these articles—a spot where they will be safe and out of the way—is the underside of basement stairs. All that is necessary is to install two screw hooks under the basement stair treads for each unit to be stored. The screen or sash is hung from these hooks by the hangers used for hanging it in the window frame. The spacing of the screw hooks on the treads should be the same as the spacing of the hangers on the screens and sash.

If the basement stairs cannot be used for storage of these items, a storage rack will make a very satisfactory substitute. The frame pictured in the illustration is made up of two independent sections which can be spaced apart at whatever distance is required.

The frame of the larger of the two parts of the rack is made of 1″ x 4″ stock. The height is 36″ and the width should be sufficient to take the number of screens and sash to be stored away. The middle and top cross pieces should be recessed into the uprights to give the framework additional support. Braces on the lower corners should also be used. 1″ x 1″ spacers should be nailed to the bottom of the framework, and 1″ x 3″ spacers to the top. These should be spaced 1/8″ farther apart than the sash is thick. If you have a few small sash or screens, spacers can be installed along the middle cross piece for these items. To prevent the sash or screens from becoming damp, nail two pieces of 2″ x 4″ stock on edge to the bottom of the framework.

The smaller, movable portion of the frame is constructed in the same fashion as the lower part of the large frame—from a piece of 1″ x 4″ with 1″ x 1″ spacers. When completed, it is placed a sufficient distance away from the large upright framework to take the screens and sash.

Materials List

4 pcs. 2″ x 4″ x 4″
2 " 1″ x 4″ x 36″
4 " 1″ x 4″, length depending on width of rack
4 " 1″ x 3″ (braces)
Required amount of 1″ x 3″ x 4″
Required amount of 1″ x 1″ x 4″

Materials Totals

2″ x 4″ — 1′ 4″
1″ x 4″ — 6′
(Remainder as itemized above)

STORING SCREENS AND STORM SASH

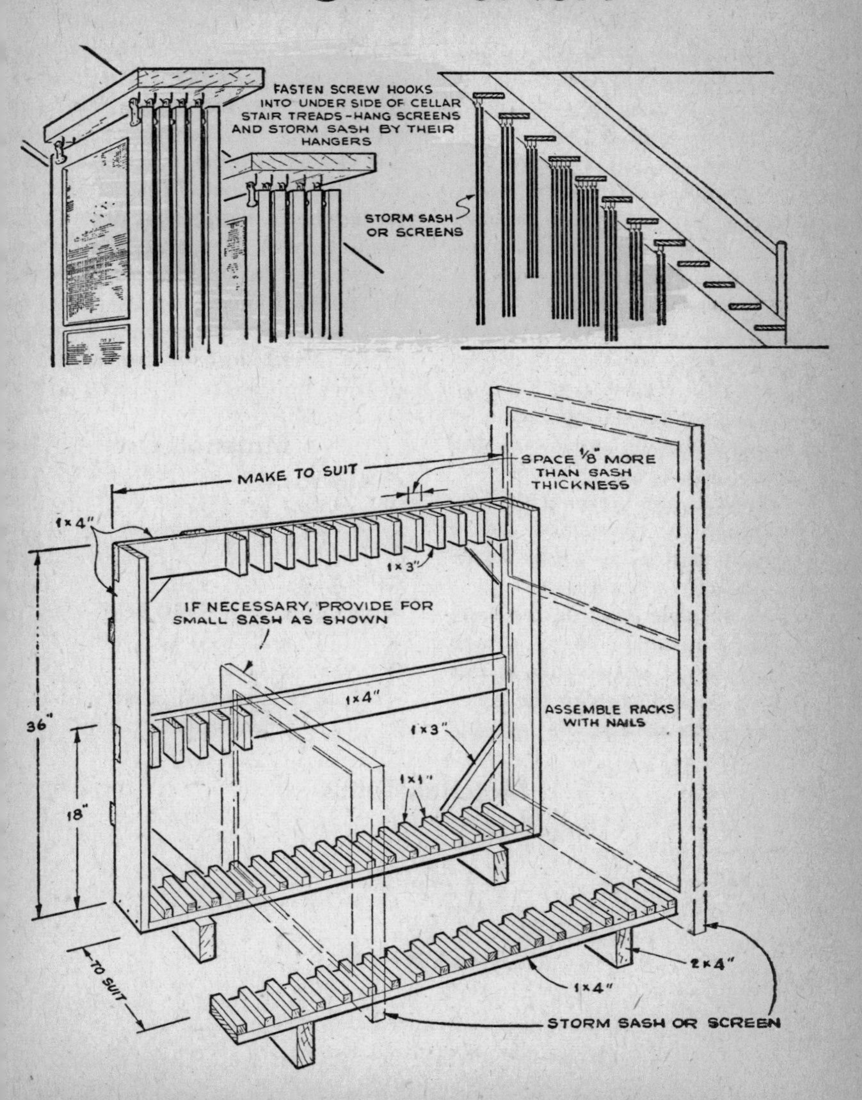

LUMBER STORAGE RACKS

Much lumber is ruined by improper storage, which often causes the boards to warp out of shape. Either lumber rack of the two shown in the illustration will keep lumber in good condition as well as out of the way though still accessible.

The top rack can be used where basement ceiling joists are exposed and where there is not enough room for a wall rack. The racks are made out of 1″ x 4″ stock supported 12″ down from the ceiling by 2″ x 4″ spaced 13 13/16″ apart. Two sets of brackets are required for each storage rack and they should not be set more than 4′ apart. Greater spacing would cause the stored boards to sag.

To eliminate the need for drilling holes through the foundation wall—which might start leaks—the wall rack is built out from a wood frame.

A 2″ x 4″ plate is set on the basement floor and anchored to it with expansion bolts. The two ends of this plate must come flush with the edges of ceiling joists so that the uprights of the frame can be nailed at the top to the joists as well as at the bottom to the plate. Uprights should not be spaced more than 4′ apart. After they are spiked into the ceiling joists, run a strip of 2″ x 2″ along the top and nail this to both the 2″ x 4″ uprights and the ceiling joists. The brackets for the lumber are made out of 1″ x 4″ strips beveled at the ends; they are nailed into the upright pieces of the frame. Additional support is given to each bracket by means of a plywood gusset. Metal supports can be used in place of plywood.

Materials List

Ceiling Rack

4 pcs. 2″ x 4″ x 24″
2 " 1″ x 4″ x 43 1/4″

Wall Rack

4 pcs. 2″ x 4″ x 7′ 10 3/8″
1 " 2″ x 2″ x 7′ 10 3/8″
9 " 1″ x 4″ x 16″
9 " 1/2″ plywood gussets (4 1/2 1-foot squares cut in half)

Materials Totals

Ceiling Rack

2″ x 4″ — 8′
1″ x 4″ — 7′ 2 1/2″

Wall Rack

2″ x 4″ — 31′ 5 1/2″
1″ x 4″ — 12′
(Remainder as itemized above)

LUMBER STORAGE RACKS

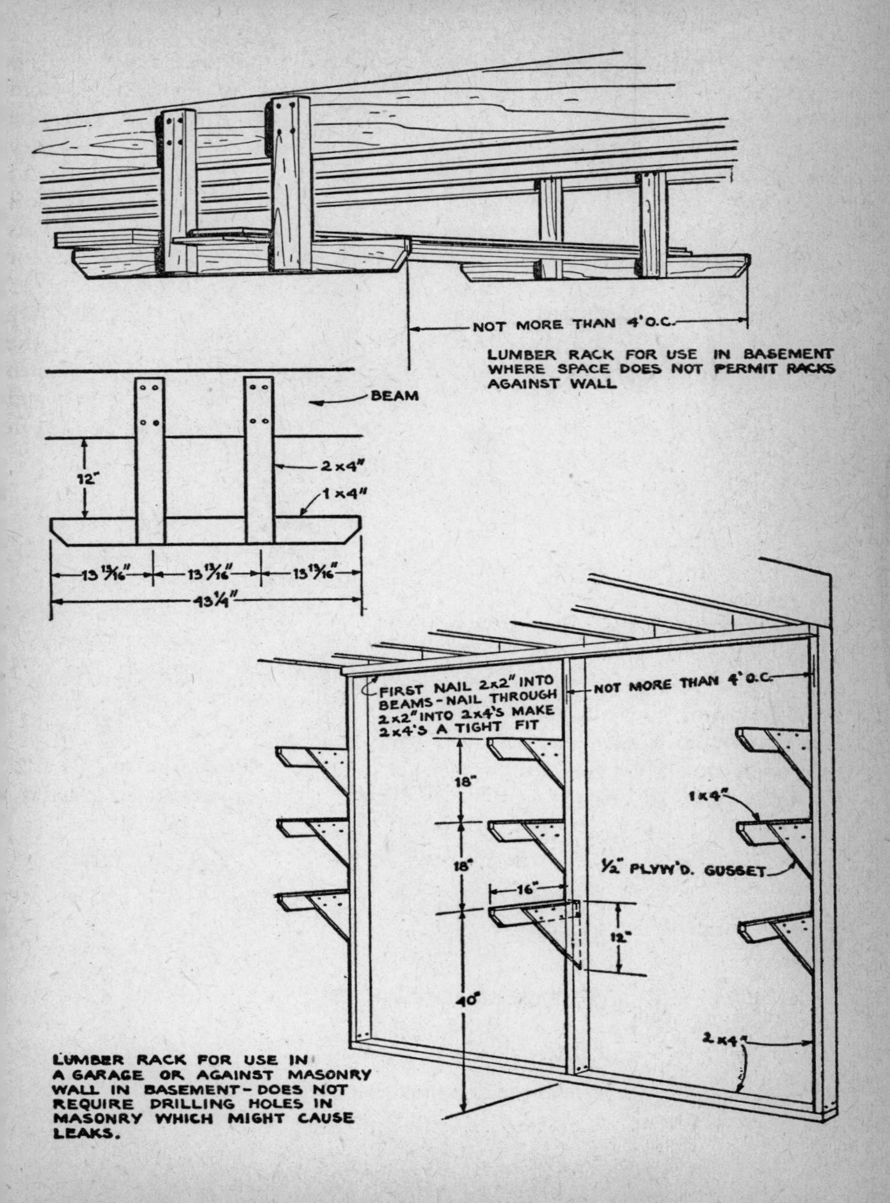

LUMBER RACK FOR USE IN A GARAGE OR AGAINST MASONRY WALL IN BASEMENT - DOES NOT REQUIRE DRILLING HOLES IN MASONRY WHICH MIGHT CAUSE LEAKS.

BED READING LIGHT

Attached to the wall over a bed, this combination reading light and bookcase makes an attractive as well as a useful piece of furniture.

But before commencing to build this item, be sure that there is a satisfactory method of connecting it to a source of electricity. If the only electric fixture in the bedroom is a light socket in the ceiling, you probably will not want a light cord running from it to a reading light.

You may have to cut the wall to connect with electric wires and install a light switch on the wall just below where the contemplated bookcase and reading light is to be, or install a base plug. You had better find out what this will cost to install.

If there already is an electrical outlet in the baseboard nearby, it will be easy to run a light cord from it to the fluorescent fixture, of course providing a light switch of some sort just below the bookcase.

Make up the top piece 9″ x 20 3/4″ out of 1″ x 10″ stock, and then make the notches at each end 3/4″ deep and 6 3/4″ wide. Cut the two side pieces 6 3/4″ x 9 1/4″ and then clamp them together and round off the upper outside corner. Clamping the pieces together during this operation insures that both curves will be equal. The side pieces can now be fastened to the top. They should extend 5 3/4″ below the upper surface of the top piece. The back piece is cut from 1″ x 4″ stock 19 1/4″ long. Fasten a 19 1/4″ x 2 3/4″ fluorescent fixture to this piece and then fasten the back to the top and side pieces.

The pattern for shaping the front piece is given in the illustration. This piece should be 5″ x 19 1/4″.

The assembly is fastened to the wall over the bed by means of long screws run through the back piece and into the wall studding in back of the plaster.

Materials List

2 pcs. 1″ x 10″ x 6 3/4″
1 " 1″ x 10″ x 20 3/4″
1 " 1″ x 6″ x 19 1/4″
1 " 1″ x 4″ x 19 1/4″
1 fluorescent unit 19 1/4″

Materials Totals

1″ x 10″ – 2′ 10 1/4″
(Remainder as itemized above)

BED READING LIGHT

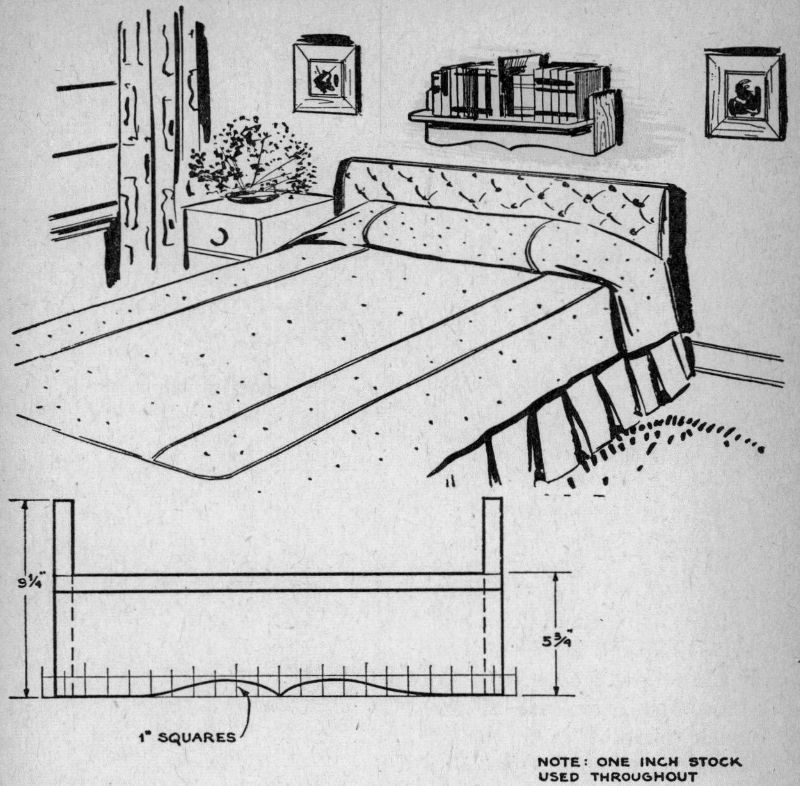

NOTE: ONE INCH STOCK USED THROUGHOUT

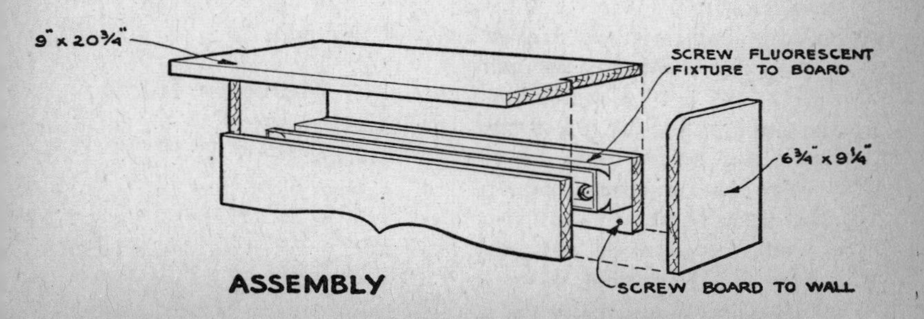

BUILT-IN BUNK

A built-in bunk with storage drawers underneath is ideal for expansion attics, guest rooms, and summer cottages.

The side and back sections for the base of the bunk are 1″ x 12″ stock. The front section is 1″ x 3″ stock. Until the drawer guides have been constructed, do not install the 1″ x 3″ vertical dividers in the front piece. Assemble the four sections of the base, using 1″ x 1″ strips on the inside of each corner for added support. A strip of 1″ x 2″ on edge should now be attached along the bottom edge of the front and back sections of the base.

The drawer guides at each end of the base are made by placing a strip of 1″ x 3″ down flat between the 1″ x 2″ strips attached to front and back of the base. Attached to this strip of 1″ x 3″ is the 1″ x 2″ drawer guide, which goes down on edge. The two drawer guides in the middle of the bunk should be spaced so that each of the three drawers will be exactly the same width. Make the base of the drawer guide out of 1″ x 6″ placed flat between the 1″ x 2″ front and back strips. At the center of each 1″ x 6″ divider a strip of 1″ x 7 1/2″ is fixed on edge lengthwise. A strip of 1″ x 2″ on edge is attached to each side of the 1″ x 7 1/2″ along its bottom edge. Support for the top of the divider strip is provided by means of 1″ x 1″ strips that run around the top of the bunk base. These strips will also support both the plywood covering for the base and the springs, so they must be securely fastened in place. The upright 1″ x 3″ divider strips of the front piece can now be installed. The main body of the drawer is made out of 1/2″ stock with a 1/4″ plywood bottom. A piece of 1/4″ plywood is attached over the front of the drawer; it should extend 1/2″ beyond the opening in the bedframe on all four sides. This is so that when the drawer is closed, there will be no open seam between drawer and bedframe base. If the drawers stick, sand guides. Fasten the 1/4″ plywood top to base with wood screws.

Materials List

2 pcs. 1″ x 12″ x 41″
1 " 1″ x 12″ x 76″
2 " 1″ x 7 1/2″ x 39″
2 " 1″ x 6″ x 70″
2 " 1″ x 6″ x 39″
2 " 1″ x 3″ x 39″
2 " 1″ x 3″ x 12″
2 " 1″ x 3″ x 6 1/2″
2 " 1″ x 2″ x 74″
6 " 1″ x 2″ x 39″
2 " 1″ x 1″ x 76″
2 " 1″ x 1″ x 39″
4 " 1″ x 1″ x 10 1/2″
1 " 1/4″ plywood 41″ x 76″
3 " 1/4″ plywood 21″ x 38″
3 drawer pulls

Materials Totals

1″ x 12″ — 13′ 2″
1″ x 7 1/2″ — 6′ 6″
1″ x 6″ — 6′ 6″
1″ x 3″ — 21′ 2″
1″ x 2″ — 31′ 10″
1″ x 1″ — 22′ 8″
(Remainder as itemized above)

BUILT-IN BUNK

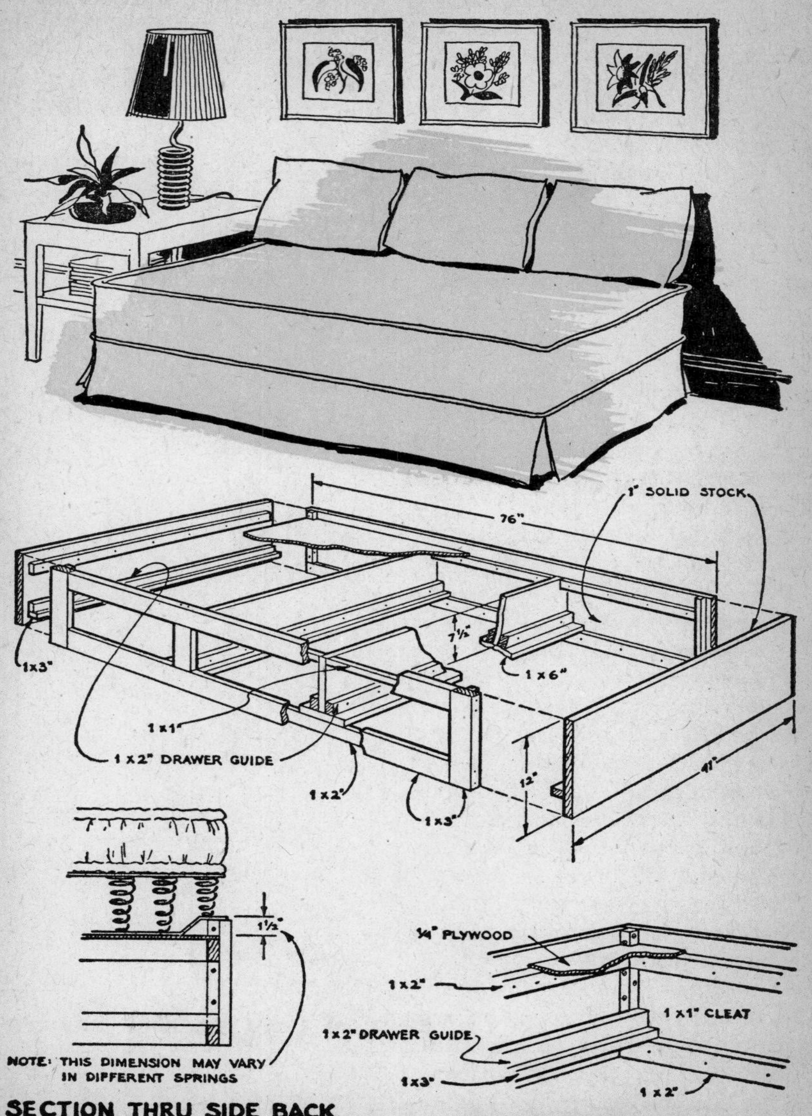

SECTION THRU SIDE BACK

VIEW OF BACK CORNER

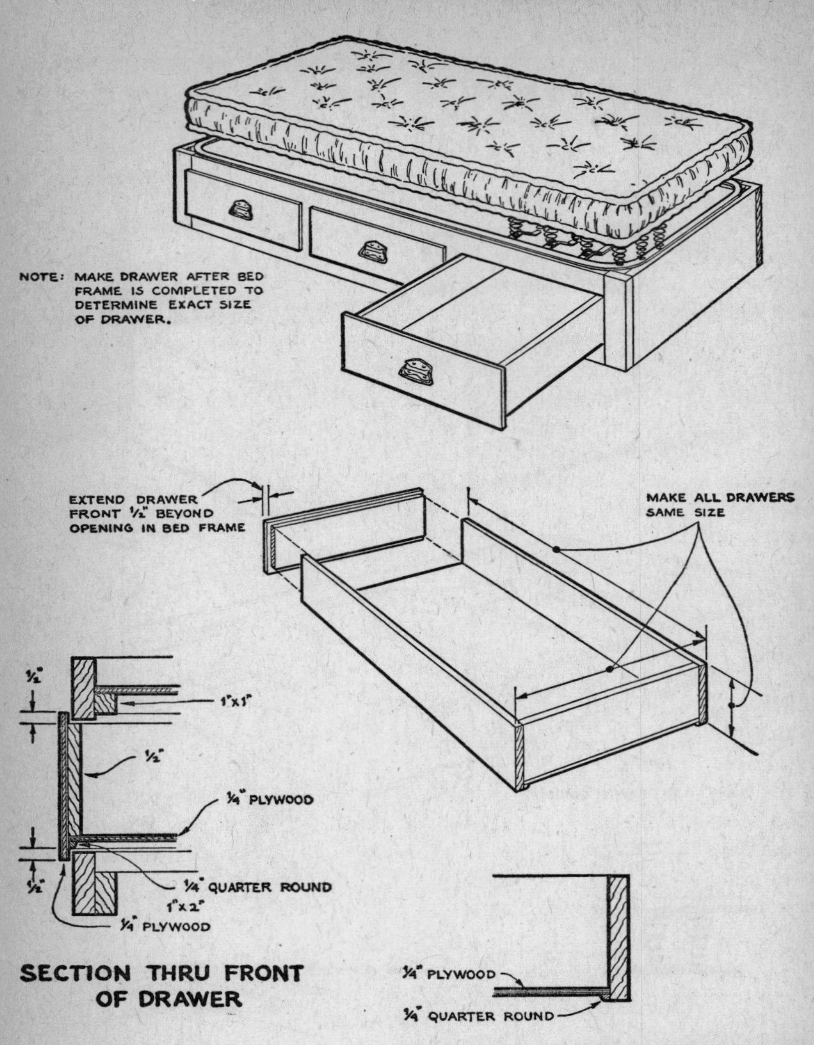

SECTION THRU FRONT OF DRAWER

SECTION THRU BACK OF DRAWER

NIGHT STAND

The two side sections are made out of 3/4″ stock. Cut them out roughly, then clamp them together for an exact fitting. Next, attach the 1″ x 1″ cleats to the sides. These cleats support the shelves. They are beveled off on the front ends. The shelves are now cut to size. Note that the bottom and top shelves are the same size, the second shelf is slightly smaller, and the top of the stand is made slightly longer so that it will fit over the side pieces. Assemble these pieces with wood screws, then cut and install the back plate, which is made of 1/4″ plywood. The inside joints, where the back plate joins the sides, are covered with 1/2″ quarter round molding. Nail the molding into the side pieces.

The base for the stand is made out of 1″ x 3″ and is joined together with butt joints and reinforced with corner blocks that are made out of 3/4″ stock and have 3″ legs. Install these blocks so that the upper edge comes flush with the top edge of the 1″ x 3″ base. Fasten them in place with glue and wood screws. When the glue is dry, the base can be attached to the stand by running wood screws up through the corner blocks into the bottom shelf of the stand. The doors should be cut to size out of 3/4″ stock. A wood handle can be fashioned out of 3/4″ stock and a finger hole drilled through it. The doors are attached in place with two cabinet hinges each. A bullet catch holds the doors closed.

Materials List

2 pcs. 3/4″ plywood 27 1/4″ x 11 1/2″
2 " 3/4″ plywood 11 1/4″ x 16 1/2″
1 " 3/4″ plywood 10 1/2″ x 16 1/2″
1 " 1/4″ plywood 16 1/2″ x 27 1/4″
2 " 1″ x 3″ x 14″
2 " 1″ x 3″ x 9 1/2″
4 " 1″ x 1″ x 10 1/2″
2 " 1″ x 1″ 9 1/2″
1 " 3/4″ x 11 1/2″ x 18″
2 " 3/4″ x 8 1/14″ x 15 3/4″
4 " 3/4″ x 3″ x 3″
2 " 3/4″ x 1 1/4″ x 7 3/4″
2 " 1/2″ quarter round 9″
2 " 1/2″ quarter round 6 1/2″
2 " 1/2″ quarter round 5 3/4″
2 pairs cabinet hinges
2 door catch

Materials Totals

1″ x 3″ — 3′ 11″
1″ x 1″ — 5′ 1″
3/4″ x 3″ — 1″
3/4″ x 8 1/4″ — 2′ 7 1/2″
3/4″ x 1 1/4″ — 1″ 3 1/2″
1/2″ quarter round — 3′ 6 1/2″
(Remainder as itemized above)

NIGHT STAND

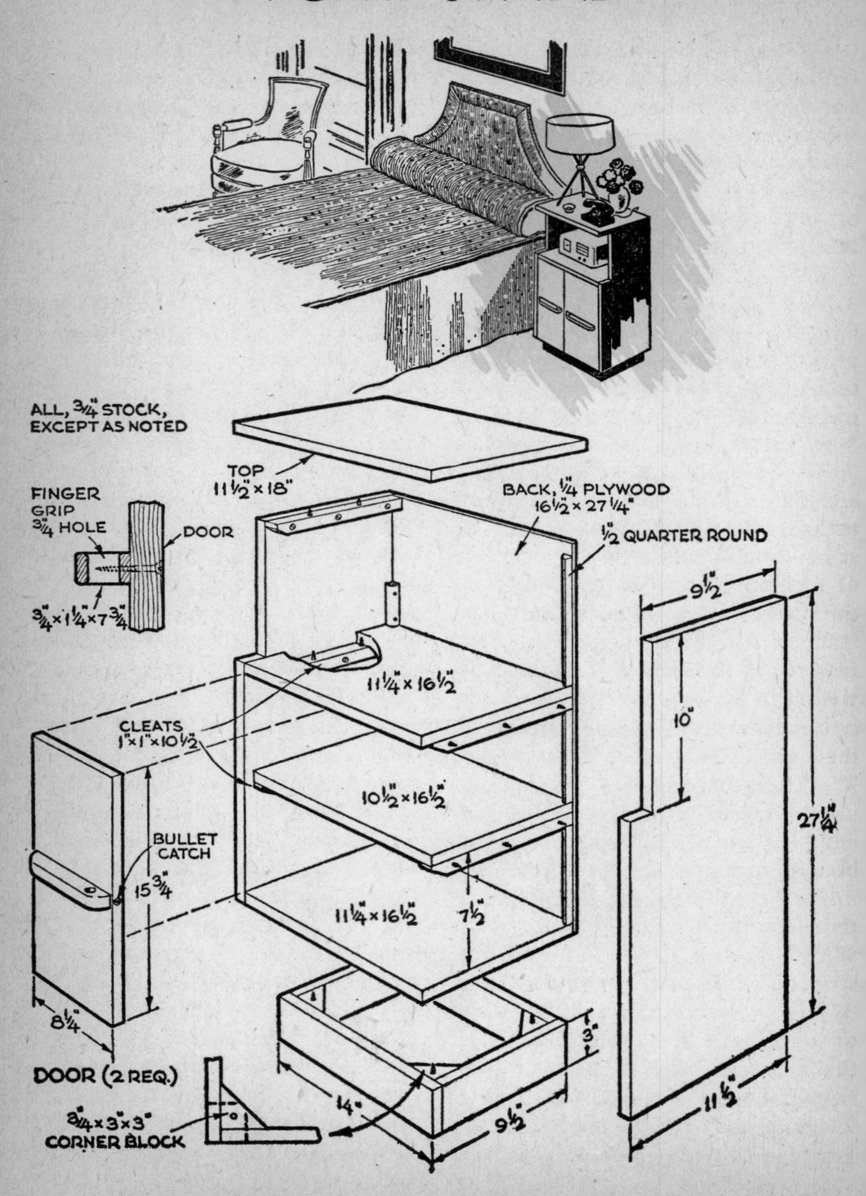
ALL, 3/4" STOCK, EXCEPT AS NOTED
TOP 11 1/2" x 18"
FINGER GRIP 3/4 HOLE
DOOR
3/4" x 1 1/4" x 7 3/4"
BACK, 1/4 PLYWOOD 16 1/2" x 27 1/4"
1/2 QUARTER ROUND
9 1/2"
10"
27 1/4"
11 1/2"
11 1/4" x 16 1/2"
CLEATS 1" x 1" x 10 1/2"
10 1/2" x 16 1/2"
BULLET CATCH
15 3/4"
11 1/4" x 16 1/2"
7 1/2"
8 1/4"
3"
DOOR (2 REQ.)
3/4 x 3" x 3" CORNER BLOCK
14"
9 1/2"

BUILT-IN WARDROBE CLOSET

Because of its size, this wardrobe cannot be moved through standard-size doors; therefore, most of its construction should be done in the room where it will be placed.

The two sides of the closet are made of 3/4″ plywood 8′ 0″ x 30 1/2″. Notch out the lower corner of each 3″ x 2 1/4″. The top of the cabinet is 3/4″ x 30 1/2″ x 6′ 4 1/2″. Similarly, the bottom of the cabinet is 3/4″ plywood 30 1/4″ x 6′ 4 1/2″. The back of the closet can be made of two pieces of 1/4″ plywood measuring 3′ 3″ x 8′ 0″ each.

Assemble the two sides, the top, and the back. In the front, between the two sides, install a strip of 1″ x 3″ at the base. Flush with the top edge of this strip, install cleats to support the bottom of the cabinet. These are made of 1″ x 1″ stock and should be fastened to the sides of the cabinet as well as to the back. The bottom piece can then be installed and fastened to the cleats and the front strip of 1″ x 3″. The front edge of the bottom should be set 1/4″ back from the edges of the side pieces. Along the bottom, measure 38 1/4″ in from the inside face of each side piece. This is the center line for a divider strip of 1″ stock 8 1/2″ x 30 1/4″. Install this strip. When in place, there should be 37 7/8″ between the divider and each of the sides of the cabinet. Mark half this distance — that is, 18 11/16″ — from the sides, and then install 1″ x 2″ guide rails for the shoe drawers. Be sure that these guide rails are parallel to the sides and to each other. On each side of the drawer guide, recess the bottom of the cabinet slightly to provide ventilation for the shoe drawers directly above.

8 1/2″ up from the bottom of the cabinet, fasten 1″ x 2″ cleats to the sides and back pieces. These will support the 3/4″ plywood shelf that carries the bottom or lower track for the sliding doors and also serves as a base for the chest of drawers. This piece of plywood is 30 1/2″ x 6′ 4 1/2″. Fasten this piece to the cleats and also to the divider piece running between it and the bottom of the cabinet.

The next step is to make the chest for the drawers. The construction of this is shown in the detail. The bottom of the chest is made out of 1/2″ plywood. It should be 36 1/4″ long and 26″ wide. Along the front edge fasten on edge a strip of 3/4″ plywood 2″ wide. Along each end of this bottom piece, fasten a 1″ x 1″ cleat. The two side pieces for the chest are of 3/4″ plywood 26 3/4″ x 19 1/2″. The back of the chest is made of 1/4″ plywood measuring 37 1/4″ x 20″. Assemble these parts and then measure up 6 1/2″ on the inside of each side of the chest and secure a strip of 1/2″ quarter round to support the 1/2″ plywood base for the drawers. The plywood base, which is 36 1/4″ x 26 3/4″, is fastened to the cleats. 6″ up from this plywood base, a second set of quarter round cleats are installed and a similar piece of plywood and a divider strip are then fastened in place. A divider strip is fastened to the upper surface of the top piece of plywood and then the top of the chest, made of 1/2″ plywood 37 3/4″ x 27″, is fastened in place. The chest is fastened in place now.

7 3/4″ down from the top of the wardrobe, a 3/4″ plywood shelf is installed. This is supported by means of 1″ x 1″ cleats attached to the sides and back of the wardrobe. The shelf should be 30 1/2″ wide and 6′ 4 1/2″ long. At the mid-point, install a 3/4″ divider 7″ wide and 30 1/2″ long between the shelf and the top of the wardrobe. 14 3/4″ down from this shelf, a second shelf is installed. This shelf, also of 3/4″ plywood, is 27″ wide and 6′ 4 1/2″ long. It is supported at each end by a 1″ x 6″ cleat fastened to the side. A 1″ x 2″ cleat is used to support the shelf along the back. Before installing the 1″ x 6″ cleats, measure 13″ in from the rear end and drill a 1″ hole 2 1/2″ down from the top edge for the clothes pole. Telescoping metal poles can be installed after the cleats are in place. If a wood pole is to be used, cut it to the correct length — 6′ 4 1/2″ — and install it at the same time that the 1″ x 6″ cleats are fastened in place.

Cut two pieces of 1″ x 3″ stock 74 3/4″ long and run one of them flush with and along the side of the chest to the upper shelf as shown in Detail X. It will be necessary to notch out the front box shelf to allow the 1″ x 3″ to pass through. Nail the other 1″ x 3″ to the chest surface and also to the first 1″ x 3″.

The chest drawer (A) and the shoe drawer (B) are now made up as shown in the drawings and installed. The 3/4″ plywood doors for the blanket storage compartments can also be installed.

Two types of sliding door runners are shown on the door detail. One is made with a metal track and metal wheels. These come in ready-made units sold at hardware stores. The other type consists of drawer rollers running on a track made of hardwood. The doors are held apart in both cases at the top by a metal center guide. The rollers at the base carry the entire weight. A 1″ x 2″ stop block should be fastened to each side of the wardrobe. The inside door should be installed first; then install the outside one. The top of the inside door is prevented from falling over by a strip of 1″ x 2″. The facing on the outside of the cabinet will prevent the doors from falling outward. Doors are made out of 3/4″ plywood. The width of each should be 38″ and the height should measure approximately 6′ 0″. Finally, 1″ x 2″ facing is installed.

Materials List

2 pcs. 1″ x 6″ x 27″
1 " 1″ x 8 1/2″ x 30 1/4″
2 " 1″ x 3″ x 7′ 4 3/4″
1 " 1″ x 3″ x 6′ 6″
2 " 1″ x 2″ x 7′ 9″
3 " 1″ x 2″ x 6′ 4 1/2″
1 " 1″ x 2″ x 6′ 3″
2 " 1″ x 2″ x 30 1/2″
2 " 1″ x 2″ x 30 1/4″
2 " 1″ x 2″ x 2″ x (stop blocks)
1 " 1″ x 1″ x 6′ 4 1/2″
2 " 1″ x 1″ x 30 1/2″
2 " 1″ x 1″ x 28 3/4″
2 " 1″ x 1″ x 26″

2 pcs. 3/4″ plywood 1′ 0″ x 30 1/2″
1 " 3/4″ plywood 6′ 4 1/2″ x 30 1/2″
1 " 3/4″ plywood 6′ 4 1/2″ x 30 1/4″
2 " 3/4″ plywood 26 3/4″ x 19 1/2″
1 " 3/4 plywood 30 1/2″ x 6′ 4 1/2″
1 " 3/4″ plywood 27″ x 6′ 4 1/2″
1 " 3/4″ plywood 7″ x 30 1/2″
1 " 3/4″ plywood 2″ x 36 1/4″
1 " 1/2″ plywood 37 3/4″ x 27″
2 " 1/2″ plywood 36 1/4″ x 26 3/4″
1 " 1/2″ plywood 36 1/4″ x 26″
1 " 1/2″ plywood 6 1/2″ x 26 3/4″
1 " 1/2″ plywood 6″ x 26 3/4″
1 " 1/2″ plywood 4″ x 26 3/4″
2 " 1/4″ plywood 39″ x 8′ 0″
1 " 1/4″ plywood 37 3/4″ x 20″
8 " 1/2″ quarter round 26 3/4″
1 closet pole 6′ 4 1/2″
Metal or hardwood sliding door track 6′ 4 1/2″
Metal center guide 6′ 4 1/2″
4 metal wheels or drawer rollers

Chest Drawer (A)

2 pcs. 1/2″ plywood 6 1/2″ x 17 7/8″
2 " 1/2″ plywood 6″ x 17 7/8″
4 " 1/2″ plywood 5 7/8″ x 26 3/4″
2 " 1/2″ plywood 5 7/8″ x 16 7/8″
4 pcs. 1/2″ plywood 5 3/8″ x 26 1/4″
2 " 1/2″ plywood 5 3/8″ x 16 7/8″
2 " 1/2″ plywood 4″ x 17 7/8″
4 " 1/2″ plywood 3 3/8″ x 26 1/4″
2 " 1/2″ plywood 3 3/8″ x 16 7/8″
6 " 1/4″plywood 26 1/4″ x 17 7/8″
12 " 1/4″ quarter round 26 1/4″
12 " 1/4″ quarter round 16 7/8″
8 " 1/4″ quarter round 5 7/8″
8 " 1/4″ quarter round 5 3/8″
8 " 1/4″ quarter round 3 3/8″

Shoe Drawer (B)

4 pcs 3/4″ plywood 8 1/4″ x 29 3/4″
2 " 1/2″ plywood 7 1/4″ x 36″
2 " 1/4″ plywood 29″ x 34 1/2″
2 " 1/4″ plywood 9 1/4″ x 36″
4 " 3/4″ quarter round 29″

Blanket Storage Space Doors

2 pieces 3/4″ plywood 6″ x 36″
2 pair cabinet hinges

Materials Totals

1″ x 6″ — 4′ 6″
1″ x 3″ — 21′ 3 1/2″
1″ x 2″ — 51′ 4″
1″ x 1″ — 20′ 7″
3/4″ quarter round 9′ 8″
1/2″ quarter round 17′ 10″
1/4″ quarter round 52′ 10 1/2″
(Remainder as itemized above)

BUILT-IN WARDROBE CLOSET

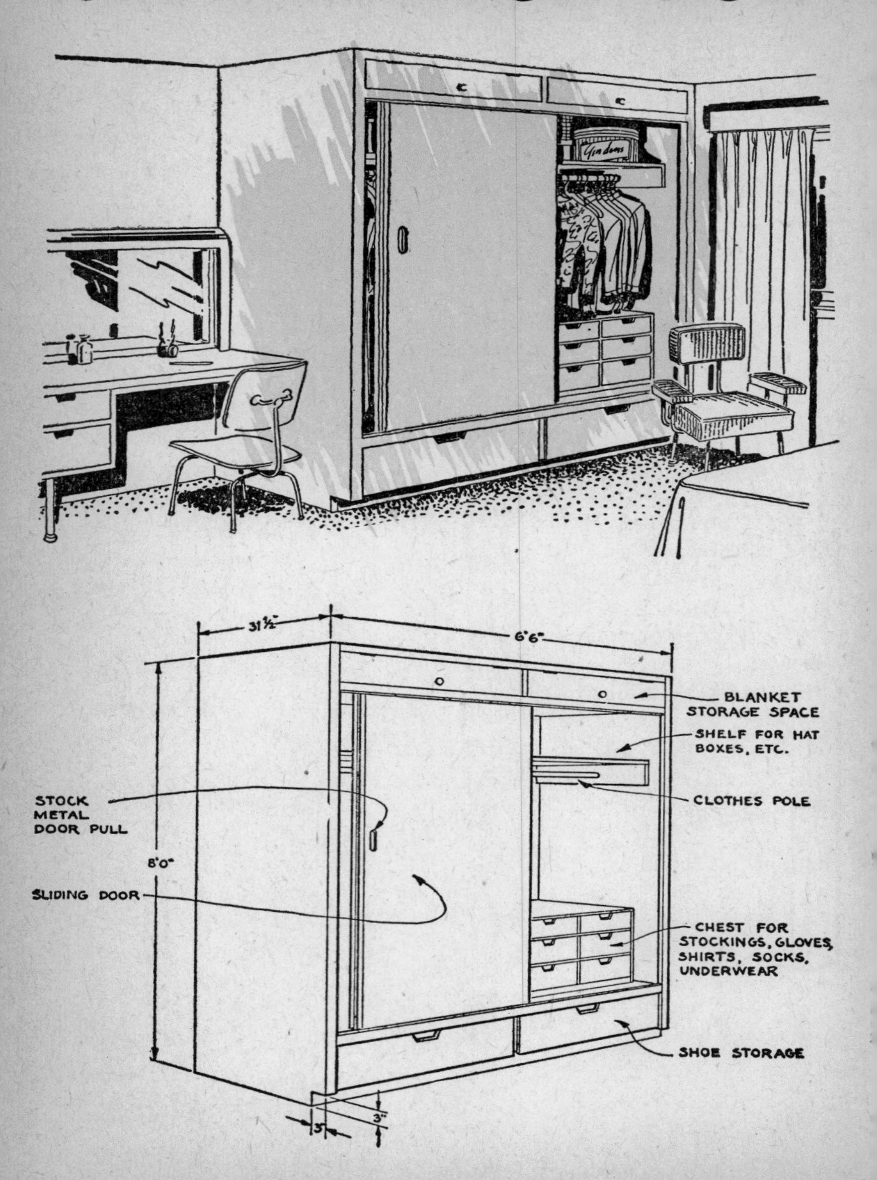

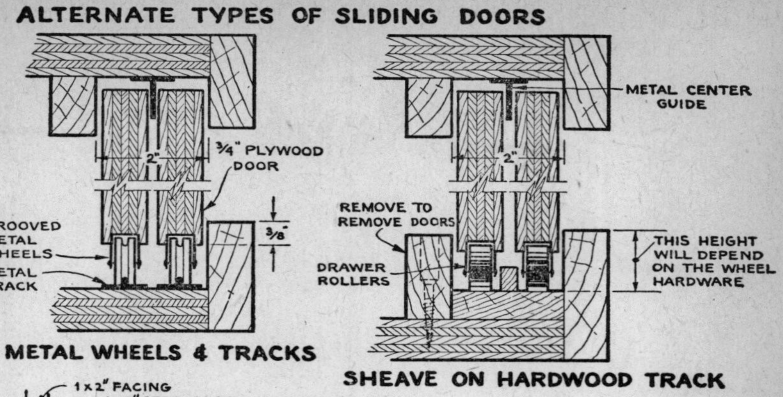
ALTERNATE TYPES OF SLIDING DOORS
3/4" PLYWOOD DOOR
2"
3/8"
GROOVED METAL WHEELS
METAL TRACK
METAL WHEELS & TRACKS
METAL CENTER GUIDE
2"
REMOVE TO REMOVE DOORS
DRAWER ROLLERS
THIS HEIGHT WILL DEPEND ON THE WHEEL HARDWARE
SHEAVE ON HARDWOOD TRACK

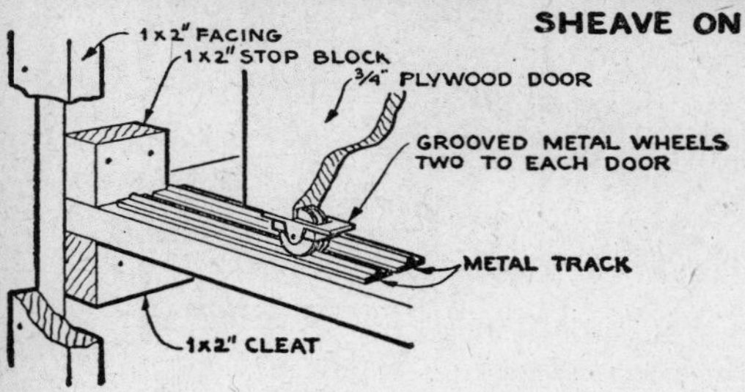
1x2" FACING
1x2" STOP BLOCK
3/4" PLYWOOD DOOR
GROOVED METAL WHEELS TWO TO EACH DOOR
METAL TRACK
1x2" CLEAT

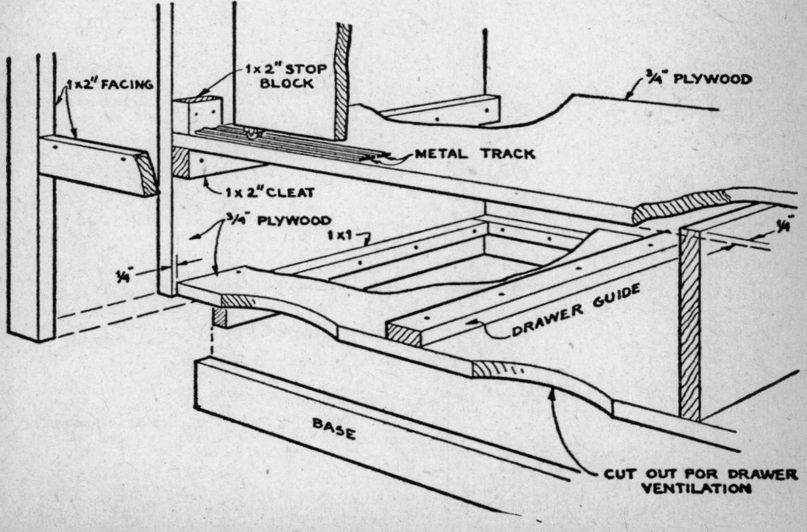
1x2" FACING
1x2" STOP BLOCK
3/4" PLYWOOD
METAL TRACK
1x2" CLEAT
3/4" PLYWOOD
1x1
1/4"
1/4"
DRAWER GUIDE
BASE
CUT OUT FOR DRAWER VENTILATION

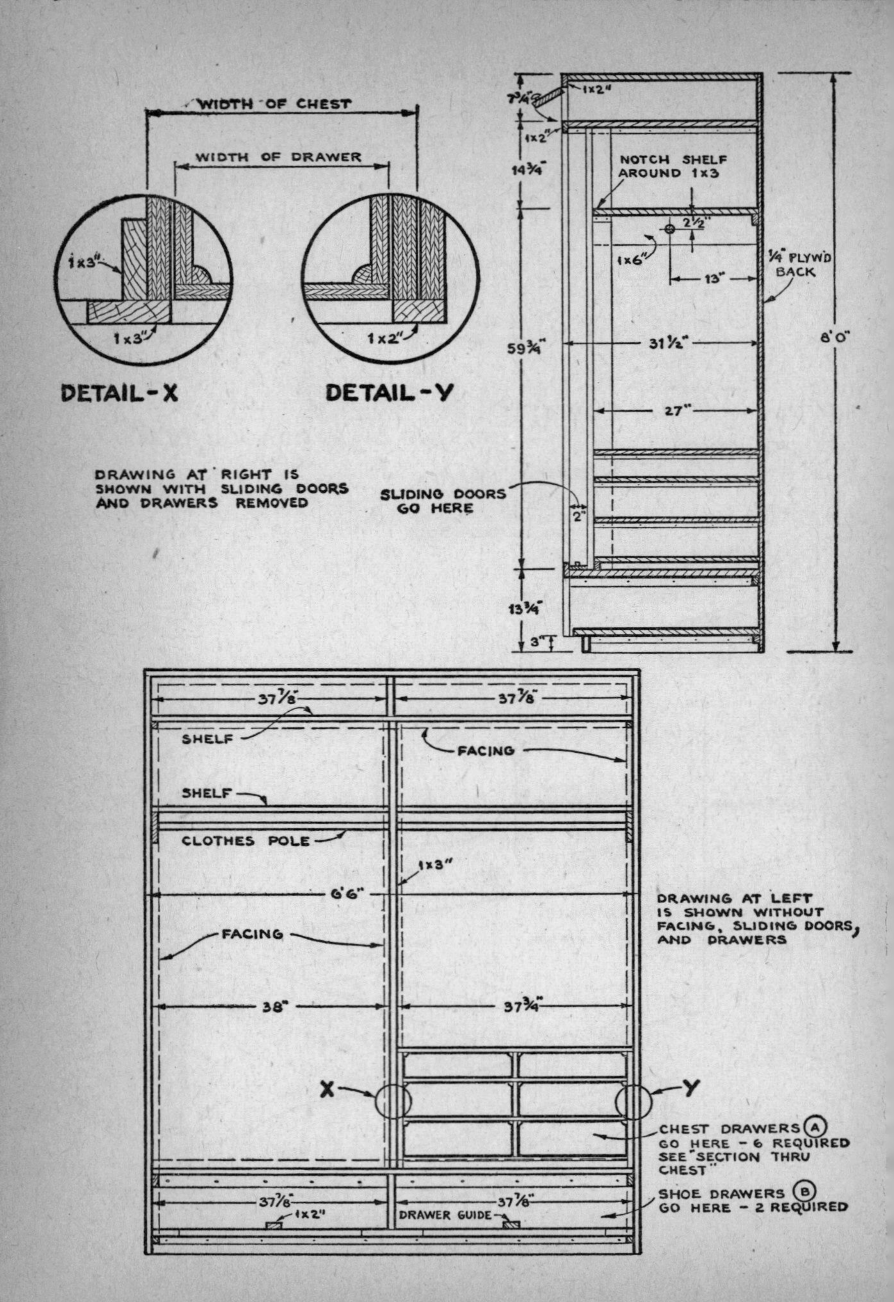
WIDTH OF CHEST
WIDTH OF DRAWER
1x3"
1x3"
1x2"
DETAIL-X
DETAIL-Y
DRAWING AT RIGHT IS SHOWN WITH SLIDING DOORS AND DRAWERS REMOVED
7¾"
1x2"
1x2"
14¾"
NOTCH SHELF AROUND 1x3
2½"
1x6"
13"
¼" PLYWD BACK
59¾"
31½"
8'0"
27"
SLIDING DOORS GO HERE
2"
13¾"
3"
37⅞"
37⅞"
SHELF
FACING
SHELF
CLOTHES POLE
1x3"
6'6"
DRAWING AT LEFT IS SHOWN WITHOUT FACING, SLIDING DOORS, AND DRAWERS
FACING
38"
37¾"
X
Y
CHEST DRAWERS (A) GO HERE - 6 REQUIRED SEE "SECTION THRU CHEST"
37⅞"
37⅞"
1x2"
DRAWER GUIDE
SHOE DRAWERS (B) GO HERE - 2 REQUIRED

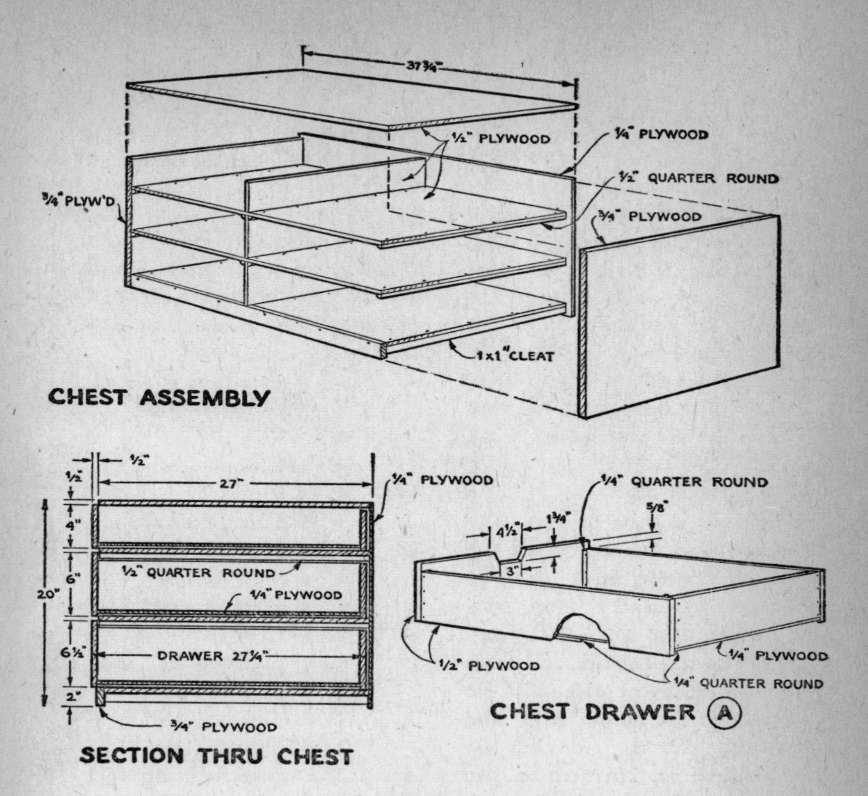

CHEST ASSEMBLY

SECTION THRU CHEST

CHEST DRAWER (A)

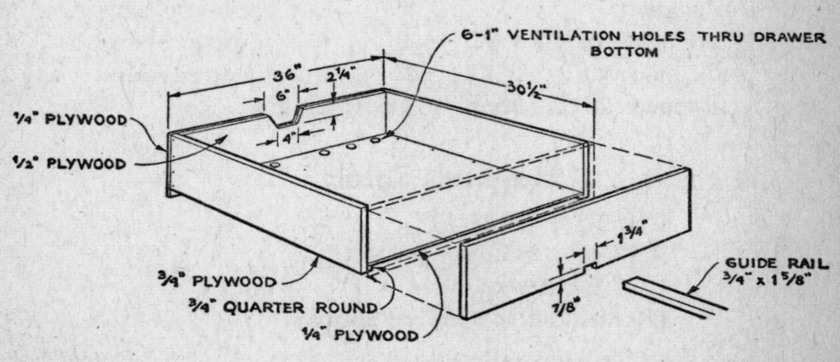

SHOE DRAWER (B)

BLANKET CHEST

Homes with limited storage space will appreciate this blanket chest, which can hold eight blankets or a similar quantity of other possessions.

The framework for the back, sides, and bottom is made out of 1″ x 3″ with butt joints. The framework for the front is made out of 1″ x 3″ for the bottom and sides and 1″ x 4″ for the top. Assemble the 1″ x 3″ using miter joints. Lay a 1″ x 4″ across them so its ends come flush with the free ends of the 1″ x 3″ side pieces. Mark the 1″ x 4″ for cutting, cut, put it back, and mark the 1″ x 3″.

Glue and nail a sheet of 1/4″ plywood to the floor frame. Let all the plywood edges come flush with the frame edges. Cover the sides with 1/4″ plywood; have it 1 1/32″ from the ends of the framework and flush top and bottom. Now assemble the four section on the floor frame. The plywood edges on the sides of the end pieces will be covered by the front and back framework.

The four legs are made of 1″ x 3″ fastened to a block made of 1″ x 3″ that in turn is fastened to the floor frame with wood screws. The two sections of each leg are mitered. The top of the chest can be made out of a solid piece of 3/4″ plywood or of tongue-and-groove lumber with batten strips. The top should extend 1″ beyond the sides and front. Trim around the top and bottom with 3/4″ cove molding with mitered joints at the corners.

Materials List

5 pcs. 1″ x 3″ x 45″
1 " 1″ x 4″ x 45″
4 " 1″ x 3″ x 19″
2 " 1″ x 3″ x 18 1/4″
2 " 1″ x 3″ x 18″
2 " 1″ x 3″ x 17 1/2″
4 " 1″ x 3″ x 13 1/2″
8 " 1″ x 3″ x 7″
1 " 3/4″ plywood 22″ x 46 1/2″
1 " 1/4″ plywood 20 1/2″ x 45″
2 " 1/4″ plywood 18″ x 43″
2 " 1/4″ plywood 18″ x 21 1/2″
2 " 3/4″ cove molding 46 1/2″
4 " 3/4″ cove molding 22″
2 " 1/2″ quarter round 41″
2 " 1/2″ quarter round 13 1/2″
3 butt hinges

Materials Totals

1″ x 3″ — 43′ 2 1/2″
3/3″ cove molding — 15′ 1″
1/2″ quarter round — 9′ 1″
(Remainder as itemized above)

BLANKET CHEST

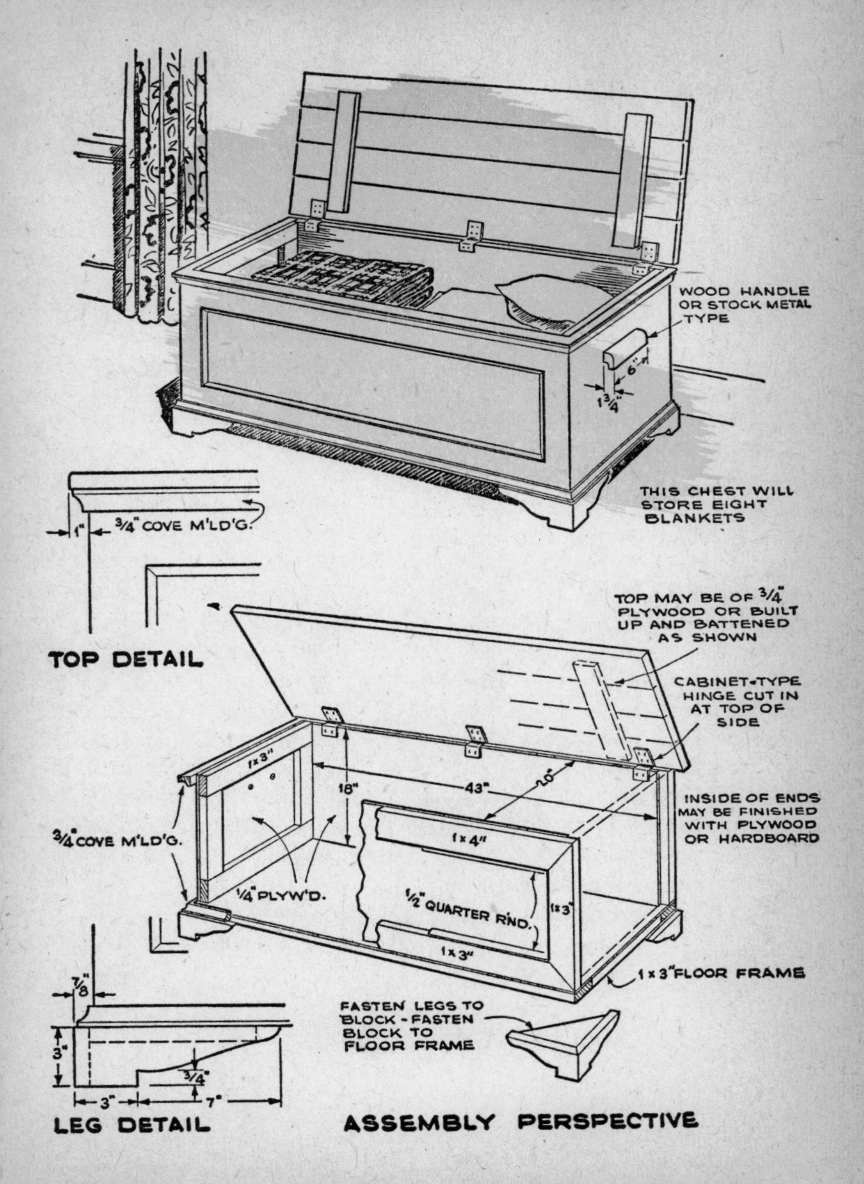

HANGING TOWEL CHEST

Whether used as an independent unit or in conjunction with the hanging medicine chest, this hanging towel chest makes an ideal storage unit for the bathroom.

The top, bottom, and sides of the chest can be made out of 3/4″ or 1″ stock. Cut these four pieces to size and assemble. After this has been done, attach the adjustable shelf standards and supports to the inside surfaces of the side pieces. These supports should be spaced about 8″ apart.

The back of the chest is made out of 1/8″ hardboard. It should not be nailed into place until the inside of the chest has been given a finish. The edges of the back piece should come flush with the edges of the chest.

Doors for the chest can be either hinged or sliding. If you wish to use sliding doors, follow the instructions given for making sliding doors for the hanging medicine chest. The only difference will be that the doors for the towel chest will be slightly larger in area; the same material can be used.

Hinged doors should be made out of 1/2″ plywood. Cut these to size and attach with semi-concealed hinges. Use hinges with a rust-resistant finish because the dampness in the bathroom will corrode ordinary steel hinges. No door stops are necessary because the top and bottom of the chest will prevent the doors from swinging too far in. Provide the doors with a latch. Handles can be stock metal ones or made of wood.

Shelves for the cabinet should be 9 1/4″ wide and 28 1/2″ long. Nail them if they do not fit in tight.

Materials List

2 pcs. 1″ x 9 5/8″ x 30″
2 " 1″ x 9 5/8″ x 16 1/2″
2 " 1″ x 9 1/4″ x 28 1/2″
2 " 1/2″ plywood 17″ x 14 1/4″
1 " 1/8″ hardboard 30″ x 18″
2 pairs semi-concealed cabinet hinges
2 metal handles
2 latches
4 adjustable shelf standards and supports

Materials Totals

1″ x 9 5/8″ — 7′ 9″
1″ x 9 1/4″ — 4′ 9″
(Remainder as itemized above)

HANGING TOWEL CHEST

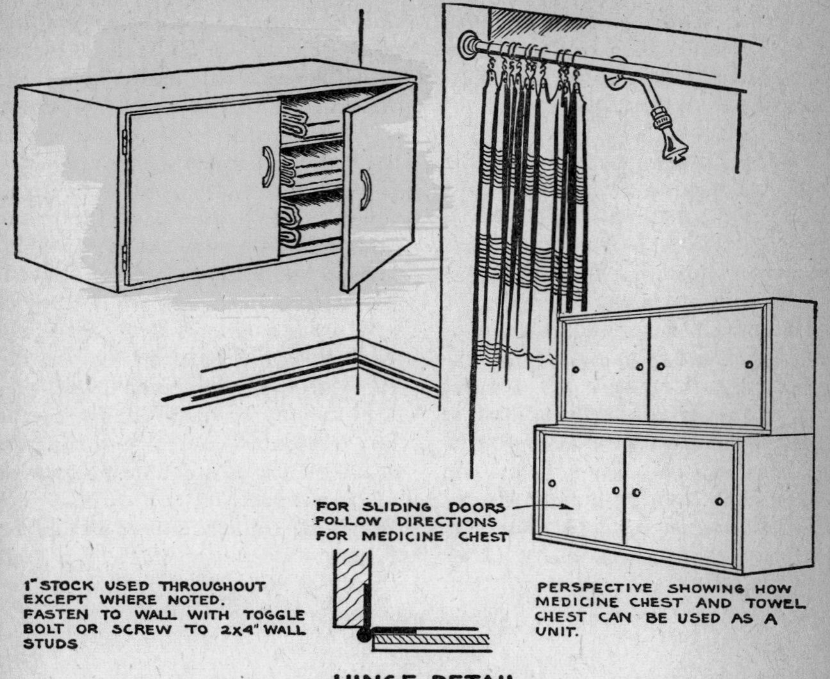

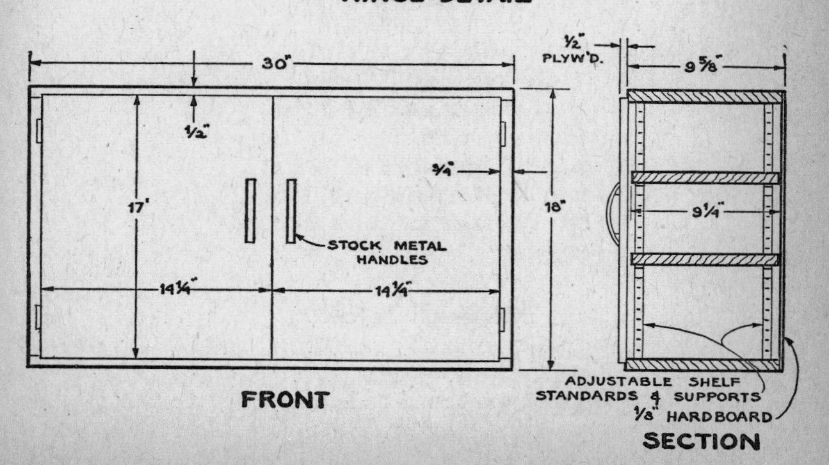

CLOTHES HAMPER

A clothes hamper of this kind can be used in the bathroom, kitchen, or bedrooms. It can effectively be used on the floor or hung from a wall.

The cabinet for the hamper is made up with a bottom and side pieces of 1″ stock. The bottom piece should measure 9 5/8″ x 22″. The side pieces are 9 5/8″ wide and 16 1/2″ long. Assemble these three pieces but do not put on the cabinet top or back until the hinged hamper has been assembled and installed in the cabinet.

The hinged hamper has a front piece made out of 3/4″ plywood. It should be 20 3/8″ x 16 1/2″. At the center of the top, cut a hand grip 1 1/2″ deep and 3″ wide at the top and 2″ wide at the base. The side pieces for the hamper are 1″ stock 8 1/2″ wide. The top ends of these pieces should be cut at an angle so that the front will measure 15″ and the rear 13″. The bottom of the hamper, made out of 1″ stock, is 8 1/2″ x 18 7/8″. Assemble these pieces and install the 1/8″ hardboard back, which is 13 1/2″ x 20 3/8″. Hamper and cabinet are joined with 3″ hinges.

Fold the hamper into the cabinet, and cut the top of the cabinet out of 1″ stock. This should be 9 5/8″ x 22″. 3/4″ in from the front edge of the top and at the midpoint, install two 1″ x 1″ x 3″ strips. These act as stops and prevent the hinged portion of the hamper from coming too far out of the cabinet. Fasten the top in place and install the 1/8″ hardboard back to the cabinet.

Materials List

2 pcs. 1″ x 10″ x 22″
2 " 1″ x 10″ x 16 1/2″
1 " 1″ x 8 1/2″ x 18 7/8″
2 " 1″ x 8 1/2″ x 15″
2 " 1″ x 1″ x 3″
1 " 3/4″ plywood 16 1/2″ x 20 3/8″
1 " 1/8″ hardboard 18″ x 22″
1 " 1/8″ hardboard 13 1/2″ x 20 3/8″
2 hinges 3″

Materials Totals

1″ x 10″ — 6′ 5″
1″ x 8 1/2″ — 4′ 7/8″
1″ x 1″ — 6″
(Remainder as itemized above)

CLOTHES HAMPER

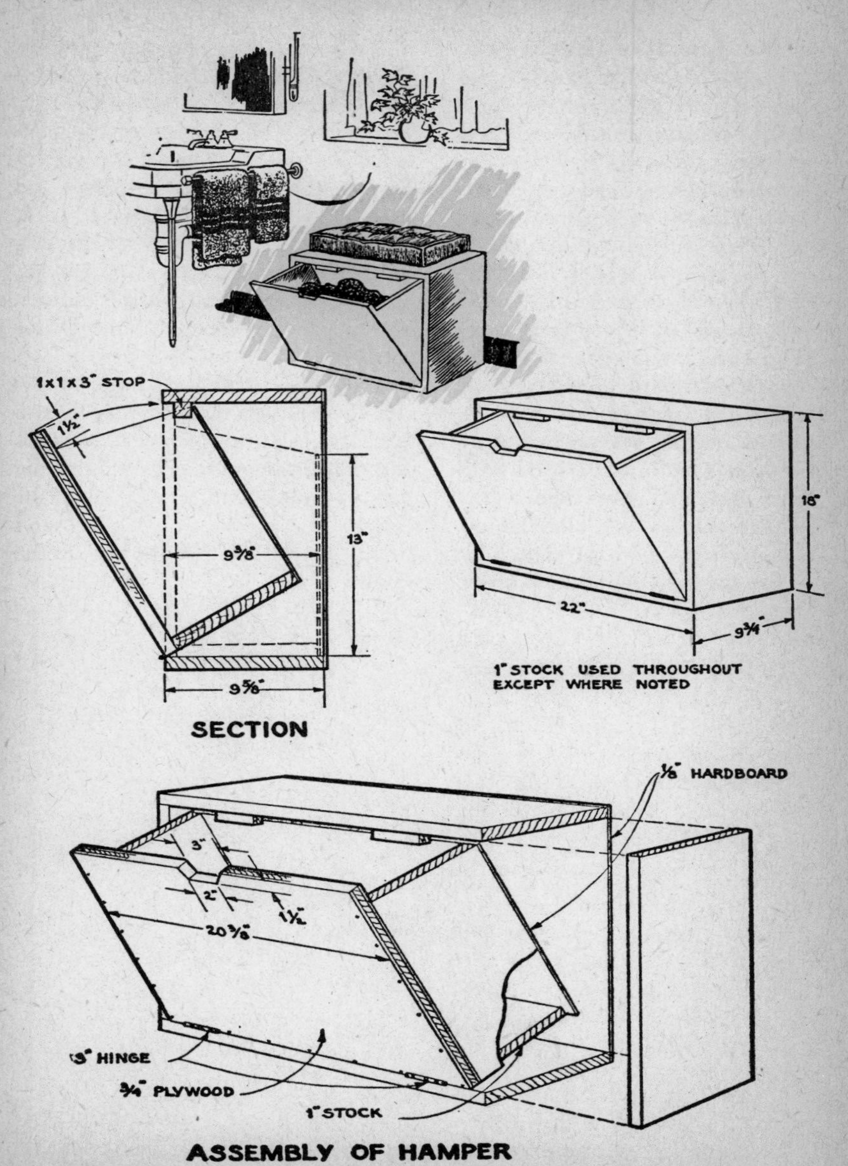

HANGING MEDICINE CHEST

As the conventional type of medicine cabinet found in most homes never seems quite large enough for a family's needs, this hanging chest should prove a popular project.

The sides, top, and bottom of the chest are made out of 1″ stock assembled with simple butt joints. As soon as these four pieces are together, install adjustable shelf standards and supports along the inside surfaces of the sides. These supports should be installed about 4″ apart to take a shelf 5″ wide.

Runners for the sliding doors are made by first installing a strip of 1/2″ quarter round molding around the front of the chest. Make the corners with miter joints. Cut two doors out of 1/8″ hardboard. Each door should measure 14 1/4″ x 16 5/16″. Working from the back of the chest, place one of these doors up against the quarter round strip. 1/4″ away from the inside face of the quarter round strip, install a strip of 1/2″ x 1/2″ to act as a separator between the two doors. One strip should run on the bottom, the other on the top. Place the second door up against this strip and then install, 1/4″ away, the final strip of 1/2″ quarter round. Check the action of the doors to be certain they move easily. Binding of the doors will probably be caused by the fact that the quarter round or separator strip is a little out of position. 3/4″ holes should be drilled in each door for finger grips. Cut and install the shelves for the chest and then install the back piece, which is made out of 1/8″ hardboard.

It will be a good deal easier to finish off the inside of the chest if the parts are painted before assembly. The sliding doors, too, should be painted before assembly.

Materials List

2 pcs. 1″ x 1 7/8″ x 30″
2 " 1″ x 7 1/8″ x 16″
2 " 1″ x 5″ x 28″
2 " 1/2″ x 1/2″ x 28″
1 " 1/2″ x 1/2″ x 15 5/16″
2 " 1/8″ hardboard 16 5/16″ x 14 1/4″
4 " 1/2″ quarter round 28″
2 " 1/2″ quarter round 16″
4 adjustable shelf standards and supports 28″

Materials Totals

1″ x 7 1/8″ — 7′ 8″
1″ x 5″ — 4′ 8″
1/2″ x 1/2″ — 6′
1/2″ quarter round — 12′
(Remainder as itemized above)

HANGING MEDICINE CHEST

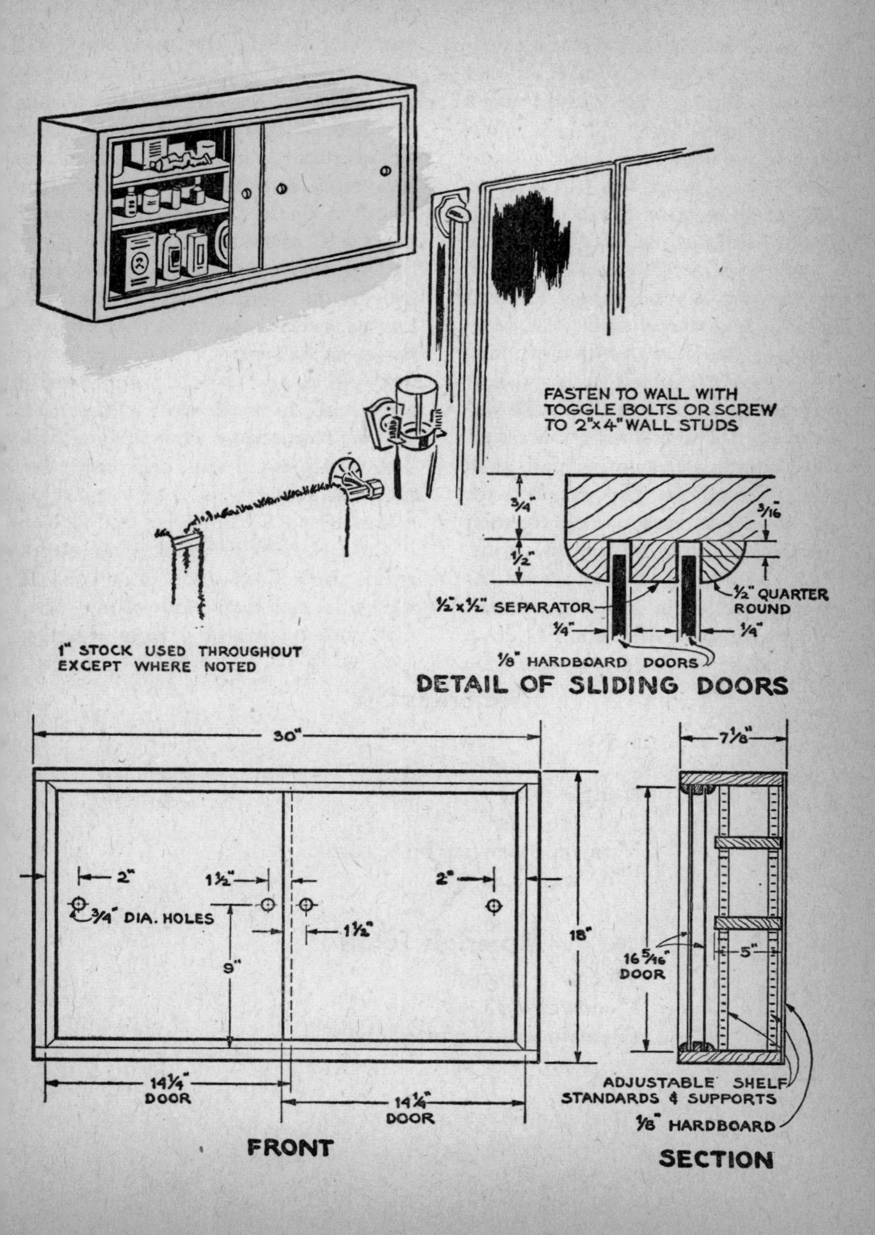

WALL TRELLIS

Here is a simple wall trellis which can be made in a very short time and will make an attractive addition to the home.

The framework is made out of 2″ x 4″ stock. Sand and plane down the wood so that the finish is smooth enough to take paint. The dimensions for the frame are given as 7′ 6″ x 8′ 6″, but these can be varied to meet individual requirements. Do not, however, make the frame too wide as this might make it difficult to remove it when necessary to paint the house siding. Joints of the framework are simple butts made with two 16d nails each and reinforced on the inside with angle irons. The framework is attached to the house siding with angle irons, too. Use only non-corrosive screws for attaching the angle irons—don't nail the framework to the house siding. The framework should either be given a prime coat of paint or be coated with a preservative wood stain before it is attached to the exterior wall. Make certain that the backside of the frame is adequately protected with a finish. The base of the frame should be kept at least 6″ above ground level.

Two methods are suggested for attaching the cord to the frame. The dowels make a somewhat more professional looking job but take much more time to install than the screw eyes. Also, non-corrosive wire staples will be required on each side of each dowel to prevent the cord from slipping off. Dowels are held in place by means of an 8d finishing nail driven in through the edge of the framework at an angle. Use some stout cord or wire attached to the dowelling. Varnish cord to protect it from weather.

Materials List

2 pcs. 2″ x 4″ x 7′ 10″
2 " 2″ x 4″ x 7′ 6″
8 angle irons
15 1″-dowels 3 1/2″
Varnished venetian blind cord or plastic wash line 85′

Materials Totals

3″ x 4″ – 30′ 8″
1″ dowel – 4′ 1/2″
(Remainder as itemized above)

WALL TRELLIS

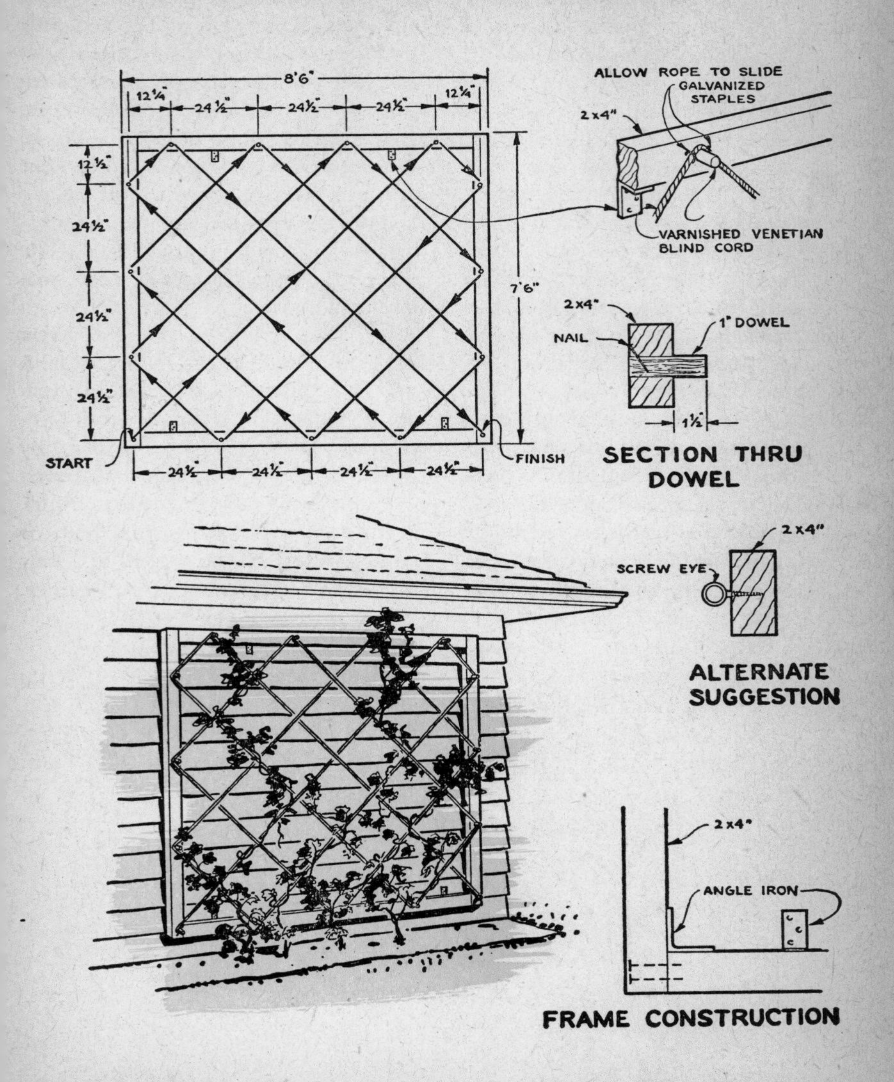

ENTRY HALL FLOWER BOXES

These two flower boxes make it possible to have growing flowers in the home throughout the year and still keep the interior woodwork dry and unmarred.

The box shown in the upper half of the illustration is built up from a base made out of a solid piece of wood 1 1/4″ thick. At each corner a block 1 1/4″ x 2 3/4″ x 2″ is attached. A middle support 1 1/4″ x 2 3/4″ x 6″ is attached along one side. The top piece of the base, the same size and thickness as the bottom, is attached over these supports. The box itself is made out of 1″ stock for sides, top, and bottom. Use butt joints on all these pieces. The box is centered on the base and attached to it with wood screws. The screws should be countersunk. The inside of the box can be lined with either zinc or copper. All seams should be soldered so that moisture from the earth inside the box will not reach the wood.

The box pictured in the lower portion of the illustration is made by building a simple rectangular box 36″ long, 8″ wide, and 8″ deep. Use 1″ x 8″ stock for the sides and bottom, and 1/4″ plywood for the ends. A strip of 1″ x 1 5/8″ is attached flush with the bottom and another flush with the top. Between these two, at the exact midpoint, a third strip of 1″ x 1 5/8″ fits in place. Line the inside of the box with copper or zinc.

Materials List

Top Box

2 pcs. 1 1/4″ x 9″ x 37″
1 " 1 1/4″ x 6″ x 2 3/4″
4 " 1 1/4″ x 2″ x 2 3/4″
2 " 1″ x 6″ x 36″
2 " 1″ x 6″ x 6″
1 " 1″ x 6″ x 34″
Copper or zinc lining

Bottom Box

2 pcs 1″ x 8″ x 34″
1 " 1″ x 6″ x 34 1/2″
3 " 1″ x 2″ x 36″
6 " 1″ x 2″ x 6 3/4″
2 " 1/4″ plywood 6 3/4″ x 7 5/8″

Materials Totals

Top Box

1 1/4″ x 9″ – 6′ 2″
1″ x 6″ – 9′ 10″
1 1/4″ x 2″ – 11″

Bottom Box

1″ x 8″ – 5′ 8″
1″ x 2″ – 12′ 4 1/2″
(Remainder as itemized above)

ENTRY HALL FLOWER BOXES

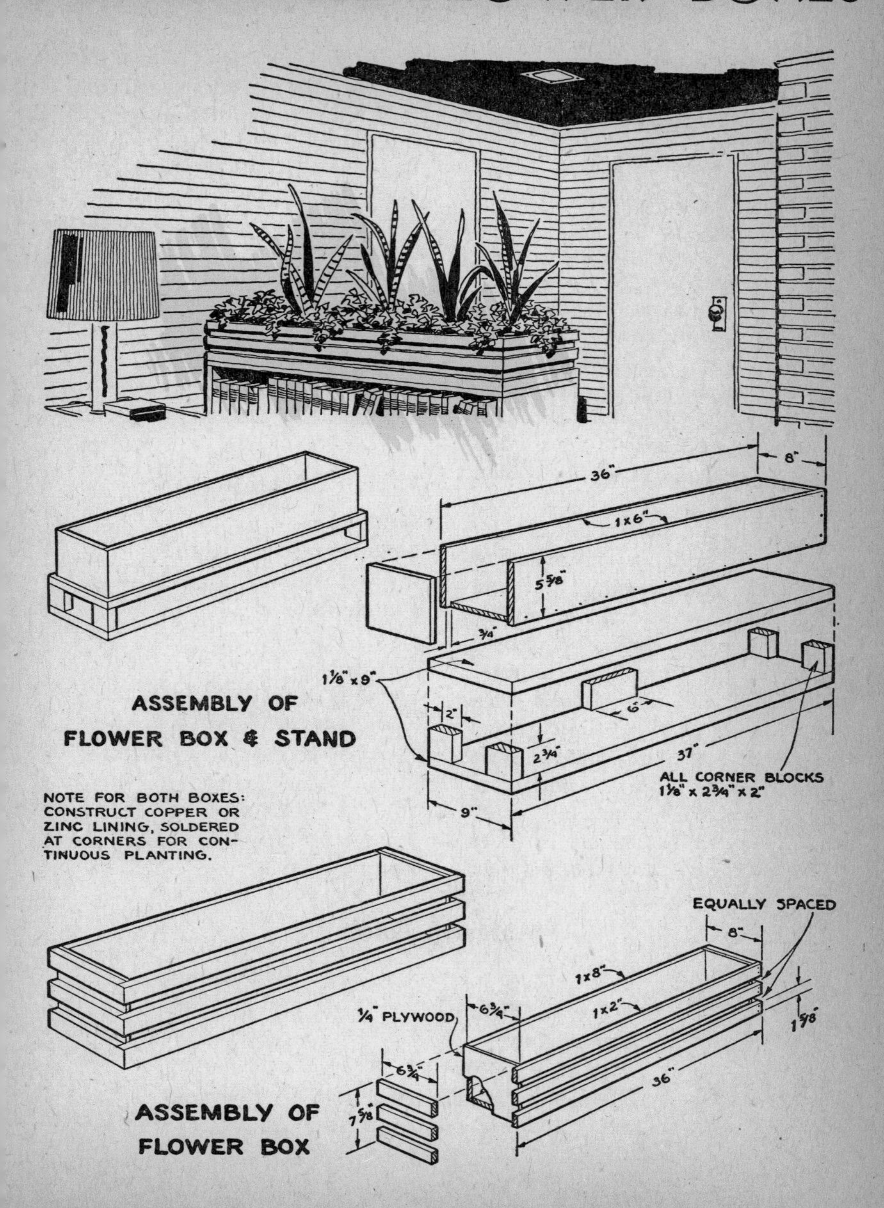

HANGING FLOWER BOXES

These two novel and attractive flower boxes are designed to be hung on exterior walls outside a window sill.

The box shown in the upper part of the illustration takes four flower pots. If smaller pots are to be used, the size of the base and the holes should be decreased according to the information given in the drawing.

Cut the board to size and then measure off the spacing for the holes for the pots. Get the exact center of the board lengthwise and use this line to locate the center of each hole. The holes can be started with a brace and bit and cut with a compass or coping saw.

End pieces for the box are cut out of 1″ stock 6″ wide, using the pattern given in the illustration. These end pieces are more for the sake of appearance since the box itself is supported from the wall by three 2″ angle irons.

The lower box has a solid back piece made out of 1″ x 6″ and a solid bottom of 1″ x 8″. The front and sides are made with 1″ x 2″ horizontal strips, to which are fastened 1″ x 2″ pickets. Cut the horizontal strips to the proper length, and then make up the pickets. Space the pickets along the horizontal strips so that they are an equal distance apart. Fasten them in place to the 1″ x 2″ strips, and then assemble the three sections and attach them to the back section of the box. Nail the ends of the pickets to the bottom piece.

The box is hung from the wall by means of a 3/4″ x 2 1/2″ angle iron at each end, and three 2″ angle irons on the bottom. The boxes should be painted—in vivid colors, if you like—to preserve the wood.

Materials List

Top Box
2 pcs. 1″ x 6″ x 10 1/2″
1 " 1″ x 10 1/2″ x 39 1/2″
3 angle irons 2″

Bottom Box
1 pcs. 1″ x 7 1/2″ x 36″
1 " 1″ x 6″ x 36″
2 " 1″ x 2″ x 7 1/2″
1 " 1″ x 2″ x 34″
16 " 1″ x 2″ x 8″
2 angle irons 3/4″ x 2 1/2″
3 angle irons 2″

Materials Totals

Top Box
1″ x 6″ — 21″

Bottom Box
1″ x 2″ — 14′ 9″
(Remainder as itemized above)

HANGING FLOWER BOXES

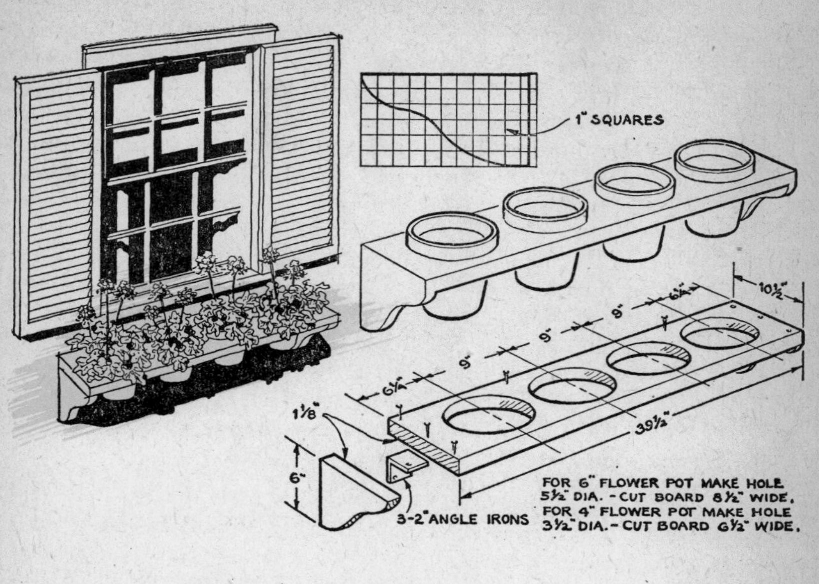

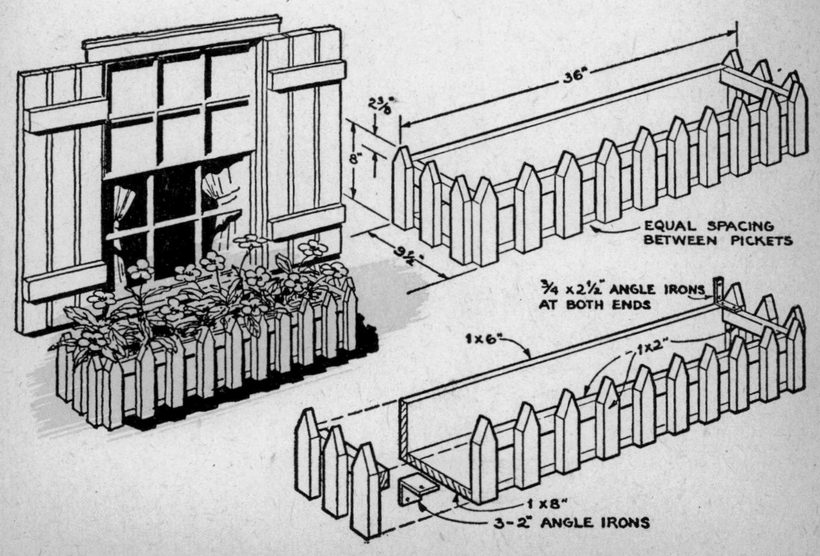

LAWN CHAIR

If you want several of these chairs, cut and shape the parts for the first and use them as patterns for the other chairs before assembling.

Patterns for the arms, arm brackets, and back legs are shown; they should be cut out of 1″ stock.

The two front legs are cut 22 1/4″ long from 1″ x 4″ stock. These are fastened in front by a 1″ x 5″. Fasten the arm brackets to their centers so the top comes flush with the top of the leg. The front legs can now be screwed to the back legs. The top of the back legs should come 13 1/4″ up from the bottom of the front legs. The back legs are joined together at the rear with a 19″ piece of 1″ x 3″ and at the front with a 20 1/2″ piece of 1″ x 5″.

The back ends of the arms are fastened together with a 1″ x 3″ that is 26 1/2″ long, and are attached to the brackets. They should overhang the front legs by 1″.

Starting at the front, install 1″ x 3″ slats 19″ long to form the seat. You will need six pieces spaced 1/4″ apart. The chair back consists of a center piece 1″ x 3″ x 38″ and three pieces of 1″ x 2″ on each side spaced 1″ apart at the top. Cut all pieces 38″ long and, after assembly, bevel the tops to obtain the curve. Using round-head wood screws, slats for the back are attached 6″ from the top of the center piece to a strip of 1″ x 3″ stock 20″ long. 5″ up from the base they are fastened to a strip of 1″ x 3″ that is 19″ long. When placed in position, this piece is secured to the rear legs. Fasten a 1″ x 3″ on top of it flat against the chair back and cut flush with the outer slats. Finally, the chair back should be fastened to the 1″ x 3″ strip between the far ends of the chair arms.

Materials List

2 pcs. 1″ x 8″ x 32″ (rear legs)
2 " 1″ x 8″ x 28″ (arms)
2 " 1″ x 6″ x 16″ (brackets)
1 " 1″ x 5″ x 20 1/2″
2 " 1″ x 4″ x 22 1/4″
1 " 1″ x 3″ x 38″
1 " 1″ x 3″ x 26 1/2″
1 " 1″ x 3″ x 20 1/2″
9 " 1″ x 3″ x 19″
6 " 1″ x 2″ x 38″

Materials Totals

1″ x 8″ — 10′
1″ x 6″ — 2′ 8″
1″ x 5″ — 1′ 8 1/2″
1″ x 4″ — 3′ x 8 1/2″
1″ x 3″ — 21′ 3 1/2″
1″ x 2″ — 19′

LAWN CHAIR

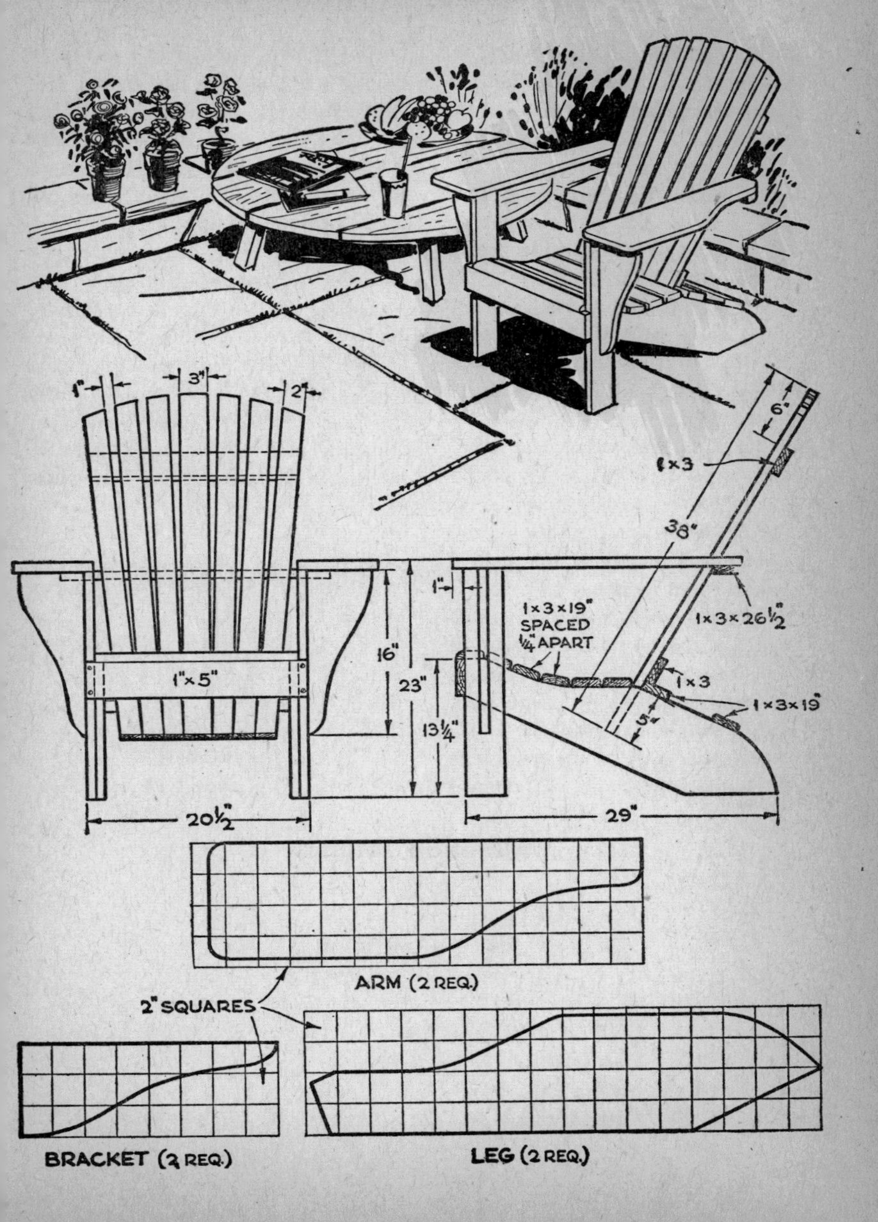
1"
3"
2"
6"
1×3
38"
1"×5"
1"
16"
23"
13¼"
1×3×19" SPACED ¼" APART
1×3×26½"
1×3
1×3×19"
5"
20½"
29"
ARM (2 REQ.)
2" SQUARES
BRACKET (2 REQ.)
LEG (2 REQ.)

DINING TABLE AND CHAIRS

Outdoor furniture like this will give years of service if made with durable wood and assembled with non-corrosive fasteners.

The first step in constructing the table is to make the apron with two pieces 1" x 4" x 28" and two pieces 1" x 4" x 29 1/2". Assemble them, and cut the legs 3" x 3" x 27 1/2". Fasten the legs to the apron corners, their tops flush with the apron top. Now fasten a 1" x 6" between opposite legs and drill a 1 1/2" hole in its exact center. Cut four 1" x 6" to tie in the leg tops and install 1" x 6" braces at opposite corners. The table top can be 3/4" weatherproof plywood or 1" stock. Cut plywood to the 4' diameter and install. If boards are used fasten them in place with 1/8"-1/4" between boards and then cut to diameter. Cut the 1 1/2" hole through the table top.

Chair legs are 1" x 3" The back legs are 24" high, the front 16 1/4". Bevel the upper part of the back legs to give the back an angle. Front and back legs are tied together at the base with 1" x 2", at the top with 1" x 3". The front legs and the back legs are tied together with 1" x 3". The seat and back can be 1/2" weatherproof plywood or 1/2" stock with 1/8"-1/4" between boards.

Materials List

Table

4 pcs. 3" x 3" x 27 1/2"
9 " 1" x 6" x 48"
1 " 1" x 6" x 41 3/4"
4 " 1" x 6" x 27 1/2"
2 " 1" x 6" x 18 1/2"
2 " 1" x 4" x 29 1/2"
2 " 1" x 4" x 28"

Chair

2 pcs. 1" x 3" x 24"
2 " 1" x 3" x 16 1/2"
2 " 1" x 3" x 16 1/4"
2 " 1" x 3" x 12 3/4"
2 " 1" x 2" x 16 1/2"
1 " 1/2" plywood 17" x 17"
1 " 1/2" plywood 11" x 17"

Materials Totals

Table

3" x 3" – 9' 2"
1" x 6" – 51' 8 3/4"
1" x 4" – 9' 7"

Chair

1" x 3" – 11' 7"
1" x 2" – 2' 9"
(Remainder as itemized above)

DINING TABLE AND CHAIRS

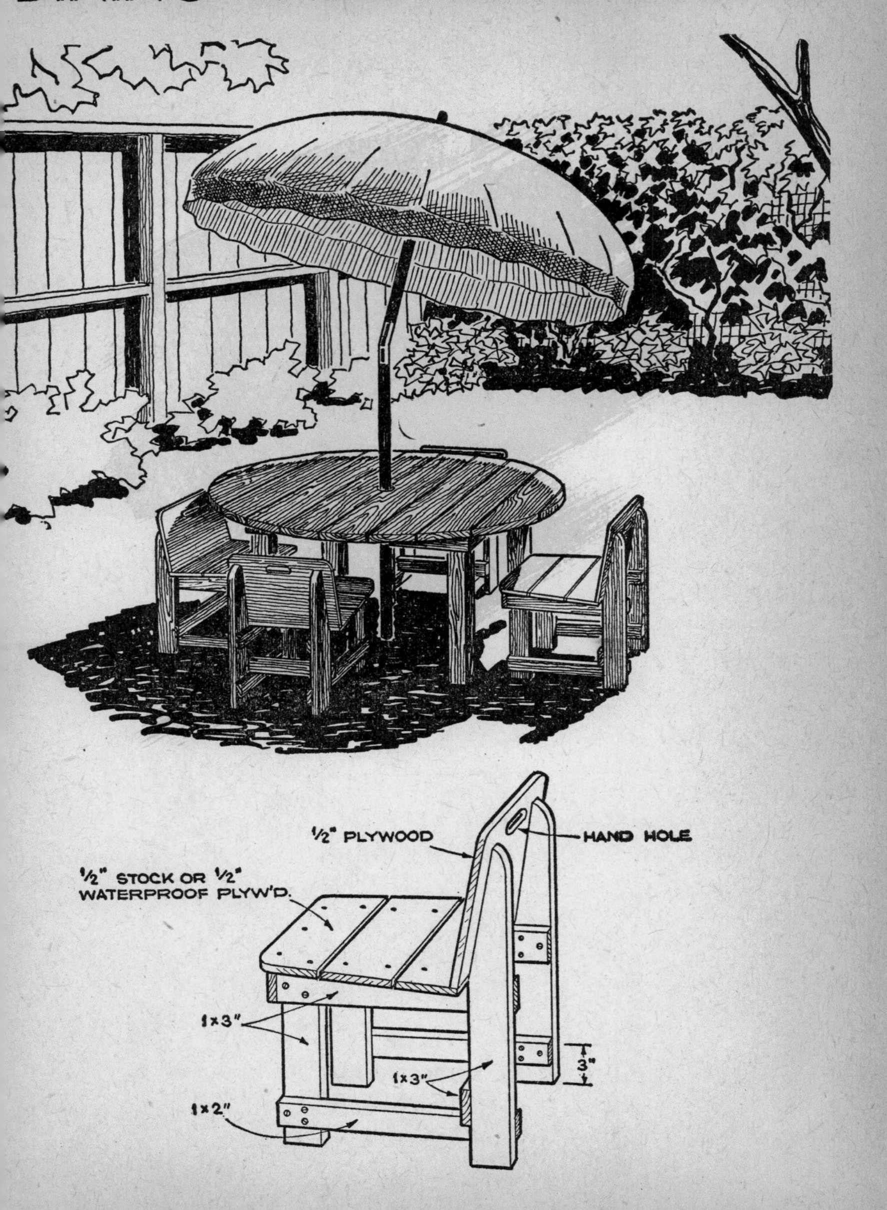

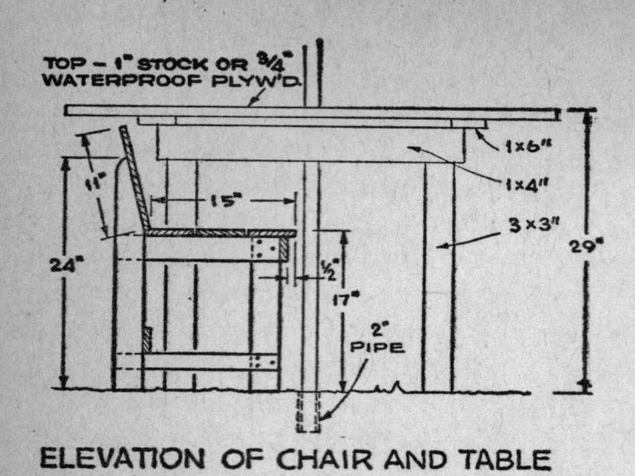

ELEVATION OF CHAIR AND TABLE

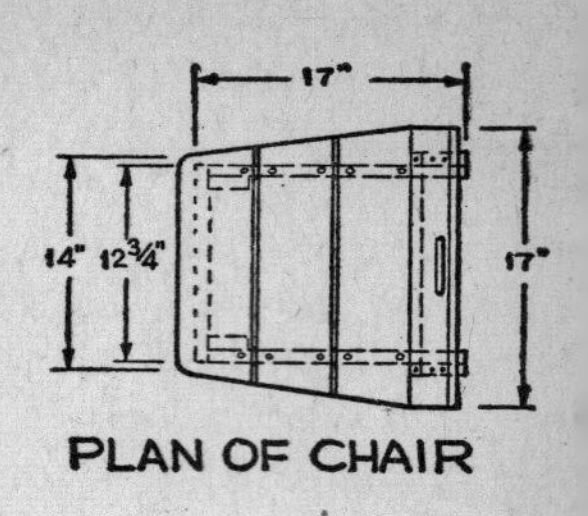

PLAN OF CHAIR

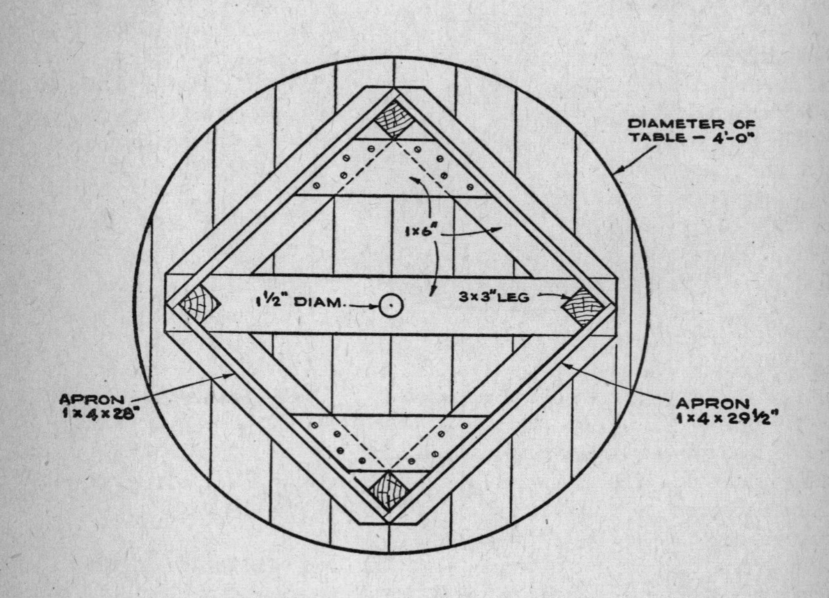

BOTTOM VIEW OF TABLE

GLIDER LAWN CHAIR

The rugged construction of this folding lawn chair makes it an ideal piece of furniture for lawn or beach. All wood used is 3/4" thick. All joints are bolted together with 3/16" x 2" stove bolts.

Cut the two front legs (5) to size. Then drill the five 3/16" holes as indicated. Next cut out the three cross bars for the front legs (2). Then, a dado 3/4" wide and 1/4" deep should be cut 3/4" in from each end of the crossbars. Holes measuring 3/16" are then drilled into each end of the cross bar and the three cross bars are attached to the legs with stove bolts. Note that the two upper cross bars go on the underside of the legs while the lower cross bar fits over the top.

The back legs (6) should be cut to size and the five holes drilled. The back legs are held together at the top by the two cross bars (1) which are 19 1/2" long, and by one cross bar (3) at the bottom measuring 21 1/2" in length. A dado 1/4" deep and 3/4" wide is cut at each end of each cross bar, as shown. Assemble the back legs and cross bars with stove bolts.

The arm and arm supports are also cut from 3/4" stock. The pattern for these pieces is given in 1" squares. Curved sections can be cut with a compass or coping saw and finished off with a rasp. The arm is attached to the arm support by three stove bolts run through both arm and arm support. Drill the holes in the arm first and place the arm in the correct position over the arm support. The location of the holes to be drilled in the support can then be accurately marked. Arm assemblies are secured to front and back legs by stove bolts with metal washers placed between the wood surfaces (see top page 159). Run the nut up until snug and test the movement of the joint to be sure it moves easily. Peen over the bolts to prevent the nut from working loose.

The bottom ends of the legs are held together by means of two tie rods (4). Each end of these rods is bolted to the legs with washers and bolts.

With the chair in the upright position, securely fasten with carpet tacks or staples a strip of 16" wide canvas to the second cross bar on the back legs. Bring it down and across and nail to the top cross bar on the front legs. Double the material under the tacks or staples.

Materials List

2 pcs. 3/4" x 1 5/16" x 19 1/2" (1)
3 " 3/4" x 1 5/16" x 22 7/8" (2)
1 " 3/4" x 1 5/16" x 21 1/2" (3)
2 " 3/4" x 1 1/8" x 17 7/8" (4)
2 " 3/4" x 1 3/8" x 35" (5)
2 " 3/4" x 1 3/8" x 48" (6)
2 " 3/4" x 3" x 14" (arm)
2 " 3/4" x 4" x 16" (arm support)
26 stove bolts and nuts 3/16" x 2"
16 bolt washers 3/16"

Materials Totals

3/4" x 1 5/16" — 10' 9 1/8"
3/4" x 1 1/8" — 2' x 11 3/4"
3/4" x 1 3/8" — 13' 10"
3/4" x 3" — 2' 4"
3/4" x 4" — 2' 8"
(Remainder as itemized above)

GLIDER LAWN CHAIR

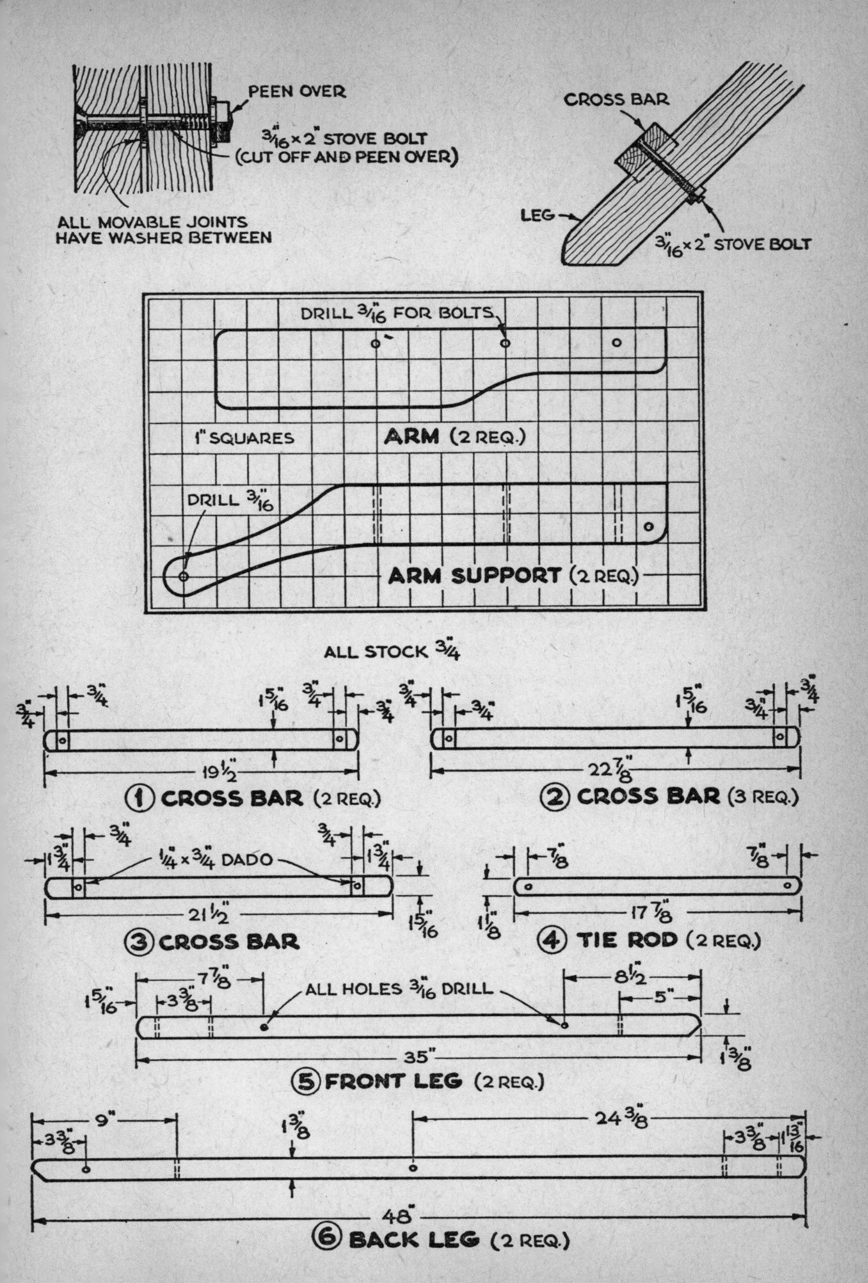
PEEN OVER
3/16 x 2" STOVE BOLT
(CUT OFF AND PEEN OVER)
ALL MOVABLE JOINTS
HAVE WASHER BETWEEN
CROSS BAR
LEG
3/16 x 2" STOVE BOLT
DRILL 3/16 FOR BOLTS
1" SQUARES
ARM (2 REQ.)
DRILL 3/16
ARM SUPPORT (2 REQ.)
ALL STOCK 3/4
19 1/2"
1 5/16"
① CROSS BAR (2 REQ.)
22 7/8"
② CROSS BAR (3 REQ.)
1/4" x 3/4" DADO
21 1/2"
③ CROSS BAR
17 7/8"
④ TIE ROD (2 REQ.)
ALL HOLES 3/16" DRILL
7 7/8"
8 1/2"
35"
⑤ FRONT LEG (2 REQ.)
9"
24 3/8"
48"
⑥ BACK LEG (2 REQ.)

SCREEN DOOR MADE FROM SHUTTERS

Old-fashion folding shutters can be easily converted into attractive, serviceable screen doors. The finished article, in fact, is somewhat superior to ordinary screen doors because it will keep out a good deal of summer heat as well as insects and will provide privacy within.

Of course it is necessary that the two shutters be as large or a little larger than the screen door is to be. The illustrations on the next page show that it is a relatively simple operation to construct such a door.

Shutters should be worked down until they fit easily in the doorway. Do not trim the sides of the shutters too much or the resulting seam between shutter and doorway will allow insects to enter.

Working from the inside of the shutters, attach a strip of 1″ x 2″ several inches up from the bottom of the shutters. Allow the strip to extend to about 2″ or 3″ from the sides of each shutter. Use wood screws to fasten this brace in place.

The screening can now be installed over the shutter openings. An unbroken strip of 1″ x 2″ should be attached along the bottom and top of the screening. These strips not only cover up the ends of the screening but they also brace the shutters so that they will no longer fold. A small 1″ x 2″ brace is also attached at about the midpoint over the joint between shutters.

All other edges of screening are covered by 1/2″ half round. Hinges of course are needed and should be put on so that the screen door will open out. A door handle or knob and lock or catch or spring are a matter of personal preference.

Materials List

3 pcs. 1″ x 2″ braces slightly shorter than total width of shutters
1 " 1″ x 2″ short brace
Screening
Half round molding
2 hinges
Door handle or knob
Lock, catch, or spring

SCREEN DOOR MADE FROM SHUTTERS

STORM DOOR

Select only well seasoned 6″ tongue-and-groove boards or random width boards and keep them in a warm dry place until the door has been assembled and painted. If exposed to damp weather, the boards will expand and later shrink, ending in a poor fitting job,

The dimensions for the door pictured in the illustration are 3″ x 6′ 8″, but these can be varied to suit individual requirements. Measure the door opening and use actual dimensions.

The assembly of the door begins with removing the groove from one of the boards with either a plane or saw. This board will be the first one on the hinge side of the door. All other boards are left with tongue and groove intact except the final board on the latch side of the door, which will have to have the tongue removed. If it is necessary to decrease the width of a board considerably to get a good fit, it is better to take an equal amount off both the first and last boards rather than all off one.

The boards are held in place by means of two 1″ x 6″ cleats. The top cleat should have its lower edge 5′ 9″ from the bottom of the door. The lower cleat should be 12″ from the bottom. Bevel the outside edges of the cleats and use flathead wood screws to fasten the boards. Be sure that all joints between boards are driven up tight and that the ends of the boards are level. As soon as all the boards are in place, cut a diagonal brace out of 3/4″ x 4″ stock to run between the cleats. The ends of this brace should fit snugly up against the cleats and it should be fastened to the door boards with screws.

The 8″ x 12″ window opening in the door is made 5′ from the bottom and should be positioned in the exact center of the door. Start the opening with a brace and bit, making a hole at each corner, and then connect the holes by cutting first with a keyhole saw and then, when the cut is large enough, with a crosscut saw. The slide for the glass consists of two pieces of 1/4″ x 3/4″ fastened 1/4″ above and below the window opening. Attached over these is a strip of 1/4″ x 1″ brought flush with the opening. The window glass slides in the 1/4″ recess at top and bottom.

Materials List

6 pcs. 6″ tongue-and-groove boards 6′ 8″
1 " 3/4 x 4″ x 6′
2 " 1″ x 6″ x 24″
2 " 1/4″ x 1″ x 1′ 11″
2 " 1/4″ x 1″ x 10″
2 " 1/4″ x 3/4″ x 1′ 11″
2 " 1/4″ x 3/4″ x 10″
1 " glass 81/2″ x 121/2″ double-strength or plate with finger grip)
2 butt strap hinges 13″

Materials Totals

6″ tongue-and-groove boards — 20 board feet
1″ 6″ — 4′
3/4″ x 4″ — 6′
1/4″ x 1″ — 5′ 6″
1/4″ x 1″ — 5′ 6″
(Remainder as itemized above)

STORM DOOR

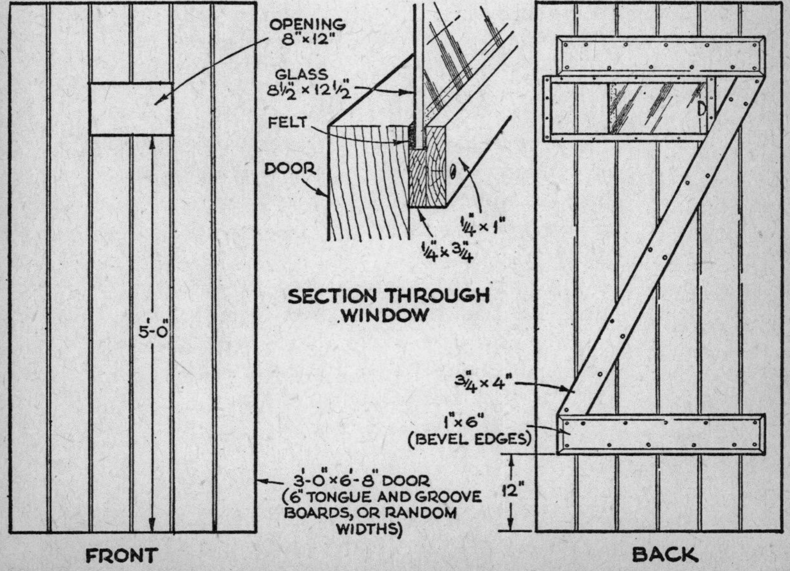
OPENING
8"×12"
GLASS
8½"×12½"
FELT
DOOR
¼"×1"
¼"×3¼"
SECTION THROUGH WINDOW
5'-0"
3¼×4"
1"×6"
(BEVEL EDGES)
12"
3'-0"×6'-8" DOOR
(6" TONGUE AND GROOVE
BOARDS, OR RANDOM
WIDTHS)
FRONT
BACK

SHUTTERS

Well-designed and constructed shutters can do much towards improving the outside appearance of a house. Besides adding a decorative note, they can make undersize windows appear larger. The four shutters shown in the accompanying illustration cover a wide range of architectural styling.

As shutters are exposed to the weather, it is best to make them out of woods such as cypress or redwood, which are highly resistant to decay. Non-corrosive screws should be used in the construction of the shutters and to fasten the hinges in place. The blind holdbacks used to hold the shutters open should also be of non-corrosive metals, as any rusting at this point would leave unsightly stains on the house siding. As is noted in the illustration, each shutter is fastened to the window trim with 3″ butt hinges.

Shutter No. 1 is a simple batten type suitable for almost and home. 1″ wide stock is used in the construction. The width will depend on the size of the window opening. Try, as far as possible, to have all the upright pieces more or less the same width.

Shutter No. 2 uses tongue-and-groove boards fastened together in the back of the shutter with lengths of strap iron.

Shutter No. 3 uses the same construction as No. 2, only here drop or novelty siding is used in place of the tongue-and-groove boards of the shutter above.

Shutter No. 4 is made of 3/4″ exterior plywood with 1/4″ x 1″ strips nailed diagonally across the face.

Shutters should be painted before installation to avoid the possibility of paint drippings on the house siding.

Materials List

No specific materials lists are given as windows vary in width. If you measure your windows and study the illustrations on the next page carefully, you should be able to easily figure out what material you need. Four 3″ butt hinges and two blind holdbacks are needed for each window; also hooks to hold the shutters shut if they are wanted to do more than merely serve as decoration.

SHUTTERS

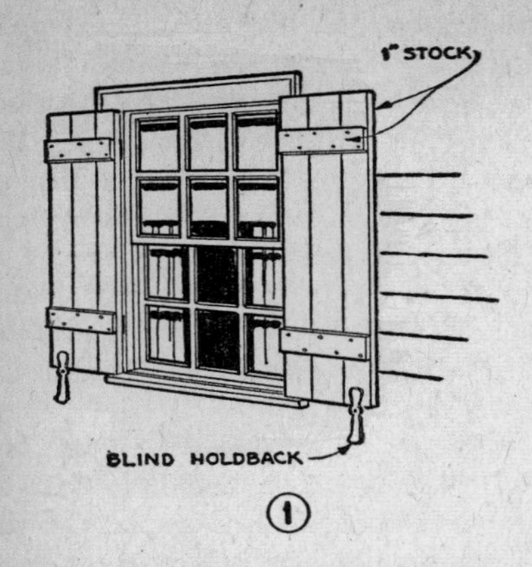

NOTE: BOTH SHUTTERS SHOWN ARE ATTACHED WITH 3" BUTT HINGES – SCREWED TO WINDOW TRIM AND BACK OF SHUTTER

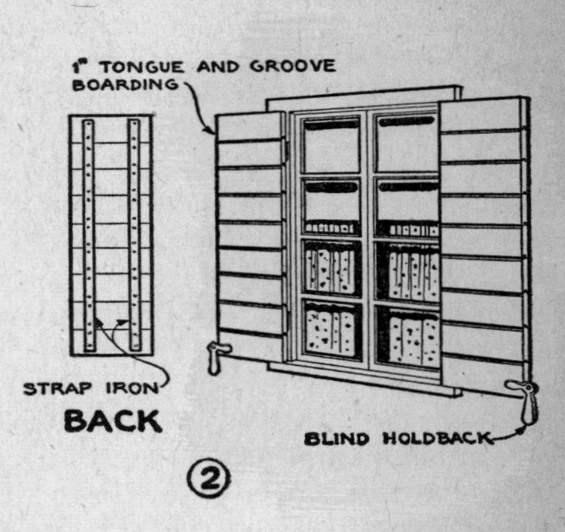

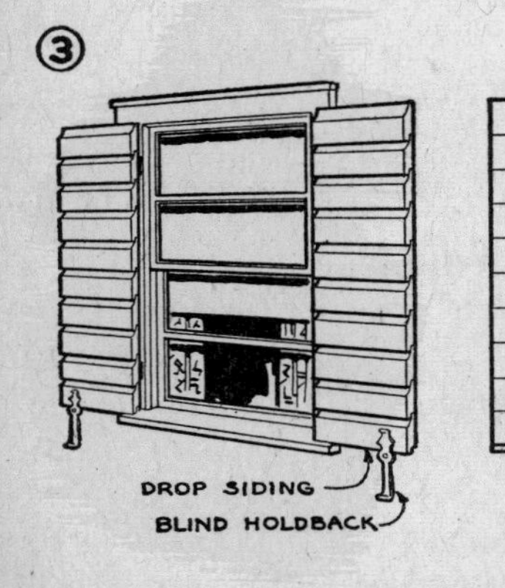

STRAP IRON

BACK

NOTE: BOTH SHUTTERS SHOWN ARE ATTACHED WITH 3" BUTT HINGES – SCREWED TO WINDOW TRIM AND BACK OF SHUTTER

PORCH SCREENS

The average outside porch can be made into a comfortable spot during the hot weather if it is tightly fitted with insect screening. The type of screening shown here can be easily made up and installed by one person. During the cold weather the panels can be removed and stored in a safe dry place.

The width of the screen frames will depend on the width of screening used. If 36″ screening is to be used, the outside width of each frame should be 39 1/2″. 2″ x 2″ supports should be installed 39 1/2″ apart running between the floor and top of the porch. The height of these, and the height of the screen panels or frames will depend on the height of the porch. Narrow panels will be required at the ends to bring the screening out to the corners.

The frames for the screens are made of 1 1/4″ x 2″ stock. Top and bottom pieces for 36″ screening should be 39 1/2″ long. Joints are made with corrugated fasteners but metal angle irons may be used to provide additional strength. The inside surface of the frames should be lined with strips of 3/4″ x 3/4″. Halfway up the frame an intermediate rail 3/4″ x 2″ is installed. The screening is fastened to the strips of 3/4″ x 3/4″ stock and the edges are covered with strips of 1/4″ x 3/4″ screen molding. 1/2″ quarter round molding can be used in place of the screen molding.

The screen frames are hung from a strip attached along the ceiling of the porch. Metal screen hangers are used for this purpose, and the screens are held closed with turn screws or metal catches.

Materials List

(For 36″ screening 7′ 6″ high)

2 pcs. 1 1/4″ x 2″ x 7′ 2 1/2″
2 " 1 1/4″ x 2″ x 39 1/2″
1 " 3/4″ x 2″ x 34 1/2″
2 " 3/4″ x 3/4″ x 7′ 2 1/2″
2 " 3/4″ x 3/4″ x 34 1/2″
2 " 3/4″ x 1/4″ screen molding 7′ 2 1/2″
3 " 3/4″ x 1/4″ screen molding 34 1/2″
1 " wire insect screening 36″ x 7′ 2 1/2″
2 metal screen hangers
1 catch

Materials Totals

1 1/4″ x 2″ — 21′
3/4″ x 3/4″ — 20′ 2″
3/4″ x 1/4″ screen molding 23′ 1/2″
(Remainder as itemized above)

PORCH SCREENS

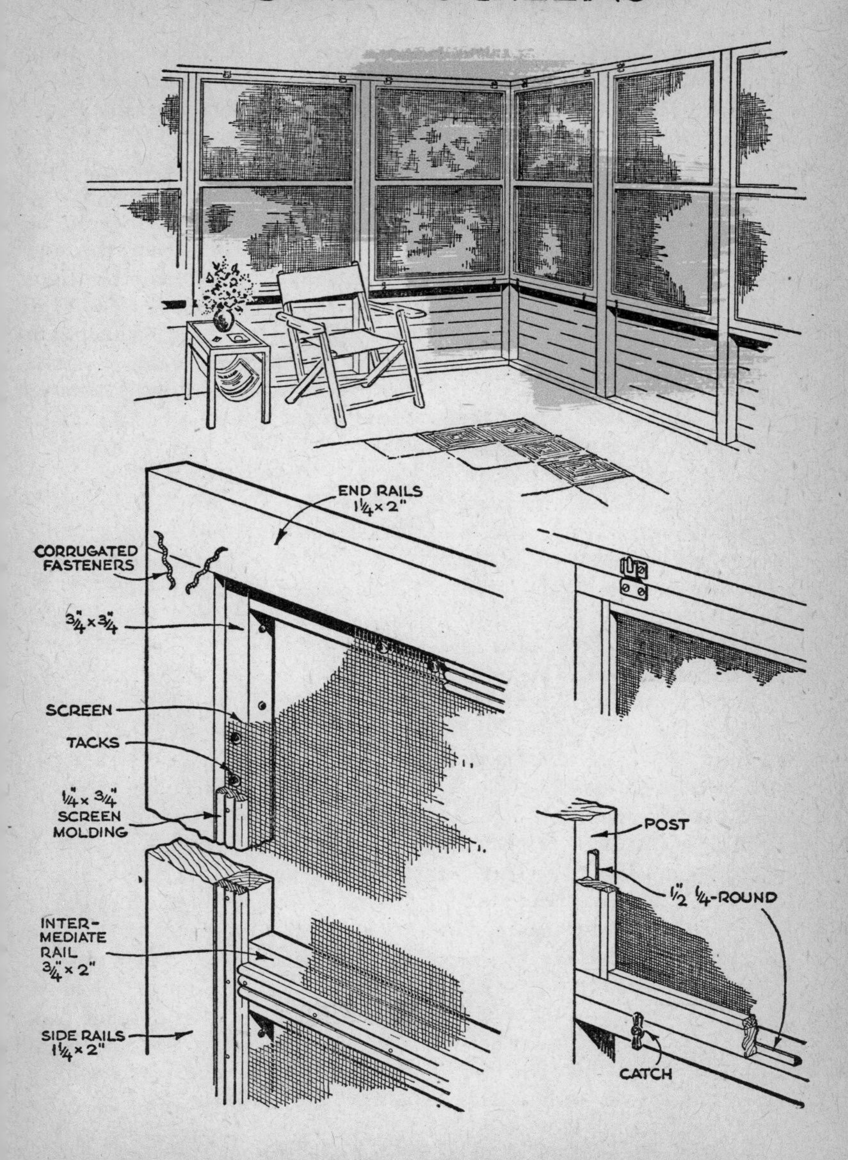

SIGNS

Anyone who has ever had to get out of his car on a stormy night to read an obscure house number will appreciate clear and conspicuous house signs.

Sign No. 1 can be used where the house is close to the road. A window close to the front door is preferable, and it would be helpful to leave a light burning near the window during waking hours.

Sign No. 2 can be used where the lawn runs close to the road. The post is made of 2″ x 2″ stock 2′ 6″ long. The end should be pointed and the top beveled slightly. A 1″ x 1″ x 5″ cleat is fastened to each side at the top of provide greater nailing area. The sign is made out of 1″ x 6″. Its length will depend on the number of letters to be placed on it. The rustic ends are made by cutting with a fine-toothed saw. The sign should be painted before metal or light-reflecting letters are installed on it.

Sign No. 3 has space for both name and house number. The two upright posts of 1″ x 2″ should be about 3′ 6″ long. The horizontal members are 1″ x 2″; their length depends on the size of panel required. The top horizontal piece should be set 1/2″ below the top of the uprights and the lower horizontal piece 10″ below this. The four corners are rounded off with a strip of 1/2″ quarter round. The top of the upright members can be rounded off with a rasp. The panel is made of 1/4″ exterior plywood 10″ wide. It is held in place with strips of 1/2″ quarter round on each side.

Sign No. 4 is attached to the house and placed where it will be illuminated. The plate is made of 1/2″ exterior plywood 4″ high; its length depends on the number of characters. Corners are rounded slightly. Paint the face white and the edges dark. Letters should be 2 1/2″ high in black.

Sign No. 5 is painted directly on concrete steps. The background should be painted white and, when this is dry, the numbers can be printed on. The easiest way to do this is to make a stencil first.

Sign No. 6 is the illuminated type. The legs are made of 1″ x 3″, 1″ x 1 3/4″, and 1″ x 2 1/4″. The recess formed by the middle piece carries the electric wire; it is closed in back by a 3/4″ x 2″ running from the bottom of the legs to the 1″ x 3″ of the back frame. The panel frame is made of 1″ x 3″, and the panel of 1/2″ exterior plywood about 26″ x 30″ but in any case 1/2″ shorter than the frame. The light cover is made of 1″ x 6″ with a 1″ x 4″ x 4″ block to hold the light socket. The socket must be a heavy-duty exterior type.

SIGNS

1. PAINTED WINDOW SIGN

(1) OUTLINE WITH CHALK ON OUTSIDE OF GLASS. USE STRAIGHTEGE AND MEASUREMENTS FOR LETTER GUIDE-LINES AND PANEL EDGE.
(2) PAINT NAME ON INSIDE OF GLASS USE LETTERING BRUSH AND BLACK ENAMEL.
(3) WHEN NAME IS DRY MASK BACK GROUND WITH DRAFTING OR MASKING TAPE. APPLY YELLOW ENAMEL WITH CLOTH BALL DAUBER.

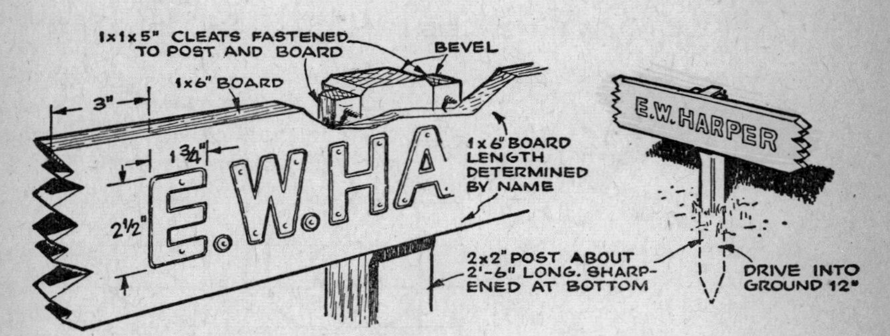

NOTE: METAL OR LIGHT REFLECTING LETTERS ARE AVAILABLE FOR THIS PURPOSE OR LETTERS CAN BE PAINTED ON CONTRASTING BACKGROUND

2. NAME SIGN

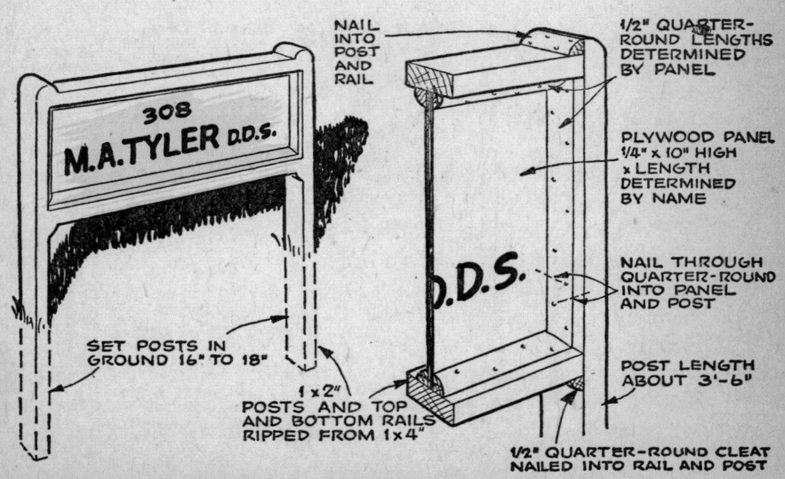

3. NUMBER & NAME SIGN

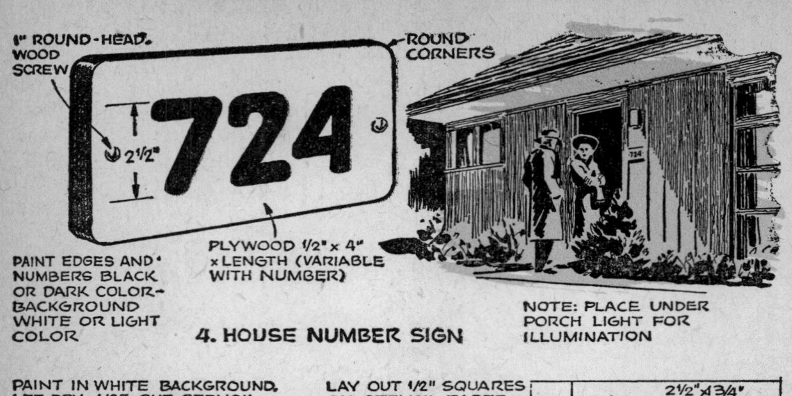

4. HOUSE NUMBER SIGN

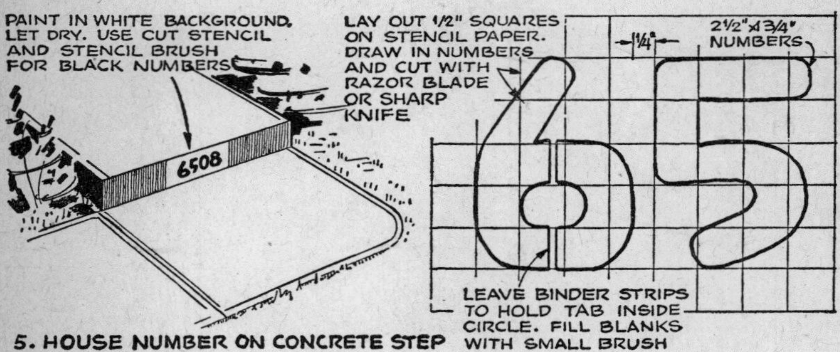

5. HOUSE NUMBER ON CONCRETE STEP

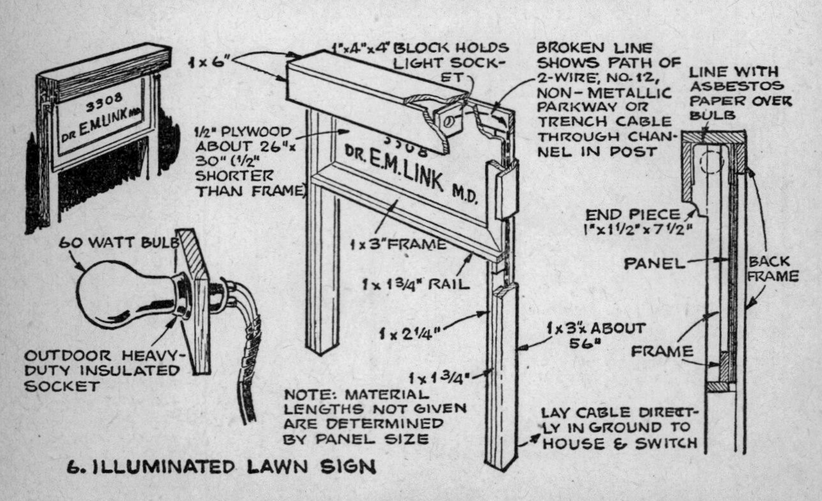

6. ILLUMINATED LAWN SIGN

GARDEN GATES

Attractive gates can add just as much to the appearance of a home as a fence or border. The proper selection of a gate depends primarily on the construction of the fence. As is the case with the fence, the wood portions of a gate that extend below the ground should be treated with a wood preservative, such as creosote, to prevent decay. Hardware and fasteners should be of non-corrosive metal. The lamp shown with gate No. 1 should be purchased where you can find one. Follow the directions for sign No. 5 on page 168 for connecting to electricity.

Materials List

Gate No. 1

2 pcs. 6″ x 6″ x 48″ (plus distance from grade to frost line)
1 " 1″ x 6″ x 46 1/2″
2 " 1″ x 6″ x 34″
2 " 1″ x 4″ x 36″
6 " 1″ x 3″ x 48″
1 " 1″ x 3″ x 34″
1 " 1″ x 2″ x 5 1/2″
2 butt hinges
1 shutter bar latch

Gate No. 2

2 pcs. 6″ x 6″ x 40″ (plus distance from grade to frost line)
3 " 1″ x 8″ x 45″
1 " 1″ x 6″ x 46 1/2″
2 " 1″ x 6″ x 34″
2 " 1″ x 3″ x 45″
1 " 1″ x 2″ x 3″
2 T hinges
1 cabinet bar latch

Gate No. 3

2 pcs. 6″ x 6″ x 47″ (plus depth from grade to frost line)
1 " 1″ x 6″ x 46 1/2″
1 " 1″ x 3″ x 36″
2 " 1″ x 3″ x 34″
1 " 1″ x 2″ x 2″
1 " 3/4″ x 8″ x 15″
4 " 1/2″ x 1 1/2″ x 42″
4 " 1/2″ x 1 1/2″ x 37″
2 butt hinges 3″
1 shutter bar

Gate No. 4

2 pcs. 6″ x 6″ x 47″ (plus depth from grate to frost line)
1 " 1″ x 6″ x 47″
1 " 2″ x 4″ x 39″
1 " 2″ x 4″ x 33″
1 " 2″ x 4″ x 32″
2 T hinges
1 square spring bolt

Materials Totals

Gate No. 1

1″ x 6″ — 9′ 6 1/2″
1″ x 4″ — 6′
1″ x 3″ — 26′ 10″
(Remainder as itemized above)

Gate No. 2

1″ x 8″ — 11′ 3″
1″ x 6″ — 9′ 6 1/2″
1″ x 3″ — 7′ 6″
(Remainder as itemized above)

Gate No. 3

1″ x 3″ — 8′ 8″
1/2″ x 1 1/2″ — 26′ 4″
(Remainder as itemized above)

Gate No. 4

2″ x 4″ — 5′ 5″
(Remainder as itemized above)

GARDEN GATES

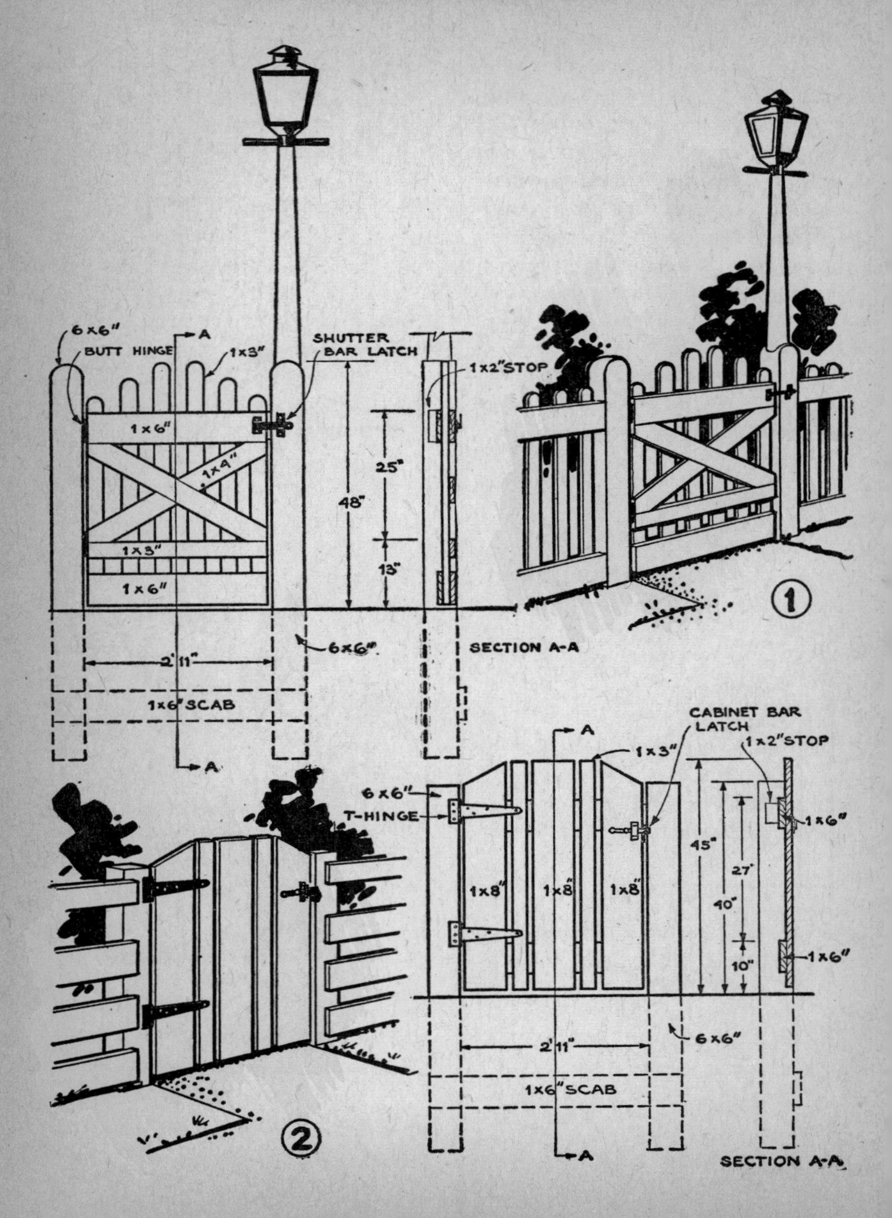

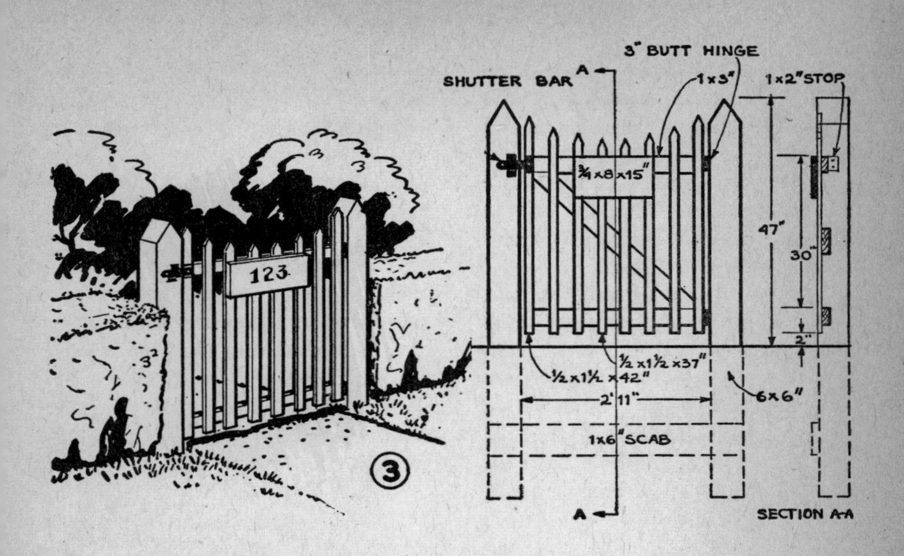
3" BUTT HINGE
SHUTTER BAR
A
1x3"
1x2" STOP
3/4x8x15"
123
47"
30"
2"
1/2x1 1/2x37"
1/2x1 1/2x42"
2'11"
6x6"
1x6" SCAB
A
SECTION A-A
3

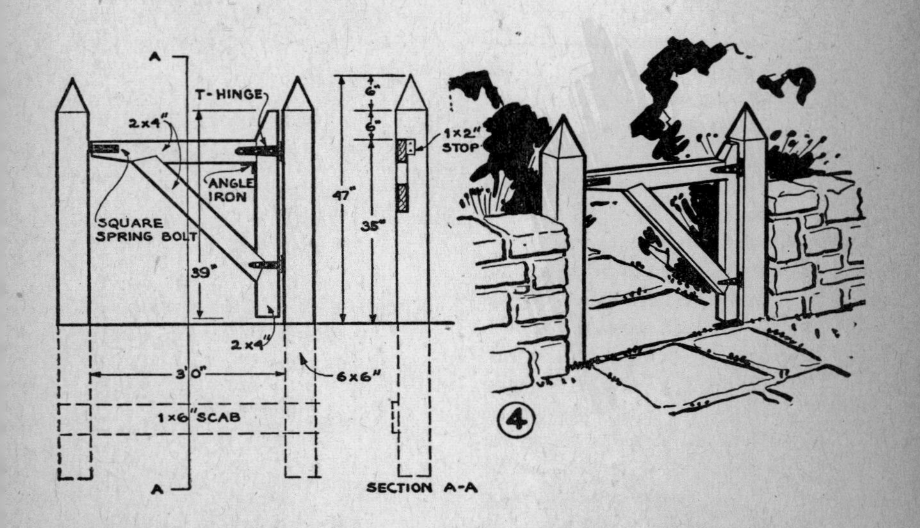
A
T-HINGE
2x4"
6"
6"
1x2" STOP
ANGLE IRON
SQUARE SPRING BOLT
47"
35"
39"
2x4"
3'0"
6x6"
1x6" SCAB
A
SECTION A-A
4

FENCES

Fences around a house have often been compared with frames around a picture. They help tie the house and grounds into a compact unit. And because of its importance, as much care should go into the selection of the right style of fence as for any architectural detail of the house.

The basic construction of the four fences shown in the accompanying illustration is similar. 4″ x 4″ posts are sunk into the ground below frost level. The exact spacing of the posts will depend on the total length of the fence, since it is desirable to have the posts spaced an equal distance apart. Spacing can be anywhere from 6′ to 10′—posts 8′ apart are ideal. The portion of the post that is underground should be treated with creosote or some other wood preservative to prevent decay and insect damage to the wood. This treated portion of the posts should extend at least 2″ above the grade.

As it is difficult to dig all the holes the same depth, set the posts into the holes and then run a level line across them so that the tops can all be cut off flush and level with each other. Notice that the top of each post is cut at a slight bevel to allow water to flow off. A trench will have to be dug between the holes for the gate posts so that the 1″ x 6″ scab that connects the lower ends of these posts together can be installed. This member must also be treated with a wood preservative. As the earth is put back around the posts, use a level so you will be sure that they are perfectly upright. Do not sink the posts into concrete unless you are unable, because of rocks or a ledge, to dig a hole of sufficient depth.

Once the posts are in position and cut to equal height, mark down from the top the location of the horizontal members of the fence. Put these parts into position, checking them with a level before nailing them in place. It is a wise idea to paint the lower portions of the fence before they are installed because once in place they are difficult to get at with a brush.

Make certain that the over-all construction is rugged and that a sufficient number of nails are used. In Northern states, the fence should be set far enough back from the road to prevent damage from snow plows or other equipment.

Materials List

Fence No. 1

(By 8′ sections)

4 pcs. 1″ x 6″ x 8′
1 " 1″ x 8″ x 8′
2 " 1″ x 4″ x 41″
2 posts 4″ x 4″ (length is figured by adding below-ground depth of frost line to 42″)

Fence No. 2

(By 8′ sections)

4 pcs. 1″ x 6″ x 8′
2 posts 4″ x 4″ (length is figured by adding below-ground depth of frost line to 40″)

Fence No. 3

(By 10′ sections)

7 pcs. 2″ x 4″ x 33″
1 " 2″ x 4″ x 10′
1 " 2″ x 4″ x 9′ 8″
2 " 2″ x 4″ x 47″
4 " 2″ x 4″ x 34″
2 posts 4″ x 4″ (length is figured by adding below-ground depth of frost line to 39″)

Fence No. 4

(By 8′ sections)

2 pcs. 2″ x 4″ x 8′
2 posts 4″ x 4″ (length is figured by adding below-ground depth to 51″)
Random width 1″ boarding cut in 54″ lengths

Materials Totals

Fence No. 1

1″ x 6″ – 32″
1″ x 4″ – 6′ 10″
(Remainder as itemized above)

Fence No. 2

1″ x 6″ – 32′
(Remainder as itemized above)

Fence No. 3

2″ x 4″ – 54′ 1″
(Remainder as itemized above)

Fence No. 4

2″ x 4″ – 16′
(Remainder as itemized above)

FENCES

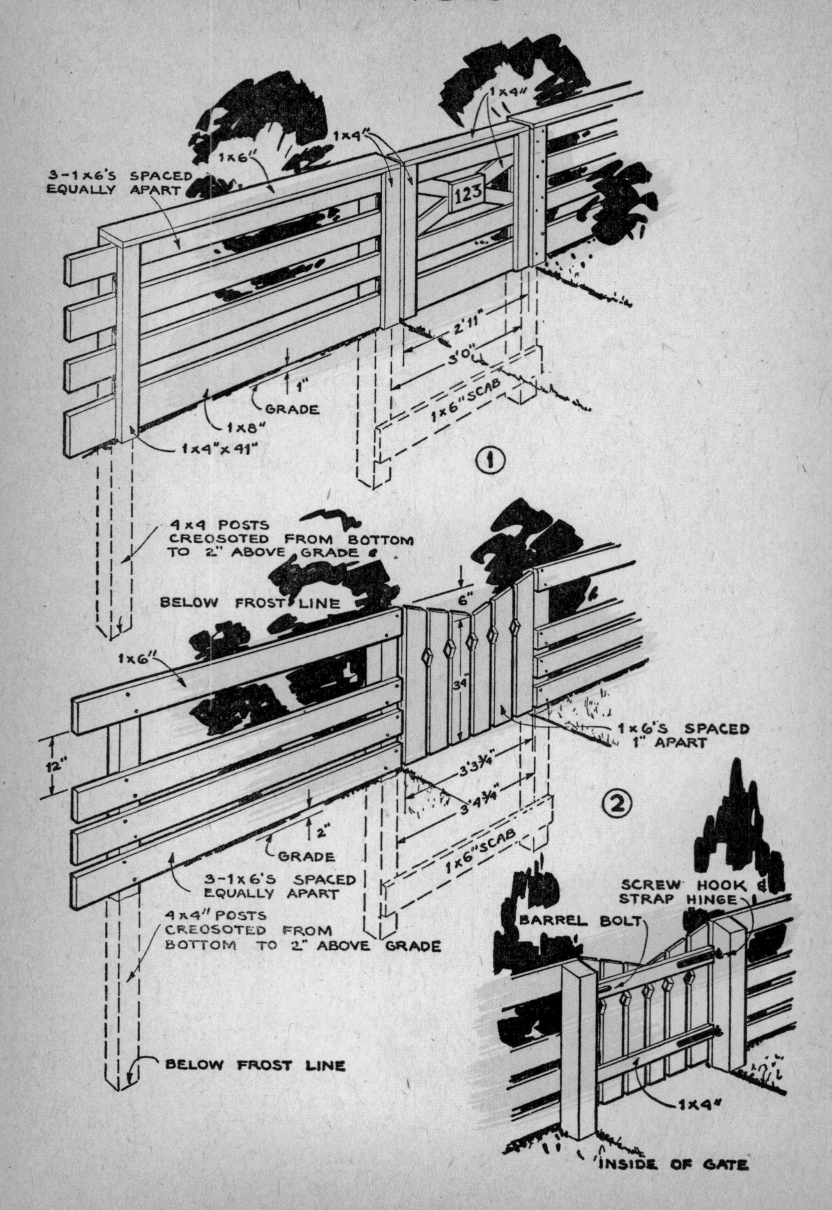
1x4"
1x6"
1x4"
3-1x6's SPACED EQUALLY APART
123
2'11"
3'0"
1x6" SCAB
1"
GRADE
1x8"
1x4"x41"
1
4x4 POSTS CREOSOTED FROM BOTTOM TO 2" ABOVE GRADE
BELOW FROST LINE
6"
1x6"
34"
1x6's SPACED 1" APART
12"
3'3¾"
3'4¾"
2
2"
1x6" SCAB
GRADE
3-1x6's SPACED EQUALLY APART
SCREW HOOK & STRAP HINGE
BARREL BOLT
4x4" POSTS CREOSOTED FROM BOTTOM TO 2" ABOVE GRADE
BELOW FROST LINE
1x4"
INSIDE OF GATE

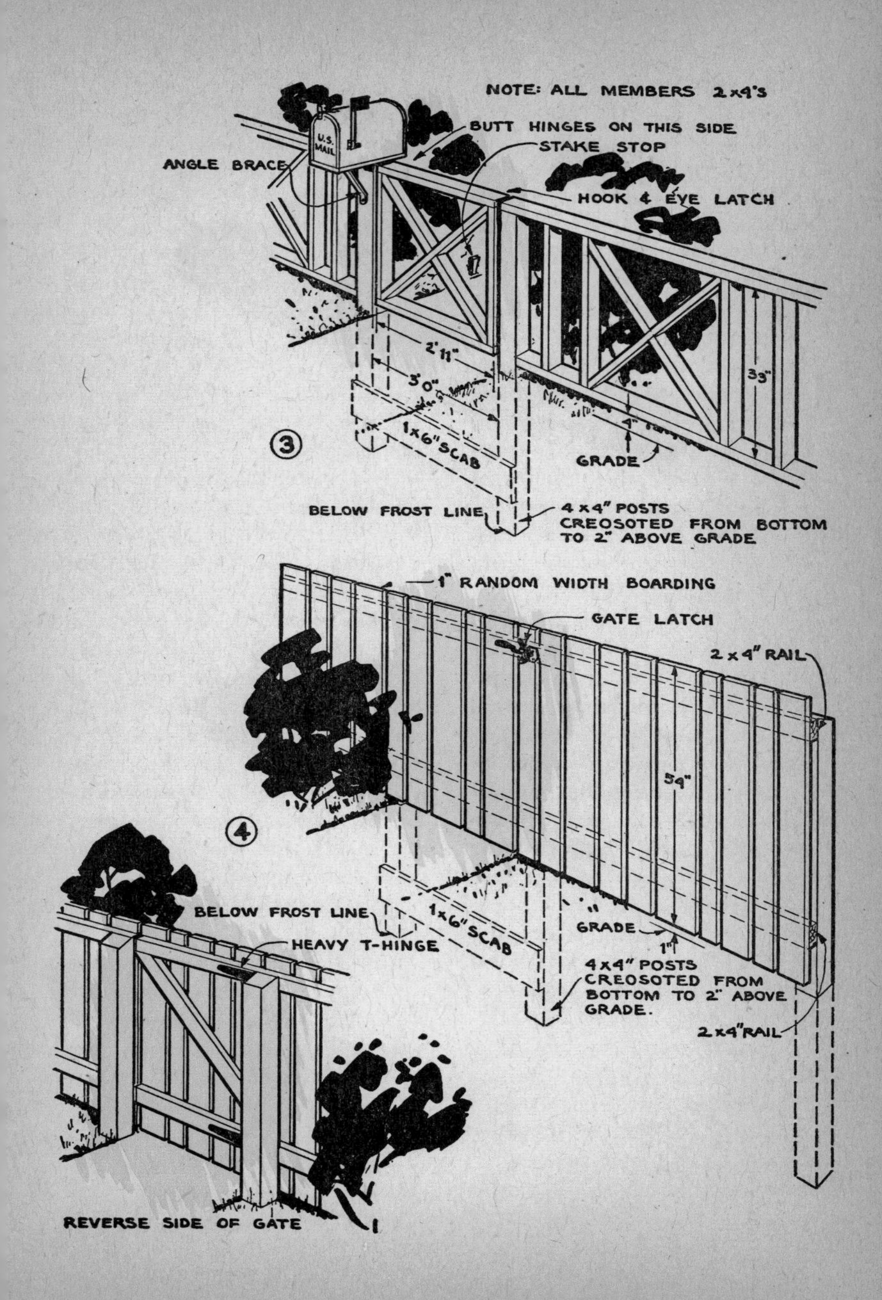

NOTE: ALL MEMBERS 2x4'S
BUTT HINGES ON THIS SIDE
STAKE STOP
ANGLE BRACE
HOOK & EYE LATCH
U.S. MAIL
2'11"
3'0"
33"
4"
1x6" SCAB
GRADE
③
BELOW FROST LINE
4x4" POSTS CREOSOTED FROM BOTTOM TO 2" ABOVE GRADE
1" RANDOM WIDTH BOARDING
GATE LATCH
2x4" RAIL
59"
④
BELOW FROST LINE
HEAVY T-HINGE
1x6" SCAB
GRADE
1"
4x4" POSTS CREOSOTED FROM BOTTOM TO 2" ABOVE GRADE.
2x4" RAIL
REVERSE SIDE OF GATE

OUTDOOR FIREPLACE

The size and depth for the excavation, fill, and foundation are given in the Foundation Detail (first illustration). Fine diagonal lines in the drawings indicate common bricks; diagonal cross-hatching indicates fire bricks.

Lay out the first course of bricks as shown in the Foundation Detail. Fill the cavity in the center with gravel and mortar, and then lay one more course. Lay fire bricks along the bottom of the fireplace opening, bringing them flush with the third course of bricks along the front of the opening. Extend the two side walls and back 12″ up from the bottom of the opening, lining them with fire brick.

12″ from the base, the fire-brick back begins to slope forward, while the side walls and common-brick portion of the back wall continue upward in a straight line. The inside surface of the back wall slopes forward until it is 4′ 0″ from the fireplace foundation; it is also 11″ out from the common bricks of the back wall, forming a throat 8″ x 3′ 6″. The space between the fire bricks and the common bricks can be filled with small stones and mortar. You can save time and trouble by making a rough wood pattern or form for the fire bricks to follow.

Bring the side walls up 2′ 10″ from the bottom of the fireplace opening and then install two angle irons — measuring 3″ x 4″ x1/4″ x 54″ — between these side walls to support the front breast of the fireplace. The back of the fireplace should be carried up so that the 11″ wide smoke shelf can be formed. Make this shelf just as flat as you can get it.

The rest of the masonry is all common brick from here on out. No more fire bricks will be required. At the point where the angle irons are installed, the side walls of the fireplace start coming together so that 18″ above the smoke shelf, the side walls are 15″ apart. This makes an opening 11″ x 15″. Smooth the side walls with mortar.

Three courses of bricks are built up on the front of the fireplace and are supported by the angle irons. After the third course, a 4″ recess is formed in the front to carry a 10″ mantle.

The brickwork for the chimney should extend 9′ 4″ above the fireplace foundation. The bricks at the top of the chimney should be capped with mortar and the mortar sloped so that water will drain off the masonry. Allow the masonry a week to harden before removing the wood forms from the inside, and then give it another week before building a fire.

The cabinets on each side of the fireplace are 3′ 1″ deep and 2′ 10″ wide. Their height, without the top covering of 2″ planks, should be 4′ 1″ from the fireplace foundation. These cabinets are fastened to the fireplace masonry with bolts set into the mortar joints during the construction of the fireplace.

The cabinets are made with a framework of 2″ x 4″ covered with 1″ and 2″ boards. Don't install the top covering of boards until the cabinets are in place and the fireplace mantle has been fastened in position. The mantle extends out along the edge of each cabinet and forms the first board of the top. After this is in place, the remaining boards can be installed.

As the cabinets will be exposed to the weather, non-corrosive hardware, such as brass, should be used for bolt, striker, and hinges. The cabinets can be covered with several coats of spar varnish or linseed oil thinned with turpentine. Either finish will preserve the wood from decay, though the best practice is to use a decay-resistant wood, such as redwood or cypress.

Materials List

Foundation

14 cubic feet of cinder or gravel fill
2 3/4 bags of cement
2/5 cubic yard of gravel or 14 cubic feet of ready-mixed concrete
1/5 cubic yard of sand

Fireplace

5 bags of cement
4 bags of hydrated lime
1 cubic yard of sand or 25 cubic feet of ready-mixed mortar
1700 common bricks
200 fire bricks
3 lbs. of fireclay (add 25% Portland cement)
2 angle irons 3″ x 4″ x 1/4″ x 54″
1 mantle 2″ x 10″ x 12′

Cabinets

8 pcs. 2″ 8″ x 34″
8 " 2″ x 4″ x 49″
2 " 2″ x 4″ x 42″
8 " 2″ x 4″ x 35 1/2″
2 " 2″ x 4″ x 34″
4 " 2″ x 4″ x 33 3/4″
4 " 2″ x 4″ x 22 3/4″
18 " 1″ x 8″ x 49″
2 " 1″ x 3″ x 38″
4 " 1″ x 3″ x 30
8 carriage bolts and nuts 1/4″ x 6″
4 butt hinges 3″
2 barrel bolts 4″
2 strap irons 1/16″ x 1″

Materials Totals

2″ x 8″ — 22′ 8″
2″ x 4″ — 87′ 8″
1″ x 8″ — 73′ 6″
1″ x 3″ — 16′ 4″
8 bags of cement
1 1/5 cubic yards of sand
(Remainder as itemized above)

OUTDOOR FIREPLACE

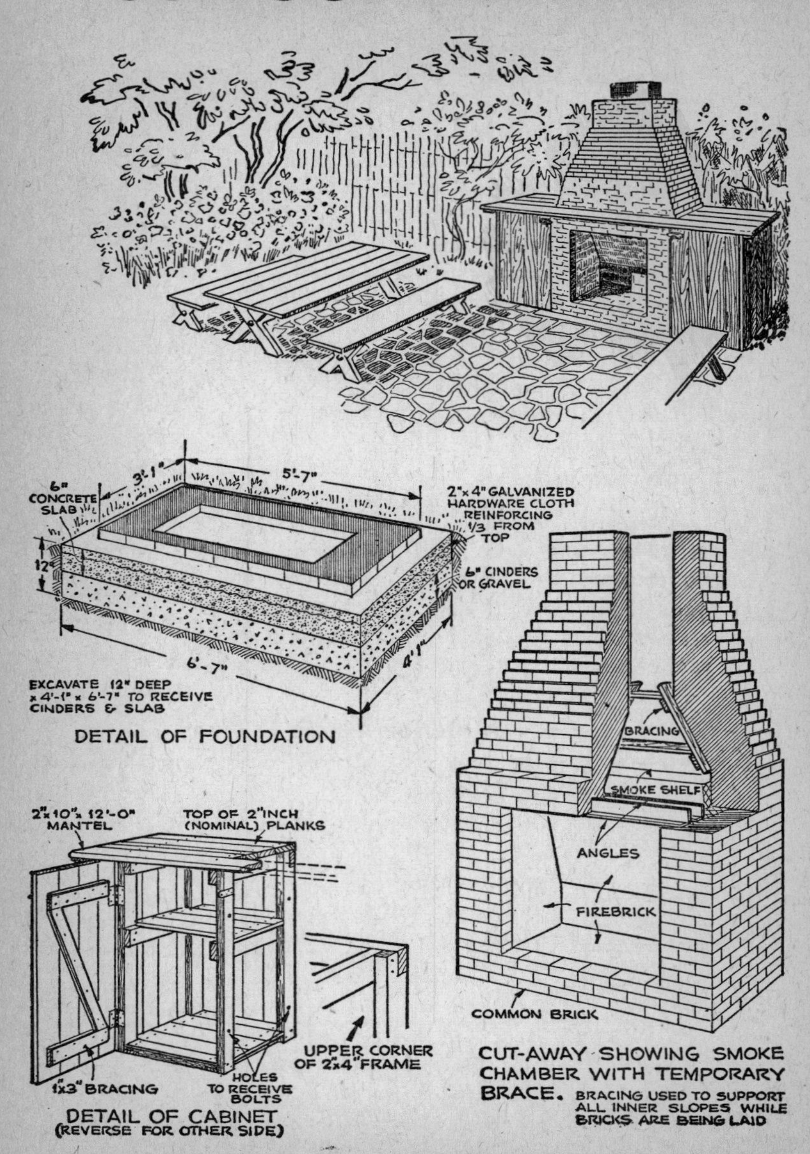

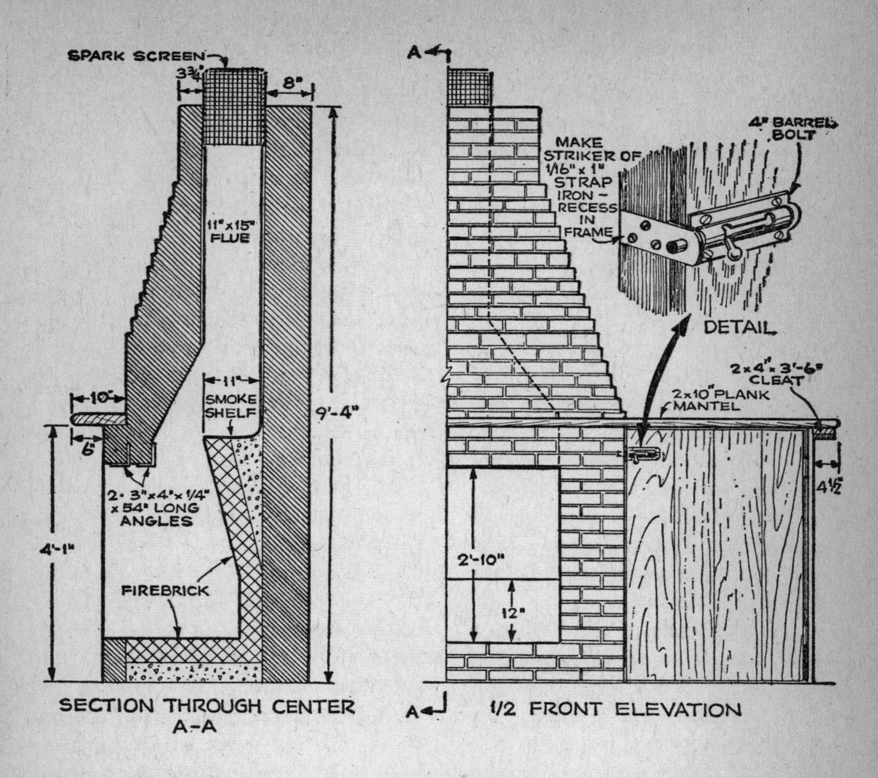

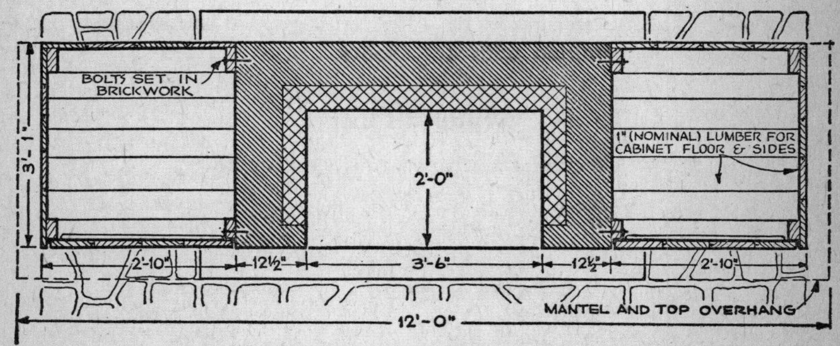

PLAN - SECTION

TWO-WALL BARBECUE

This simple two-wall barbeque will help transform any yard or lawn into a real recreation spot for the family and friends.

Place the front opening of the fireplace so that it faces in the direction of local prevailing winds. This will prevent smoke from getting in everyone's eyes.

Step 1: Make an excavation 12″ deep and 41″ x 45″. Pour in 6″ of gravel or cinders, tamping it down so it forms a compact base. Now pour in 6″ of concrete and bring to a level surface. The concrete is made by mixing 1 part Portland cement, 2 3/4 parts sand, and 4 parts gravel. Allow this base to set for several days before starting the brickwork.

Step 2: The walls of the barbeque are made of common bricks with an inner lining of fire bricks. Common bricks are laid in a mortar made with 1 part cement and 3 parts sand. Mix only the amount of mortar you can use in a half-hour. The bricks should be soaked in water or sprinkled with a garden hose before use. Mortar joints should be about 1/2″ thick; this can be varied so the brickwork will come out even. Be sure that all vertical and horizontal joints are thoroughly packed with mortar.

Step 3 shows the proper arrangement of the bricks. Note that the vertical joints in one row never come directly in line with those in the rows above and below it. You will need six courses, or rows, of bricks to get the proper height. The fire bricks on the inside surface should be fastened in place with fireclay, a heat-resistant type of mortar used on the inside surfaces of fireplaces and furnaces. The fire-brick lining stops one course below the common bricks and the resulting recess makes a support for the three 12″ x 25″ metal grilles.

Allow masonry ten days to two weeks to harden before building a fire. Never put out a fire in the barbeque with water because this sudden change of temperature would crack the masonry.

Materials List

8 cubic feet cinders or gravel for fill
8 " " concrete
20 " " sand
20 " " gravel
1/4 bag aggregate for cement mix
2 lbs. fireclay
200 common bricks (approximate)
70 fire bricks (approximate)
3 metal grilles 12″ x 25″

TWO-WALL BARBECUE

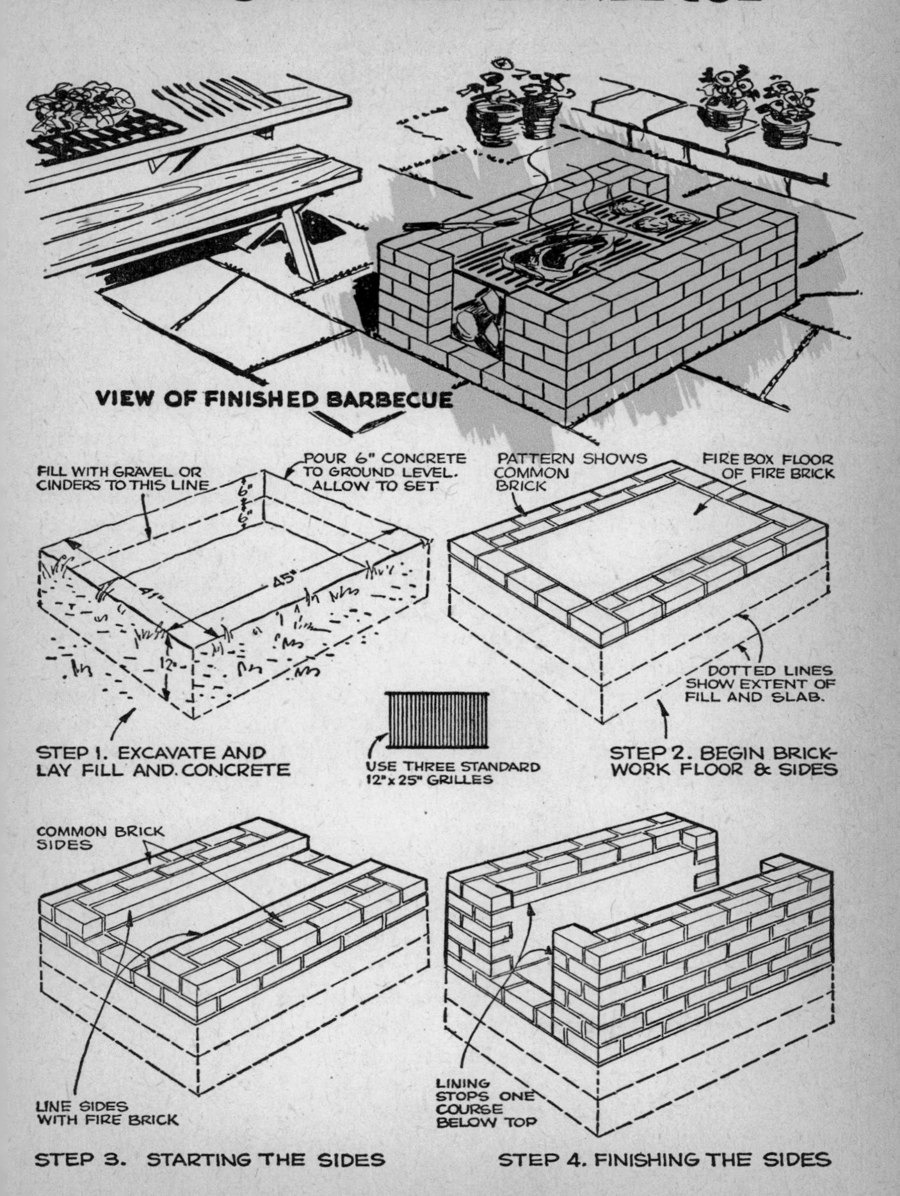

THREE-WALL BARBECUE

Although designed to be built of local stone, this barbeque can also be made out of bricks or concrete blocks. The position of the opening and the construction of the base are the same as those for the two-wall barbeque. Mortar for stone is the same as for bricks or blocks—one part cement and three parts sand. Brush stones clean before applying the mortar and make sure all joints are thoroughly packed. Avoid using very large stones as they are difficult to handle and hard to hold in place.

Build the four walls to a height of about 1′ 3″ with a cavity in the middle. This can be filled with stone and concrete and leveled off at the top. Build up the side and back walls another 10″, leaving enough room on the inside surfaces for a lining of fire bricks about 4″ thick. Imbed a 3/8″ section of pipe in each side wall to support the spit. Pour a 3″ bed of concrete at the base of the pit and give this a slight downward slope. Line the three inside wall surfaces with fire brick.

Then carry the rear wall up another 10″ to 12″ and place two hooks in it directly above the last course of fire brick to serve as fasteners for the folding metal grille. The grille assembly consists of two standard 12″ x 25″ grilles fastened together with wire hinges.

The support for the spit is a 5/16″ metal rod that is bent at the top and fitted down into the 3/8″ pipe. If you do not possess the equipment for bending the rod to shape, it can be done for you at small expense by a forge or a garage specializing in body repair work.

Materials List

7 cubic feet cinders or gravel for fill
7 " " concrete
18 " " sand
18 " " gravel
1/4 bag aggregate for cement mix
1 lb. fireclay
60 fire bricks (approximate number)
8 cubic yards stone
2 metal grilles 12″ x 25″
2 3/8″-I.D (inner diameter) pipe, with cap, 18″
2 5/16″-rods 26″

THREE-WALL BARBECUE

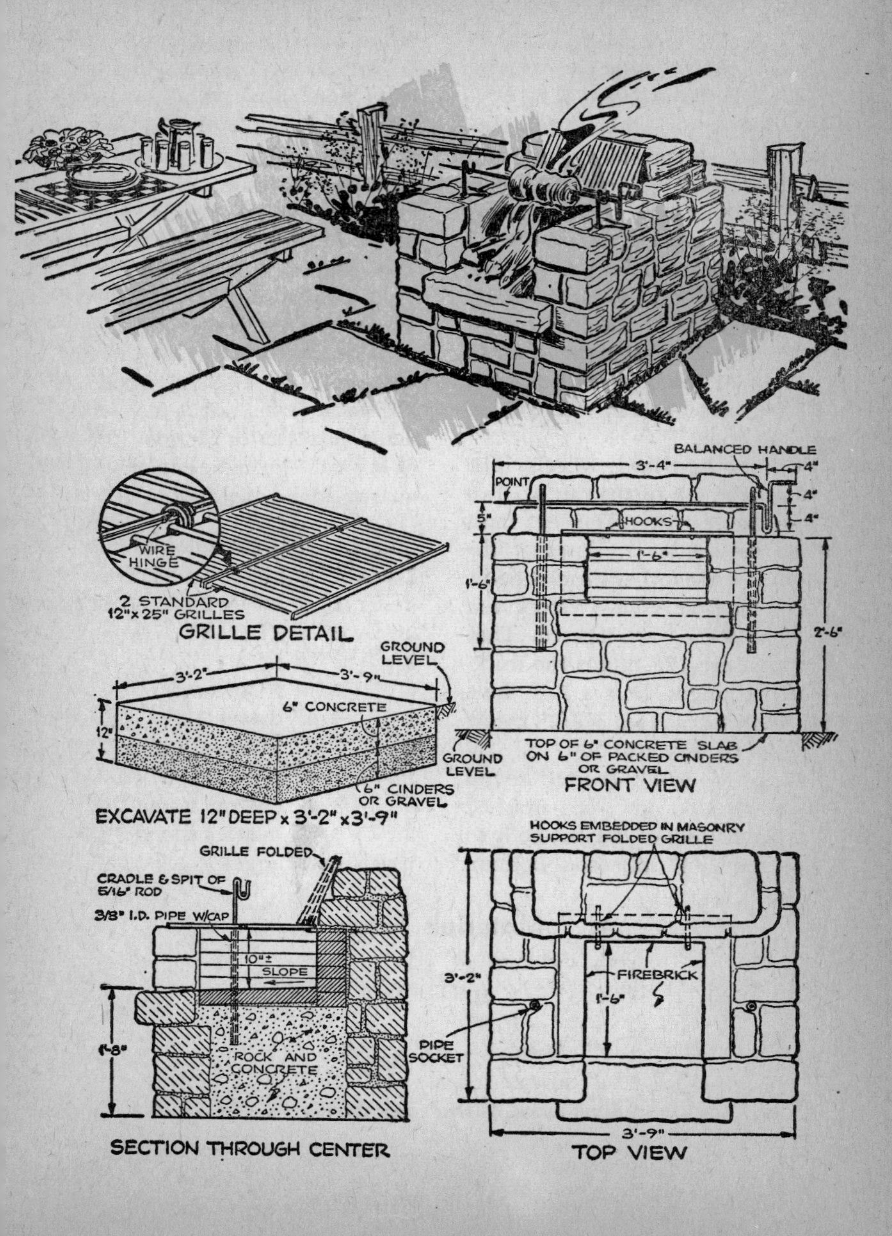

OUTDOOR SERVING CART

This little cart makes a handy serving table and a place to store articles used either on the porch or lawn.

The body of the cart is made out of 1" x 12" stock. The sides of the cart body measure 27" and the ends 18 1/2" long. Assemble these pieces with butt joints, using flathead wood screws. The two rear legs of the cart are cut from 2" x 3" stock 18" long. The bottom ends of the legs are tapered down to 2". Fasten the legs into the corners of the body with the top of each leg coming flush with the top of the cart body.

The front legs have wheels. The hinges for the top of the cart are fastened to the leg tops. The legs must therefore be set the thicknes of the hinges below the top of the cart body. Legs are cut from 2" x 3" stock and their bottom ends are tapered. They should measure 17" minus the thickness of the hinges. Bore a 7/8" hole in the center of each leg 3 1/2" below the bottom of the cart body.

A strip of 3/4" quarter round molding should now be attached around the bottom of the cart body to support the 1/4" plywood bottom. Notch out the plywood so it will fit around the legs and fasten it in place. Make each wheel out of two pieces of 1" stock cut to a 5" diameter. Glue these together, placing wood grain at right angles. Now drill the holes for the 3/4" wood dowels, slip 3/4" dowel through the holes in the front legs, and slip the wheels over the ends. Use finishing nails to secure the wheels to the dowel.

Make the top for the cart out of two pieces of 1/2" plywood 20" x 25" each. If the cart is to be left outdoors, use exterior plywood. The sides of the cart top can be edged with 3/4" quarter round molding.

Materials List

2 pcs. 1" x 12" x 18 1/2"
2 " 1" x 12" x 25"
2 " 2" x 3" x 18"
2 " 2" x 3" x 17"
4 " 1" x 5" (wheels)
1 " 3/4" dowel 21"
2 " 1/2" plywood 20" x 25"
1 " 1/4" plywood 17" x 25"
6 " 3/4" quarter round 20"
2 " 3/4" quarter round 13"
1 pair butt hinges

Materials Totals

1" x 12" — 7' 3"
2" x 3" — 5' 10"
1" x 5" — 1' 8"
1/2" plywood — 40" x 25"
3/4" quarter round — 12' 2"
(Remainder as itemized above)

OUTDOOR SERVING CART

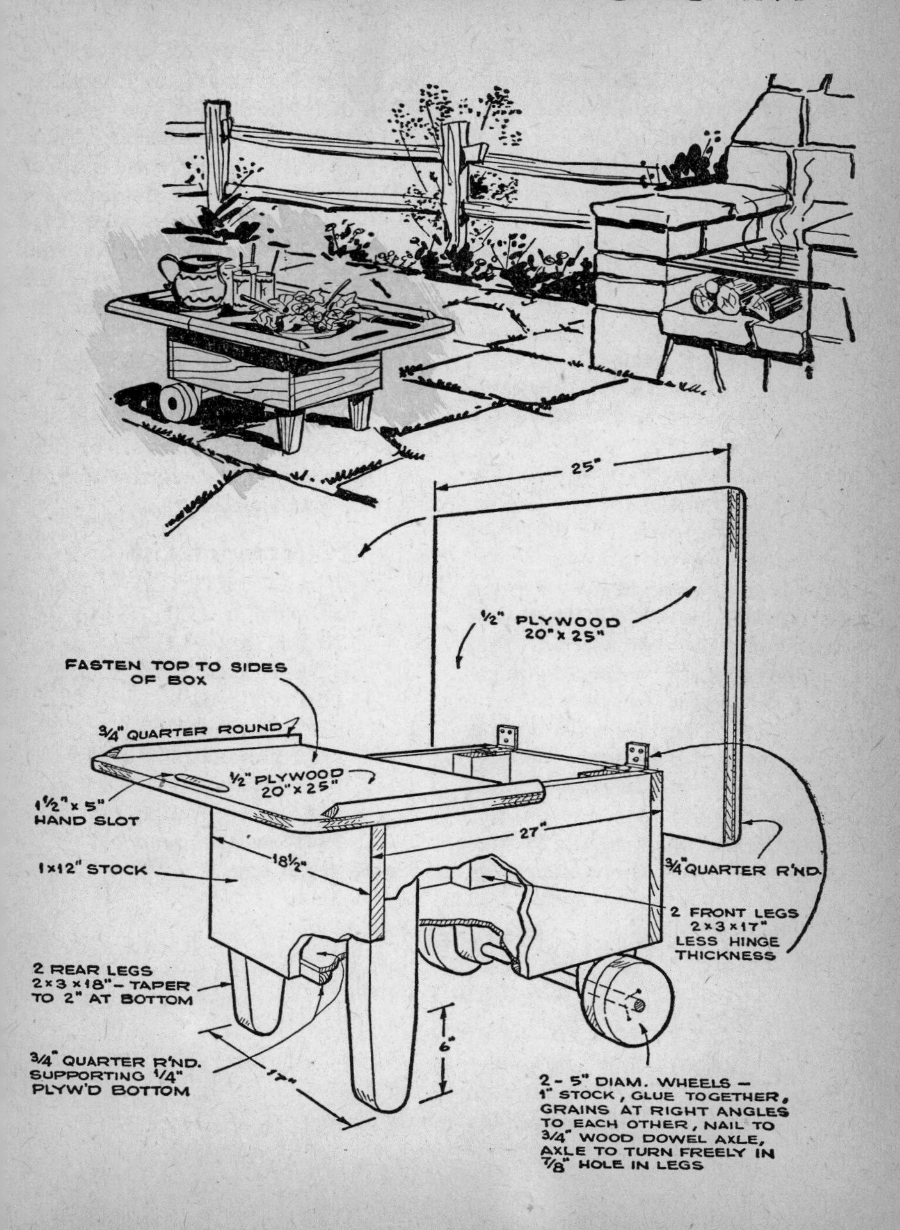

COLLAPSIBLE TRAY-STAND

You'll find many uses for this stand and tray set indoors and out. When not in use, it can be folded and stored.

Make up the four legs out of 1″ x 1″ stock 3′ 7″ long. Bevel the ends of the legs slightly and round off the tops. 5″ from the bottom of each leg, bore a 1/2″ hole on the *inside* surface about two-thirds of the way through the wood. 20″ from the center of this hole bore a similar hole. The legs are then connected in pairs by means of 1/2″ dowels about 19 3/8″ long set into these holes. The dowels should be cut so that the legs are 18″ apart.

The legs are joined at the top by hinges as shown. A strip of 1″ x 3″ stock 20″ long is fastened with flat-head wood screws to the front or rear pair of legs and will serve as a hand grip. The lower center portion of this piece is cut out so that it is 2″ rather than 3″ wide. Now fasten the hinges in place and attach the legs.

The bottom tray is made out of 1/2″ stock and is 3″ deep. The top tray is the same. Before the pieces are assembled, cut the 1/4″ dado in the front, back, and side pieces of the top tray to accommodate the dividers. Assemble the tray and then install the plywood dividers.

The trays are fastened to the dowels by means of strap iron brackets and small tool clips. This allows the trays to be folded but still holds them when the stand is set up. A small hook fastened to the top and bottom trays locks the assembly when folded.

The top tray on the dowels should overhang the legs at front and back by 3 1/2″. Use braces to hold the frame in this position and then mark the underside of the tray where the strap brackets are to be installed. Install the tool clip at the other edge of the tray so it fits down over the dowel.

Materials List

4 pcs. 1″ x 1″ x 43″
1 " 1″ x 3″ x 20″
4 " 1/2″ x 3″ x 17 1/2″
4 " 1/2″ x 3″ x 14 1/2″
2 " 1/2″ plywood 17 1/2″ x 16 1/2″
8 " 1/4″ plywood 3 3/4″ x 3″
2 " 1/4″ plywood 3″ x 17″
4 " 1/2″ dowel 19 3/8″
2 pair hinges
4 strap iron brackets
4 small tool clips
1 small hook
1 screw hook pin

Materials Totals

1″ x 1″ – 14′ 4″
1/2″ x 3″ – 10′ 8″
1/2″ dowel – 6′ 5 1/2″
(Remainder as itemized above)

COLLAPSIBLE TRAY-STAND

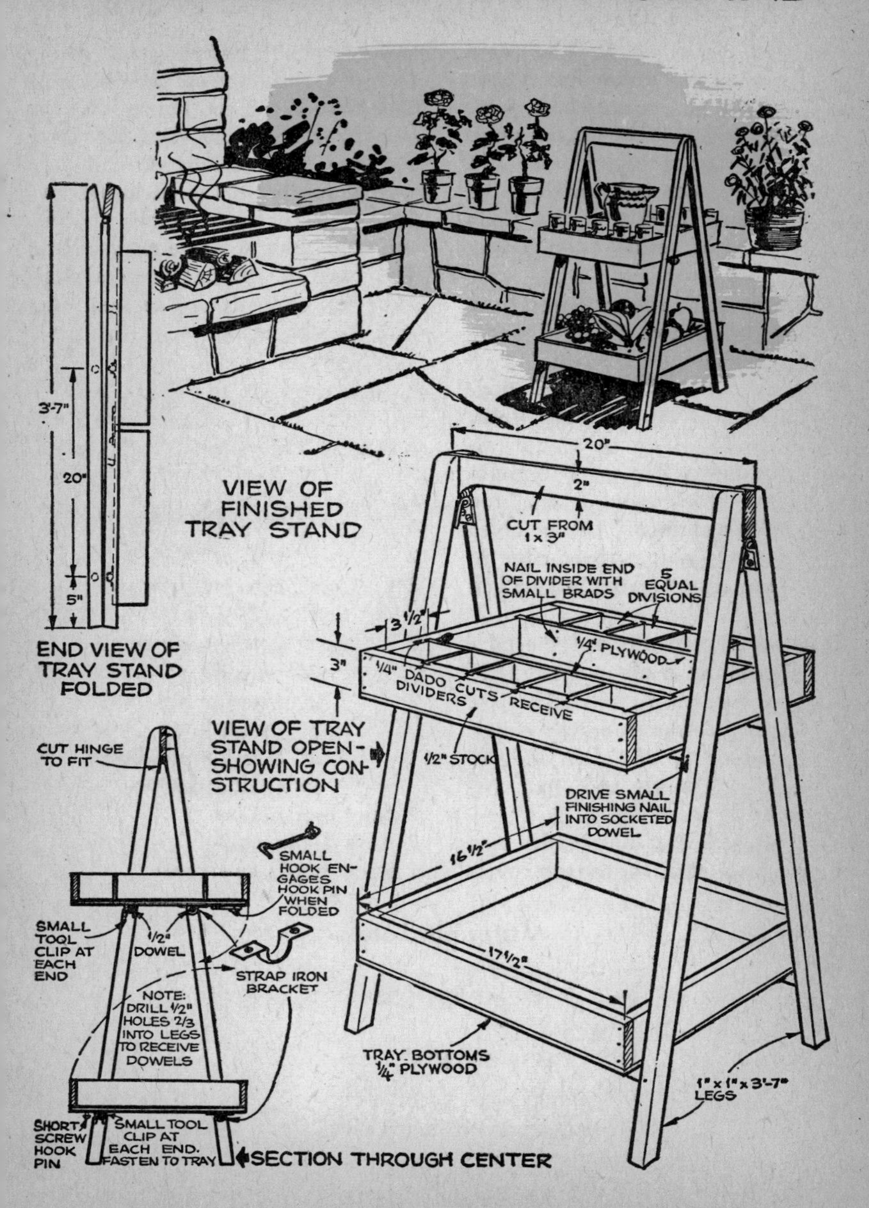

GARBAGE ENCLOSURE

The appearance of the back yard will be improved considerably if garbage is stored in this enclosure. Garbage is emptied into the cans through the top openings of the enclosure, and the cans are removed through the front openings. Latches on the doors prevent dogs and vermin from getting in.

Build the grille for the base of the enclosure out of two 1″ x 2″ pieces 54″ long with cross pieces of 1″ x 3″ that are 26″ long. Use 1 1/2″ non-corrosive screws to assemble these. The upright pieces are of 2″ x 2″ attached by screws and given a slight bevel at the top. The two 1″ x 2″ top horizontal pieces should also be given a slight bevel on the upper edge so that the top covers of the box will fit snugly.

The two side pieces and the back piece should be made out of 1/2″ exterior or outdoor plywood. They are attached to the framework by waterproof exterior wood glue and 1″ wood screws. The top and front covers should be made out of 3/4″ exterior plywood. Use butt hinges of a non-corrosive metal for the top covers and T hinges for the front doors. A 1/2″ x 1″ strip should be attached to each edge of the dividing piece at the front to serve as door stops. Use hooks and screw eyes for latches.

It is best to set the enclosure on a concrete base that is about 4″ thick and an inch or so above ground level. The base should be given a slight slope in one direction so that water will drain off easily.

Materials List

3 pcs. 2″ x 2″ x 41″
3 " 2″ x 2″ x 34″
13 " 1″ x 3″ x 26″
4 " 1″ x 2″ x 54″
2 " 1/2″ x 1″ x 29″
2 " 3/4″ exterior plywood 27 1/2″ x 30″
2 " 3/4″ exterior plywood 24″ x 29″
2 " 1/2″ exterior plywood 30″ x 38 1/2″
1 " 1/2″ exterior plywood 38 1/2″ x 55″
2 pairs butt hinges
2 pairs T hinges
2 screw hooks and eyes

Materials Totals

2″ x 2″ – 18′ 9″
1″ x 3″ – 28′ 2″
1″ x 2″ – 18′
1/2″ x 1″ – 4′ 10″
(Remainder as itemized above)

GARBAGE ENCLOSURE

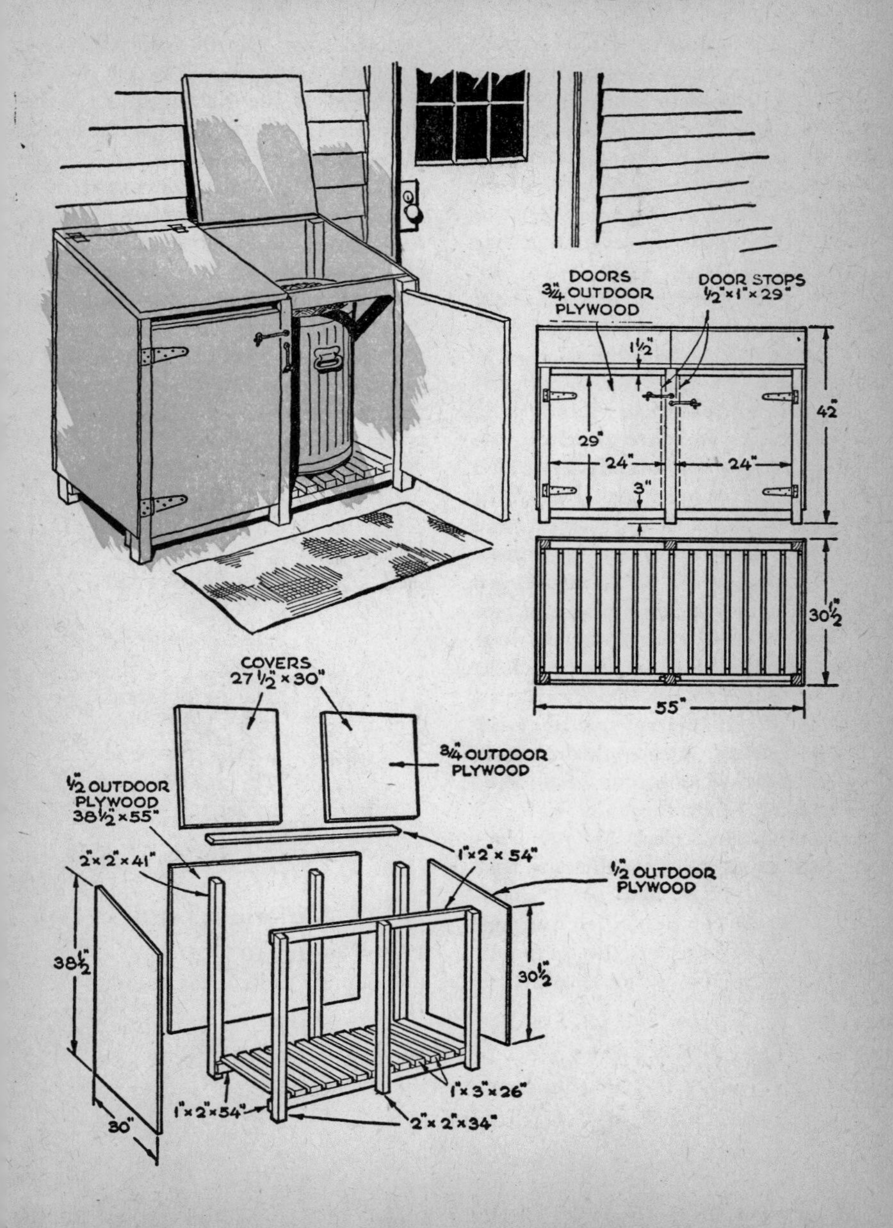

GARDEN HOSE REEL

A sturdy garden reel makes handling the hose easier and will lengthen its life by a good many years.

The cradle for the reel is made of two pairs of legs that are joined at a right angle at the top by cutting the end of each at a 90 degree angle. The bottom ends of the 23″ legs are rounded off while the 26″ legs are beveled off at the base. Braces to hold the legs together are made from 1″ x 4″ stock cut flush with the outer edge of the legs. These braces are fastened in place by driving nails through the leg and brace and then clinching the nail end against the grain. The two sets of legs are held apart by a piece of 1″ x 6″ stock 13 1/2″ long at the base of the 26″ legs, and by a piece of 1″ x 4″ stock 13 1/2″ long between the shorter legs. A small wooden brace (see wheel detail) is installed between the 1″ x 4″ and the legs so that wheels may be attached.

Each side of the reel is made from one piece 30″ long and two short pieces, each 13″ long. The short pieces are butted against the long piece and held in place by a cleat. The two sides of the reel are held together by four 1″ x 4″ strips 10″ long. A 1″ diameter hole should be drilled through each end of the reel at the midpoint. Corresponding holes should be drilled in the cradle. Now set the reel into the cradle and run a 1″ dowel through the holes. Cut the dowel flush with the outside surface of the cradle and fasten each end to the cradle with a long finishing nail. The reel should rotate freely on the dowel. Wheels for the reel can be cut out of 1″ stock and should be 6″ in diameter. They are fastened in place by running a 2 1/2″ screw through a hole in the center of the wheel and into the brace in back of the cradle leg. A washer should be placed on each side of the wheel.

Materials List

1 pcs. 1″ x 6″ x 13 1/2″
2 " 1″ x 4″ x 30″
2 " 1″ x 4″ x 26″
2 " 1″ x 4″ x 23″
1 " 1″ x 4″ x 13 1/2″
4 " 1″ x 4″ x 13″
2 " 1″ x 4″ x 12 1/2″
2 " 1″ x 4″ x 11″
4 " 1″ x 4″ x 10″
2 " 1″ x 4″ x 6″
1 " 1″ dowel 14″
2 wood or metal wheels 6″ diameter

Materials Totals

1″ x 4″ — 26′ 10 1/2″
(Remainder as itemized above)

GARDEN HOSE REEL

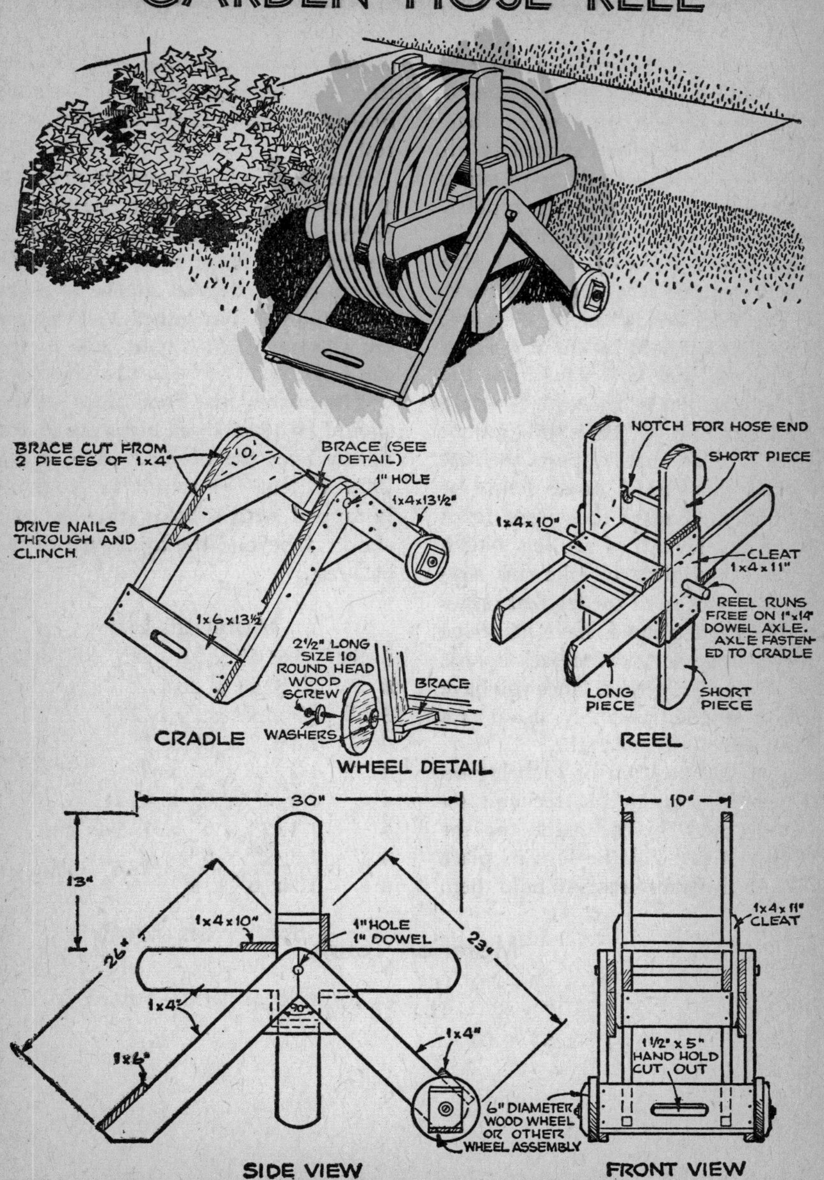

BENCH AROUND A TREE

Set under a favorite shade tree this bench will prove a popular piece of outdoor furniture during hot weather. As the bench will be exposed to all sorts of weather, use a decay-resisting wood such as redwood or cypress. Your bench will then stand up well.

The legs for the bench will also serve to support the seat and backrest. They are made out of 2" x 4". The bottoms should be cut at a slight angle so the legs will slant in at the top. Set one leg at the proper angle and mark a line 18" from the ground. Set the 2" x 4" that supports the seat 1" below this line. A brace should be run from the end of this piece down to 2" from the end of the leg. Notch out the leg slightly to take this support. The portion of the leg that serves as a backrest should have its edge beveled down so that the back boards will fit tightly together. Once you have made up one leg assembly, use it as a pattern for the other eight.

Locate the position of each leg on the ground around the tree and set stone or brick in the earth for the legs to rest on. Put the legs in place and use temporary braces to hold them at the correct angle and position until they can be tied together with the boards that serve as the seat and backrest.

The seat and backrest are made of 1 1/2" x 5". The four boards that form the outer edge of the seat should be cut 7' 0" long; their ends should be cut at 45 degree angles to make miter joints. The other seat boards are spaced 1 1/2" apart and joined similarly.

The boards that form the backrest should be beveled off at the ends to fit tightly over the beveled edge of the 2" x 4" leg. The top of the backrest is capped with a board that extends about 1" beyond the top board of the backrest.

Materials List

8 pcs. 2" x 4" x 36 1/4"
8 " 2" x 4" x 20 1/2"
8 " 2" x 4" x 19 1/2"
4 " 1 1/2" x 6" x 7'
4 " 1 1/2" x 6" x 6'
4 " 1 1/2" x 6" x 4' 11"
4 " 1 1/2" x 6" x 4' 3 1/2"
4 " 1 1/2" x 6" x 4'
4 " 1" x 6" x 4'

Materials Totals

2" x 4" — 50' 10"
1 1/2" x 6" — 104' 10"
1" x 6" — 16'

BENCH AROUND A TREE

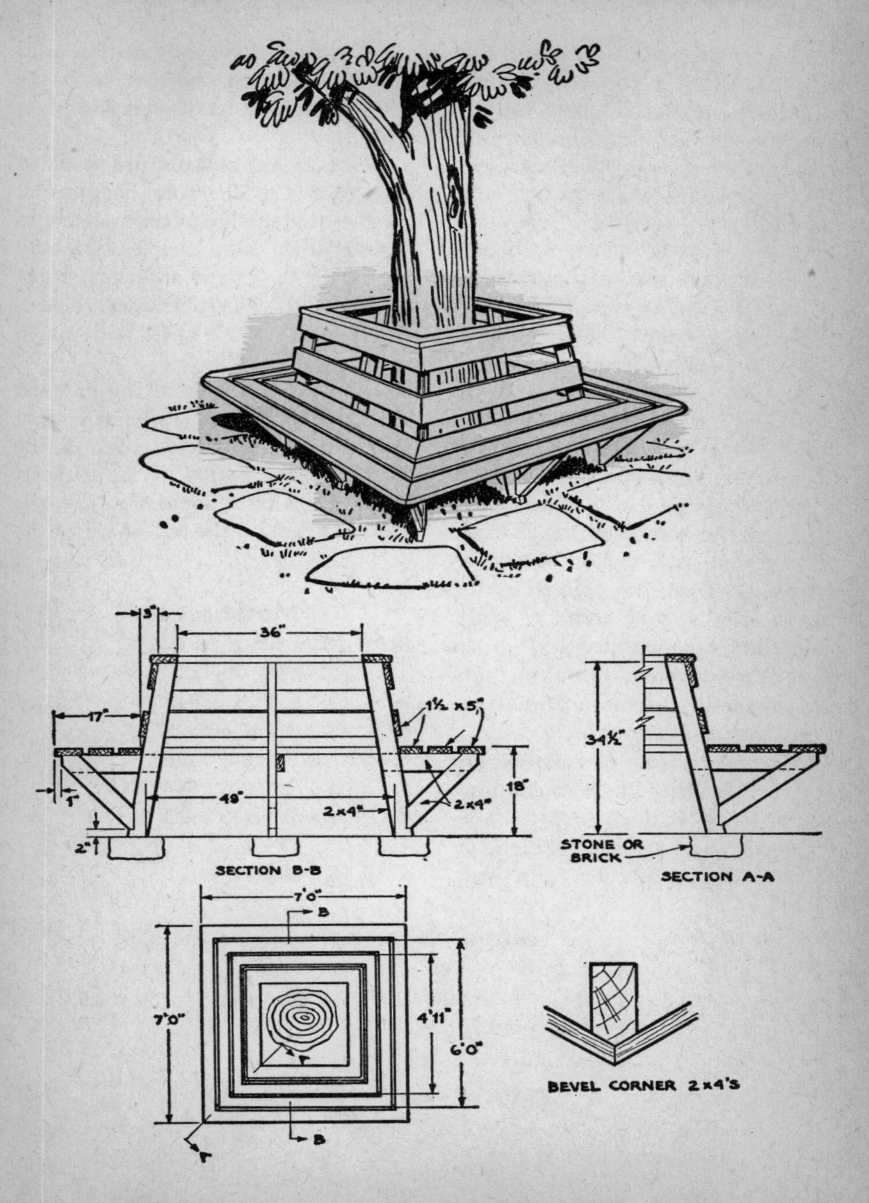

BIRD FEEDING STATION

This bird feeding station will add a decorative note of color to the outside of the house as well as make a safe and convenient place to feed your feathered friends, rain or shine.

The base is made out of 1/2" plywood 13 3/4" x 13 3/4". Notches spaced an equal distance apart should be cut along the four edges. Strips of 1/2" x 3/4" should be tacked around the edges. In the center of the plywood base, fasten a piece of 2" x 2" that is 1 1/2" high. Bevel down the top so that the sides slope in the same manner as a house roof. The two sides for the hopper are made out of 1/2" stock or 1/2" plywood 11 1/2" long and 2" wide. Cut a hole in the base of each piece as indicated in the drawing. Fasten these two pieces to the 2" x 2" hopper base and then make up the end pieces. After the end pieces have been shaped to size, cut one into three parts, as indicated in the drawing, for the hopper door.

1/2" stock or 1/2" plywood is fastened around the base of the hopper to form a feeding trough.

The roof of the feeding station is made of 1/2" exterior plywood 8" x 15". Strips of 1/2" stock or 1/2" plywood are used along the ends and as a ridge. The pattern for the hanging bracket is shown in the drawing in 1" squares. This bracket should be cut out of 1" stock.

Materials List

1 pcs. 1/2" plywood 13 3/4" x 13 3/4"
2 " 1/2" plywood 8" x 15"
1 " 2" x 2" x 1 1/2"
1 " 1" x 10" x 20"
1 " 1" x 3" x 30"
1 " 1" x 3" x 19"
2 " 1/2" x 7" x 12"
2 " 1/2" x 2" x 11 1/2"
2 " 1/2" x 2" x 3"
1 " 1/2" x 1" x 15"
4 " 1/2" x 1" x 8"
2 " 1/2" x 1" x 7"
4 " 1/2" x 3/4" x 14 3/4"
4 screw eyes
2 leather hinges
1 catch
Light chain or wire 12"

Materials Totals

1" x 3" — 4' 1"
1/2" x 7" — 2'
1/2" x 2" — 2' 5"
1/2" x 1" — 5' 1"
1/2" x 3/4" — 59"
(Remainder as itemized above)

BIRD FEEDING STATION

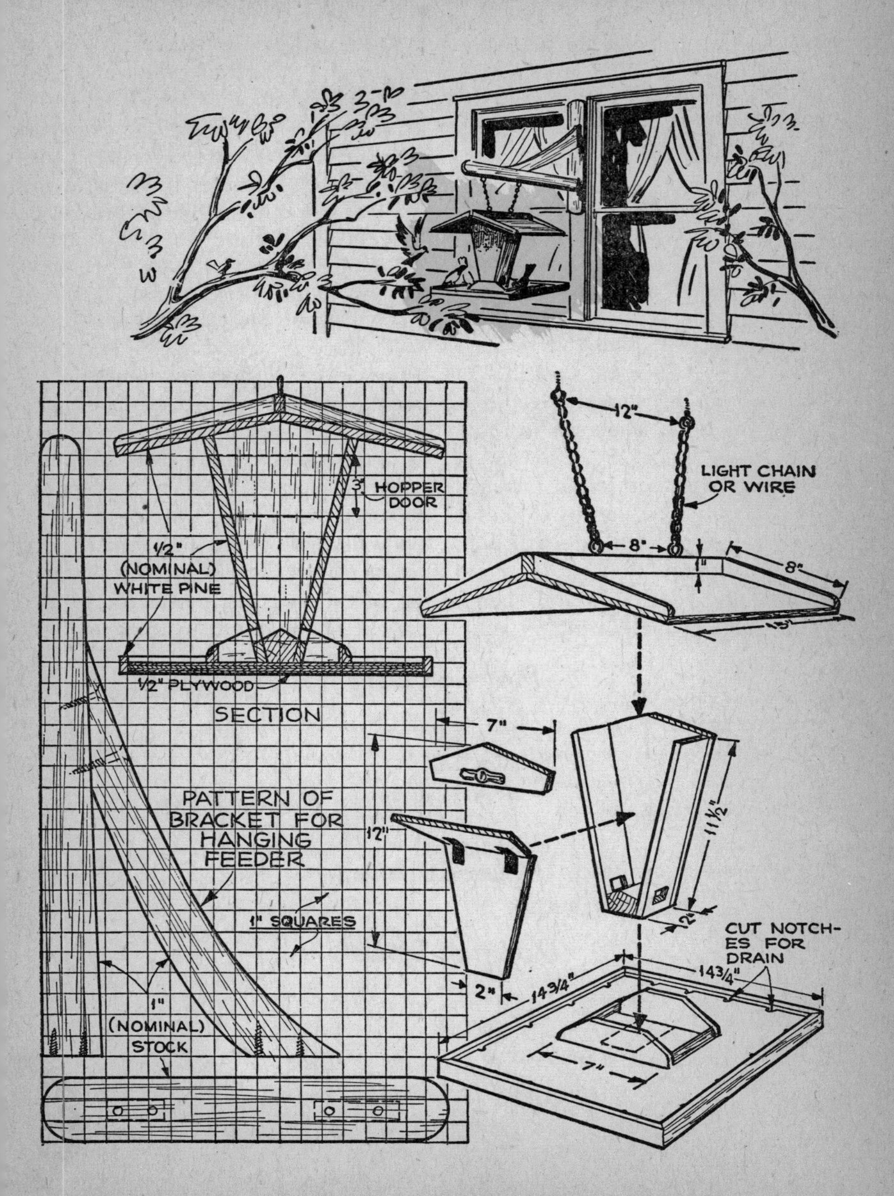

SHOE SHINE CABINET AND STOOL

Whichever method of construction you select for this job, the finished article will prove useful around the home.

The legs for the cabinet are made out of 2″ x 2″ stock. Bevel these down, starting 8″ from the top, so that the ends are 1″ square; this can be done with a wood plane. Now assemble the body of the cabinet. The four sides are made out of 1″ x 8″ stock 14″ long. These can be joined together with miter joints or, as shown in the encircled insert labeled "Alternate Construction," with butt joints. If butt joints are used, 1″ x 1″ strips around the bottom edge of each side will be required for support.

Assemble the four sides and then install the legs. Bevel or round off the top of the legs so that the top of the cabinet will fit properly. The bottom of the cabinet is made out of 1/4″ plywood, and this will have to be notched out at the four corners to fit around the legs. Cut these notches with care so that you get a good fit around each leg.

The top of the cabinet consists of a stationary piece and to this is hinged a piece with a shoe rest mounted in place. The shoe rest is made by gluing wood pieces together until the desired height is obtained and then working down to shape. It can then be fastened in place with wood screws. Ready-made metal rests are available, if you prefer to use them. Correct positioning of the shoe rest on the top is important for a snug fit of box top.

Materials List

4 pcs. 2″ x 2″ x 16″
4 " 1″ x 8″ x 14″
2 " 1″ x 7″ x 14″
3 " 1″ x 3″ x 9″ (foot rest)
4 " 1″ x 1″ x 8″ (alternate construction)
1 " 1/4″ plywood 14″ x 14″
1 pair hinges

Materials Totals

2″ x 2″ — 5′ 4″
1″ x 8″ — 4′ 8″
1″ x 7″ — 2′ 4″
1″ x 3″ — 2′ 3″
1″ x 1″ — 2′ 8″ (alternate construction)
(Remainder as itemized above)

SHOE SHINE CABINET AND STOOL

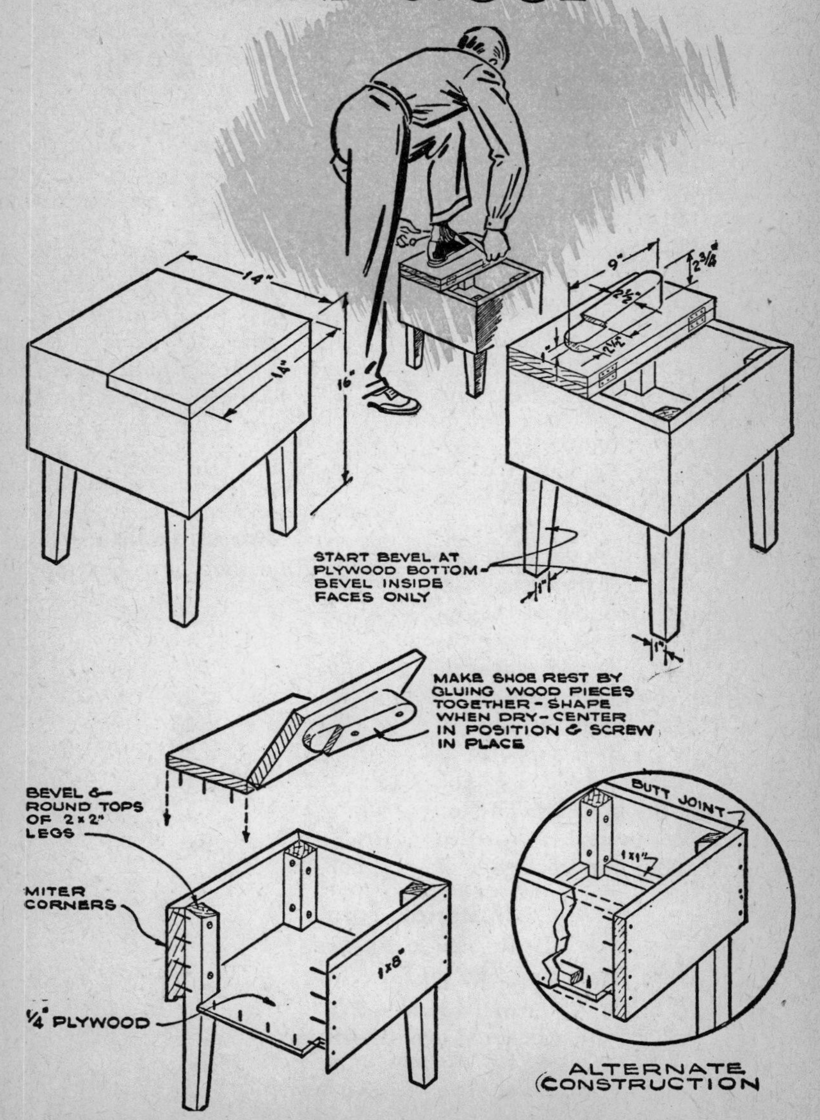

SHOE RACK

This shoe rack not only contains space for a good many pairs of shoes, but the cabinet at the base has storage area for shoe trees, brushes, and similar equipment for maintaining footgear.

Construct the base cabinet first, with with the exception of the top pieces, which go on after the rack is built up. The cabinet consists of two side or end pieces 8″ x 11″ x 4″. The back piece is 7 1/4″ x 18 1/2″, the bottom is 10 1/4″ x 18 1/2″, and the front is 4″ x 18 1/2″. Use 1″ stock throughout. At the top center of the front piece, make a notch 3/4″ deep and 4″ wide. Cut the two uprights for the rack out of 4″ stock 43 3/4″ long. If there is no baseboard where the rack is to be set, the back edges of these uprights can be flush with the back edge of the base cabinet. If there is a baseboard, cut out the bottom of the uprights so that they will fit over the baseboard and set them back this same distance when you fasten them to the base cabinet (see detail in illustration). Cut out the shelf supports, as shown in the detail, from 1″ x 4″ and fasten them to the uprights. The top shelf and racks can also be installed at this time. Along the front edge of each rear rack, a strip of 1/2″ quarter round molding is attached to hold the shoes in place.

After the rack has been assembled, the top of the base cabinet can be cut to size. The upper surface of the cabinet back may have to be beveled slightly so that the strip of 1″ x 4″ to which the cabinet top is hinged can be set in at the proper angle. Nail this strip to the back of the cabinet and drive nails in through the uprights into each end of it for additional support. Cut the cabinet top to size and attach in place with two butt hinges. A strip of 1/2″ quarter round molding is then attached in back of the hinges to the stationery 1″ x 4″.

Materials List

1 pcs. 1″ x 10 1/4″ x 18 1/2″
1 " 1″ x 8″ x 20″
2 " 1″ x 8″ x 11″
1 " 1″ x 7 1/4″ x 18 1/2″
1 " 1″ x 6″ x 22″
2 " 1″ x 4″ x 43 3/4″
7 " 1″ x 4″ x 20″
1 " 1″ x 4″ x 18 1/2″
6 " 1″ x 4″ x 12″
4 " 1/2″ quarter round 20″
2 butt hinges

Materials Totals

1″ x 8″ – 3′ 6″
1″ x 4″ – 26′ 6″
1/2″ quarter round – 6′ 8″
(Remainder as itemized above)

SHOE RACK

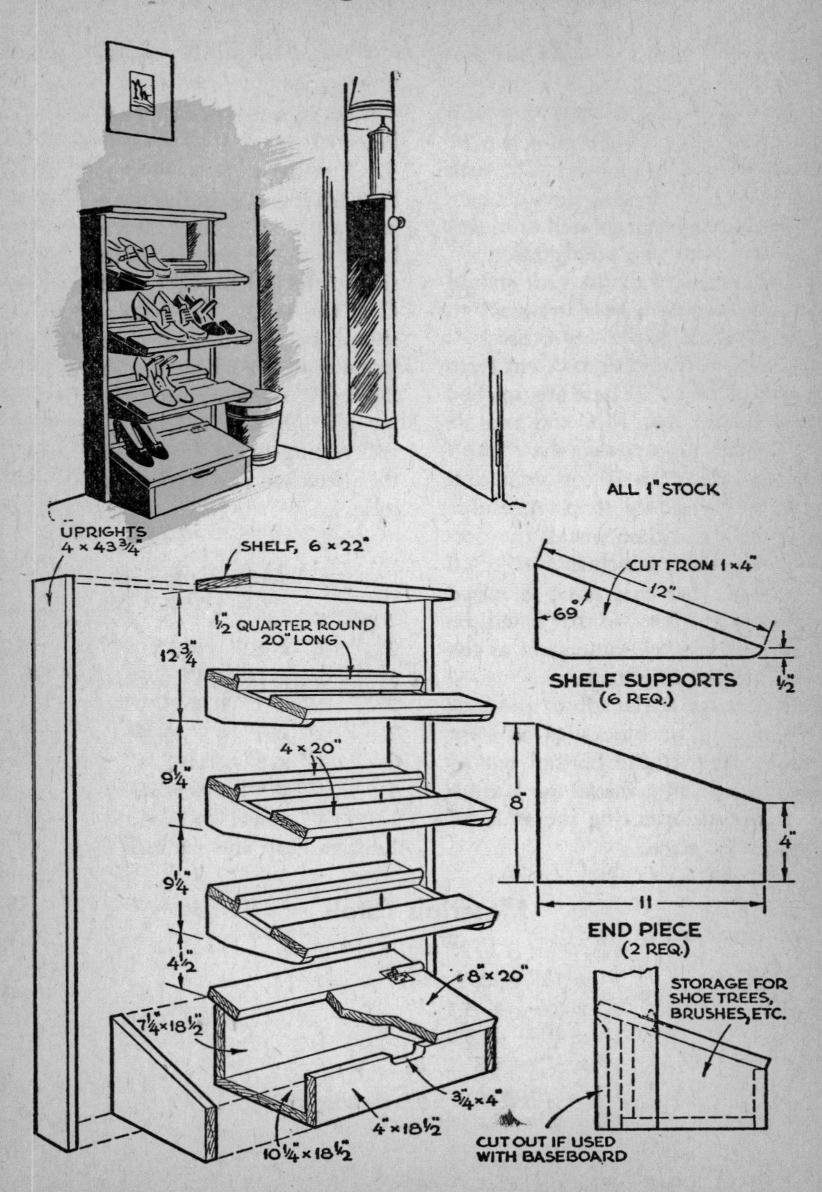
ALL 1" STOCK
UPRIGHTS 4 × 43¾"
SHELF, 6 × 22"
½" QUARTER ROUND 20" LONG
12¾"
9¼"
9¼"
4½"
4 × 20"
8" × 20"
7¼" × 18½"
3¼ × 4"
4" × 18½"
10¼" × 18½"
CUT FROM 1 × 4"
12"
69°
½"
SHELF SUPPORTS (6 REQ.)
8"
4"
11
END PIECE (2 REQ.)
STORAGE FOR SHOE TREES, BRUSHES, ETC.
CUT OUT IF USED WITH BASEBOARD

GUN RACK WITH LOCKING DEVICE

Every man who owns a gun will appreciate a rack where guns can be displayed but not removed. The rack shown here has a locking device which will prevent children, as well as adults, from tampering with your guns.

The dimensions of the rack should be varied slightly where necessary to fit the guns you happen to possess.

The two side pieces can be cut from a piece of 1″ x 12″. These are notched out at the bottom, top, and middle of the outside edge to take the 1″ x 5″ base strip, the 1″ x 4″ top strip, and the 1″ x 4″ middle strip. Assemble these pieces and then install the bottom of the rack, which is a 1″ x 10 1/4″. Note that this piece is raised 1/2″ up in the back so that it will be on more or less the same slant as the butt end of the rifle stock.

Spacer strips at the top of the rack are made out of blocks 1″ x 3″ x 1 3/4″, those at the bottom out of 1″ x 3″ x 10 1/4″. Install the bottom spacers before installing the 1″ x 5″ front bottom piece.

The locking device consists of a block of wood 1 3/4″ x 3 1/2″ x 4 3/4″ with a 1 5/8″ hole drilled through it and a similar block of wood with a 1 5/8″ U cut in at the top. The block with the hole is attached to one side of the rack and the block with the U at the other. The hole and the U should be in line with each other. A wood dowel or a broom stick 1 1/4″ x 24 1/4″ is then inserted, one end pushed into the hole and the other end resting in the U. A hinge hasp is then attached and secured with a padlock.

Materials List

2 pcs. 1 3/4″ x 3 1/2″ x 4 3/4″
2 " 1″ x 12″ x 48″
1 " 1″ x 10 1/4″ x 24 1/4″
2 " 1″ x 5″ x 25 3/4″
2 " 1″ x 4″ x 25 3/4″
6 " 1″ x 3″ x 10 1/4″
4 " 1″ x 3″ x 1 3/4″
1 1-1/4″ dowel 24 1/4″
1 hinge hasp and padlock

Materials Totals

1 3/4″ x 3 1/2″ — 9 1/2″
1″ x 12″ — 8′
1″ x 5″ — 4′ 3 1/2″
1″ x 4″ — 4′ 3 1/2″
1″ x 3″ — 5 8′ 1/2″
1 1/4″ dowel — 24 1/4″
(Remained as itemized above)

GUN RACK WITH LOCKING DEVICE

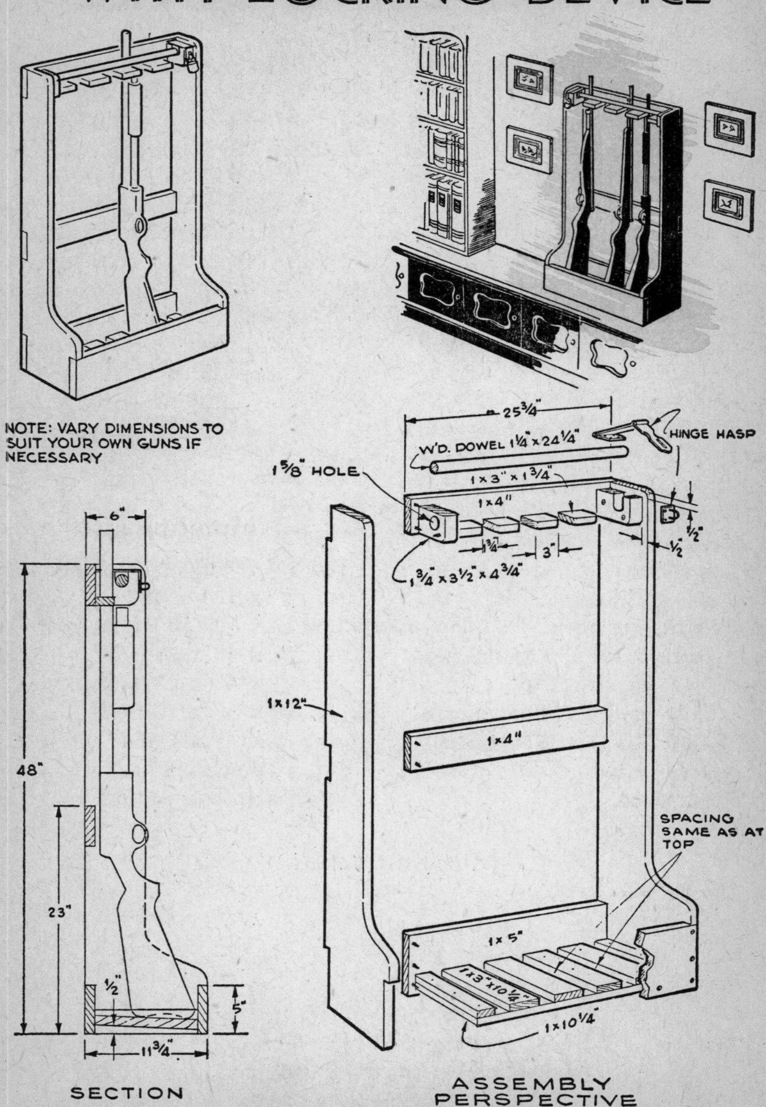

SECTION

ASSEMBLY PERSPECTIVE

CLOSET HAT HOLDERS

Closet hat holders take advantage of the space on the back of closet doors, which is usually wasted. Besides two hats, this shelf has storage space for clothes and hat brushes and neckwear.

The over-all length of the holder is given as 26″, but this should be varied according to the size of the door so that the holder is 4″ less than the width of the door to insure clearance at all times.

The back piece of the holder is made out of 1″ x 8″ stock. 1″ up from the bottom edge, drill holes for 1/4″ dowels 1″ apart. These holes should be drilled at a slight angle so that when the dowels are installed they will have a slight upward pitch. Holes can be drilled right through the 1″ x 8″ stock.

The shelf for brushes and other items is made out of 1″ x 4″ stock. It should be fastened on edge with flathead wood screws 3″ up from the lower edge. Along the outside edge of this shelf, install a strip of 1/4″ plywood 1 1/4″ wide with finishing nails. This will prevent articles on the shelf from falling off if the door is slammed shut.

Flush with the top edge of the 1″ x 8″ piece, install with flathead wood screws a piece of 1″ x 1 1/2″. Nail to the edge of this piece the hat holder, which is cut from 1/4″ plywood. Slots are cut along the top of this piece an equal distance apart to accommodate the crowns of hats.

Dowels for neckwear are cut 2 3/4″ long and fastened with wood glue into the holes already drilled for them.

Materials List

1 piece 1″ x 8″ x 26″
1 " 1″ x 4″ x 26″
1 " 1 1/2″ x 1″ x 26″
1 " 1/4″ plywood 8 1/4″ x 26″
1 " 1/4″ plywood 1 1/4″ x 26″
1/4″ dowels 5′ 8 1/4″

CLOSET HAT HOLDERS

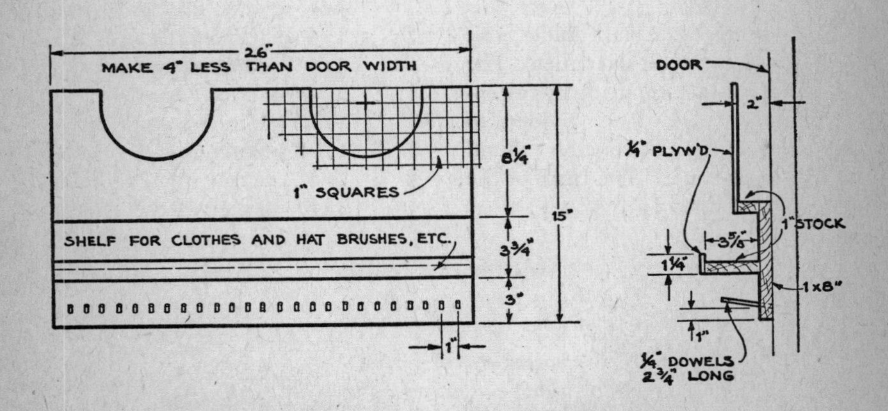

SEWING BOX

The sides, back, and bottom of the box are 1/2″ plywood. The sides are 10 1/2″ x 8″; the back 8″ x 12 1/2″; the bottom 10″ x 12 1/2″. Assemble these pieces.

Make drawer B of 1/2″ plywood. Its front is 3″ x 13 1/2″. Its sides of 5/16″ stock or 1/4″ plywood are 10″ x 2 1/2″ set in from each end of the front piece 9/16″. The back is 5/16″ x 2 1/2″ x 11 3/4″ (if sides are 1/4″, back is 11 7/8″). Corners are made with 1/2″ quarter round. The bottom is 1/4″ plywood 11 3/4″ x 11 7/8″ (depending on sides) x 10″. Set completed drawer in the box and fasten 1/4″ quarter round guides to the box sides. 1/4″ plywood 10″ x 12 1/2″ is placed over the guides and fastened to the quarter round with brads.

Drawer A is made similarly except the front is 2 1/4″ wide and the width of sides and back is 2″. Place this drawer in the box, install guides, and fasten 1/4″ plywood over them. The top compartments are made by fastening 5/16″ or 1/4″ x 2″ dividers to this covering; 1/4″ quarter round makes a strong joint. The front of the top is 1/2″ plywood 2 1/4″ x 13 1/2″ nailed to the box sides. At the top center, cut a recess 3/4″ x 3″.

The box top is 1/2″ plywood 13 1/2″ x 11″ hinged to the back with butt hinges.

Materials List

2	pcs.	1/2″ plywood 10 1/2″ x 8″
1	"	1/2″ plywood 13 1/2″ x 11″
1	"	1/2″ plywood 10″ x 12 1/2″
1	"	1/2″ plywood 8″ x 12 1/2″
2	"	1/2″ plywood 2 1/4″ x 13 1/2″
1	"	1/2″ x 3″ x 13 1/2″
2	"	1/4″ plywood 11 3/4″ x 10″
2	"	1/4″ plywood 10″ x 12 1/2″
1	"	5/16″ x 2 1/2″ x 11 3/4″
2	"	5/16″ x 2 1/2″ x 10″
1	"	5/16″ x 2″ x 11 3/4″
3	"	5/16″ x 2″ x 10″
1	"	5/16″ x 2″ x 8 3/16″
1	"	5/16″ x 2″ x 4 3/16″
4	"	1/4″ quarter round 10 1/2″
1	"	1/4 quarter round 10″
1	"	1/4″ quarter round 8 1/2″
1	"	1/4″ quarter round 8″
1	"	1/4″ quarter round 5 1/2″
4	"	1/4″ quarter round 4 3/16″
4	"	1/4″ quarter round 2 1/2″
4	"	1/4″ quarter round 2″

Materials Totals

5/16″ x 2 1/2″ — 2′ 8″
5/16″ x 2″ — 4′ 7″
1/4″ quarter round — 8′ 11″
(Remainder as itemized above)

SEWING BOX

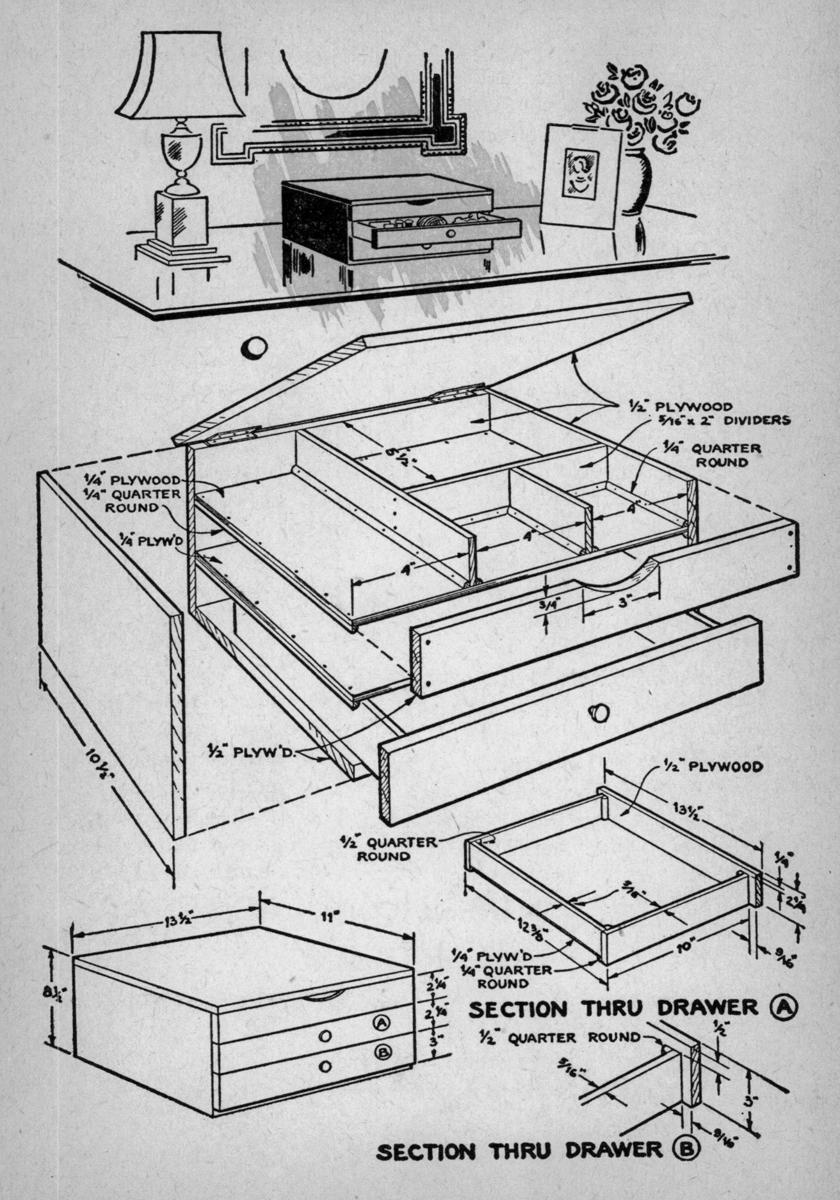

1/2" PLYWOOD
5/16" x 2" DIVIDERS
1/4" QUARTER ROUND
1/4" PLYWOOD
1/4" QUARTER ROUND
1/4" PLYW'D
5 1/2"
4"
4"
4"
4"
3/4"
3"
1/2" PLYW'D.
10 1/2"
1/2" PLYWOOD
13 1/2"
1/2" QUARTER ROUND
1/4"
2 1/4"
3/16"
12 3/8"
10"
9/16"
1/4" PLYW'D
1/4" QUARTER ROUND
13 1/2"
11"
8 1/2"
2 1/4"
2 1/4"
3"
SECTION THRU DRAWER Ⓐ
1/2" QUARTER ROUND
1/2"
5/16"
3"
9/16"
SECTION THRU DRAWER Ⓑ

WOMAN'S SHOE CABINET

Shoes will last longer and require less upkeep if kept stored in this dust- and dirt-proof cabinet.

Make up the two sides of the cabinet and attach 1" x 1" cleats to the inside faces to support the shelves for the shoes. Correct spacing of these cleats is given in the section drawing. The cleats should be given an equal downward slope. A strip of 1/2" quarter round molding should be attached to the rear inside edge of each side piece. Cut the top and bottom to size and assemble the four pieces. Attach the 1/4" plywood back in place.

The base for the cabinet is made out of 1" x 2 3/4" stock. It is fastened to the bottom of the cabinet by four glue blocks. The shelves should now be cut to size. The rear corners of each shelf will have to be notched out slightly to fit around the 1/2" quarter round molding attached to the back of the side pieces. Along the front edge of the bottom shelf, attach a strip of 1" x 1" stock. Three inches down from the back of the remaining three shelves, attach a strip of 1/2" x 1/2" stock. The shelves should be attached securely to the cleats provided on the sides of the cabinet.

Along the bottom of the outside edge of the cabinet top, attach a strip of 1" x 2" to act as a door stop. The four outside edges of the cabinet are trimmed with 1" x 2" stock. The four corners are mitered. The cabinet door can now be cut to size and fitted in place. It is hinged from the side trim with two butt hinges. The door handle is made out of 3/4" x 1" x 6" stock.

Materials List

1 pcs. 1/4" plywood 22" x 35 3/4"
1 " 1/4" plywood 18 1/4" x 35" (approximate, for door)
1 " 1" x 18" x 32 3/4"
2 " 1" x 10" x 35 3/4"
6 " 1" x 10" x 21 1/2"
1 " 1" x 2 3/4" x 21 1/2"
2 " 1" x 2 3/4" x 10"
2 " 1" x 2" x 35 3/4"
2 " 1" x 2" x 22"
1 " 1" x 2" x 21 1/2"
1 " 3/4" x 1" x 6"
3 " 1/2" x 1/2" x 21 1/2"
2 " 1/2" quarter round 35 3/4"
2 butt hinges
4 glue blocks

Materials Totals

1" x 10" — 16' 8 1/2"
1" x 2 3/4" — 3' 4 1/2"
1" x 2" — 12' 5"
1/2" x 1/2" — 5' 4 1/2"
12" quarter round — 5' 11 1/2"
(Remainder as itemized above)

WOMAN'S SHOE CABINET

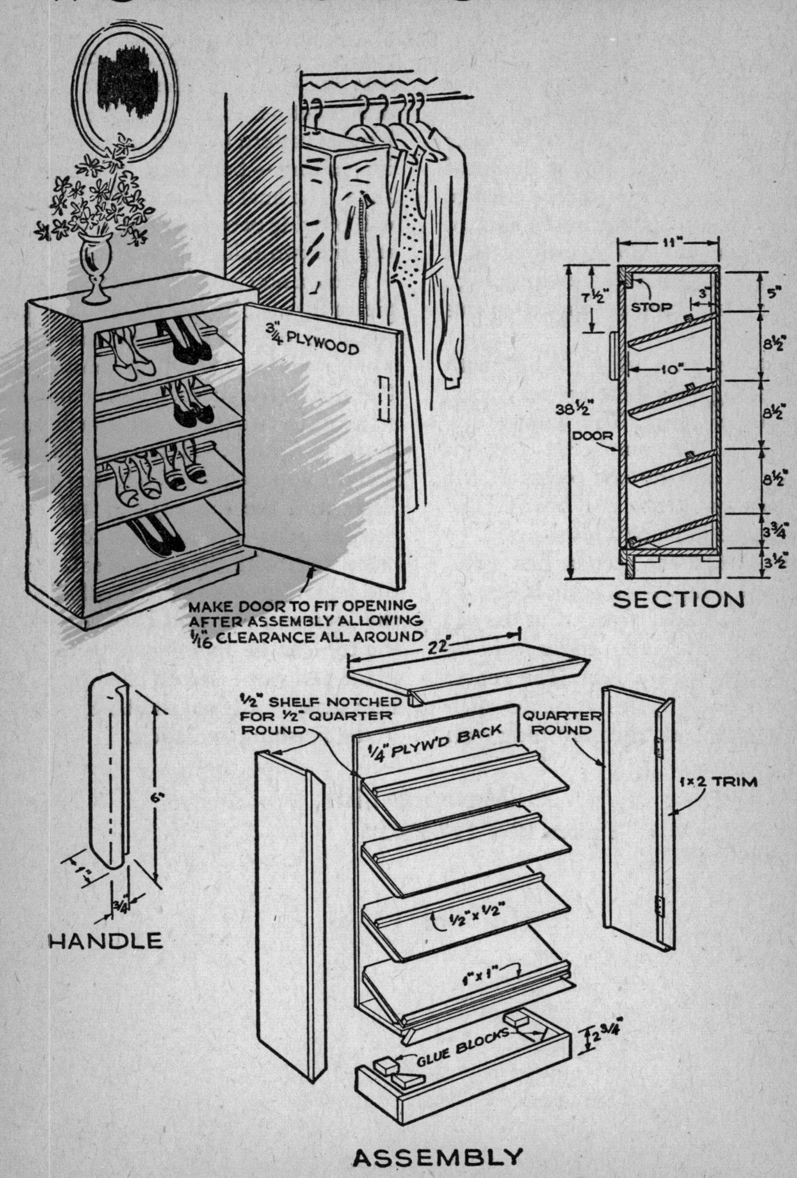

UTILITY STOOL

A sturdy utility stool is a useful addition to practically every room in the house. All the lumber for this stool can be cut from a single 1″ x 12″ only 42″ in length. This stool is designed for a child to carry; it can be used to stand in front of a bathroom sink or bookshelves, for TV viewing, as a handy step-up stool for reaching high places, or as a stand for miscellaneous items.

Select the piece of 1″ x 12″ with care, making sure there are no cracks, checks or warping. The oblong diagram with the numbered sections shows how the various pieces of the stool are cut from the board. The shaded areas indicate unused wood.

Cut the first leg section first (No. 1). Use a compass or keyhole saw to form the rounded corners. Cut the top next (No. 2). The edges can be rounded off with a rasp. The center cut-out is made by drilling holes with a brace and bit and then finishing with a wood chisel, or a gouge, or a compass saw and rasp. The second leg section is cut next (No. 3). Use the first leg as a pattern to mark the second leg for cutting — both legs will then be alike. The final section of the 1″ x 12″ will provide two cleats (Nos. 4 and 7) and the two rails (Nos. 5 and 6).

Make a notch on each side of the leg pieces that is 3″ high and has a depth equal to the thickness of the stock, which will be 25/32″ in most cases. Plane a bevel on each lower outside edge of the two cleats, and attach them in place with wood screws. Be sure that the upper edge of each cleat comes flush with the top edge of the legs. Set the rails, making sure the ends come flush with the outside surface of the legs. The top is now nailed onto the legs and the rails. The edges of the top can be rounded down with a plane and rasp; and all the other corners should be given similar treatment in the finishing operation.

Materials List

1 piece 1″ x 12″ x 42″

UTILITY STOOL

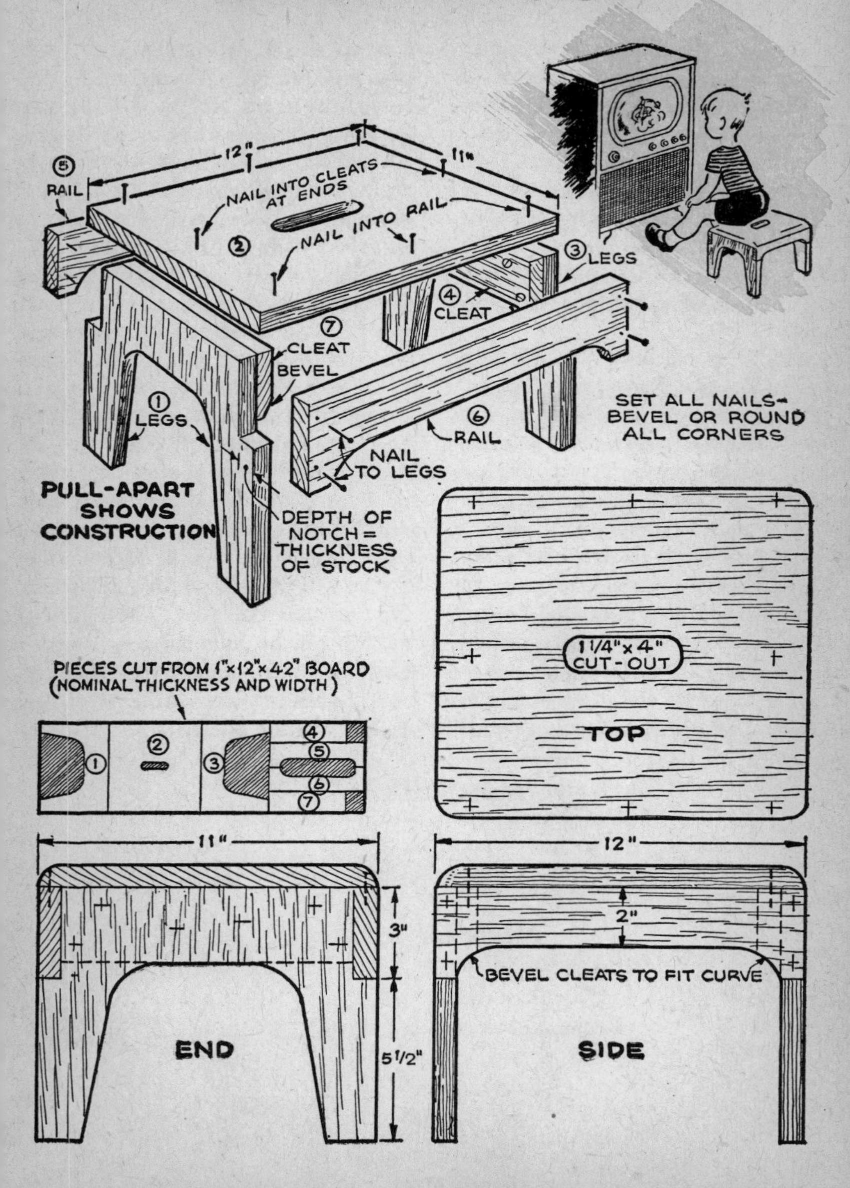

TOY STORAGE CHEST

Any child should be delighted to put his toys away at night if he has this chest to store them in. There is even a special place for keeping comic books.

The four sides of the chest are made out of 3/4″ plywood. At the top rear of each end piece leave a tongue 1 5/8″ high by 3 5/8″ wide for the 2″ x 4″ to which the top of the chest is hinged.

Assemble the four sides, using 1″ x 2″ strips at the corners. Around the bottom inside edges install 3/4″ quarter round molding to support the 1/4″ plywood bottom. Install the 2″ x 4″ between the two end pieces and fasten it to both ends and the back piece.

The top of the chest is in two parts. The back section is firmly secured to the top of the 2″ x 4″. The other part is hinged to the 2″ x 4″. This movable portion is made with a frame consisting of a 2″ x 2″ back piece and 1″ x 2″ strips used for the sides and front. The side pieces are doubled to provide additional support. The bottom is covered with a sheet of 1/8″ hardboard cut out along one edge to serve as a storage place for magazines, comic books, etc. The top consists of 3/4″ plywood projecting 1/2″ beyond the sides of the chest. Three butt hinges should be used to fasten the movable portion of the top in place. A lift for the top is made out of 1″ x 1″ x 4″. Handles at the sides of the chest are made out of wood brackets and 3/4″ dowels. A 3/4″ rope is nailed around the base of the chest and under the 1/2″ projection at the top.

Materials List

1 pcs. 3/4″ plywood 18″ x 40″
1 " 3/4″ plywood 14 1/4″ x 40″
2 " 3/4″ plywood 14 1/4″ x 18″
1 " 3/4″ plywood 13″ x 40″
1 " 1/4″ plywood 16 1/2″ x 38 1/2″
1 " 1/8″ hardboard 16 1/2″ x 38 1/2″
1 " 2″ x 4″ x 38 1/2″
1 " 2″ x 2″ x 38 1/2″
1 " 1″ x 2″ x 38 1/2″
4 " 1″ x 2″ x 12″
4 " 1″ x 2″ x 11 1/4″
1 " 1″ x 1″ x 4″
2 " 3/4″ quarter round 38 1/2″
2 " 3/4″ quarter round 16 1/2″
3 butt hinges

Materials Totals

1″ x 2″ — 10′ 11 1/2″
3/4″ quarter round — 9′ 2″
(Remainder as itemized above)

TOY STORAGE CHEST

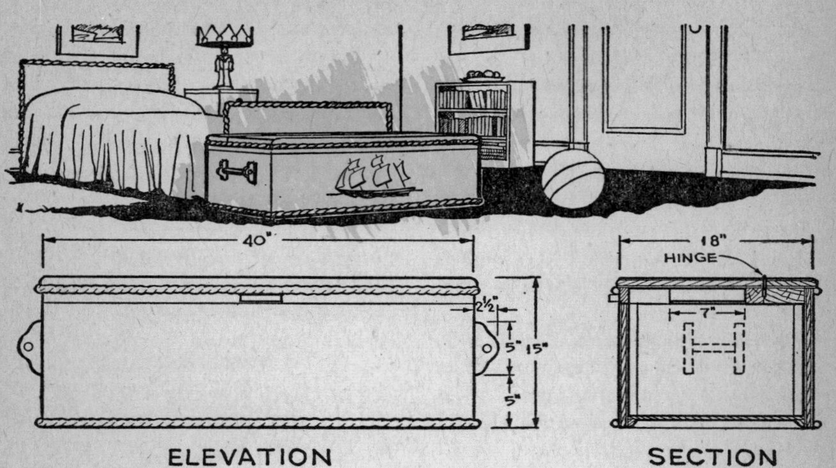

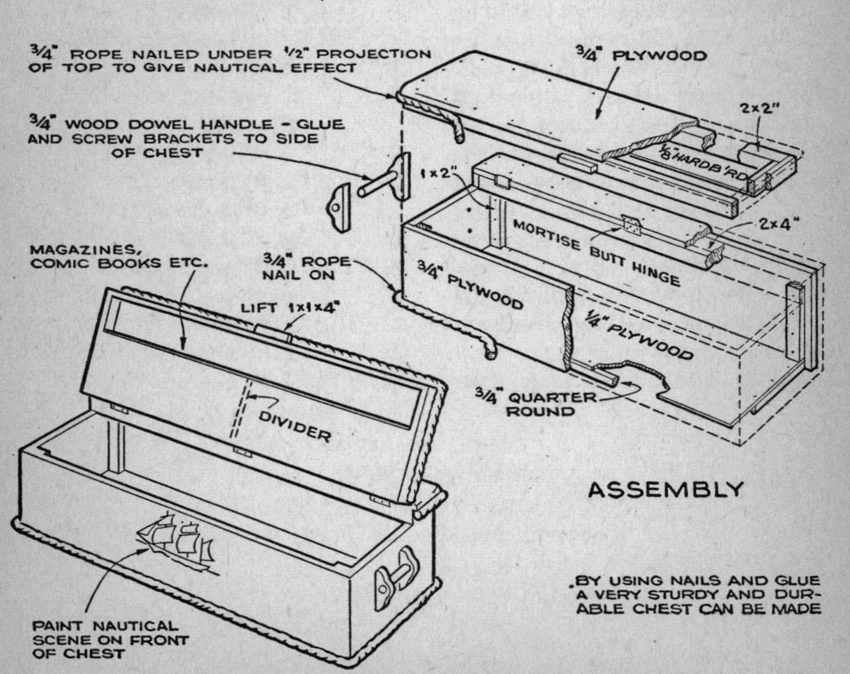

OVERSHOE AND RUBBER STORAGE CABINET

Placed in the hall or entry way, this cabinet solves the problem of where to store rubbers and overshoes.

The back section, made of 3/4" plywood, should be 17" high and 22 1/2" wide. Along its bottom edge and sides fasten strips of 1" x 1" stock and along the top edge attach a strip of 1" x 2" stock.

The front of the cabinet, which is a louver, consists of a piece of 2" x 3" stock 22 1/2" long with two 1" x 1" uprights 16 1/4" high at each end. The 2" x 3" is fastened along the bottom and then the louver is built up from this. Spacers for the louver are made out of 1" x 1" stock 3/4" wide. The starter spacing block is made by cutting one of these in half, which establishes the 45 degree angle. The louvers are made of 1/2" plywood cut 2" wide. They are nailed to the spacer blocks. The 2" x 2" top piece is set perfectly flat against the 1" x 1" uprights. The ends of the louver are covered on the front with a strip of 1" x 3".

Make the two side pieces of 3/4" plywood 17" x 14 1/2". Now assemble all four pieces. Install 1" x 1" x 10 5/8" strips along the bottom edge of the sides. Then make the bottom out of 1/4" plywood; its corners will have to be notched out to fit around the 1" x 1" corner pieces. A 1" x 2" hinge strip planed down to 3/4" x 2" is fastened along the back of the cabinet and the cover can then be installed with two or three butt hinges.

Materials List

2 pcs. 3/4" plywood 17" x 14 1/2"
1 " 3/4" plywood 17" x 22 1/2"
1 " 3/4" plywood 13 5/8" x 24"
7 " 1/2" plywood 2" x 22 1/2"
1 " 1/4" plywood 12 1/8" x 22 1/2"
1 " 2" x 3" x 22 1/2"
2 " 2" x 2" x 22 1/2"
2 " 1" x 3" x 17"
1 " 1" x 2" x 24"
2 " 1" x 1" x 22 1/2"
2 " 1" x 1" x 14 3/8"
2 " 1" x 1" x 16 1/4"
2 " 1" x 1" x 10 5/8"
14 " 1" x 1" x 3/4"
1 pair butt hinges

Materials Totals

2" x 2" — 3' 9"
1" x 3" — 2' 10"
1" x 1" — 11' 6"
(Remainder as itemized above)

OVERSHOE AND RUBBER STORAGE CABINET

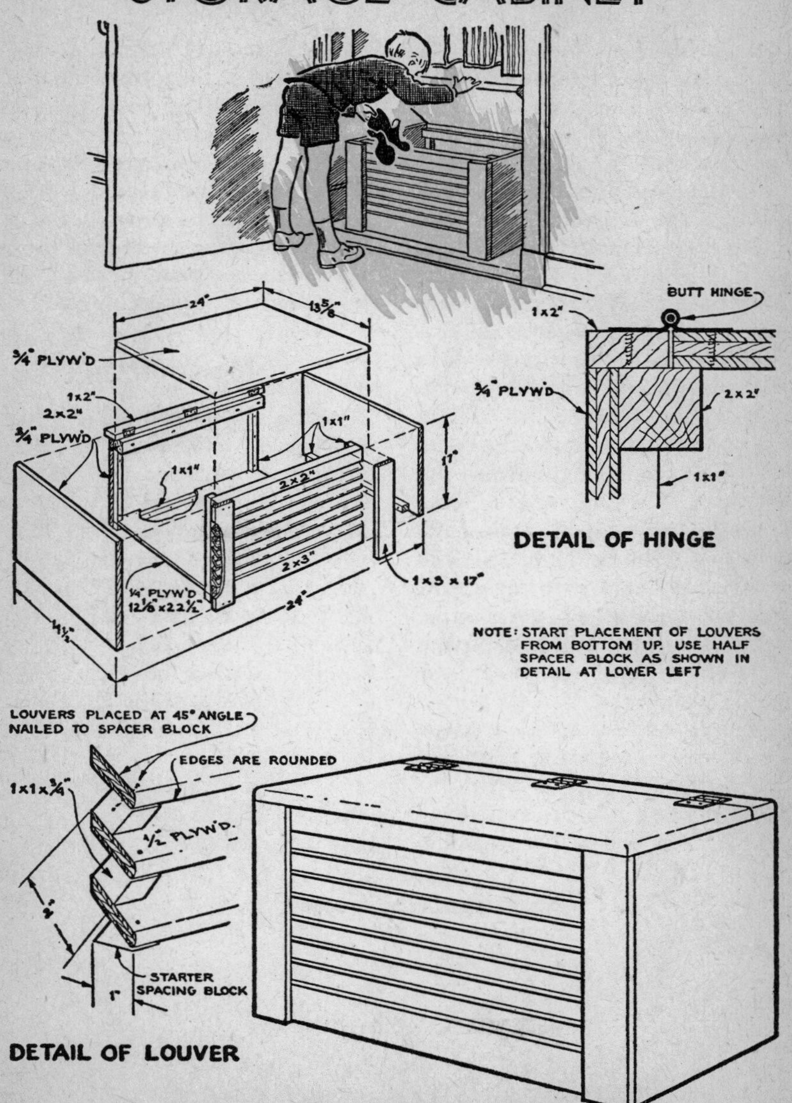

TABLE-TENNIS TABLE

The table-tennis table shown is standard size—5′ x 9′ and 36″ high. It can be unhooked when not in use and set one section atop the other for storage. That is a very attractive feature of this table.

The top of the table is constructed out of a single piece of 1/2″ plywood 5′ x 9′. This is somewhat larger than the conventional sheet of plywood and is made primarily for table-tennis table tops. If your local lumber yard does not have this size of sheet in stock, it can be ordered for you. If the table is to be used outdoors, be sure to specify exterior plywood.

The plywood sheet should be cut in half so that each section measures exactly 5′ x 4′ 6″. A framework for each section of the top should be made out of 1 1/8″ x 3″ stock. Each section of the table top is secured to the frame with glue and screws that are either set flush or countersunk into the top of the table.

Each section of the table requires four legs, each of which is made out of 2″ x 2″ stock 29 1/2″ long. The tops of the legs are placed inside the corners formed by the framework of each section and are held in place by 1 1/2″ wood screws run in through the framework. Additional support is given the legs by the two 6″ corner blocks at each corner and by the strap iron supports. Place metal glides on the bottom of each leg.

The edges of the plywood top can be left as they are or covered with a strip of 1/2″ half round molding. The table top should be stained or painted dark green. When this is dry, the white lines can be painted. A quick, accurate way to mark out lines is to mask their edges by putting transparent tape directly on the table after the green paint has dried. The white lines should be 3/4″ wide, and they run along the outside edges and lengthwise down the center.

Materials List

2 pcs. 1/2″ plywood 5′ x 4′ 6″
8 " 2″ x 2″ x 29 1/2″
4 " 1 1/4″ x 3″ x 4′ 6″
4 " 1 1/4″ x 3″ x 5′
16 " 1 1/4″ x 3″ x 6″
16 strap irons 1/8″ x 3/4″
8 metal glides
1/2″ half round 28′

Materials Totals

1 1/4″ x 3″ — 46′
2″ x 2″ — 19′ 8″
(Remainder as itemized above)

TABLE-TENNIS TABLE

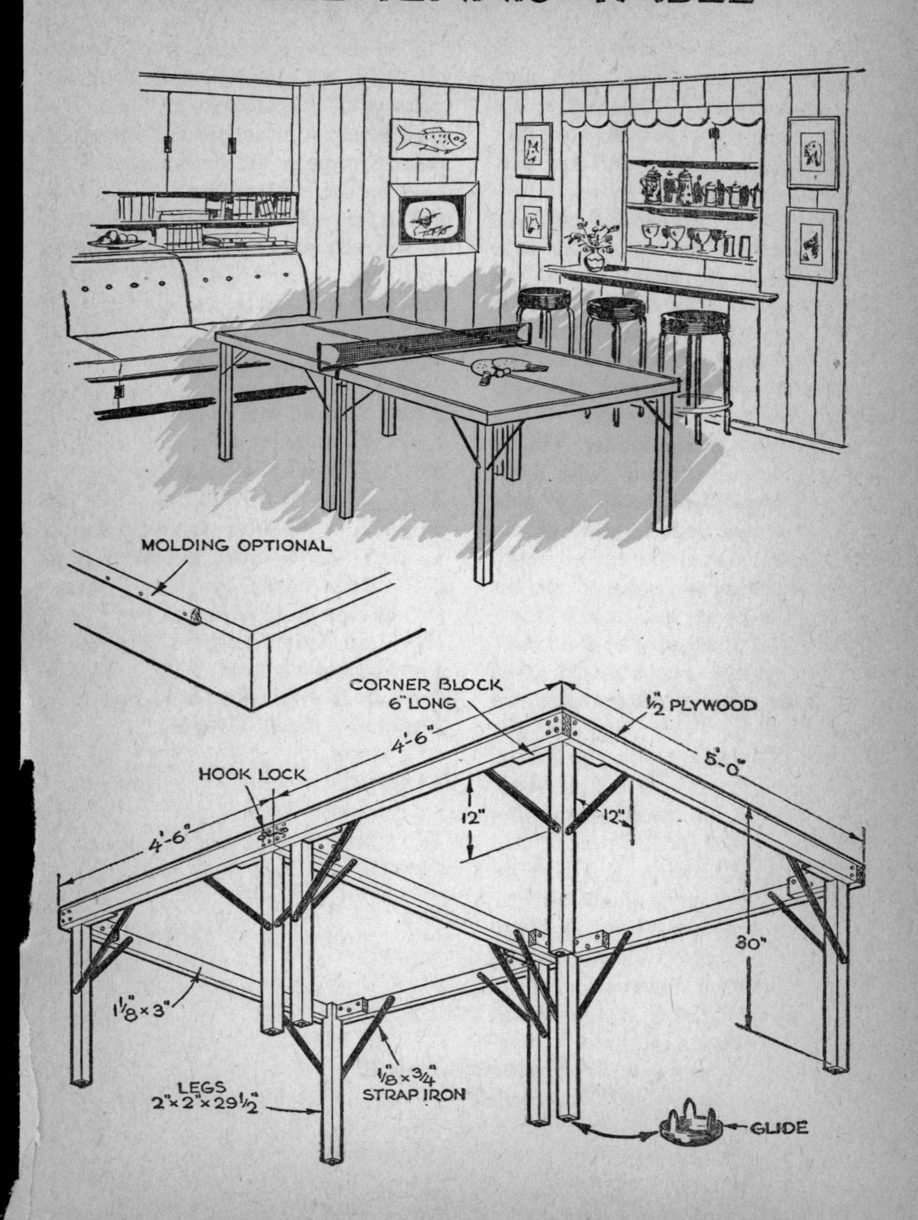

SWING-LADDER-SEESAW

This swing-ladder-seesaw will transform any back yard into a real playground for several children.

Before assembly, all woodwork that will be in direct contact with the earth should be treated with a wood preservative to prevent decay. Sand all pieces smooth to prevent splintering.

The base of the swing consists of three pieces of 2″ x 6″ that are 10′ long. They are notched out at the bottom to take a 2″ x 4″. Bevel the pieces at the ends. Use two 16d nails to fasten the 2″ x 4″ in place.

Next, construct the ladder. This is made out of two 4″ x 4″ with 3/4″ pipe for rungs. Place the 4″ x 4″ side by side and mark the location of the holes for the rungs. The rungs are 8″ apart. Use a depth gauge on the bit so that all holes are drilled to 1 1/2″. Notch out the bottom of each 4″ x 4″ so it will fit over the middle 2″ x 6″. Notch out the top of the two uprights to take a 2″ x 4″ on edge. Cut the rungs to size and assemble the ladder, using temporary braces to hold it together. Raise it into position and hold it plumb with temporary braces until the final braces can be cut and installed. These are put on with carriage bolts. Install the third upright and then put the 2″ x 4″ on edge across the top. Additional support is given at this point by metal angle braces, which can be bent slightly to fit; they are fastened in place with heavy wood screws. Holes are now drilled through the 2″ x 4″ on edge to take the eye bolts for the swing.

The seesaw is made out of a piece of 2″ x 10″ sanded smooth. Two strips of 2″ x 4″ that are 9 1/2″ long are nailed on either side of the midpoint to prevent the board from slipping on the ladder rung.

The base should be partially buried in the ground. To prevent it from "walking," drive 3/8″ x 18″ metal rods into the soil.

Materials List

3 pcs. 4″ x 4″ x 9′
1 " 2″ x 10″ x 12′
3 " 2″ x 6″ x 10′
2 " 2″ x 4″ x 9 1/2″
3 " 2″ x 4″ x 6′
1 " 1″ x 8″ x 21″ (seat)
2 " 1″ x 4″ x 7 1/2″ (seat cleats)
6 " 1″ x 3″ x 6′
11 " 3/4″ iron pipe (rungs)
2 metal angle braces
2 eye bolts 1/2″ thread dia., 6″ long
2 thimbles for 1/2″ rope
1/2″ rope 20′
12 carriage bolts 6″
12 carriage bolts 5″
12 carriage bolts 4 1/2″
4 metal rods 3/8″ x 18″

Materials Totals

4″ x 4″ — 27′
2″ x 10″ — 12′
2″ x 6″ — 30′
2″ x 4″ — 19′ 7″
1″ x 4″ — 1′ 3″
1″ x 3″ — 36′
(Remainder as itemized above)

SWING-LADDER-SEESAW

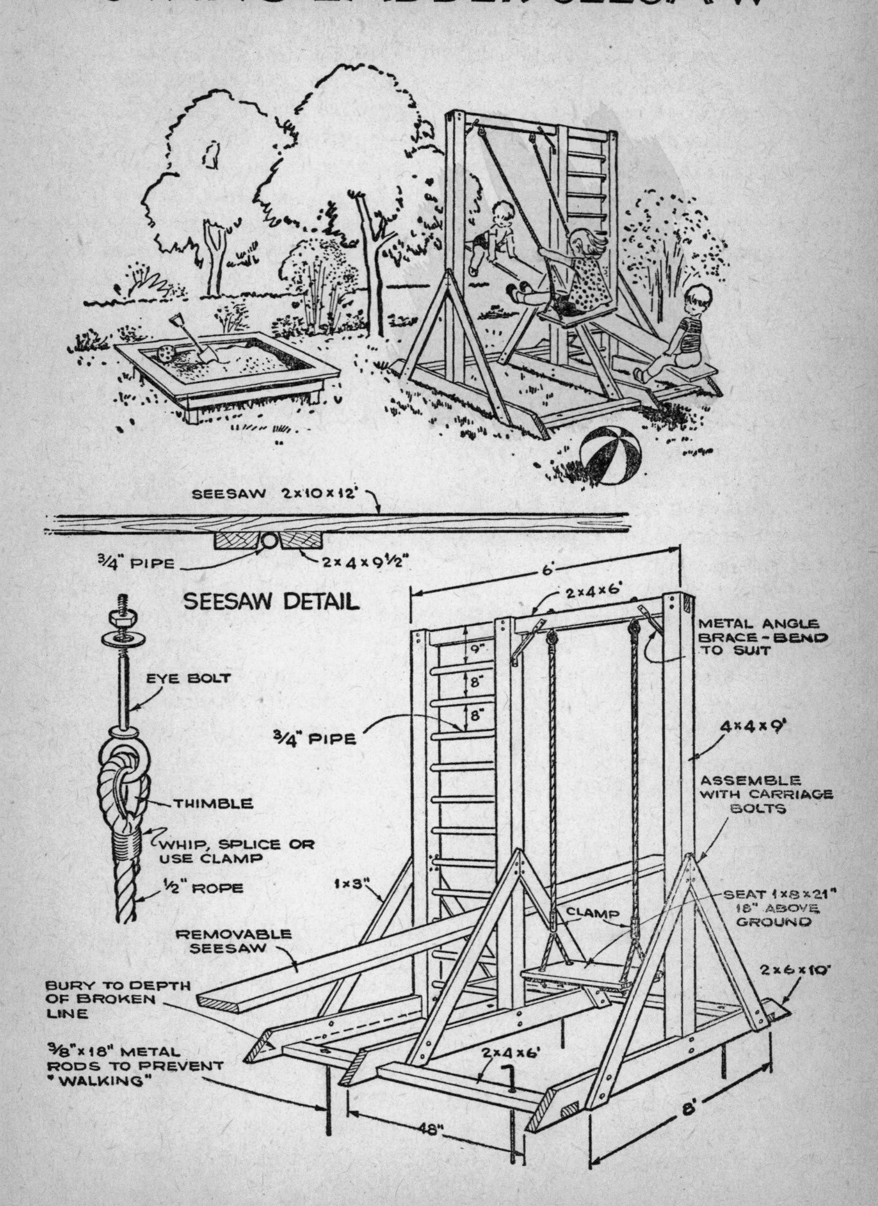

CHRISTMAS TREE STANDS

Anyone on the look-out for something a little different in the line of Christmas decorations should be interested in one of these Christmas tree stands.

The stand shown in the upper portion of the drawing has a base approximately 2″ thick. This can be made up of two layers of 3/4″ plywood covered on the top with a piece of 1/2″ plywood. The base should measure 18″ x 18″. In the center of the base cut a hole 3″ in diameter. The bottom of this hole should be covered with a piece of 1/4″ plywood 4″ x 4″. This is necessary to prevent the end of the tree trunk from damaging the finish of the table that the stand may be set on. Also to prevent damage to furniture finish, blocks of wood 1/2″ x 2″ x 2″ are fastened to each corner of the stand and felt is cemented to the underside of these blocks. The first star for the stand is made out of 3/4″ plywood. The second star is made of 1/2″ plywood and its perimeter lies 1″ inside the perimeter of the first star. 3″ holes are drilled in the center of each.

The lower stand has a base made of four pieces of 1″ x 4″. Use boards or plywood for the top of the stand. The top should be 26″ square. The circles at the corner are marked out with a square and a compass, and their outside curves are cut with a keyhole saw. A 4″ square opening is made at the center of the top. Four 1″ strap irons are installed to support the tree.

Materials List

Upper Stand

3 pcs. 3/4″ plywood 18″ x 18″
1 " 1/2″ plywood 18″ x 18″
1 " 1/2″ plywood 17″ x 17″
1 " 1/4″ plywood 4″ x 4″
4 " 1/2″ x 2″ x 2″
4 screw eyes

Lower Stand

1 pcs. 1/2″ plywood 26″ x 26″
2 " 1″ x 4″ x 26″
2 " 1″ x 4″ x 24 1/2″
4 strap irons 1″ x 24″

Materials Totals

Upper Stand

1/2″ x 2″ — 8″
(Remainder as itemized above)

Lower Stand

1″ x 4″ — 8′ 5″
(Remainder as itemized above)

CHRISTMAS TREE STANDS

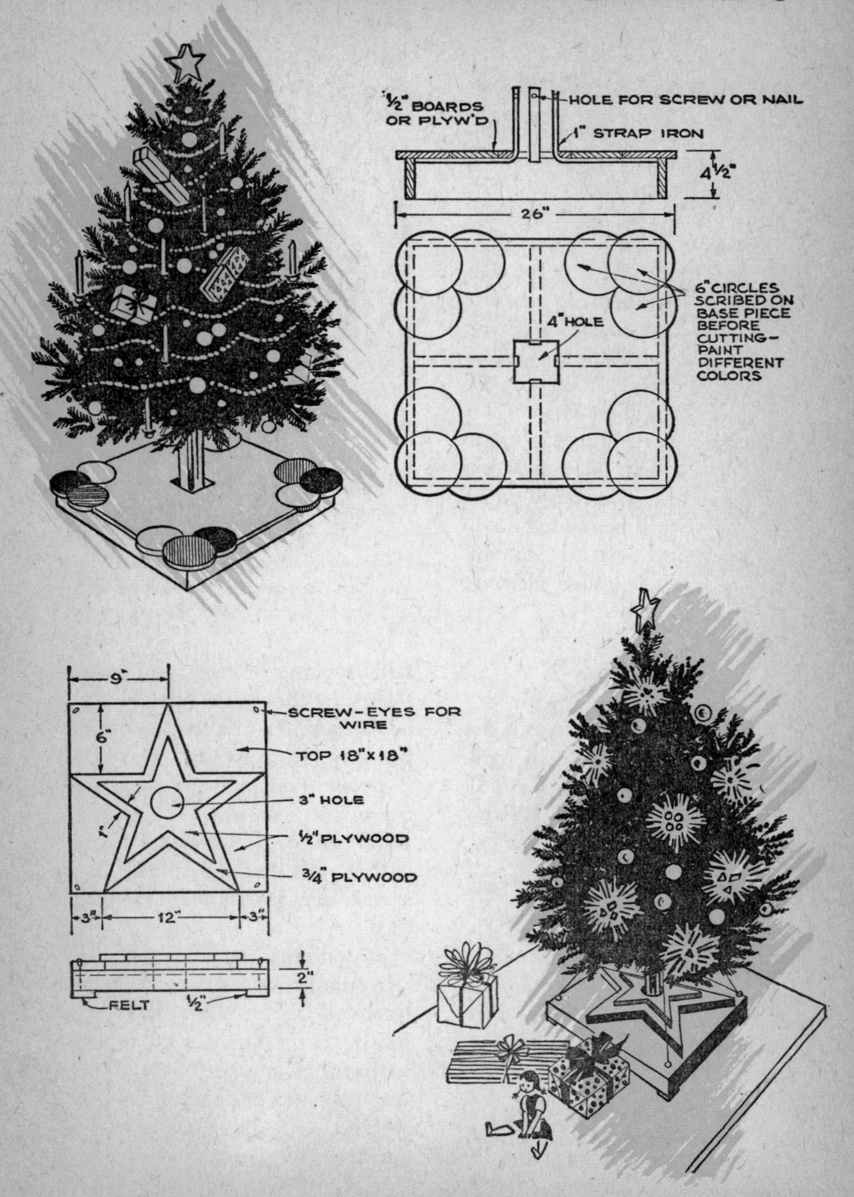

PAINTING AND FINISHING

FINISHES AND FINISHING

The success of any furniture building project depends largely on how well the piece is finished; and the success of any finishing operation depends on how well the wood surface has been prepared. A simply constructed piece of furniture can be made into a most attractive article by giving it a good finish. An elaborate piece of furniture, on the other hand, can be ruined if given a poor finish.

The first step in finishing is to remove any marks left on the wood during construction. The rough edges left by the saw should be sanded down with sandpaper until perfectly smooth. If they are very rough, touch them up with a plane or rasp, and then sand. Dents in the wood left by the head of a hammer can be eliminated by pricking slightly the wood with a sharp-pointed tool and then applying a few drops of water to the area. The water will make the wood fibers swell back to the original shape. After the area is dry, sand down the rough surface.

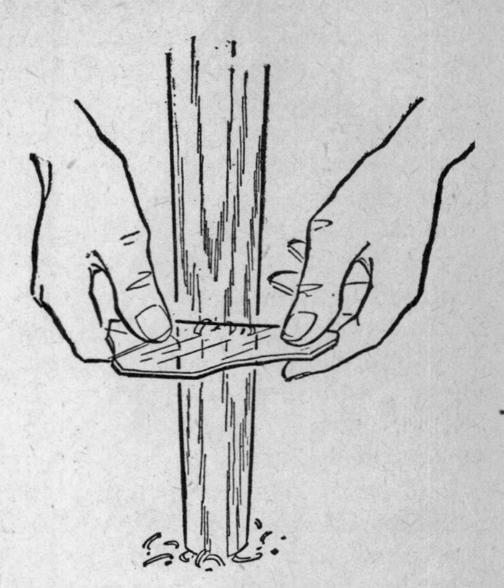

Fig. 2. A broken piece of glass makes an excellent scraper for smoothing off rough portions of wood.

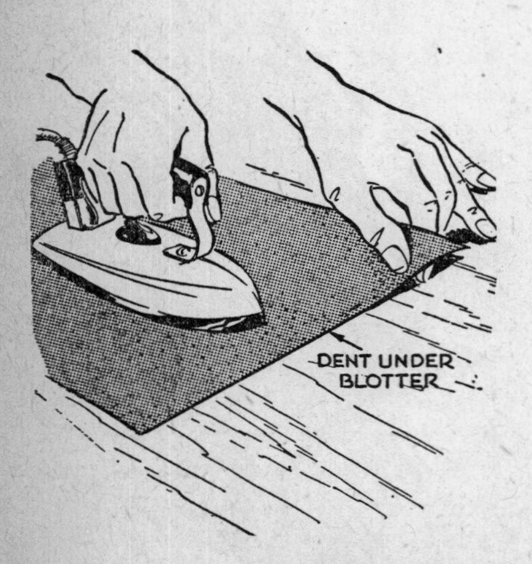

Fig. 1. Dents in wood can be removed with a piece of wet blotting paper and a warm iron.

Wood surfaced at a mill may contain small rough spots. These must be removed before the wood is given a finish. The spots can be removed by sanding, planing, or scraping with a wood scraper or piece of broken glass. A piece of glass, by the way, makes an excellent scraper, especially for small spots difficult to remove with an ordinary wood scraper.

Joints between sections of wood that are not as tight as they should be can be filled with a wood filler. The seam should be first cleaned out and then packed with a wood filler such as plastic wood or spackle. As these fillers shrink slightly when dry, use a little more than is required. An excellent home-made filler is wood glue mixed with sawdust — use the same sort of sawdust, when possible, as the wood to be filled. After the filler is dry, shave down the excess with a razor blade and then sand. Similarly, cracks in end grain and other spots should also be filled.

Nail heads should be punched below the wood surface and the resulting hole filled with wood filler. Screw heads that have been countersunk can be treated in the same manner. But a more professional method is to glue a wood plug on top of the screw head. The wood plug is cut off flush with the wood surface after it is in place.

Fig. 3. An electric sander is a great time-saver.

Wood plugs made from different kinds of hardwood are available at some of the larger hardware stores and lumber yards.

Check all the joints on the piece to be sure they are solid. If they do not appear to be too strong, now is the time to do something about them. Additional nails or screws may be necessary. In some cases, metal angle irons or wood blocks may be required. In any event, do not begin finishing until you are certain that the project is good and solid.

SANDING

The next step in preparing the wood for a finish is to give all surfaces a thorough sanding. Start out with a No. 1 1/2 grade paper followed by No. 0, No. 2/0 and finally No. 4/0.

All sanding should be done in the direction of the wood grain. If the sanding is done by hand, make a sanding block with a felt pad attached to the underside. This does a better, faster job than if the sandpaper is pushed by your hand alone. Sanding blocks can be purchased at paint and hardware stores. A good deal of time can be saved on large projects by using a power sander. Belt or oscillating sanders are excellent for this purpose.

Most rotary sanders are not quite as good, as it is difficult to control the sander. Also, a rotary sander works against as well as with the grain. Areas that cannot be reached with sandpaper can be smoothed out with steel wool.

SELECTING A FINISH

There are several ways in which a project can be finished. It can be finished with a paint suitable for furniture, such as an enamel. If the wood grain has an attractive appearance, a natural finish can be used or the wood can be bleached out to a lighter color and given one of the many attractive modern finishes.

The usual reason for painting a piece of furniture is that the wood is unattractive and ought, therefore, to be completely covered. Several coats of enamel properly applied will completely hide the defects in the wood and produce a finish with a high or semi-gloss. Much modern furniture is finished with enamel or lacquer. To match these pieces you would use a similar kind of finish.

If the wood in the project has an attractive wood grain, that is usually enough reason for wanting to preserve the natural finish. The wood may be darkened by staining before the finish is applied. The finish used to produce a natural effect is usually either varnish or shellac. Staining will also help to bring out the wood grain. A natural finish should only be used on woods that are naturally attractive.

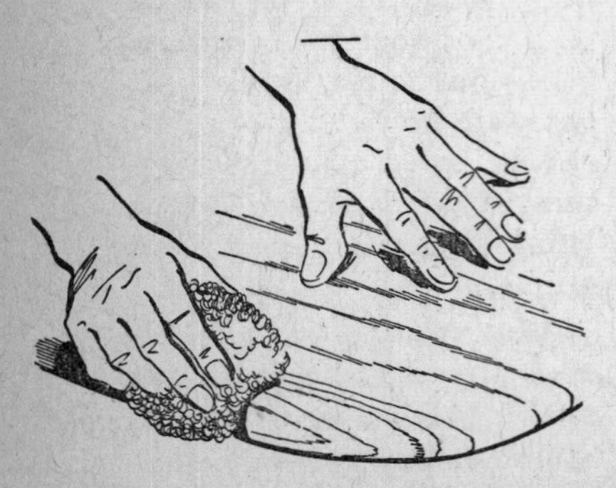

Fig. 4. Steel wool is better than sandpaper for smoothing off rounded edges.

Many homes are furnished with pieces done in the modern blonde effect. To match these, a blonde finish of one sort or another is required. Factory finished articles are almost impossible to match exactly as there are several methods used to obtain the same general appearance. But it is possible to come pretty close.

Of all the finishes, paint is the easiest to apply and usually requires the least work. It is also the most likely to turn out the way you expect. On the other hand, amateur builders who are willing to take the time can produce excellent results with other, more complicated types of finishes.

Where to Work

To obtain the best results, all finishing operations should be conducted in a room free from dust. If there is dust present, it is almost sure to stick on the freshly applied finish, usually spoiling your work.

Workshops are usually not suitable for finishing because of the amount of sawdust present. This is especially true where power saws and sanders have been used. Basements, too, are usually dusty. The best course is to select a room in the house which is not only free from dust but has good ventilation and where the temperature is about 70 degrees. This is important in getting the most out of a finish. Furniture and floors may be covered with dropcloths or old newspapers during the finishing operation. Good illumination is most important, especially when working with the lighter finishes.

Separate as many parts of the piece as possible before finishing, and treat each as a separate unit. This, you will find, is easier and actually quicker than trying to finish the entire unit as a whole. Also, it will eliminate the possibility that doors and drawers will stick due to hardened paint or varnish in the seams or around the edges. On very fine work, it will be wiser to remove the hardware.

Small articles, such as chairs and the like, should be placed on a table for finishing. Nails driven into the end of each leg will raise the piece high enough to allow you to get at the under parts with ease. As a rule, it is better to do the small and hard-to-get-at portions first. Leave the large areas till last. By doing the inconspicuous portions first you also have an opportunity of seeing if the finish is going to come out as you expect.

Fig. 5. For finishing, use tacks or small nails to lift the table or chair off the floor.

Fig. 6. How to take paint on a brush.

ENAMELING

It is assumed that the wood has been sanded down until it is very smooth and that it is clean and dry. If the wood is plywood, the first step is to apply a special plywood primer. This is necessary because the grain in plywood, especially fir, is very pronounced and difficult to conceal unless many extra coats of paint are applied. Applying a special plywood primer will save you both time and paint. After this primer is dry, an enamel undercoater is brushed on. This can be either an ordinary flat white paint or a special enamel undercoater. If the finish is to be a color other than white, the undercoater can be tinted either by mixing some colors in oil into it or by adding a little of the enamel you plan to use as the finish

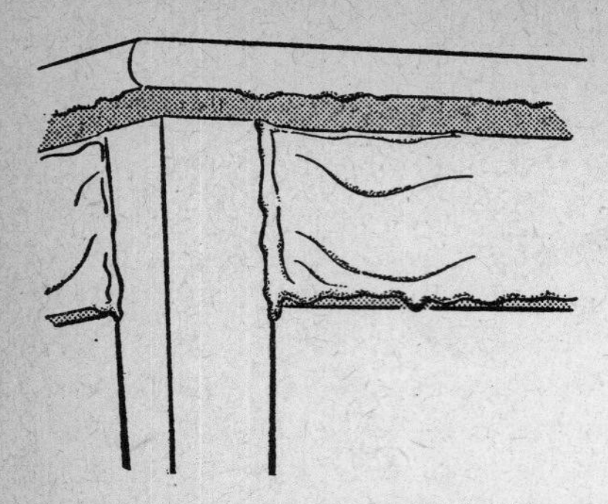

Fig. 7. Heavy coats of enamel improperly applied will run and sag around the edges.

coat. Allow the undercoater to dry at least twenty-four hours and then give the surface a sanding with No. 2/0 sandpaper. Remove all traces of dust with a clean cloth dampened in turpentine. The surface is now ready for the enamel. Enamel is best applied with a special enamel brush having a chisel tip. Enamel, unlike paint, is flowed onto the surface and the action of the enamel removes the brush marks so that the surface dries out completely smooth. Once the finish has been applied, do not go back over it for additional brushing as this may leave marks which will not flow out. Be careful of accumulations of enamel

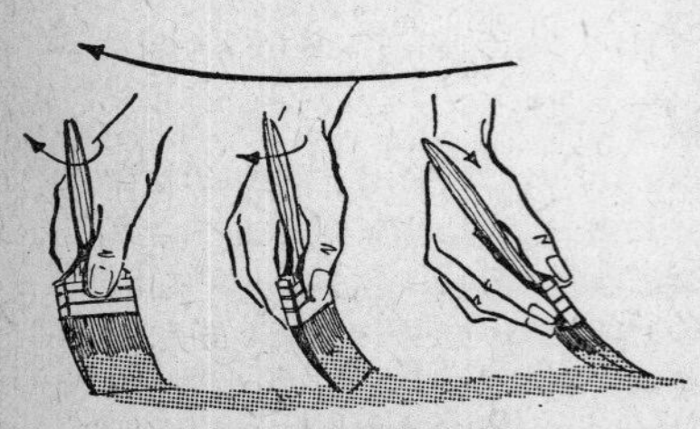

Fig. 8. Enamel should be applied lightly with not too much paint on the brush.

around edges. These must be removed at once before they dry.

In most cases, one coat of enamel will be sufficient. If it is not, allow it to dry thoroughly, give it a light sanding and dusting, and then apply a second coat.

TRANSPARENT AND SEMI-TRANSPARENT FINISHES

Many of the more expensive and better woods have very attractive natural coloring and grain, which you will naturally want to emphasize. There must, however, be some sort of protective coating over the wood. If there is not, the wood colors may soon fade and become dark due to dirt absorbed by the wood pores. Also, unprotected wood stains easily and discolors with water and other liquids. For some purposes, a finish as transparent as obtainable may be required. In other cases, the finish may be semi-transparent to darken the wood slightly. The most common kinds of transparent and semi-transparent finishes are varnish, shellac, and lacquer.

If you wish to darken the wood slightly and emphasize the wood grain, then a stain is applied before the finish. A stain is unlike a paint, for while a paint is opaque and completely hides the wood, a stain is similar to a dye in that it merely colors the wood grain without hiding it. There are different kinds of stains. Each has certain characteristics which recommend it, so you must make your choice according to your own circumstances.

Water Stain

This is the least expensive kind of stain you can buy. It comes in powder form and is mixed with hot water for use. The main disadvantage of this stain is that the water leaves the wood surface very rough, and therefore the surface must be sanded smooth again after the stain is dry. The advantages of this stain, aside from its low cost, are that it is non-fading, and non-bleeding, and gives an even coloring. A water stain may be applied with either brush, spray gun, or cloth. Before the stain is applied, the wood should be sponged with water so that the grain rises, and then it must be sanded smooth. This eliminates some of the sanding necessary after the wood has been stained. When applied with a brush, the stain should be distributed freely. Allow the stain twenty-four hours to dry.

Oil Stains

These are sold ready-mixed at paint and hardware stores. They are applied with a brush or cloth. These stains do not penetrate very deeply into the wood and therefore are easy to control. If, when the stain is dry, it seems too dark, a light sanding will remove some if not all of the stain. Special shades can easily be mixed by thinning the stain with turpentine.

Non-Grain-Raising Stains

Most professional furniture builders prefer to use a non-grain-raising stain. These stains come in a wide range of colors, which can be made into the desired shade. They have the permanency of water stains without causing the grain to rise. They can be applied either with a brush or with a spray gun.

Use of Stains

Before deciding to use a stain, there are several points to keep in mind. First, stains can only be used to darken wood — they will not make the wood lighter. The longer a stain is left on the wood surface before wiping it off, the deeper it will penetrate and the darker will be the final effect. If you wish to tint the wood only slightly, apply a thin coat of stain and wipe it off immediately. Remember that it is always possible to get a darker effect by applying another coat of stain once the first is dry. But if the first coat dries out too dark, the only way to lighten up the wood is to sand out the stain. Also, the end grain of wood absorbs stain more readily and faster than the other areas, so use especially light coats on such places so they will not darken more than the rest of the wood.

Fig. 9. Most of the stains you will use can be applied with a brush.

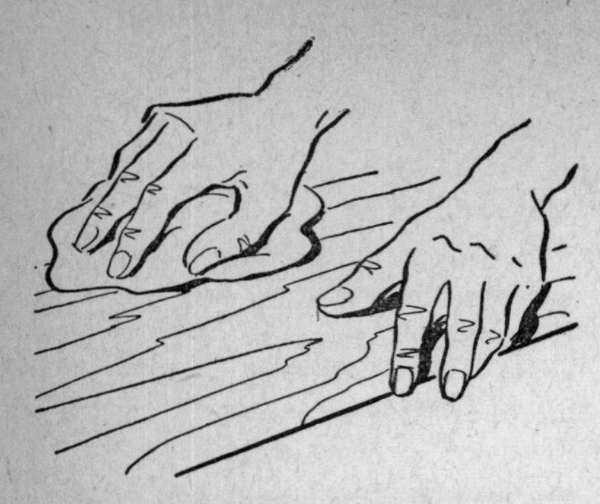

Fig. 10. Excess stain on the wood surface may be wiped off with a clean lintless cloth.

Bleaching

Just as stains are used to darken wood and bring out the grain, bleaching is used to make the wood lighter. Bleaching is done in most of the blonde finishes. The best sort of bleach to use on wood for furniture is a commercial type of bleach sold at the better paint and hardware stores. When applying these bleaches, follow the instructions on the container. Drying time for bleaches will differ, but it is well to allow forty-eight hours or so. After the bleach is dry, the wood should be sanded lightly to remove traces of the bleaching solution as well as to smooth out the grain raised by the bleach. *Avoid inhaling any of the dust.* After the surface has been dusted, it should be given a very thin coat of shellac to prevent the wood from becoming darkened by the oils in the filler.

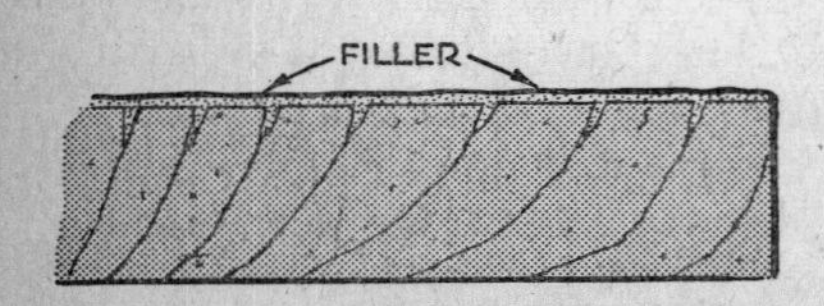

Fig. 11. This cross-section shows filler in the wood pores.

FILLERS

Some woods, such as oak and chestnut, are called open-grained woods. The wood pores, or cells, in these woods are very large, and if a finish were to be applied directly to the wood, it would dry out rough and uneven due to the fact that some of it would sink down to fill the pores while the rest would be on the surface.

It is possible, of course, to sand this first coat smooth and then apply a second and third coat of finish, sanding each until at last you have built up a smooth surface for the final finish. It is much easier and faster, however, to fill these wood pores with a wood filler so that the surface is built up level before the first coat of finish is applied. Fillers may be stained or tinted, if desired, to produce additional coloring. Some woods which have a very close grain, such as cedar, cypress, and basswood, require no filler at all. Ash, beech, butternut, chestnut, elm, and hickory do require a filler.

There are two types of fillers—paste and liquid. As a rule, the paste fillers are used on woods with open-grain while liquid fillers are used for the close-grain varieties.

Paste fillers can be purchased in neutral wood color and in several common wood colors. It is best to use a filler of the same color as the wood to be treated. If no such filler is available, a natural filler can be tinted with colors in oil.

Paste fillers must be thinned down somewhat before they are applied to the wood. Naphtha is usually used for this purpose. The amount of thinning required depends on the size of the wood pores. Fillers for use on oak and chestnut need not be thinned as much as fillers used on close-grain woods, such as walnut.

Application of Filler

The filler, when properly thinned, is applied rather freely to the wood with a brush. Do not cover too great an area with the filler because it will set in fifteen minutes or so and must be wiped off at this time. Brush the filler on, working with the wood grain.

After the filler has been brushed over the wood surface, it should be rubbed in a circular motion with a felt pad. This operation, known as "padding in," forces the filler into the wood pores.

It usually takes about fifteen minutes for the filler to set. As the filler begins to set, it becomes dull and starts to harden. This is the time to wipe off the excess filler on the wood surface. If the filler is allowed to set for too long, it will become so hard that the excess can only be removed by sanding. On the other hand, if it is wiped off before it has begun to set, there is a chance of pulling out the filler that has gone into the wood pores — and this defeats the purpose of the filler. It will require a little practice on the part of the amateur before he is able to gauge exactly the

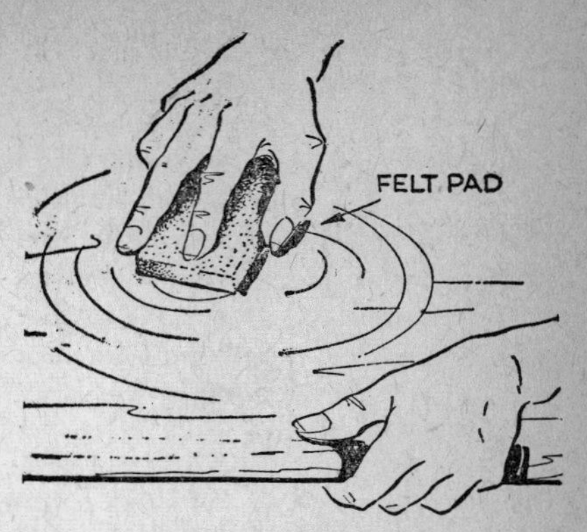

Fig. 12. Brush the thinned filler on in the direction of the grain.

right moment to remove the excess filler.

The process of removing the excess filler from the wood surface is called "towing off." This is done with a coarse piece of cotton or a piece of burlap. Wipe first across the grain with pressure and then with the grain. If some portions of the filler are too hard they can be softened up somewhat by adding a little naphtha. Coating the surface with a fresh coat of filler will also soften the hardened filler.

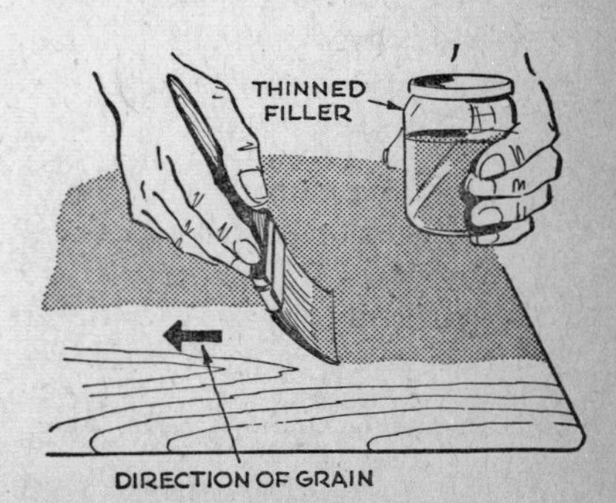

Fig. 13. Filler being padded in.

After the excess filler has been removed, dampen a piece of felt cloth in naphtha and wipe the surface very lightly. Allow the filler to dry hard and then sand the surface smooth with No. 2/0 sandpaper. After this operation, dampen a piece of lintless cloth in naphtha and wipe the surface down to remove any of the filler dust which may have been left by the sanding operation.

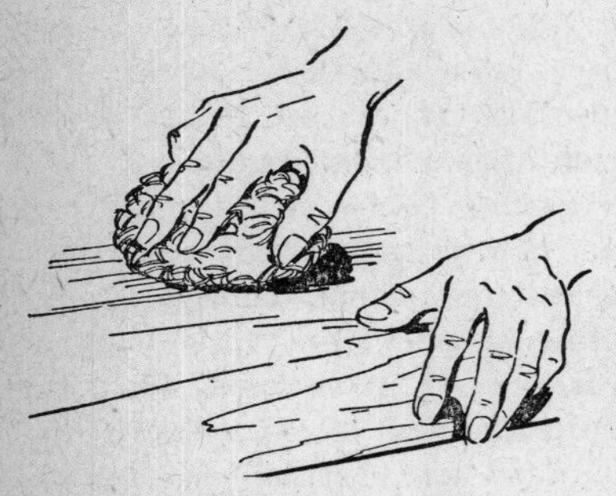

Fig. 14. This operation is known as towing off.

If, after the final sanding, you find that all the wood pores are not completely filled, another coat of filler should be applied.

Liquid Fillers

The most common type of liquid filler is shellac thinned down to a very light coat with denatured alcohol. One or two light coats are applied with a light sanding between coats to remove the shellac from the wood surface. Bleached shellac should be used for light colored finishes and orange shellac for darker finishes.

SEALING

This process is usually referred to as "washcoating." It consists of applying a thin coat of sealer to the wood before the finish is applied. This sealer serves many purposes. It provides a good bond between the finish coats and the wood and at the same time prevents the absorption of the first coat of finish by the wood. This usually eliminates the need for an additional coat of finish, for highly-absorbent woods will completely absorb the first coat of finish so that little or none of it remains on the surface. The sealer also prevents the filler or stain from discoloring the finish. In very fine work, it is wise to use a sealer after the stain as well as after the filler. The sealer between stain and filler prevents any possibility of discoloration at this point. A sealer before the filler is applied is most important on bleached finishes because, if it is not applied before the filler, the oils in the filler will discolor the bleached wood.

Shellac makes an excellent sealer. Orange shellac is used for darker finishes and white shellac for light finishes. A 3 1/2-pound cut is used for ordinary work. The shellac can be applied either by brush or with a spray gun. Another common kind of sealer is thin lacquer. This is best applied with a spray gun.

FINISHING PLYWOOD

Many of the projects outlined in this book call for the use of plywood, and by far the most common—as well as the least expensive—kind of plywood is made from fir. While this is an excellent material in many respects, it is a difficult one to finish because of the wild grain found in fir and the fact that the wood tends to fuzz, producing a rough surface. Before attempting to finish off this material, a special primer and sealer should be applied. This is applied in a heavy coat and allowed to dry thoroughly. If the wood is to be stained, the sealer can be tinted with stain before it is applied or a stain may be applied after the sealer is dry. Another finishing problem connected with plywood is the treatment of the edges, which expose the various layers of veneer. These can be filled out smooth with filler and then painted, but a somewhat more satisfactory solution is to cover them with strips of half-round molding of the same diameter as the thickness of the plywood.

FINISHES OR TOP COATS

The most common materials used for the final finish or top coat are varnish, shellac, lacquer, wax, and oil.

Varnish

Varnish is a very old finish, and over a period of years many different types of varnish have been developed for special uses. For most woodworking purposes, only a few of the many kinds are of any interest.

Spar Varnish: Also called marine varnish, this type is very hard and very tough when dry. It is used mostly for exterior work, but it is also useful for interior work, especially in the kitchen, where it will be subject to moisture. It dries in twelve to twenty-four hours.

Rubbing and Polishing: This group of varnishes is designed for use on furniture. These varnishes contain less oil than do some of the others and this prevents gumming of the abrasives used to sand out any irregularities.

Polishing Varnish: This is used as a top coat over rubbing-and-polishing varnish. It can be polished out to a high gloss.

Table Top Varnish: This dries out to a very tough surface which is very resistant to scratching and staining from moisture and alcohol.

Varnish Stain: This is a varnish tinted with stain. It is used, where appearance is not too important, in place of a regular stain followed by varnish. As it combines two operations in one, it is a time-saver.

Flat Varnish: This type of varnish dries out to a dull gloss and is useful for most general work.

Application of Varnish

To get good results with varnish it is necessary to fulfill certain rather

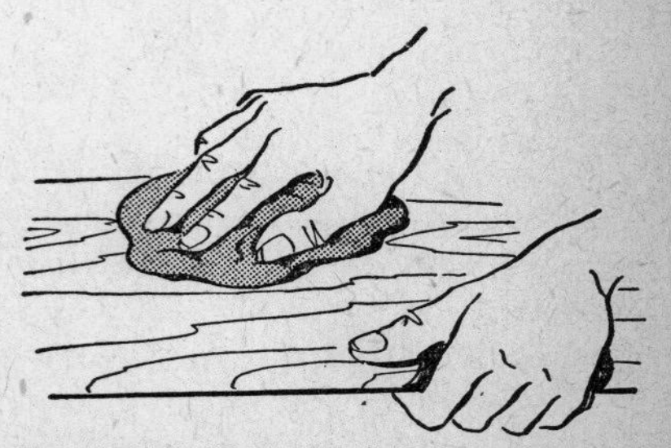

Fig. 15. Before varnishing, remove traces of dust from the surface with a lintless cloth dampened in varnish.

exacting conditions. First, the wood surface must be sanded out until it is perfectly smooth. It must also be clean and dry. Before the varnish is applied, dampen a piece of lintless cloth in a little varnish and wipe the surface with this. The small amount of varnish in the cloth will pick up dust which would not otherwise be caught with a dry cloth. It is best not to try to varnish in the same room where you have been working with wood because the sawdust in the air may fall on the freshly varnished surface and spoil it. It is better to do the varnishing in a room as free from dust as you can get it.

Varnishing should not be done during wet weather or when the humidity is very high. For best results select a warm dry day and be sure that the room in which you work is not damp.

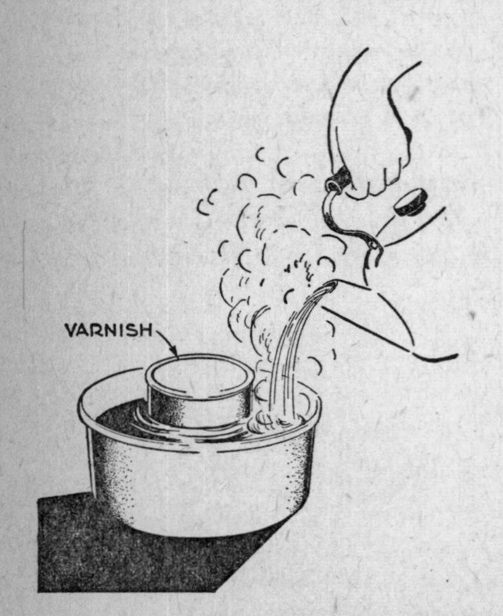

Fig. 16. Cold varnish can be brought to the proper temperature by placing the container in a pan of hot water.

Varnish applied in a damp basement will not dry properly. The temperature of the air has a good deal to do with how well varnish dries out. For best results, the temperature should be between 70 and 80 degrees.

This means that during the winter months varnish must be applied indoors in a heated room. If the varnish container has been stored in a cold room, place it in a pan containing warm water until the varnish has reached a good working temperature.

Because varnish can so easily be ruined by dust or dirt, it is best not to put the brush directly into the varnish container. Pour a quantity of varnish—the amount you expect will be required for the job at hand — into a clean container, and use this for brushing. When the job is finished, do not pour this varnish back into the original container. Instead, cover it and use it for some other job where the appearance of the varnish is of no importance.

The best kind of brush to use for varnishing is a varnish brush with a chisel point. These brushes should be used only for varnish—never for paint. The reason for this is that once a brush has been used for paint or enamel, no matter how well it is cleaned some of the paint or enamel will remain at the base of the bristles, and when the brush is next used for varnish, this paint will discolor the varnish. Keep varnish brushes just for varnishing and have a good selection of them in different sizes for both large and small jobs.

The application of varnish by brush is divided into three operations. The first step is called "cutting in." In this operation the brush is dipped about one-third the length of the bristles into the container. The varnish is then applied to the surface with smooth strokes. The next step is "cross brushing"—the brush is drawn across the wood grain. Start from either side and work the brush half-way across. The final step is "tipping off." Here the brush is drawn with the wood grain so that the tips of the bristles just touch the surface. Excess varnish around the edges of the piece or in the molding should be removed immediately before it has set. Make a careful inspection of the piece to be sure that there are no areas which have been missed. Give the first coat of varnish about twenty-four hours to dry and then give it a light sanding to cut the gloss. Use No. 6/0 paper for this operation. Dust the surface and then apply the second coat. The number of coats required is a matter of personal taste. Two coats will produce a very adequate finish for most jobs. For very fine work, three or even four coats can be applied. For the final step in obtaining an attractive finish with varnish, the surface should be polished down. This operation is covered later in this section.

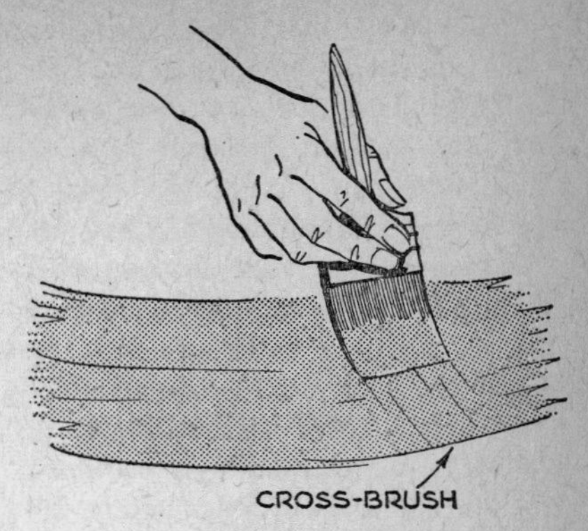

Fig. 17. Cross-brushing.

Shellac

Shellac may be used for the final finish in place of varnish. As is the case when using a shellac sealer, use white or bleached shellac for finishing light woods and orange shellac for the darker woods. When used as a finish, a standard 4-lb. cut of shellac must be thinned down. Use 3/4 quart of denatured alcohol to each quart of shellac. Shellac spoils if kept too long, so be sure to purchase fresh, pure shellac and do not get more than you can use over a period of six months. Also, shellac should not be stored in a metal container. Store it either in a special lead-lined container or in a glass container. Take the same precautions when applying shellac as outlined above for varnish. Shellac sets and dries rather rapidly, so you must work fairly fast to get it on properly. On the other hand, since it dries rapidly, there is less chance of its picking up dust.

Fig. 18. Shellac should be stored in a lead-lined or glass container.

After the first coat of shellac is hard and dry, rub it down with No. 2/0 sandpaper, dust, and then apply the second coat. Two or three coats is enough.

French Polishing: This is one of oldest methods of finishing fine furniture. White shellac should be thinned down to a 1-lb. cut. This is done by adding two quarts of denatured alcohol to each quart of shellac, assuming the shellac is originally a standard 4-lb. cut. The shellac is applied to the surface with a piece of soft lintless cloth rolled into a ball. The cloth is dipped into the shellac and then rubbed over the wood in straight strokes. Use very light pressure. Allow the surface to dry and then sand lightly with No. 6/0 sandpaper. Dust and then apply a second coat of shellac in the same way as the first. Additional coats are applied until a light glow begins to appear on the finish. At this stage, add several drops of boiled linseed oil to the shellac and apply this mixture to the surface with the cloth using a circular motion. Add additional drops of oil to each coat until the deep finish you want has been obtained.

Dip and Rub Finish: This is another type of shellac finish. It is somewhat easier and faster to apply than the French polishing method. Fill one saucer with pure turpentine and another saucer with white shellac from a 4-lb. cut. Roll a piece of lintless cloth into a pad and dip it first into the turpentine and then into the shellac. Rub the pad over the surface with a circular motion. Apply four or five coats in the same fashion. When the final coat is dry, rub the surface down with a cloth dipped in linseed oil.

Lacquer

Roughly speaking, lacquer can be divided into two groups — brushing lacquer and spraying lacquer. Lacquer dries through the absorption by the air of the solvent or thinner in it. As this solvent has a fast rate of evaporation, lacquers dry very rapidly. The brushing lacquers dry more slowely than spraying lacquers. Spraying lacquers dry so rapidly that they cannot be applied by brush—they must be used only with a spray gun. The solvent used with lacquer for thinning or other purposes, such as cleaning brushes, is lacquer thinner. Thinners suitable for paints and varnish should not be used with lacquer. While paints and varnish can be applied over lacquer, lacquer should never be applied over paint or varnish because the solvent in the lacquer will soften up these base coats.

There are several special types of spraying lacquer which can be used for various finishing operations:

Clear Gloss Lacquer: This is a clear lacquer which dries to a high gloss in four hours or so. When dry, the surface may be rubbed and polished.

Clear Flat: This is the same as clear gloss except that it dries out flat.

Rubbing and Polishing Lacquer: This is a very high grade of lacquer especially suitable for rubbing and polishing.

Shellac-Mixing Lacquer: This is a special type of lacquer which mixes with shellac to provide better surfaces for sanding.

Water White Lacquer: That is a perfectly clear lacquer used on blonde finishes.

Application of Lacquer

Brushing Lacquer: While brushing lacquer dries much more slowly than spraying lacquer, it does dry fast. To apply it properly you must work with a good deal of speed. The lacquer should be flowed on and brushed out as little as possible. As speed is important, use as large a brush as is effective and let the brush carry as much lacquer as possible without dripping. Apply the lacquer in one direction only. If a second coat is required, it must be applied with even more speed or the solvent in the second coat will soften up the first coat.

Spraying Lacquer: By far the best method of applying lacquer is to use a spray gun, but this calls for a very high-class piece of equipment—not the ordinary kind found in many homes. (See SPRAY GUNS, below.)

RUBBING AND POLISHING

To produce a really fine finish of varnish, shellac, or lacquer, the final coat should be rubbed and then polished. On very fine work, all coats are rubbed down before the succeeding coat is applied.

Rubbing is the first operation. It removes any rough spots, brush marks, or bits of dust or dirt from the finish. The rubbing is done with a felt pad. The abrasive used for the operation is FFF grade powdered pumice stone mixed into a paste with water or light oil. Rubbing is faster with a water paste than with an oil paste. Rubbing should be done in the direction of the wood grain. From time to time, clean the surface of the work and examine it to be sure that the rubbing action is uniform. When the entire surface is flat and free from any flaws, remove all traces of the rubbing abrasive. Areas which cannot be rubbed easily with the felt, such as legs of tables or chair and trim, can be rubbed with a cloth saturated with the abrasive paste.

Polishing is a continuation of the rubbing operation, except that an even finer abrasive, such as rottenstone, is used to remove any of the marks left by the coarser pumice stone. Instead of polishing, a high sheen can also be produced by buffing. This is done with a buffing wheel attached to an electric drill. The buffing wheel should be several inches thick and the buffing compound should be applied either to the surface of the work or to the wheel itself. The final buffing is accomplished with a dry and clean wheel.

SPECIAL TECHNIQUES

Special effects can be achieved during the finishing operation by the use of various techniques to produce special results.

Shading

In some work it is desirable to have contrasting shades. The best time to achieve this is during the application of the stain with a spray gun. All that is required is to spray some areas lightly and others more heavily. More control over the degree of shading can be achieved by first spraying on a very light coat of stain and, before this is dry, spraying again with the same mixture where you wish to have the darker areas. In some cases, an article will have been made from several kinds of wood, all of different

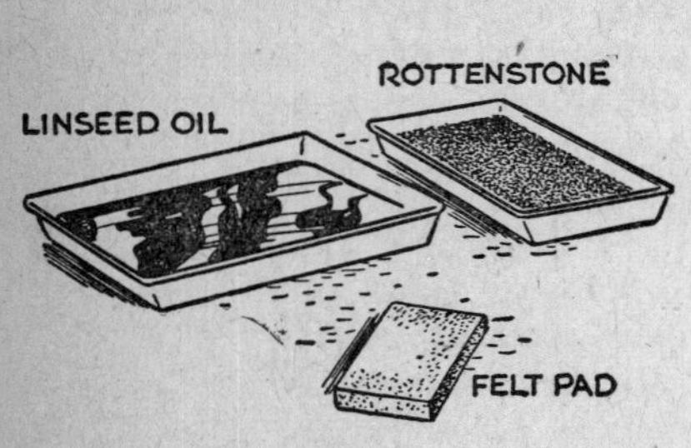

Fig. 19. Equipment required for polishing.

shades or colors. In this case, if you wish to have a uniform finish, it will be necessary to bring the various pieces to a uniform color. Shading is best accomplished with a non-grain-raising stain applied with a spray gun. If the staining must be done with a brush or cloth, then a wiping stain can be used.

Highlighting

This is very useful when trying to match period pieces such as Colonial American. Highlighting can be produced by first giving the wood a coat of stain so that the color is uniform. After the stain is dry, the areas you wish to make lighter are sanded with very fine sandpaper or steel wool. The technique of highlighting calls for a good deal of practice and skill, for if too much of the color is removed during the sanding operation, it is usually necessary to remove all the stain and start out anew. Trying to patch up the spots with more stain is all but impossible.

Glazing and Antiquing

Another method used for finishing period pieces and for achieving interesting shades is through the use of a glaze. Glazing liquid can be purchased in various shades at paint and hardware stores. In some cases, paint or even stain is used in place of the liquid glaze. The wood is first given a base coat of enamel, paint, or sealer. The exact shade of glaze to use will depend on the color used for the base coat. If the base coat is light, then a rather light glaze will be sufficient to produce the desired amount of shading. As darker base colors are used, darker glazes must be also used to produce the right amount of contrast. The glaze is applied over the entire surface with a brush. Before it has a chance to harden, it is wiped off with a piece of clean cheesecloth. The wiping should begin in the center of the surface and should be done with a circular motion. The amount of glaze left on the surface depends on the amount of pressure used in wiping. More and more glaze is allowed to remain as the wiping gets closer to the edges of the surface. The final effect should be a gradual blending, starting with little or no glaze at the center and with a greater and greater intensity of glaze as the edges are reached. If the glaze appears to be too heavy in some places, or if it becomes too stiff for easy wiping, dampen the cloth with a little turpentine. Interesting effects can be achieved by using your fingers or a brush instead of a cloth. On large surfaces it is best to add a little linseed oil to the glaze to slow up the drying so that the work can be accomplished unhurriedly.

Getting the proper technique with glaze will require a little practice. Your first attempts may not be all satisfactory. If so, it is a simple matter to remove all the glaze with some turpentine and start again.

The glaze in molding, carvings, and the like can be blended out for the desired effect with a brush.

Stencils

Many pieces of furniture, both modern and period, can be improved considerably by stenciling designs on them in contrasting colors. Ready-made stencils are available at paint and art supply stores, but it is a simple matter to make your own. Draw out the design and then transfer it to stencil paper. The design is then cut out with a very sharp knife or a razor blade. The cuts must be very sharp or the final transfer will have rough edges. After the stencil has been cut out, it should be coated with shellac or lacquer to stiffen the paper. The stencil is then placed on the work and held securely with masking tape. If you are going to use a spray gun, mask a sufficiently large area around the stencil.

Paint can be applied either with a spray gun or with a stencil brush. A spray gun will produce better results than applying the paint by hand, but care must be taken not to allow the paint to become too thick. And don't hold the gun in such a fashion that some of the paint gets under the edges of the stencil and spoils the design. If the paint is to be applied witth a brush, then a special stencil brush should be used.

Ordinary paint is too thin for good stenciling. Colors in oil are far superior. As they come from the tube too thick for application with the stencil brush, they must be thinned down to the proper consistency with turpentine.

Fig. 20. Buffing can be done with a buffing wheel attached to a small electric drill.

After the paint is dry and the stencil has been removed, the design can be protected against wear with a thin coat of clear varnish.

Decalcomanias

Another method of transferring designs is the use of decalcomanias, or "decals," as they are popularly known. There are two kinds of decals available for use. One is the water type, which is soaked in water for a short period before it is applied to the surface to be decorated. The paper is then removed, leaving the design. This type is suitable for most work.

The other type is the varnish decal. It leaves no overlap at the edges as does the water decal, and, therefore, it more closely resembles freehand painting.

SPECIAL FINISHES

Over the years, special finishes have been developed to meet certain requirements or to simulate certain effects. Various kinds of so-called "modern finishes" are especially popular today. As different methods are employed by professionals in obtaining these finishes, duplication is difficult unless you happen to know the exact technique used on the original. On the other hand, it is possible for the amateur working with a home-constructed article to finish it so that its appearance is professional.

Wax Finish

This is a relatively easy technique to use and one that will provide a long-wearing, durable finish. The wood should be sanded smooth, stained if desired, filled, and then given two coats of thin shellac or one coat of varnish or lacquer. After the final coat is dry, sand lightly with steel wool and then apply a rather heavy, but even, coat of good paste wax. Allow the wax to dry for about one hour and then rub the wax with a piece of felt. Rub it in the direction of the wood grain. Allow the wax to dry for a day or so and then apply a second coat somewhat more lightly than the first. Several additional coats should be applied in the same manner, allowing a day for drying between each coat. The success of this finish depends on the quality of the wax used and the thoroughness of the rubbing.

Linseed Oil Finish

This finish produces excellent results, especially on walnut. The final finish is extremely resistant to heat and scratches. When wear begins to show in certain areas, it is a simple matter to patch them up with additional coats of oil. There are several methods used in producing this finish. A simple method is to mix two-thirds boiled linseed oil to one-third turpentine. This solution may be tinted with a stain, but it should be remembered that the linseed oil alone will darken the wood somewhat, and this usually gives enough color.

Warm the linseed oil solution in a double boiler. Don't place it over an open flame as the solution is a highly inflammable one. The oil mixture is applied to the wood with a brush or clean cloth and rubbed into the surface. Put on a fairly heavy coating. Allow the oil to remain on the wood for several hours and then wipe off the excess with a clean cloth. The piece should then be rubbed down with a piece of felt wrapped around a block of wood. Allow the oil to dry for several days, and then apply a second coat of linseed oil in the same manner. This process is repeated until the wood will no longer absorb oil. Additional rubbings at frequent intervals over a period of many weeks will improve the appearance of the finish. Rubbing several times a year will maintain it.

Another method of applying this finish calls for the application of linseed oil without the turpentine. The oil is applied with a cloth or brush and then rubbed into the wood by hand until the wood will no longer absorb oil. Frequent hard rubbings by hand over a period of months is necessary to produce the final effect. But many people consider it well worth the trouble.

An oil finish is often used on knotty-pine paneling and on other pine articles where a natural finish is desired. The mixture used here is one part linseed oil to two parts turpentine.

Limed Oak

This type of finish is used extensively in modern furniture. The wood must first be bleached out with a commercial bleaching agent. After this, the wood may be tinted with stain or left as it is. Seal it with a wash coat of water-white lacquer and then fill with a white filler (made by adding zinc white color to natural filler). The top coat of the finish must be water-white lacquer.

Pickled Pine

This finish can be used on a wide variety of woods. Dark woods must first be bleached out to a light color. This is not required on the lighter woods. In the case of pine, a gray stain is applied to the wood. This is followed by a thin wash coat of white shellac. A light filler is then applied or a light wiping stain. Finally a thin coat of white shellac is applied.

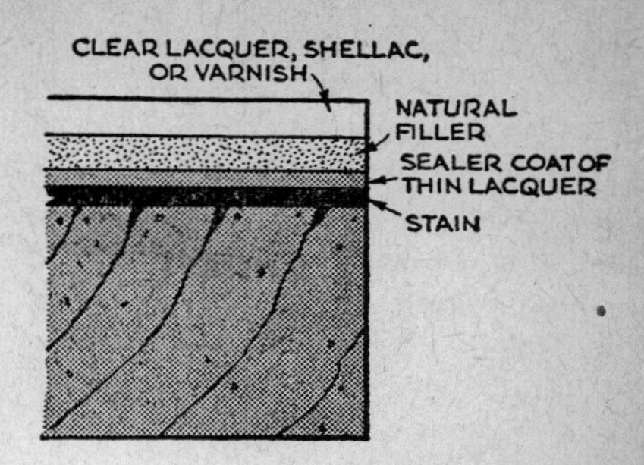

Fig. 21. This cross-section shows the average number of steps in finishing.

Honey-Tone

This finish is particularly effective on light-colored woods like maple and birch. If dark woods are to be used, they must first be bleached out. A toner of one part white lacquer and four parts clear lacquer is applied directly to the wood. This produces a thin and transparent coating. Several applications of the toner are made. The final coating consists of two coats of water-white lacquer.

Bone White

The base needed for this finish is a coat of bone-white enamel, which comes ready-mixed. After this dries a glaze or brown wiping stain is applied and then wiped away, but with traces left in the corners, on edges, and so on. When the glaze or stain is dry, apply a top coat of clear or water-white lacquer.

Heather Mahogany

In this case the effect desired is created by using a white filler in the wood. Remove the excess filler by wiping across the grain and then apply a top coat of water-white lacquer.

Blonde Finishes

There are a wide variety of finishes that fall under the general classification of "blonde finishes." The blonde effect can be obtained with light-colored woods by the application of a tinted coat of flat varnish or of a blonde sealer. Either will produce a blonde effect without covering the wood grain. The top coat must produce a transparent covering. In the case of dark woods, it is necessary to bleach them to a lighter shade.

Cedar Finish

This is a type of paint which produces the aromatic odor of cedar. It is used for coating the inside of closets and chests.

Crackle Finish

This is an extremely popular type of finish and falls in the "novelty" group. After the wood has been sanded smooth, a coat of lacquer is applied.

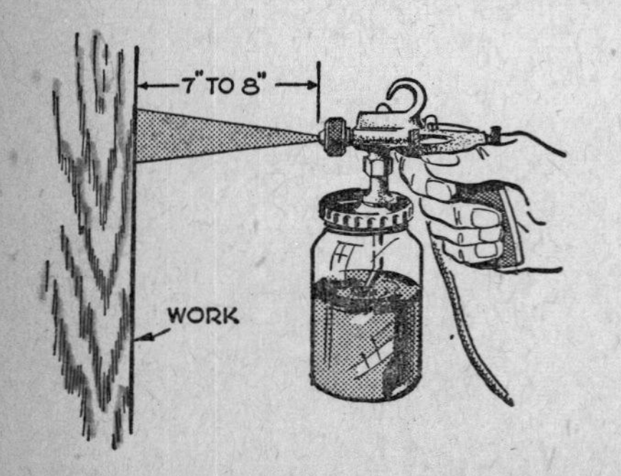

Fig. 22. Hold the spray gun perpendicular to your work and about 8" away.

When this is dry, a coat of crackle enamel is applied. As this enamel dries out, it shrinks and cracks into small sections.

BRUSHES AND SPRAY GUNS

Brushes

To produce fine results when finishing furniture and other articles, it is essential to have a good selection of high-quality brushes. The number and size of brushes to buy for a finishing job depend on your needs. The brushes range in size from the very fine type necessary for getting into small corners to the fairly large ones used in applying fast-drying finishes, such as for brushing lacquers on large surfaces. Before using a new brush, work it back and forth on the palm of your hand to remove any loose bristles that might otherwise come out on the finish. After use, thoroughly clean the brushes in the proper solvent and wrap them in wax paper with all the bristles straight, so the brush will be ready for the next project.

Brushes used with paints and enamel should be cleaned with turpentine, naphtha, benzine, or linseed oil. Shellac brushes are cleaned with denatured alcohol. For lacquer brushes, use lacquer thinner.

Spray Guns

While not absolutely essential, a spray gun is a great convenience and time-saver in applying professional-looking finishes. It is also necessary for applying lacquers other than brushing lacquer because of their fast-drying properties. If you should decide to get a spray gun, get a good one and be sure that it is suitable for use with lacquer. Some kinds of spray guns cannot operate with fast-drying materials.

Much of the trouble encountered with spray guns is due to improper adjustment and inadequate cleaning. Either of these can ruin a finish. Be sure you understand the proper adjustment of the gun as well as the mixing of the paint. Be sure, too, that the gun is properly cleaned after use.

The spray gun must always be held perpendicular to the work. Pointing the gun up or down will result in an uneven coating. The gun should be held about eight inches from the work. In any event, do not hold the gun more than ten inches or less than six inches away from the work. As the gun is moved across the surface to be finished, try to keep it an even distance away. Move the gun across the work with an even, free sweep of the arm. The trigger of the gun should be pulled before the gun hits the edge of the work and not released

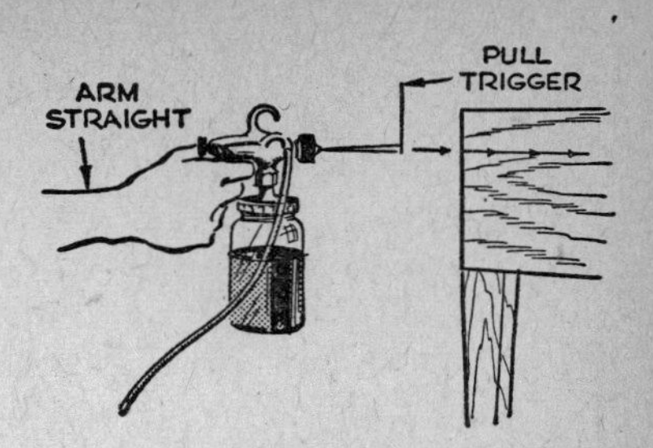

Fig. 23. The triggering of the gun should start at the beginning of the stroke to insure getting a clean edge.

until after the gun has passed the other edge. This gives you an even coat of finish along the entire surface.

It is best to spray the small and difficult-to-reach areas first, before you do the large sections. If you do the large sections first, you will have trouble preventing additional spray from getting on these pieces when you begin working on the small pieces. Outside corners can be sprayed head on. For inside corners, do the two adjacent sides independently, trying, as much as possible, to prevent overlapping.

INDEX

A

B

C

D

E

F

G

H

I

J

K

L

S

T